DATE DUE

Wolf- fac			
GAYLORD			PRINTED IN U.S.A.

THE PREHISTORY OF THE TEHUACAN VALLEY

THE PREHISTORY OF THE TEHUACAN VALLEY

VOLUME TWO

Nonceramic Artifacts

By Richard S. MacNeish, Antoinette Nelken-Terner
and Irmgard W. Johnson

Published for the
ROBERT S. PEABODY FOUNDATION
Phillips Academy, Andover

UNIVERSITY OF TEXAS PRESS • AUSTIN & LONDON

Published in Great Britain by the
University of Texas Press, Ltd., London

Library of Congress Catalog Card No. 67-17873

The preparation and publication of
The Prehistory of the Tehuacan Valley
has been assisted by grants from
the National Science Foundation.

Typesetting by Service Typographers, Indianapolis, Indiana
Printing by The Meriden Gravure Company, Meriden, Connecticut
Binding by Universal Bookbindery, Inc., San Antonio, Texas

PREFACE

The Tehuacan Valley lies in southeastern Mexico, extending from the southern portion of the state of Puebla into the northern portion of the state of Oaxaca. It forms a part of the great structural trench known as La Cañada Poblana-Oaxaqueña which lies between the Sierra de Zongolica—a branch of the Sierra de Oaxaca —and the Sierra de Zapotitlan—a branch of the Sierra de Mixteca. In this position it lies in a rain shadow, and consequently its climate is hot and arid. Xerophitic vegetation which today covers the valley floor may best be described as cactus and spiny scrub. The crest of the Sierra de Zongolica supports a cloud forest, and the Sierra de Mixteca once was more heavily forested than it is today. Between the mountain forests and the valley floor, a wide variety of vegetal and animal resources was available to ancient inhabitants of the region.

Forces of diastrophism and erosion have produced cliffy faces at many places in the valley. Only some of these were sufficiently undercut to provide protection, and still fewer were situated above a nearly level land surface which would tempt people to settle at their base. These few rock shelters offered dry areas, where the occasional rain did not penetrate, and they have preserved dry rubbish in which was buried the lost, the broken, the outworn or discarded treasures of nearly ten millennia. Here, too, the dead were sometimes laid to rest. From the great rock shelter of Coxcatlan has come the key stratigraphic sequence, spanning, with only one great interruption, almost the entire known pre-Hispanic history of the Valley. Two other shelters lay not far from Coxcatlan—Purron Cave, with a deep stratified deposit with a high percentage of stone debris and mineral soil, and Abejas, which was smaller than the other two but yielded some important finds. On the other side of the valley, and at a higher elevation lies Tecorral Canyon in which are San Marcos Cave and Tecorral Cave. North of these sites, El Riego Cave lies but a short distance from Tehuacan, itself.

Open sites in the floor of the valley were selected because test excavations suggested that they might fill gaps in the sequence, or contribute to a fuller understanding of cultural units poorly represented in deposits in rock shelters. Most of these excavated sites lay near the center of the valley.

Excavations in southern Puebla were undertaken in the belief that dry deposits in rock shelters would preserve remains of primitive maize and other plants first domesticated in the general region of southern Mexico. At the same time, it was anticipated that excavators would uncover material remains of the culture of the inhabitants which might shed light on their transition from hunters and collectors of wild plant food to sophisticated city dwellers. Reasons for selecting the Tehuacan Valley are more fully explained in another volume in this series.

In this volume our interest in the nonceramic materials from Tehuacan was primarily in terms of chronology and cultural change. We classified them in such a way as to determine archaeological "types" which could serve as time markers for the pre-Hispanic period of the region's history, and particularly for the era preceding ceramic times. Although the stone, wood, bone, shell, fiber, and other nonceramic remains are not as numerous as ceramic remains, they may be typed to establish sequences and to determine intra- and extra-areal relationships. They are an aspect of the lives of the ancient peoples that should not be ignored; only through studying them can we discover the length of the periods of slowly evolving culture, and the continuity which persists in primitive societies, not only within a small region such as the valley, but by comparison with artifacts from other places, among groups of people in a similar stage of culture over wide areas of the continent. We hope that this volume will stimulate others to undertake similar studies in Mexico, and that these, in turn, will provide additional cultural time markers for comparative purposes and thus lead to a fuller knowledge of the life of the pre-Hispanic peoples.

The artifacts discussed in this volume were collected during the years 1960–64 by members of the Tehuacan Archaeological-Botanical Project—Arturo Arvide, Douglas S. Byers, Robert Chadwick, Angél García Cook, Melvin L. Fowler, Frederick Johnson, Francisco Molina, Antoinette Nelken, Frederick A. Peterson,

Narciso Tejeda, their various crews, and myself. A few tools were picked up by visitors, who included Donald Collier, Bruce Warren, José Luís Lorenzo, Michael D. Coe, and our youngest visitor, at the age of five years, Nicholas Coe. Analyses of these materials were almost entirely accomplished by Antoinette Nelken, Irmgard Weitlaner de Johnson, and myself. All three of us are the creators and authors of this volume. To Irmgard Johnson goes credit for the chapter on textiles. As I have written the final draft of that part of the volume which does not treat of textiles, responsibility for any shortcomings there rests with me.

It would not have been possible to carry to fruition researches undertaken by the Tehuacan Archaeological-Botanical Project without the generous and encouraging support of the National Science Foundation and the Rockefeller Foundation. A grant from the Rockefeller Foundation supplemented our first grant from the National Science Foundation and made possible botanical investigations during the summer of 1961 that were of inestimable value to the entire project. The National Science Foundation has given support not only for field research, but also for preparation of manuscript and the manufacture of this volume, without which it could not have been published.

To these foundations, I give my sincere thanks.

The Robert S. Peabody Foundation of Phillips Academy, Andover, Massachusetts, has administered these funds and taken care of our wants while in the field. To the Foundation, and through the Foundation to Phillips Academy, I owe a great debt. Invaluable assistance by Frederick Johnson, Curator, R. S. Peabody Foundation, has made possible the preparation of the excellent illustrations in this volume. His assistance in this and other ways in its preparation is gratefully acknowledged. Douglas S. Byers, Director, has assisted in many ways, and acted as Editor-in-chief. To him and to Chase J. Duffy I owe sincere thanks for their help in presenting my thoughts in nearly readable form.

RICHARD S. MACNEISH

CONTENTS

ILLUSTRATIONS

Credits

Photographs of artifacts illustrated in Parts I-III are by Alvin H. Towne for the Robert S. Peabody Foundation, Phillips Academy, Andover, Massachusetts. Photographs of textiles in Part IV, unless otherwise noted, are by Luis Torres, Departamento de Prehistoria, Instituto Nacional de Antropología e Historia, Mexico.

TABLES

The Prehistory of the Tehuacan Valley

NONCERAMIC ARTIFACTS

Introduction

THIS SECOND volume in the Tehuacan Archaeological-Botanical series is concerned with the 20,000 or so nonceramic artifacts found in the Tehuacan Valley of southeastern Mexico during the years 1960-64. Over half of these tools came from well-controlled excavations, and the others were collected in archaeological reconnaissance.

These nonceramic artifacts are part of the historic and scientific record, and as such, it behooves one to describe them. After all, they were associated with basic technologies and economic activities, as well as with other social phenomena, and were a facet of the ancient life that cannot be ignored. Obviously, for practical reasons we cannot describe individually each of these 20,000 artifacts. Fortunately, the various man-made nonceramic remains can be grouped together according to a number of different kinds of criteria such as style, form, and function. A study based on any of these or other characteristics would be a valid classification in terms of one's own reasons for grouping the artifacts into logical units.

However, I feel that before the artifacts are classified or studied in terms of wide cultural implications or interpretations, one should first establish a firm chronological framework for the region. Therefore, while we may consider the nonceramic artifacts from many other standpoints in later volumes, in this volume they shall be considered in terms of chronology and cultural change. Here the nonceramic artifacts of the Tehuacan Valley will be classified into groups that may serve as time markers and as a mechanism for establishing a chronology.

Our classification of artifacts into groups of time markers—or into archaeological types—is based upon the following assumptions about culture (Ford 1962):

1. Culture is a continuum of interrelated concepts, ideas, and beliefs through time and space. In other words, any group of people living at a particular time and in a specific place have received a set of concepts, ideas, and beliefs from their predecessors and ancestors. What is more, their culture (or that of their ancestors) always has been influenced by the culture of peoples surrounding them. Further, the culture of this particular group at this time and this place will be passed on to future generations.

2. Culture is constantly changing, owing to a variety of cultural mechanisms. This change may show considerable variation, both as to the particular aspects of the culture which may change and in regard to the speed and rate of change.

3. Culture both patterns and gives consistency to customary behavior. In other words, culture has an internal order. At any one moment in time, a culture will have a certain core of ideas and beliefs about what is "the right way" to make a pot or a tool, and this "right way" will appear to the maker as consistent with the other aspects of his culture and environment.

4. Artifacts are reflections of culture. As such, they are part of the cultural continuum, are constantly changing, and reflect the internal order of a culture.

In terms of these assumptions, let us consider the method by which artifacts may be studied so that they become types or time markers. All artifacts have at least form and dimension. Artifacts are also made by different techniques and are constructed from different materials. The multiple variation of the interrelated aspects of an artifact are considered to be the artifact's attributes. For example, consider projectile points. All of them have shape or form, dimension, and weight, and can be manufactured from different kinds of materials by a number of techniques. In terms of form, the tips of projectile points may be sharp or blunt; their bodies may be triangular, lanceolate, diamond-shaped, tear-drop-shaped, or pentagonal; their bases may be notched, concave, straight, or convex; they may be stemless or stemmed; they may have corner notches or side notches and different shapes of stems and barbs, and so on. They may also vary in length, width, thickness, and weight, and may be made of stone, metal, or bone. Further, they can be made by either percussion-chipping or pressure-flaking, or they may be ground into form, carved, molded, and so forth. All in all, they have between 600 and 1,000 possible features or attributes. To determine and record the attributes of artifacts is one of the first tasks of the archaeologist. This must be done by observation, study, and actual handling of the material.

Once the attributes have been determined for a series of artifacts, comparisons may be undertaken to discover the modes—that is, those attributes which have significance in time and space (Rouse 1939). When a series of artifacts from one occupation are compared with those from another occupation of a different time period or with those from a different place, some of their features or attributes may be found to be the same, while others will differ. Those attributes that are significantly different are modes and are thus time and space markers. Once the significant artifactual changes are determined, a major portion of our study has been accomplished. In concentrating on the abstracted modes alone, however, we have focused on only a small, temporally sensitive portion of the whole artifact, and it becomes difficult to discern the over-all artifactual changes—nor can we see the culturally compulsive internal order to which the artifact and its various attributes belong.

Further comparisons therefore must be made with "whole" artifacts from sites or occupations of either different time periods or different places. One is then able to determine those groups of artifacts which possess a series of modes clustered together—often along with other attributes having no temporal or spatial significance. These groups of artifacts with mode-attribute clusters—that is, a series of interrelated features having significance in time and space—are called artifact types. Artifact types are tools for establishing chronology and are abstracted by the archaeologist from the continuum of culturally patterned ideas and concepts utilized by the ancient toolmakers. If our types serve as well-defined time and space markers, they are valid types for that purpose, and it does not really matter whether the ancient Tehuacaneros would recognize them as types or not.

Besides serving as time markers to segment the lengthy cultural sequence in the Tehuacan Valley, the artifact types are useful in determining the chronological relationship between a number of different sites in the Tehuacan region. The types from any one excavation with a series of superimposed levels of different time periods, of course, show cultural change and trends. When the artifact types from two or more excavations, each with a series of superimposed occupations, are compared, the various occupations may then be aligned in chronological order in terms of the over-all trends established by the artifact types. Further, when types from a single occupation, or even from a surface collection, are compared with the artifact types derived from multi-occupied sites, these single-period components may be placed in their relative chronological position on the basis of similarity or difference. Thus, if a site with types A, B, and C in the top floor, types C, D, and E in the middle floor, and types E, F, and G in the lower floor is compared with a single-occupation site containing types D, E, and F, it seems safe to conclude that the single-occupation site existed during the period occurring between the middle and lowest occupations of the multi-occupied site. Therefore, trends of artifact types allow one to discern the temporal relationships of a series of sites from a single area. This relative dating of sites or components within one region by artifact trends, of course, tests, supplements, and confirms other methods of relative and absolute dating.

The use of our artifact types, however, need not be confined to determining relationships within the Tehuacan Valley. Comparing our types with those from other areas may indicate relationships which may become the basis for aligning the cultural sequence of Tehuacan with other sequences. In fact, during the period 1960 to 1965, our comparisons not only showed temporal relationships but allowed one tentatively to date the cultural phases of related regions.

On a higher level of abstraction, extra-areal comparisons of artifact types give us insights into the diffusion of culture. Comparisons between the artifact types of Tehuacan and those from other areas give information about the origin and spread of certain types of artifacts. For example, in the Tehuacan Valley split-stitch basketry with a coiled bundle foundation originated about 4000 B.C. This type of basketry did not appear in Tamaulipas until 1500 B.C. and did not reach the southwestern United States until almost A.D. 500. Thus this type of basketry obviously diffused northward.

A final by-product of typology is that it allows us to discern significant periods or stages of cultural development. When all sequences of all classes of artifact types within this volume are compared, it becomes apparent that there are specific periods within the span of pre-Hispanic Tehuacan history when clusters of new types appear. In other words, cultural change, in terms of artifact types, appears in spurts of new types, rather than as a gradual accumulation of new types. We believe that these "spurts" of new types represent periods of significant cultural change. These periods or segments of our sequence having a new complex of reoccurring types are called "phases."

These periods, or phases, of rapid change in nonceramic artifacts still must be considered tentative, for the nonceramic artifacts are but a part of the whole cultural inventory. However, when periods of change in nonceramic artifacts are compared with periods of change in ceramic types, in burial types, in settlement patterns, and in subsistence patterns—and if the changes in all of these cultural phenomena show a high correlation—then our tentative phases may be considered to be true or confirmed periods, or phases, of cultural change. We might add here that there is a very high correlation between the tentative phases of nonceramic artifactual change described in this volume and the various other types of cultural change uncovered by the Tehuacan project. That is to say, the tentative periods of cultural change indicated by the sequence of nonceramic artifact types are extremely sensitive reflections of the major cultural phases in the Tehuacan Valley.

We collected in the Tehuacan Valley about 20,000 nonceramic artifacts which showed definite evidence of having been intentionally fashioned into tools of various kinds. We set aside, or only cursorily studied, a much larger number of chips, pebbles, cores, and rocks found with these artifacts. (I have no idea exactly how many there were, but they filled six fifty-pound gunnysacks.) Our sample study of some of this unfinished material indicated that although it did reveal minor changes through time and gave some inklings about changing technology, it was not nearly so sensitive an indicator of cultural change as were the finished artifacts. This material was catalogued but not further studied and was given to the Instituto Nacional de Antropología e Historia in Mexico.

The 20,000 "finished" artifacts described in this volume came from a variety of sources. About 13,000 came from excavation and the rest from surface collections gathered at the 454 sites discovered during our reconnaissance. About 12,000 of the artifacts from excavations

Major stratified sites	No. of zones	No. of artifacts
Coxcatlan (Tc 50)	27	5268
Purron (Tc 272)	25	415
Coatepec (Ts 368)	18	1055
Abejas (Tc 307)	11	238
Ajalpan (Ts 204)	10	1075
Quachilco (Tr 218)	9	1000
El Riego, West (Tc 35w)	7	1016
San Marcos (Tc 254)	7	292
El Riego, East (Tc 35e)	6	873
Coxcatlan Terrace (Ts 51)	5	321
Las Canoas (Ts 367)	5	236
Ajalpan Test (Ts 204D)	5	41
Tecorral (Tc 255)	3	163

were uncovered in "major digs" in stratified sites, as the accompanying tabulation shows. Approximately 5,300 nonceramic artifacts were found in the twenty-seven stratified occupational zones of Coxcatlan Cave (Tc 50). Some 1,016 artifacts came from seven stratified layers in the West Niche of El Riego Cave (Tc 35w). Over 400 tools were unearthed in the twenty-five superimposed floors of Purron Cave (Tc 272). Abejas Cave (Tc 307) had eleven superimposed floors which yielded 238 artifacts; Tecorral Cave (Tc 255) had only three floors which contained 163 artifacts. The San Marcos site (Tc 254), although it had seven separate occupational zones, yielded only 292 nonceramic artifacts, but it contained a considerable number of plant remains. Located in the brickyards near Ajalpan was the Ajalpan site (Ts 204). The 1,075 nonceramic artifacts from this site (and there were many more ceramic ones) came from ten strata containing human remains; four of these strata were capped by definite house floors. Nearby was the Coatepec site (Ts 368), where a pit seven meters deep revealed eighteen strata of cultural debris that contained 1,055 artifacts, and bags and bags of potsherds. Five unconnected test trenches in different parts of the Quachilco site (Tr 218) yielded from five to nine occupational zones, even more pottery than Coatepec, and about 1,000 nonceramic artifacts. The final major excavation was the East Niche of El Riego Cave (Tc 35e), which had six stratified zones full of sherds and vegetal material, along with 873 nonceramic artifacts.

Three of the smaller tests had stratified deposits. A long trench (Ts 51) through the terrace in front of Coxcatlan Cave revealed five zones with 321 artifacts. A somewhat shorter but wider trench near Ajalpan, in a particularly dry section of the clay pits, was called Las Canoas (Ts 367). Here we uncovered five stratified zones containing mainly pottery but also 236 nonceramic artifacts. The final test square having stratigraphy was a small cut made near the Ajalpan site (Ts 204D). It yielded forty-one nonceramic artifacts in five zones. The accompanying map (Fig. 1) shows the geographic location of these sites in the Tehuacan Valley.

The 12,000 artifacts, then, from the 138 stratified zones of the major excavated sites are the basis for our artifact typology and for our trends of artifact types. In this volume, however, we shall not attempt to describe the methods by which we dug these strata, nor their contents, nor their extent, nor the criteria on which we differentiated between them. These matters will be fully explained in Volume V, and it would be repetitious to discuss them here. This being the case, we ask the reader to make two more assumptions: first, that we did use careful excavating techniques and methods and

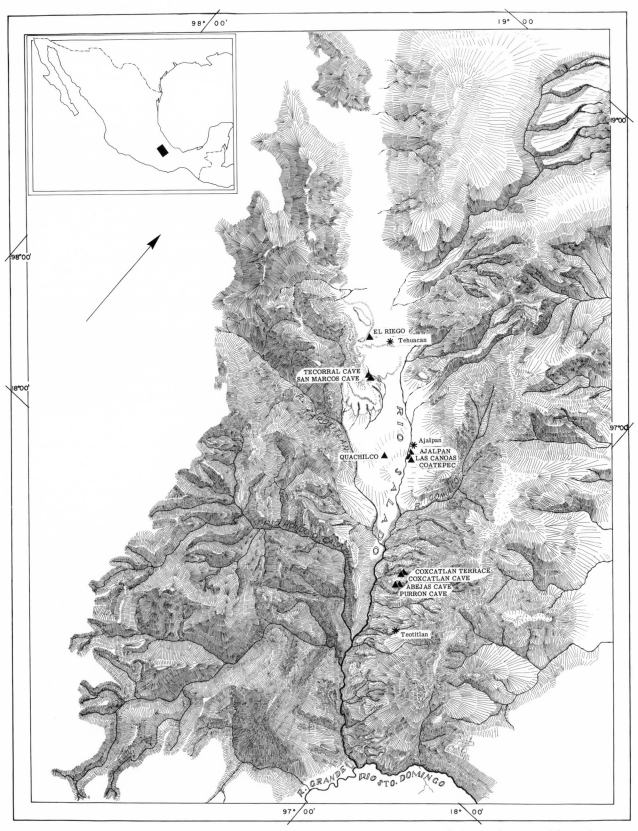

Fig. 1. The Tehuacan Valley, showing the principal towns and major stratified sites (in capital letters).

that we were able to strip off extra strata; second, that we had the ability to distinguish between the different strata apparent in our digging. Here I must admit that in the beginning there were some among us who were "strata-blind," but "strata-vision" became, with practice, a shared characteristic.

About 1,000 nonceramic artifacts were exhumed in some twenty-five test digs, but the stratigraphy was so poor, or the samples so small, that we did not use these tools in the basic typology. These artifacts, along with the 7,000 tools collected from the 454 surveyed sites, were used only to check our final type descriptions. Both sets of artifacts, however, were compared with the trends of artifact types from the stratified sites and were used to align the surface sites and tested components in their relative chronological positions.

Cataloguing, of course, came before any actual study of the artifacts themselves. In order to catalogue, we separated the artifacts into various categories—such as bifaces, unifaces, and so forth—so that they could easily be numbered. In fact, as we were digging and bagging the material, the first sorting for cataloguing began. Each set of material, as it came out of the ground, from the very beginning of digging Coxcatlan Cave in 1961, was sorted into corn, vegetal material, projectile points, pottery, bones, textiles, ground-stone artifacts, blades, and all other chipped-stone artifacts. When each level in each square was completely excavated, the materials in each category were wrapped in foil and tagged as to content and location—site, square, zone, and level. Then all the packages were placed together in a single, larger cloth bag which had duplicate tags inside and out giving the site number, the square number in the site, the level, the zone, the depth of the zone, the date of excavation, and the name of the excavator.

After these bags of roughly sorted materials were brought to the headquarters in Tehuacan, the real numbering of the specimens began. Every specimen received a number, or a numbered tag, indicating its exact, original, excavated locus. The numbers themselves were expressed as fractions, with the site number in the position of the numerator. For example, in terms of our survey system, Coxcatlan Cave's number was Tc 50—i.e., *T* for Tehuacan, *c* for cave, and "50" because it was the fiftieth site found in the survey. On rare occasions, particularly with some of the larger sites found during the latter part of the survey, *e* or *w* was added to the site number, indicating the east or west part of the site.

The denominator portion of the catalogue number was divided into four parts. The first number was that of the square excavated. The first square excavated in a

cave, regardless of its map number, was for purposes of cataloguing, called number 1. The square number was followed by a dash and a second number corresponding to the level, and often to the zone, of the particular square of that particular site. Affixed to the final number was a letter indicating the kind of material; for, as we have mentioned, excavated material often had to be kept wrapped in foil and the type of specimen inside could not always be visually identified.

The catalogue number was also recorded in a loose-leaf notebook, along with all the information written on the original bag tag. Later, when a site was completely catalogued, the handwritten notebook pages were typed and checked against the original tag and the field notes. Thus our half-million or so specimens gradually became numbered and catalogued.

The next task was the sorting of the numbered and catalogued specimens. The specimens from a single site were first separated into boxes according to the various categories—pottery, blades, scraper-planes, plants, and so forth. The boxes were labeled, indicating the site and contents—such as "Tc 50—projectile points"—and in time, labeled boxes from various sites, with special categories of artifacts in each, began piling up. As we sorted these piles, we put aside certain of the excavated materials for specialists who would be visiting the project.

The materials from the surface collections, after being washed, numbered, and catalogued, were sorted into bags—one set for ceramic and another for nonceramic artifacts—and put aside until after the typology based on excavated materials had been completed.

At this point, we were ready to start classifying the chipped-stone artifacts from stratified excavated sites. Our basic equipment was a large laboratory containing four large tables, rolls of wrapping paper to cover the tables, colored chalk to mark the paper on the tables, pliers, glue, hand lenses, a microscope, and reams of graph paper.

To illustrate how we classified the chipped-stone artifacts, I shall describe in detail our analysis of the blades. We began with the boxes of blades from our best stratified site, Coxcatlan Cave, and a table top marked off into twenty-seven rows, representing the twenty-seven zones of the cave. The blades from each zone were then laid out in the appropriate rows. As we studied this arrangement, we soon saw that certain attributes of the blades, such as their size and form and the number of dorsal ridges, showed little significance; but it was also apparent that some attributes did have definite temporal significance and were therefore modes. For instance, we immediately recognized that crude blades were dominant in the early levels and that fine blades were more popular in later levels, and this gave us our first set of modes.

Another series of modes became apparent when we inspected the various kinds of striking platforms adhering to the blades. Unprepared, prepared, pointed, and ground striking platforms appeared in our sequence in the order mentioned. We also compared the fragments of blades without striking platforms and discovered that tips of blades occurred throughout our sequence in no regular manner, but that broken blades with both tips and striking platforms snapped off appeared in significantly large proportions in the upper levels.

A number of other attributes, such as the specific part of the blade that had been worked or retouched, the kind of material used, the relationship of thickness to width, and so on, were also examined, and some of these had modal value. The occurrence and percentile frequency of these modes were then recorded on large sheets of graph paper, with the levels in rows and the modes in columns.

Once the modes became apparent, we began reshuffling the blades to determine the mode-attribute clusters. Groups of blades were laid out according to levels and divided into little piles in terms of their combination of modal characteristics. In this way, for instance, piles emerged of crude blade tips and of fine blade tips; of fine snapped blades with retouched ends and of fine snapped blades with one edge retouched and with two edges retouched. There were piles of crude blades with one edge retouched and with two edges retouched and piles of fine blades with one and with two edges retouched; there were crude blades with unprepared and with prepared striking platforms and with or without retouched edges; there were fine blades with unprepared, prepared, pointed, or ground striking platforms and with one edge or two edges retouched, and so on. After a number of reshufflings, we noticed that some of the categories on the table appeared in large amounts only in certain of the rows representing excavation zones. For example, in the rows representing the upper three occupational zones—and nowhere else—there were three different piles of fine blades with ground striking platforms; the blades in one group had no lateral retouching, the blades in another group had one edge retouched, and the blades in the third pile had two edges retouched. It was thus apparent that the blades with ground striking platforms with or without retouching in various places had the same stratigraphic or temporal significance. These three piles, therefore, were combined to serve as a single "trial type."

We also discovered that our lowest zones contained only crude blades with unprepared striking platforms, although some of these blades were not retouched at all and others were retouched or worked along one or both edges. Thus all the crude blades with unprepared striking platforms could be combined into a single trial type. By a series of such manipulations, we eventually arrived at nine trial types of blades, along with two other categories for fragments of crude and fine blades, and these eleven groupings had temporal significance.

It was now time to test these trial types from Coxcatlan Cave with the blades from the West Niche of El Riego Cave. The El Riego blades were laid out in groups of trial types, according to the stratum from which they came. It immediately became apparent that for the most part the El Riego and Coxcatlan blades had the same significance in time. However, in classifying some of the other kinds of artifacts, we found it necessary during this comparative stage to modify or redefine our trial types.

Our next step was to calculate the percentage of blades of each trial type from each time level of El Riego Cave and compare them, one at a time, with the similar percentages from Coxcatlan Cave. When a level from El Riego Cave contained percentages which seemed to fall between two sets of percentages from two zones of Coxcatlan Cave, a space on the larger Coxcatlan table was marked off, and the group of trial types from El Riego Cave were placed in that appropriate row. For example, Zone B of El Riego Cave had 26 percent snapped blades and 74 percent blades with ground striking platforms. This set of percentages seemed to fall between those of Zones III and IV of Coxcatlan Cave, which had respectively 75 and 25 percent of blades with ground platforms and 25 and 75 percent of snapped blades. Eventually, all the trial types from both caves were dovetailed on the same table, in terms of the percentage trends of each trial type.

The same process was undertaken with the blades from Purron, San Marcos, and Tecorral caves, and later with blades from the other stratified sites. Our laboratory tables were now covered with piles of blades according to trial types, one next to the other, showing the trends in blade types with all modal characteristics taken into account, as well as the chronological alignment of the occupational zones from all stratified sites. These data were recorded on large sheets of graph paper, with the types being the abscissa, the aligned zones of all stratified sites being the ordinate, and the exact number of each type, at each level, being at the junction of the appropriate abscissa and ordinate rows.

We now assumed that we had determined the mode-attribute clusters of the blades and had determined valid types, and that we knew the trends in popularity of these types. We were now ready to fit the single-period excavations and surface collections that contained blades into their relative chronological position with respect to the stratified sites. The percentages of each type from each single-component site were calculated and were compared with those from the components of the stratified sites, then the sites were aligned in the same manner as the stratified components. Another chart, organized in the same way as the first one, was drawn for the single-component sites.

Next, all blades of one type were sorted by site and were stored in boxes labeled by type to await description and further study. All that remained to be done in preparation for this volume was to record the measurements of an adequate sample of blades of each type and to study their distribution in areas outside the Tehuacan Valley.

When we finished with the blades, we analyzed and described in the same manner the other chipped-stone tools, the ground-stone artifacts, the materials made of bone, shell, and wood, and the baskets, petates, knots, and cordage. In the meantime, Irmgard de Johnson studied the nets and textiles and prepared a description of them.

For the most part, the study of each class of artifacts was relatively independent. But at the termination of each study, the chronological alignment of sites was compared one with the others, and the differences, when they existed, were analyzed. Since samples varied from component to component and since some types were better time markers than others, we occasionally had to adjust our chronological alignment of components. Eventually, we compared this adjusted alignment with the chronological order of components based on ceramic typology and made further modifications. We believe, however, that we have finally arrived at a fairly correct relative chronology on the basis of the trends of our 250 nonceramic artifact types.

As our studies progressed, we noticed that a series of new types in a single class of artifacts would suddenly appear within a sequence. These sudden appearances of new types tentatively allowed us to separate the sequence into segments or complexes, which we named. As more and more different classes or types were studied, together with the other cultural aspects, it became apparent that not only did new types of a single class appear at specific time periods within the sequence, but that whole complexes of new types emerged in specific parts of the sequence. This occurrence of an assemblage of new types appearing at specific times within the sequence, together with the re-

occurrence of this assemblage in a series of different components, became the basis for the establishment of the following tentative cultural periods, or phases. From early to late these phases are Ajuereado, El Riego, Coxcatlan, Abejas, Purron, Ajalpan, Santa Maria, Palo Blanco, and Venta Salada. The phases are usually named after the site or location which provided the first recognizable assemblage of characteristic artifacts. As we shall show in later volumes, and as the data concerning subsistence in Volume I indicate, the tentative phases based on nonceramic artifacts correlate closely with the major changes in ceramics, subsistence patterns, settlement patterns, and other aspects of the culture of these prehistoric Tehuacan people.

Ajuereado Phase

The earliest assemblage of artifacts represents the Ajuereado phase. In the caves, we uncovered evidence of six different occupations, while surface collections have yielded four more sites of this cultural complex. As yet we have only three dates, obtained by the radiocarbon technique, on the final stages of this phase. The phase seems to have ended by at least 6500 B.C. Examination of these floors indicates that in this period the inhabitants were grouped together into small, nomadic families or microbands who changed their camps three or four times a year with the seasons. As means of subsistence they collected wild plants, and they hunted and trapped. Although they hunted such animals as horses and antelope of now extinct species during the earliest part of the phase, even then most of their meat came from smaller game, such as jack rabbits, gophers, rats, turtles, birds, and other small creatures. In the later part of the phase they trapped only species that exist today. These people, in the so-called "big-game hunting stage" or "mammoth-hunting period," were far from being the great hunters they are supposed to have been. As one of my colleagues said: "They probably found one mammoth in a lifetime and never got over talking about it—like some archaeologists."

The manufactured tools of this group were not numerous, and all were made by chipping flint. They include a series of bifacially chipped leaf-shaped knives and projectile points, keeled and ovoid end-scrapers, flake and bifacial choppers, side-scrapers, gravers, and crude prismatic blades struck from even cruder polyhedral cores. No ground stone was utilized. The floors held few perishable remains, hence we know nothing about the weaving industry or the traps and perishable tools of these people. No burials have been found, though there is one fragment of a charred human bone.

El Riego Phase

Gradually the Ajuereado phase developed into one which we call the El Riego cultural phase. This is extremely well known, for we have dug up twenty-three floors and have found fourteen open camp sites. Ten dates, obtained by the radiocarbon method, allow us to estimate the time of this cultural phase fairly accurately. It seems to fall between 6500 and about 4800 B.C. The people of this period were seasonally nomadic like their predecessors, but there had been a definite increase in population, and some changes in the settlement pattern seem to have taken place. The sites are almost equally divided between very small camps, which obviously represent the family groups or microbands of the dry seasons, and much larger sites, representing camps of related families or macrobands which gathered together in the spring and wet seasons. The means of subsistence was basically plant and animal collecting, supplemented by some hunting—not very different from the previous period, although these peoples seem to have hunted deer instead of horse and antelope, and the cotton-tail rabbit instead of the jack rabbit.

As for the hunting and trapping activities, there were no fundamental changes; nor do the people seem to have been "forced by the changing climatic conditions that followed the end of the Wisconsin Glaciation to make readjustments." The preserved plant remains, however, seem to show that plant collecting was even more important than it had been in the previous culture. Nevertheless, it was only a seasonal affair. During the dry season, apparently, people still hunted and trapped in small groups and probably nearly starved, but when the spring came, and later the rains, a number of microbands seem to have gathered together in larger groups to live off the lusher vegetation. There is evidence that they were collecting a large variety of plants, and I would guess that this was the period when they first conceived the idea that if you drop a seed in the ground a plant comes up. By the close of this period they may have domesticated the avocado and perhaps the chili pepper, one species of squash (*Cucurbita mixta*), and amaranth.

The development of such a subsistence and settlement pattern undoubtedly caused some change in social organization. From comparative ethnological data, one might guess that these groups, if related, were patrilineal bands with some sort of weak temporary leadership in the hands of a male, and perhaps some concept of territoriality. Further, there apparently were shamans, or witch doctors, who had considerable power in both the medicinal and the ceremonial fields. These, of course, would not have been full-time specialists.

The tools we dug up gave considerable evidence about the industrial activities of these peoples. For example, they manufactured a number of varieties of contracting-stemmed and concave-based projectile points. These are very neatly chipped and were probably used to tip atlatl darts used in the chase. The most prevalent artifacts were, however, the large plano-convex scrapers and choppers chipped from pebbles or nodules of flint. These tools could have been used for preparing skins, but it seems more probable that they were used for pulping various vegetal materials. Some blades, burins, and end-scrapers of types found in the previous horizon were still made and utilized. The most noticeable change in the material culture was the use of ground-stone and pecked-stone implements. Mortars and pestles were particularly numerous, and there were many milling stones and pebble manos. Tools of both types were probably used to grind plant and animal remains into some sort of palatable (or unpalatable) stew.

In addition, it is in this period that we found the first evidence of weaving and woodworking—knotted nets, a few small fragments of twined blankets and coiled baskets, fragments of dart shafts, and pieces of traps.

To me, one of the most surprising findings for the El Riego period was evidence of relatively elaborate burials, which indicate the possibility of complex beliefs and ceremonies. We uncovered two groups of multiple burials. In the first were the skeletons of two children; their heads had been removed and were exchanged in burial. The head of the older child seems to have received ceremonial treatment before being placed in a basket found resting on the chest of the younger child, an infant under six months old. The other multiple burial included an elderly man, a woman of at least middle age, and a child of less than one year. There was evidence that the elderly man had been intentionally burned, and the heads of both the woman and the child had been smashed, perhaps intentionally. These findings could indeed be interpreted as involving human sacrifice, but the correctness of such an interpretation is difficult to prove. In both these burials the bodies were wrapped in blankets and nets and were richly furnished with basketry. Is it not possible that the ceremonialism which is so characteristic of the later Mexican periods began at this time?

Coxcatlan Phase

The phase developing out of the El Riego phase was termed Coxcatlan. It probably extended from about 4800 to 3500 B.C. Nine components of this phase were uncovered in cave excavations, and four open camps were also found. Although fewer occupations were

10

found than in the El Riego phase, most of them were larger. However, the way of life may have been much the same, with nomadic microbands in the dry season and macrobands in the wet season. The macrobands seem to have been larger than those of the earlier phase, and they seem to have stayed in one place for longer periods. Perhaps this was due to their rather different subsistence pattern.

Although the Coxcatlan people were still basically plant collectors who did a little animal trapping and hunting, all through this period they acquired more and more domesticated plants. Early in the period they were using corn, *Cucurbita mixta*, chili, avocados, amaranth, and gourds. By the end of the phase they had acquired common beans, *Cucurbita moschata*, and black and white sapotes. It would appear, however, that all these domesticated plants combined did not make up more than 15 percent of their total diet.

It seems that microbands still came together at some favorite collecting spot in the spring, and it may be that while they were there they planted some of their domesticates. This would have given them food to continue living at that camp after they had consumed their wild foods. As the numbers of domesticates increased, the group could, of course, have stayed together as a macroband for longer and longer periods. But with the onset of the dry season and the depletion of their agricultural "surpluses," they would have broken up again into nomadic microbands.

The changing subsistence and settlement pattern may have been connected with the changes in social organization. The bands may still have been patrilineal. But one wonders whether the use of gardens and the more settled way of life might not have resulted in bands having definite collecting territories and ideas about property "garden rights." Moreover, a greater dependence upon agriculture (and rainfall) may have made the shaman even more powerful, not only in medicine and in birth and death ceremonies, but also in regard to rituals connected with plantings and harvestings. In addition, the more settled life involving larger numbers of people may have resulted in some kind of macroband leadership, more stable than that vested in the oldest or most powerful male in a family.

The industrial activities of the group were not vastly different from those of their predecessors, although different types of tanged projectile points were manufactured. Blades were more delicately made, scrapers and choppers were of new types, and true metates, with manos, were replacing the mortars, pestles, and milling stones. Some minor improvements were also made in the manufacture of nets and coiled baskets.

Abejas Phase

The Abejas phase follows the Coxcatlan phase, and we estimate that it existed from about 3500 to 2300 B.C. Fifteen occupations have been uncovered, and eight sites were found in reconnaissance.

The settlement pattern seems to have changed significantly in this period. Of the cave occupations, seven were hunting (dry-season) camps of macrobands, while eight of the macroband settlements were on river terraces in the valley. The latter appear to have been larger settlements of five to ten pit houses, and some of them may have been occupied all year round. This even more settled way of life was made possible by more efficient food production. This was accomplished with plants already known and, in addition, with domesticated jack beans, perhaps pumpkins (*Cucurbita pepo*), and tepary beans, as well as some varieties of hybrid corn with *teosinte* introgression. The people also used cotton and had dogs. However, even with the increase in domesticates, botanical studies and studies of feces reveal that more than 70 percent of their foods still came from wild plants and animals.

Again, many of the older techniques of artifact manufacture continued in use, though the types of artifacts are a little different. Some of the types which carry over into much later times originated during this period. These include: split-stitch basketry, stone bowls, oval metates and large plano-convex manos, obsidian blades made from long cylindrical cores, and other objects.

Purron Phase

The next phase, Purron, probably falls between 2300 and 1500 B.C. It is the least clearly understood phase in the sequence and is represented by only two excavated floors. The excavated materials include a few plant remains, early tripsacoid corn cobs, manos, metates, scrapers, fine obsidian blades, and a number of very crude, crumbly pieces of broken pottery. The pottery, the earliest so far found in Mesoamerica, has the same vessel forms as the stone bowls of the previous period. This pottery, as well as the stone bowls, may not be the first vessels made in Mexico but only a duplication of still earlier pottery (as yet unfound) in some other area. One might surmise that the subsistence and settlement pattern and social organization of the Purron phase was much the same as that of the Abejas phase.

Ajalpan Phase

The following phase, Ajalpan, which extends from 1500 to about 900 B.C., is much better understood. Sixteen floors were found in the diggings, and two open sites were found during survey. The Ajalpan people were full-time agriculturists; they planted early hybrid corn; mixta, moschata, and pepo squashes; gourds; amaranths; beans; chili; avocado; sapotes; and cotton. They seem to have lived in small wattle-and-daub villages of from 100 to 300 inhabitants. Whether they built religious structures is not yet known, but their figurines, mainly female, attest to a complex religious life. Male priests and chiefs certainly must have had considerable power, although the rich female burials and the figurines hint that kinship and property ownership may have had a matrilineal emphasis.

Many stone tools of the older types were still made, but one of the more notable industries of this period was pottery making. The pottery, though well made, is usually unpainted, although a few examples of monochrome, specular-hematite red ware are found. A limited number of forms were modeled; the tecomate, or small-mouthed seed jar, is the dominant type of receptacle.

The figurines show an interesting development throughout this period. The earliest ones are very crude with spherical heads and with features marked by punctations, and they have crude, standing, sexless bodies. These give way to large solid figurines that have rather realistic facial features and female bodies. In the final part of the phase there are large, red, hollow, female dwarfs (proto-Olmecoid?). The figurines are unlike any found in highland Mexico, but the large solid figurines resemble the earliest ones found in the lowlands.

Santa Maria Phase

In the subsequent Santa Maria period the pottery still shows resemblances to pottery of the Vera Cruz coast. It also has a resemblance to the earliest pottery remains of Monte Alban, the Valley of Mexico, and other highland regions. Thus we have good evidence for correlating a number of sequences from a number of regions, not only with Santa Maria of Tehuacan, but also with each other.

The Santa Maria period lasted from before 900 B.C. to about 200 B.C. The culture is well known, for we excavated forty-three components and found about fifteen surface sites. The settlement pattern reveals that the people lived in small wattle-and-daub houses in villages that were oriented toward a single, larger village with a ceremonial structure. The people were full-time farmers, using all of the plants previously known, plus manioc, tomatoes (*Physalis* sp.), and *Phaseolus coccineus*. However, more productive hybrids had been developed from many of these plants. This may also be the period in which true irrigation was first used.

Although a few new types of chipped-stone tools, woven cotton fabrics, and new kinds of ground-stone tools appear, the great majority of the materials we uncovered consisted of pieces of broken pottery. The vessels were well made. They were mainly monochrome (white or gray), though there were a few bichromes. About half of all the vessels found were flat-bottomed bowls; the rest were ollas, water bottles, composite silhouette bowls, and other forms. Decoration was usually achieved by incising on the interior bottoms of bowls or on the rims of lips, but a few of the vessels have plain rocker stamping, negative painting, and engraving.

Palo Blanco Phase

The Santa Maria period developed into the Palo Blanco period, which extends from before 200 B.C. to about A.D. 700. On the basis of information and materials from seventeen excavated components and about 200 sites found in survey, we are able to make the following reconstruction about the way of life of the people of this phase. They too were full-time agriculturists, and they systematically used irrigation. Besides the previously known domesticates, they had also acquired peanuts, small lima beans, guavas, and turkeys. They lived in wattle-and-daub villages or hamlets either oriented toward or adjacent to large hilltop ceremonial centers with elaborate stone pyramids, plazas, ball courts, and other structures. Some of these ruins covered whole mountain tops and, in terms of population, might be considered cities, albeit sacred cities. Perhaps these centers were under the authority of priest-kings; if so, the priest-kings certainly must have been assisted by full-time specialists and a hierarchy of bureaucrats, at least to run the irrigation works.

The manufactured products were varied and more elaborate than those of previous phases. The fine gray and orange pottery, the obsidian working, the bark cloth, and the elaborately woven cotton fabrics are particularly distinctive.

Venta Salada Phase

The final period, Venta Salada, dates from before A.D. 700 to 1540. Study of the records of early Spanish conquerors of the Tehuacan Valley should shed further light on this phase. Studies made so far reveal that the people were full-time agriculturists and relied upon irrigation. Further, their economy was greatly supplemented by commerce with other regions. Local salt-making and cotton-processing industries made products for exportation. Politically, the valley seems to have been divided into a series of little kingdoms, each of which had urban centers with surrounding hamlets. These units may have been subsidiary to the rulers of the Mixtec Empire. Among the manufactured articles were such distinctive artifacts as polychrome pottery, a variety of cotton fabrics, bark cloth, and chipped-stone tools and arrow-points. We have excavated over fifteen occupations of this final phase and have found about 200 sites in surface surveys.

Initially, this long sequence was classified into evolutionary stages called Paleo-Indian, Archaic or Incipient Agriculture, Formative, Classic, and Postclassic. Each of these stages was thought of as having a series of well-defined artifact characteristics which seemed applicable to all of Mesoamerica. However, the more I compared the artifacts and subsistence patterns of each of our Tehuacan phases with other sequential cultural manifestations in Mesoamerica, the less convinced I became that there had been a neat evolutionary stage development for the whole area. In later volumes this problem will be pursued further.

In spite of these doubts about a unilineal evolution, I did find it useful to employ the terminology usually applied to stages, but for time periods, not developmental stages. Thus, I shall speak of there being a Paleo-Indian period, which lasted until about 7000 B.C. ± 1000 years. Our Ajuereado phase falls into this period. The El Riego, Coxcatlan, and Abejas phases seem to fall into the second period, called Archaic, extending from 7000 B.C. ± 1000 years to 2000 B.C. ± 500 years. The Purron, Ajalpan, and Santa Maria phases belong to the Formative period from 2000 B.C. ± 500 years to 200 B.C. ± 200 years. This period can be divided into three sub-periods: early Formative from 2000 B.C. ± 500 years to 900 B.C. ± 100 years; middle Formative from 900 B.C. ± 100 years to 500 B.C. ± 100 years; and late Formative from 500 B.C. ± 100 years to 200 B.C. ± 200 years. Purron and Ajalpan can thus be considered as early Formative, while early Santa Maria is middle Formative and late Santa Maria is late Formative. The Palo-Blanco phase was thought of as being of the Classic period, from 200 B.C. ± 200 years to 700 A.D. ± 100 years. Venta Salada was of the Postclassic period, from 700 A.D. ± 100 years to the time of the Spanish conquest.

Admittedly, there are cultural similarities in terms of trade materials, horizon styles, and overlapping types over wide areas of Mesoamerica during each of these periods which gives them the superficial appearance of being evolutionary stages. I, however, have considerable doubt that these artifactually similar periods can be directly correlated with wide-spread Mesoamerican similarities in subsistence pattern, settlement pattern, social organization, and other cultural aspects that would be basic to the establishment of any evolutionary scheme. Certainly our present archaeological evidence cannot justify the classification of the meager sequential data into stages.

Before we can start establishing or even criticizing the sweeping generalizations about evolutionary stages of cultural change, we must have long sequences of artifacts and the resultant archaeological cultural phases from a number of different regions. The following descriptions and classifications of the nonceramic artifacts in this volume from the Tehuacan region are, I hope, a start toward amassing these necessary data.

REFERENCES

FORD, JAMES A.
1954   "The Type Concept Revisited." AA, 56:42–54.
1962   A Qualitative Method for Deriving Cultural Chronology. Technical Manual 1, Pan American Union. Washington.

KRIEGER, ALEX D.
1944   "The Typological Concept." Am. Ant., 9:271–88.
ROUSE, IRVING
1939   Prehistory in Haiti. Yale University Publications in Anthropology, No. 21. New Haven.

PART I: CHIPPED-STONE ARTIFACTS

CHAPTER 1

Blades and Polyhedral Cores

BLADES, for the purposes of this study, are chipped-stone tools with roughly parallel lateral edges, a dorsal surface divided by one or more lengthwise ridges, and an unworked ventral surface, usually with a bulb of percussion near the end adjacent to the remains of the striking platform. The striking platform usually forms one end of the blade and is at an acute or right angle to its dorsal surface. Blades are removed from the fluted or parallel-chipped sides of polyhedral cores, or nuclei, by either percussion or pressure techniques—that is, they are struck from the core directly by blows against the striking platform or indirectly through use of a punch, or they are removed by pressure exerted against the striking platform. Obviously, different types of cores produce different types of blades. Since we uncovered few polyhedral cores but many blades in the Tehuacan excavations, our typology is based mainly upon the blades and only secondarily upon the cores. Many of the core types described below, in fact, are largely derived from inferences drawn from the study of the blades themselves.

Crude blades with unprepared striking platforms are the earliest type found in the Tehuacan Valley. By a crude blade, we mean a blade whose sides are only roughly parallel and whose dorsal ridges are poorly defined, running in the same direction as the sides but not really parallel to them. Crude blades are usually made of flint, although a few are obsidian. They were probably struck from conical or hemiconical nuclei with striking platforms nearly at right angles to their poorly fluted surfaces. These cores probably resemble the domed scraper-planes described in Chapter 2—some of which may have been cores for blades and not true scrapers at all.

Crude blades with unprepared striking platforms are the only blades appearing in the earliest period, Ajuereado, of the Tehuacan sequence. They were also found

in the other early periods, but always as a minority type. A single blade with an unworked striking platform was found with the second Iztapan mammoth in the Valley of Mexico, and other crude blades have been uncovered in the earliest horizons of Hidalgo and Chiapas. In South America, crude blades have been uncovered with the El Jobo remains in Venezuela. In the earliest horizons of North America, crude blades appear to have a distinctive distribution. On the one hand, they seem to be absent from the big-game-hunting horizons of the Great Plains, such as Sandia, Clovis, Folsom, Plainview, and the like. They are found, however, in the Rocky Mountain chain, at sites seemingly of similar antiquity, such as Five Mile Rapids in Oregon, the Fraser Canyon site in British Columbia, the Klondike sites in the Northwest Territories of Canada, the Kluane and Flint Creek complexes of the Yukon, and the Kayuk complex in the Brooks Range of Alaska. Is it not possible that this crude-blade trait was ultimately derived from the Upper Paleolithic culture of eastern Asia and became part of the cultural tradition which spread southward from the Bering Strait through western North America into Mesoamerica?

Following our earliest blade type—originating and reaching a maximum popularity in the second, or El Riego period, of the Tehuacan sequence—are crude blades with prepared striking platforms. These blades were struck from conical or hemiconical nuclei with prepared striking platforms at an acute angle to their fluted surfaces. They may well be a Mesoamerican development based upon concepts involved in the manufacture of the earlier type. But I make this conjecture on limited data, since the only crude blades of this type I am familiar with in Mesoamerica were found either in the Tehuacan Valley or in the Santa Marta Cave in Chiapas.

Having a somewhat similar distribution and possibly

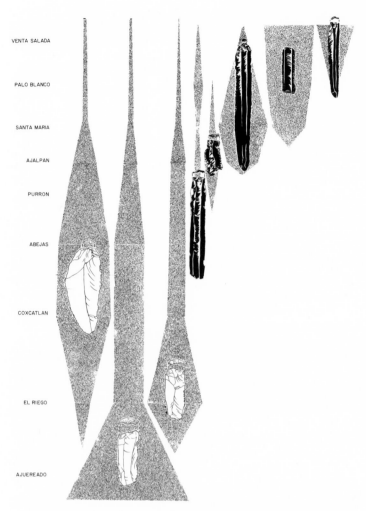

VENTA SALADA

PALO BLANCO

SANTA MARIA

AJALPAN

PURRON

ABEJAS

COXCATLAN

EL RIEGO

AJUEREADO

Fig. 2. Distribution of blade types in the Tehuacan cultural sequence.

a similar development are crude blades with pointed striking platforms. Although they were first manufactured almost as early as the previous two types of blades, they did not become popular until the third or Coxcatlan phase of the Tehuacan sequence. This particular type of crude blade could have been derived from either of the former types of cores by the use of especially skillful flint-knapping techniques, but many of the characteristics of these blades suggest that they were removed by indirect percussion.

The first fine blades appeared at about the same period that crude blades with pointed striking platforms were most popular. Fine blades have parallel central ridges and parallel lateral edges, and they are generally made of obsidian. The first distinctive type of fine blade —those with unprepared striking platforms—appeared at the end of the Coxcatlan phase and in the subsequent Abejas phase. Some of these blades may have

been struck from conical cores, not unlike the crude conical cores or scraper-planes, but most of them were derived from longer, finer, bullet-shaped cores with striking platforms at right angles to their tapering fluted sides. Some of the more flattened bullet-shaped cores superficially resemble the tongue-shaped cores of northwestern America and northeastern Asia. However, the Techuacan cores lack the retouched edge at the tip of the tongue and so cannot be said to be the same. Therefore, fine blades with unprepared striking platforms are probably a local development.

Just about the time that pottery appeared in the Tehuacan sequence, about 2000 B.C., fine blades with prepared striking platforms were being manufactured. These, too, were usually removed from bullet-shaped cores, but ones that had prepared striking platforms at an acute angle to their fluted surfaces. Some of the fine blades with prepared striking platforms also came from conical nuclei. This type of blade was never very popular, and it died out in the Palo Blanco period, about the time of Christ.

About 1500 B.C. fine blades with pointed striking platforms made their appearance, and these are the horizon markers for the Formative period, or the Ajalpan and Santa Maria phases of the Tehuacan sequence. Almost all of these blades appear to have been made from long, narrow, cylindrical or bitapered cores, with striking platforms usually at both ends and roughly at right or obtuse angles to the fluted sides.

In somewhat earlier levels we began to find blades with their striking platforms and tips deliberately snapped off and with one or both ends retouched. These tools probably were used as end-scrapers, and they are described as such in Chapter 2. In the Ajalpan period another type of snapped blade appeared, with worked or retouched lateral edges. These blades may have been used as side-blades, and if so, the idea may ultimately have been derived from Asia. This type of blade reached its greatest popularity in the Palo Blanco phase, which corresponds to the Classic period, and lasted into the Postclassic Venta Salada phase.

Our final type of fine blade had a ground striking platform and was struck from what Paul Tolstoy calls an Amantla core—a bullet-shaped core with a ground or abraded striking platform. These blades first appeared in Palo Blanco or Classic times and became horizon markers for the Venta Salada or Postclassic period.

As this brief summary indicates and as Fig. 2 shows, the blade types (and inferentially the core types) are excellent time markers for the Tehuacan cultural sequence. Perhaps future studies will show that blades are horizon markers for all Mesoamerica. Unfortunately,

	Ts 372	Ts 391	Ts 380	Ts 387	Ts 390	Ts 388	Ts 377	Ts 381	Ts 379	Ts 384	Ts 252	Ts 338	Ts 385	Ts 373	Ts 365	Ts 376	Ts 386	Ts 381e	Ts 375	Ts 253	Ts 273	Tc 274	Tr 363	Tr 212	Tr 25	Tr 67	Tr 4	Tr 366	Tr 73	Tr 79	Tr 213	Tr 232	Tr 16	Tr 24	Tc 9	Tr 28	Tc 13	Tr 48	Tr 251	Tr 229	Tr 243	Tr 147	Tr 69	Tr 90	Tr 207	Tr 153	Tr 173	Tr 175
					EL R	IEGO							COX	CAT-L	AN				ABE	JAS			SA	NTA M	ARIA						PALO	BLAN	CO								PALO	BLAN	CO W					
Fine Cores																																																
Ground platforms																																																
Prepared platforms																																																
Bitapered																																																
Unprepared platforms																																																
Crude Cores																																																
Cylindrical							1																																									1
(Hemi) conical, prepared platforms						1	1																																									
(Hemi) conical, unprepared platforms	1						1		2																																							
Core Fragments																							1																1								1	1
TOTAL CORES	1					1	3		2														1																1								1	2
Fine Blades																																																
Ground platforms																							1	1					2											4				1			1	
Snapped, two edges retouched																				1			2	1	6	1	1		10	1	1			1	1	1	1	3	2	5	6	1		1			4	3
Pointed platforms																							1	1	2						1										3					1		
Prepared platforms																					1								1															1				
Unprepared platforms																	1						2	1																								
Crude Blades																																																
Pointed platforms									2					1	3	2	1						1																1									
Prepared platforms					1	1		2	1	1				4		1	2		1										1																			1
Unprepared platforms	2	1	3	1	1	2	1	3	2			1	1				1	2	1				1																									1
Blade Fragments																																																
Fine																													1	1		1																1
Crude			2	1				2				1		3			1			1			1					1	1	1									1					1			1	
TOTAL BLADES	2	1	5	1	2	4	1	9	3	1	1	2	1	8	3	5	3	6	2	2	1	1	6	4	10	2	1	1	16	1	1	2	1	1	1	1	1	4	3	10	9	1	1	2	1	1	7	3

these tools usually are picked up by archaeologists, sometimes are counted, and often are displayed, but they are not always adequately studied or described. For those who may become interested in typological studies of blades in Mesoamerica, the occurrence of every blade type is listed, by site or by component within the site, in Tables 1 and 2.

Blades—*Type Descriptions*

Crude Blades, Unprepared Striking Platforms

Fig. 3

253 specimens; 182 excavated, 71 collected.

Dimensions in cm. of 50 specimens: length, 2.0–8.4, average, 3.8; width, 1.2–3.4, average, 2.2; thickness, 0.3–1.9, average, 0.7.

These blades vary in outline from rough rectangles to elongated isosceles triangles, with the triangular form more common. Ventral surfaces are usually concave and have a relatively small bulb of percussion at the wider end. Dorsal surfaces are convex and have a lengthwise medial ridge roughly parallel to the lateral edges. Some blades have two dorsal ridges, and a very few have three. Although the ridges are more or less parallel to the edges, they are more likely to be curved than straight. One end of the blade is almost always very thin and is either somewhat rounded or pointed. The other end, the striking platform, is usually straight and fairly thick, and is at an acute or right angle to the dorsal surface. This end generally is the thickest part of the blade.

These features indicate that the blades were struck from conical or subconoidal nuclei without prepared striking platforms. The cores were probably fairly crude, with only a few fluted facets. They may very well have been similar to the scraper-planes described in Chapter 2. A small portion of the excavated blades had retouched lateral edges; twenty-four had one retouched edge and eight had both edges retouched. One of the latter blades had been sharpened to a point as well.

Similar blades are found from Bering Strait at least as far south as Mexico. This type of blade occurs throughout the entire Tehuacan sequence and was most popular in the earliest Ajuereado phase. In the Valley of Mexico, one blade of this type was found with the second Iztapan mammoth; although the blade material from this region is unstudied, one would suspect that this type would range over a similarly long span. In Chiapas these blades are found in the Santa Marta complex, as well as in all the later horizons. In Tamaulipas in northeastern Mexico they are not found earlier than the Almagre horizon, but they do last through the rest of the sequence in that area.

On a more general level, this type of blade seems to be associated with the Cordilleran tradition which extends from below Mexico through western North America to Bering Strait. Since this type of blade is the only type known from the so-called Paleolithic culture of northeastern Siberia, it seems likely that it was one of the early artifact types to spread from the Old World into the New World.

Crude Blades, Prepared Striking Platforms

Fig. 4

199 specimens; 157 excavated, 42 collected.

Dimensions in cm.: length (54 specimens), 1.8–6.5, average, 3.6; width (56 specimens), 1.1–3.5, average, 2.0; thickness (57 specimens), 0.2–1.5, average, 0.6.

These blades range in outline from rectangles to long, narrow triangles, with a long oblong form the most prevalent. Lateral edges vary from slightly convex to relatively wavy. Striking platforms are straight or very slightly convex, and the opposite end varies from straight to almost pointed and is most often convex. Ventral surfaces are generally concave, with a well-marked bulb of percussion near the striking platform. The thickest part of the blade is usually the striking platform itself, although a few specimens were thickest near the midpoint. The striking platforms are at an acute angle to the dorsal surface and always give evidence of having been prepared by percussion. Lateral edges are rarely worked; only seventeen blades had one worked edge, and only twelve had two worked edges. The working along the edges is not the product of intentional pressure-flaking. It most likely is the result of the blades' having been used by human beings.

These blades probably were manufactured from crude conical or hemiconical nuclei with striking platforms at an acute angle to the fluted sides. The fluted surfaces probably had a limited number of lateral ridges, since only nine of the excavated blades had two parallel dorsal ridges, and the rest had a single dorsal ridge. The cores definitely had striking platforms that were prepared by percussion-chipping.

In the Tehuacan region, crude blades with prepared striking platforms were first manufactured and were predominant in the El Riego period. They last into the later periods, but only as a minority type. This particular type of blade is unknown in Tamaulipas, but it is found in Chiapas from Santa Marta times onward. Whether it exists in the Valley of Mexico is not known. It is also found in the Hopewell and Poverty Point cultures of the eastern United States. The type is unknown in Alaska and the Canadian Arctic, although it does appear in the so-called Mesolithic culture of Japan. Its

Fig. 5. Crude blades, pointed striking platforms.

rather singular distribution in southern Mexico, the eastern United States, and Japan perhaps suggests independent invention of a similar type in the three areas, or at least an independent modification from the earlier conical nuclei with unprepared striking platforms.

Crude Blades, Pointed Striking Platforms

Fig. 5

197 specimens; 170 excavated, 27 collected.

Dimensions in cm.: length (49 specimens), 2.1–8.2, average, 3.7; width (51 specimens), 0.8–3.7, average, 1.7; thickness (51 specimens), 0.2–1.5, average, 0.5.

These blades are predominantly long and leaf- or lance-shaped, although a few of the broken ones are long and triangular. Ventral surfaces vary from slightly convex to definitely concave, with the majority being very slightly concave. None of the specimens has a well-marked bulb of percussion. Striking platforms are difficult to discern and very small, but they show evidence of working and are roughly oval to pointed in shape. They seem to be at right angles to the dorsal surface. Dorsal surfaces usually have a single medial ridge roughly parallel to the lateral edges; many of these ridges are rather wavy. Only eight blades of this type from excavation have two dorsal ridges. Twenty-nine

of the excavated blades were retouched or worked along one edge, and only seven showed working along both edges. On all but four of these thirty-six blades, the working along the edges seems to be the result of use. Each of the four exceptions, however, had one worked edge that was definitely the product of pressure-retouching. The fact that the tiny striking platforms are roughly at right angles to the dorsal surface, considered in conjunction with the blades' relative lack of curvature and their length in relation to their narrow width, indicates that these blades probably came off long, relatively cylindrical cores with striking platforms at right angles to their fluted surfaces. The blades may have been removed from these cores by indirect percussion. The relative crudeness of the dorsal ridges suggests as well that the cores were crude and were worked from only one end.

In the Tehuacan Valley this type of crude blade first appears as a minority type in the El Riego phase and becomes the majority type in both the Coxcatlan and Abejas phases. It is also one of the dominant types found in the early ceramic Purron and Ajalpan phases. In the Queretaro and Hidalgo findings of Cynthia Irwin-Williams, as well as in the state of Tamaulipas, this type of blade seems to be the predominant type in the later preceramic periods. Crude blades with pointed striking platforms were not found in preceramic levels in Chiapas, but the few blades that have been found there in association with ceramics are of this blade type. It was the contention of Byers (1954) that blades (type not specified) may have served as preforms for points at Bull Brook and at the Williamson site, and that they were characteristic of the Lindemeier industry. Green (1963) has stated that crude blades with pointed striking platforms are an integral part of the Clovis industry. Byers (personal communication) now feels that industries of eastern sites of the Llano complex are based on flakes rather than blades. Green further notes that similar crude blades are found in the later Agate Basin and Folsom assemblages, but these are not usually of the same specific type.

Perhaps crude blades with pointed striking platforms diffused southward from the United States to Mexico, as had the earlier types of crude blades. It is difficult to decide on present evidence, however, whether this type of crude blade is a New World invention, or whether it was ultimately derived from Asia.

Fine Blades, Unprepared Striking Platforms

Fig. 6

72 specimens; 51 excavated, 21 collected.

Dimensions in cm. of 32 specimens: length (10 specimens

Fig. 6. Fine blades, unprepared striking platforms.

only), 2.1–7.0, average, 5.5; width, 0.7–2.5, average, 1.4; thickness, 0.2–0.6, average, 0.3.

These blades in outline are long, narrow rectangles or oblongs. They tend to be widest near the midpoint. Ventral surfaces vary from straight to very slightly concave. The dorsal surfaces of all but two of the excavated blades have two long, straight ridges parallel to the lateral edges but not always exactly parallel to each other. For example, the ridges on a few of the blades are closer together near the striking platform, and on other blades they converge away from the striking platform. The thickest portion of the blade is usually at the striking platform, but this end is only very slightly thicker than other parts of the blade. The striking platform itself is unprepared and is at right angles to the dorsal surface. These narrow blades tend to be thick in relation to their width. This tendency, the character

of the dorsal ridges, and the position of the unprepared striking platform indicate that the blades were struck from beautifully fluted, long, cylindrical or bullet-shaped obsidian cores. Also, the cylindrical cores may have been worked from both ends.

In the Tehuacan Valley this type of blade is first found in components of the Abejas phase. At that time it represented only about 3 percent of the total number of blades, and it was found in about the same proportion throughout all of the ceramic periods. The absence of similar blades in Queretaro, Tamaulipas, and Chiapas at the same time period leads me to suspect that the cylindrical core and the resultant long, straight blades with unprepared striking platforms are a central Mexican invention.

Fine Blades, Prepared Striking Platforms

Fig. 7

38 specimens; 16 excavated, 22 collected.

Dimensions in cm.: length (one complete specimen), 4.0; width (9 specimens), 1.1–3.3, average, 1.8; thickness (10 specimens), 0.3–1.0, average, 0.6.

This type is the crudest of the fine blades, for the dorsal ridges are often jagged. It differs from the earlier crude blades in that all examples of it are made of obsidian. Ventral surfaces vary from slightly concave to slightly convex. The widest portion of the blade is usually near the striking platform, which is itself the thickest part of the blade and is usually at a slightly acute angle to the dorsal surface. The dorsal surfaces of all but one of the specimens from excavation have two roughly parallel ridges. The striking platforms have been prepared by percussion, which seems to indicate that these blades were removed from roughly conical or hemiconical nuclei by indirect percussion. Three specimens are definitely pressure-retouched along the

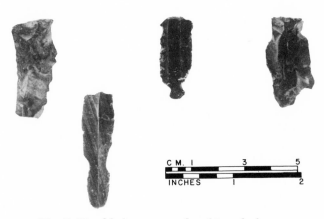

Fig. 7. Fine blades, prepared striking platforms.

22

Fig. 8. Fine blades, pointed striking platforms.

These blades are obviously derived from the earlier crude blades with prepared striking platforms (see Fig. 4). Fine blades with prepared striking platforms are also found in the eastern United States in the Hopewell horizon, and I suspect that there may have been a diffusion of this type of blade from Mesoamerica into the Woodlands of eastern North America.

Fine Blades, Pointed Striking Platforms

Fig. 8
269 specimens; 178 excavated, 91 collected.
Dimensions in cm. of 67 specimens: length (35 specimens only), 1.8–11.8, average, 3.4; width, 0.6–2.7, average, 2.0; thickness, 0.2–1.0, average, 0.3.

These blades vary in outline from a thin leaf-like shape to long narrow oblongs. Ventral surfaces range from straight to quite definitely concave, and whether straight or concave, tend to possess an extremely well-defined bulb of percussion. Dorsal surfaces usually have two long medial ridges, but blades with a single ridge and with three parallel ridges were found in significant proportions. Most of the blades are thickest at the mid-point. The very small, almost pointed striking platforms are unprepared. In general, the blades are relatively wide in proportion to their thickness, which gives them a flat appearance. These blades may have been derived from cores that were roughly bullet-shaped, cylindrical, or bitapered. The extreme smallness of the striking platform suggests that the blades were removed by indirect percussion.

This type of fine blade does not appear in the Tehuacan sequence until Formative times. It reaches its greatest popularity in the middle and late Formative periods and by the Postclassic period it has become a minority type. Tolstoy noted that this blade is a dominant type in the Formative period in the Valley of Mexico. Although rarely found at Chiapa de Corzo in Chiapas, the blades appear there most frequently in the Chiapa de Corzo 2, 3, and 4 periods. Fine blades with pointed striking platforms therefore may be good time markers for the middle and late Formative periods throughout Mesoamerica.

This seems to be another type of blade that was invented in Mesoamerica and did not spread out of the area. It may ultimately have been derived, of course, from earlier types of crude blades.

Fine Snapped Blades, Two Edges Worked or Retouched

Fig. 9
984 specimens; 371 excavated, 613 collected.
Dimensions in cm. of 52 specimens: length (51 specimens

lateral edges, and two of these have shallow notches on opposing edges.

These blades were popular only in the Purron and Ajalpan periods of the Tehuacan sequence, although four were found in Santa Maria and three in Palo Blanco complexes. This blade type has not been recorded elsewhere in Mexico.

Fig. 9. Fine snapped blades, two edges retouched.

only), 2.1–6.4, average, 3.4; width, 0.7–2.0, average, 1.1; thickness, 0.2–0.6, average, 0.4.

The two ends of the blades of this type have been deliberately broken off, and the resulting shape is rectangular. Ventral surfaces range from slightly concave to straight, suggesting that these blades derive from fine blades with pointed or with ground striking platforms; but they may, in fact, have originated from any type of fine blade. Most specimens had two dorsal ridges parallel to the lateral edges. Both edges had been worked or retouched. About half of the sample had two finely retouched edges, but the rest of the blades had only one finely retouched edge and one edge that was nicked from use. The retouching suggests that perhaps these snapped blades were inserted into the sides of handles to be used as side-blades, or perhaps they were used as side-blades in clubs.

In the Tehuacan Valley this type of blade first appears in late Formative or Santa Maria levels. It reaches maximum frequency in components of the Postclassic or Venta Salada period. It is extremely widespread throughout Mesoamerica, and similar types of blades are found in the eastern United States. The use of blades and side-blades as knives or weapons has been known from very early times in both the New World Arctic and northeastern Siberia. Perhaps, then, the basic

Fig. 10. Fine blades, ground striking platforms.

Fig. 11. Crude conical and hemiconical nuclei. *Left,* conical core, unprepared striking platform; *upper right,* hemiconical core, unprepared platform; *lower right,* hemiconical core, with separate view of prepared platform.

idea of the snapped blade diffused from Asia and southward through the New World. However, the insertion of a series of these blades on either side of a paddle-like object to serve as a battle-ax or sword is unique to Mesoamerica. I suspect that this type of fine snapped blade was used in the latter manner and that it is a Mesoamerican invention based on Asian concepts.

Fine Blades, Ground Striking Platforms

Fig. 10

438 specimens; 157 excavated, 281 collected.

Dimensions in cm. of 60 specimens: length (42 specimens only), 1.9–7.2, average, 4.6; width, 0.7–1.8, average, 1.1; thickness, 0.2–0.4, average, 0.2.

Most of these blades are long and thin, though the shapes and the width vary. Almost all of the blades have a slightly concave ventral surface, with a poorly defined bulb of percussion. Dorsal surfaces, with only a few exceptions, have two long roughly parallel ridges.

The widest part of the blade is usually near or at the ground striking platform, which is at a right angle to the dorsal surface. Forty-one excavated blades had two lateral edges retouched by irregular pressure-flaking. The blades seem to have been struck from bullet-shaped cores whose flattened striking platforms had been ground in some manner, probably to facilitate the removal of the blades by indirect percussion or by pressure.

A blade of this type from Zone II of Coxcatlan Cave was provided with a bark-cloth handle. The strip of bark cloth was wrapped closely in overlapping layers around the lower half of the blade and was bound with a strand of fine untwisted fiber. The handle is nearly three times the length of the visible part of the blade.

In the Tehuacan area fine blades with ground striking platforms are found mainly in the Postclassic period, although they first appeared in Classic levels. Two examples, both probably intrusive, were found with

25

very late Formative remains. Blades of this type have a similar distribution in the Valley of Mexico. They also have been unearthed in Yucatan during what appears to be the Postclassic period. The type is unknown north of the Valley of Mexico. It seems to be a further modification of the fine blade with pointed striking platform. It also seems likely that the type has been modified or invented somewhere in Central Mexico.

Polyhedral Cores—*Type Descriptions*

Crude Conical Nuclei, Unprepared Striking Platforms

Fig. 11

13 specimens; 9 excavated, 4 collected.

Dimensions in cm. of 4 specimens: length, 3.2–6.0, average, 5.6; diameter, 1.9–6.3, average, 4.8.

These cores were fashioned from either flint or pebble nodules which had been split in half. The newly created surface was used as a striking platform. Blows struck against the edges of the platform removed a series of long flakes from the sides of the nodules, thus fluting them. Our specimens varied in having from two to nine flutes. Carefully controlled blows struck on the striking platform just above the ridges separating the flutes removed blades of the type crude blades with unprepared striking platforms.

Conical nuclei with unprepared striking platforms appear throughout the Tehuacan sequence, although they are more common in preceramic phases. They are also found and recorded throughout much of North and Central America; Mesoamerican archaeologists, however, seldom record their existence.

Crude Conical or Hemiconical Nuclei, Prepared Striking Platforms

Fig. 11

9 specimens; 7 excavated, 2 collected.

Dimensions in cm. of 3 specimens: length, 2.1, 3.4, and 4.2; width, 2.4, 6.7, and 3.9; thickness, 1.3, 2.1, and 3.5.

Six specimens were made from split nodules or pebbles of flint. The surface created by the split had been chipped so that it was at an acute angle to the fluted sides and served as a striking platform. The other three cores were merely large, thick flakes that had been chipped so that one portion was at an acute angle to the adjacent surface and thus served as a prepared striking platform. A series of parallel blows struck near the edges of these platforms created from two to seven flutes along the sides of the cores. The blows may have been struck by the technique that Jeremiah Epstein calls billet-flaking, in which a percussion tool that is softer than stone is used. Further blows on the platform, just

26

Fig. 12. Crude cylindrical nuclei. *Left,* three views of a core showing the fluted sides and the unprepared striking platforms at each end; *right,* two views of a second core.

Fig. 13. Fine Nuclei. *Row 1:* Bullet-shaped core with prepared striking platform; two cylindrical cores with unprepared platforms. *Row 2:* Two bitapered cores with battered platforms; bullet-shaped core with prepared platform. *Row 3:* Bullet-shaped cores with ground platforms.

above the ridges separating the flutes, would have spalled off crude blades with fragments of the prepared platforms adhering to them.

In Tehuacan these nuclei are found mainly in preceramic levels dating from the El Riego phase, but a

few come from ceramic horizons. Similar cores come from Middle Woodland cultures in the eastern United States and from northwestern North America and Asia.

Crude Cylindrical Nuclei

Fig. 12

5 specimens; 2 excavated, 3 collected.

Dimensions in cm. of 2 specimens: length, 4.2 and 5.3; diameter, 3.2 and 4.6.

These crude nuclei are made from roughly cylindrical nodules of flint. Indirect percussion applied to the striking platforms at the end or ends of the clyinders produced two to four flutes along the sides. The spalls scaled off the sides probably were of the type crude blades with pointed striking platforms.

These nuclei have been recorded only in the Tehuacan Valley, and the only two found in excavation appeared in components of the Coxcatlan and Abejas phases.

Fine Cylindrical or Bullet-Shaped Nuclei, Unprepared Striking Platforms

Fig. 13

5 specimens; 1 excavated, 4 collected.

Dimensions in cm.: length, 2.7 to over 6.1; diameter, 1.4 to over 3.0.

These cores were made from elongated nodules of obsidian. One end or both ends of the nodules were flattened by the removal of a single large chip in order to make striking platforms. Then long, parallel flakes were removed from the sides—probably by direct or indirect percussion—producing fluted cylindrical cores if the blows were struck from both ends, or fluted bullet-shaped cores if the blows were struck from one end. Long, fine blades with unprepared striking platforms were spalled from these cores.

Cores of this type are widely distributed in Mesoamerica. They date from late preceramic times to the Conquest and were slightly more popular in the earlier part of this span.

Fine Bitapered Nuclei, Battered or Small Unprepared Striking Platforms

Fig. 13

8 specimens; 1 excavated, 7 collected.

Dimensions in cm: length 3.9–7.3; width 1.6–2.5; thickness 1.1–1.9.

All our cores of this type seem to have been almost completely exhausted, and this section is partly a reconstruction of what these cores were like. Our specimens were long, roughly cylindrical nodules of ob-

27

sidian, with unprepared striking platforms at both ends. The edges of the platforms have been battered by the removal of numerous small chips during the process of spalling off blades. These battered edges, together with the fact that the resultant pointed blades have very low bulbs of percussion, indicate that the fluting of the sides and the removal of blades were probably accomplished by the billet-flaking technique. Both ends of the cores were worked in this manner. Some of the specimens are relatively flat and superficially resemble the tongue cores of northeastern Asia and northwestern America, but they lack the retouched ends opposite the striking platforms. However, some of the smaller pointed blades removed from this type of core do resemble microblades from northern America.

Although only one core was found in excavation in the Tehuacan region, the distribution of pointed blades suggests that this type of core was first used about 1200 B.C. and that it continued in use until the Spanish conquest. These blades, and inferentially these cores, were popular in the Formative Ajalpan and Santa Maria phases, and they may be sensitive time markers for the Formative period in Mesoamerica.

Fine Hemiconical or Conical Nuclei, Prepared Striking Platforms

Fig. 13
9 specimens; 1 excavated, 8 collected.
Dimensions in cm.: length, 2.8–5.7; width, 1.8–2.7; thickness, 0.7–1.9.

Some of these obsidian cores are roughly conical in shape, and some are hemiconical. They have chipped, prepared striking platforms at an acute angle to their tapering, fluted sides. The relatively greater depth of the negative bulb of percussion suggests that blades were removed by percussion with a hammerstone. Por-

tions of the prepared striking platform may have adhered to the blades.

These cores and the blades struck from them probably originated in earliest ceramic times in the Tehuacan region and lasted to the Spanish conquest. They were more popular in the earlier half of this period. This type of core has not been commonly recorded from Mesoamerica, except for the early El Arbolillo phase in the Valley of Mexico.

Fine Bullet-Shaped Nuclei, Ground Striking Platforms

Fig. 13
19 specimens; 4 excavated, 15 collected.
Dimensions in cm.: length, 3.4–7.3; width, 1.5–2.9; thickness, 1.2–2.5.

These bullet-shaped obsidian cores have ground striking platforms at about right angles to the long delicately fluted sides. The intentionally roughened platforms with their battered edges, as well as the small and deep negative bulbs of percussion, indicate that blades were produced from the cores by impulsive pressure-flaking. The ground surface of the platform perhaps prevented the punch used to push off blades from slipping. This technique was described by Juan de Torquemada in 1616 and by Francisco Hernandez in 1580. (See below, Fig. 83.) The blades removed from these nuclei retain small portions of the ground striking platforms.

Although bullet-shaped cores may have been manufactured a few hundred years earlier, they were popular only in the Venta Salada or Postclassic period of the Tehuacan sequence. Paul Tolstoy has recorded a similar distribution of this type of core in the Valley of Mexico. The type has not been recorded beyond the limits of Mesoamerica.

REFERENCES

ALEXANDER, HERBERT L.
1963 "The Levi Site: A Paleo-Indian Campsite in Central Texas." *Am. Ant.*, 28:510–28.

AVELEYRA ARROYO DE ANDA, LUIS
1956 "The Second Mammoth and Associated Artifacts at Santa Isabel Iztapan, Mexico." *Am. Ant.*, 22:12–28.

BONCH-OSMOLOVSKY, G., AND V. GROMOV
1936 "The Paleolithic in the Union of Soviet Socialist Republics." *International Geological Congress, XVIth Session, 1933*. Washington.

BORDEN, C. E.
1960 "DjRi 3, An Early Site in Fraser Canyon, British Columbia." *Contributions to Anthropology, 1957*. National Museum of Canada, Bulletin No. 162. Ottawa.

BYERS, DOUGLAS S.
1954 "Bull Brook—A Fluted Point Site in Ipswich, Massachusetts." *Am. Ant.*, 19:343–51.

CAMPBELL, JOHN M.
1959 "The Kayuk Complex of Arctic Alaska." *Am. Ant.*, 25:94–105.

CRESSMAN, LUTHER S.
1960 *Cultural Sequences at The Dalles, Oregon.* APS-T, Vol. 50, Part 10.

CRUXENT, J. M., AND IRVING ROUSE
1956 "A Lithic Industry of Paleo-Indian Type in Venezuela." *Am. Ant.*, 22:172–79.

EPSTEIN, JEREMIAH F.
1964 "Towards the Systematic Description of Chipped Stone." *XXXV Congreso Internacional de Americanistas, Mexico, 1962,* I:155–69. Mexico.

GREEN, F. E.
1963 "The Clovis Blades: An Important Addition to the Llano Complex." *Am. Ant.*, 29:145–65.

GROMOV, V. I.
1945 "Twenty-five Years of the Quaternary of the U.S.S.R." *AJS*, Vol. 243.

KIDDER, ALFRED V.
1947 *The Artifacts of Uaxactun, Guatemala.* CIW, Publication No. 576.

LARSEN, HELGE
1951 "De Dansk-Americanske Alaska-ekspeditioner, 1949–50." *Geografisk Tidsskrift,* 51:63–93. Copenhagen.

MacNEISH, RICHARD S.
1958 *Preliminary Archaeological Investigations in the Sierra de Tamaulipas, Mexico.* APS-T, Vol. 48, Part 6.
1959 "Men out of Asia: As Seen from the Northwest Yukon." *Anthropological Papers of the University of Alaska,* 7:41–59. Fairbanks.
1960 "The Callison Site in the Light of Archaeological Survey of the Southwest Yukon." *Contributions to Anthropology, 1957.* National Museum of Canada, Bulletin No. 162, pp. 1–51. Ottawa.
1964 "Archaeological Excavation, Comparisons, and Speculations." *Investigations in the Southwest Yukon.* Papers of the Robert S. Peabody Foundation for Archaeology, Vol. 6. Andover.

MacNEISH, RICHARD S., AND F. A. PETERSON
1962 *The Santa Marta Rock Shelter, Ocozocoautla, Chiapas, Mexico.* Papers of the New World Archaeological Foundation, No. 14. Provo, Utah.

MARINGER, JOHN
1950 *Contributions to the Prehistory of Mongolia.* Sino-Swedish Expedition, Publication 34, No. 7. Stockholm.

OKLADNIKOV, A. P.
1950 *Lenskiye Drevnosti,* Vyp. 3 (Antiquities of the Lena, Part 3). Moscow.

ROUSE, IRVING
1939 *Prehistory in Haiti.* Yale University Publications in Anthropology, No. 21. New Haven, Connecticut.

TOLSTOY, PAUL
——— "Stone, Bone, and Antler Tools of Central Mexico from Preclassic to Aztec Time." To be published in *Handbook of Middle American Indians.* Austin: University of Texas Press.

VAILLANT, GEORGE C.
1930 *Excavations at Zacatenco.* AMNH-AP, Vol. 32, Part 1.

YOSHIZAKI, M.
1959 *Tachikawa Preceramic Industries in South Hokkaido.* Hokkaido Municipal Museum Research Bulletin, No. 6. Tokyo.

CHAPTER 2

End-Scrapers

ALTHOUGH the term "end-scraper" implies function, our definition of this chipped-stone tool is morphological: an end-scraper is a plano-convex artifact with a flat, unworked ventral surface and a convex, worked dorsal surface. Furthermore, the most well-defined working or retouching is most frequently found along one of the shorter edges, or sides, of the dorsal surface. In order to clarify other terminology which will be used in describing end-scrapers, we should explain that the sharp junction of the ventral and dorsal surfaces is referred to as an edge or side; the retouched edge at the narrow end of the convex dorsal surface is called the cutting edge; and the opposite narrow edge is the base.

The characteristics or attributes associated with end-scrapers stem from the various chipping techniques used in their manufacture, from the types of flakes employed, from the specific area of the flake selected for retouching, and from the geometrical form or shape of the finished artifact. When the attributes of end-scrapers from different time levels in the Tehuacan sequence are compared and contrasted, it becomes possible to determine the particular characteristics, or modes, that have temporal significance for the Tehuacan region.

We began the analysis of end-scrapers with the specimens from the stratified levels of Coxcatlan Cave. The 760 unifaces from this site with one narrow edge retouched were spread out on a large table according to the levels or zones from which they were excavated. We first examined the chipping techniques used to make the cutting edges of these specimens and determined that three different techniques were employed. These were pressure-retouching, rough percussion-flaking, and a third technique which was more difficult to determine, but which was finally considered to have been either very well-controlled percussion-flaking or very poor pressure-flaking. (These chipping techniques are, of course, possible attributes of any scraper.) The end-scrapers from Coxcatlan Cave were then classified in terms of these three methods of manufacture, and the distribution of each type was counted, level by excavated level (see Table 3).

Well-controlled percussion-flaking (or poor pressure-flaking) was the dominant technique used for specimens from early levels, and its use gradually died out in the later levels. Rough percussion-flaking was a dominant technique of the middle levels, although it was also used for scrapers from the early levels and remained a popular technique in the late levels. Pressure-retouching originated as a minority technique in the middle levels and became dominant in the more recent time levels of the cave.

As we were analyzing and counting the attributes concerned with chipping techniques, it became obvious that another important set of attributes were associated with the types of flakes selected for making end-scrap-

Table 3. Chipping Techniques
Used to Make Cutting Edges
(Based on 760 end-scrapers from Coxcatlan Cave)

Zones	No. of end-scrapers	Controlled percussion or poor pressure-flaking		Rough percussion		Pressure retouching	
		No.	Percent	No.	Percent	No.	Percent
I-III	11	2	9	4	36	5	55
IV-VI	29	5	17	13	45	11	38
VII	22	5	27	13	45	4	28
VIII-IX	56	19	35	27	48	10	18
X-XIII	129	31	24	84	65	14	11
XIV-XXII	470	147	32	312	67	11	2
XXIII-XXIV	43	26	61	17	39	0	0

30

ers. Study of the materials used reduced numerous tentative categories to but five basic types of flakes. Continued work with these five categories eventually proved their temporal significance throughout the levels of Coxcatlan Cave.

As Table 4 shows, crude prismatic flakes were used to make end-scrapers only during the earlier levels of occupation. Large flat flakes were employed throughout the history of the cave but were dominant material only in the early levels. Broken nodules were also used to make end-scrapers throughout the cave's history, but they were dominant largely during the middle levels of occupation. Very thin, fine flakes began to be made into end-scrapers in the middle levels and became the preferred kind of flake near the end of the cave's occupation. Prismatic blades struck from polyhedral cores were used only in the latest levels.

By this stage of the analysis, there were three modes associated with the type of chipping techniques used to make end-scrapers and five modes associated with the types of materials selected. The next step was to see if any of the fifteen possible combinations of these two sets of modes had temporal significance. Once again the end-scrapers were laid out by levels and were regrouped according to the fifteen possible combinations. It became apparent at once that four of the combinations could be eliminated: neither controlled percussion-flaking nor rough percussion-flaking was used to make scrapers from prismatic blades; percussion-flaking was never used to make scrapers from thin, flat flakes; and pressure-flaking was never used to make scrapers from large, thick, flat flakes. The remaining combinations were, however, susceptible to study, and the results of our analysis are shown in Table 5.

Table 4. Materials Used for End-Scrapers
(Based on 760 end-scrapers from Coxcatlan Cave)

Zones	No. of end-scrapers	Large flat flakes		Crude prismatic flakes		Broken nodules		Thin flakes		Prismatic blades	
		No.	Per-cent	No.	Per-cent	No.	Per-cent	No.	Per-cent	No.	Per-cent
I-III	11	2	18			4	37	2	18	3	27
IV-VI	29	4	14	1	3	13	45	10	35	1	3
VII	22	4	18			13	59	4	18	1	5
VIII-IX	56	16	29	3	5	27	48	10	18		
X-XIII	129	34	27	1	*	80	62	14	11		
XIV-XXII	470	154	37	25	1	273	58	18	4		
XXIII-XXIV	43	21	50	16	37	6	13				

*Less than one percent.

It was obvious that some of the eleven combinations had a similar distribution through time and could therefore be grouped to form rough trial types. For example, large flakes manufactured into end-scrapers by controlled percussion-flaking were dominant in the early levels and then gradually died out. Large, flat flakes worked only by rough percussion-flaking followed the same general trend, although they were slightly less prevalent numerically. Therefore, since we were trying to establish time markers, we combined these two groups with a similar temporal distribution. Some of the other modal combinations with similar temporal distribution were also regrouped, until we eventually arrived at only six modal combinations, or trial types, which proved to have significance in time and space (see Table 5).

Table 5. Modes Derived from Chipping Techniques and Materials
(Based on 760 end-scrapers from Coxcatlan Cave)

Zone	Total end-scrapers	Large Flakes				Prismatic Flakes						Thin Flakes				Nodules						Blades	
		Controlled percussion		Rough percussion		Controlled percussion		Rough percussion		Pressure retouching		Controlled percussion		Pressure retouching		Controlled percussion		Rough percussion		Pressure retouching		Pressure retouching	
		No.	Per-cent	No.	Per-cent	No.	Per-cent	No.	Per-cent	No.	Per-cent	No.	Per-cent	No.	Per-cent	No.	Per-cent	No.	Per-cent	No.	Per-cent	No.	Per-cent
I-III	11	2	18											2	18			4	36			3	27
IV-VI	29	3	10	1	3					1	3	1	3	9	31	1	3	12	42			1	3
VII	22	3	14	1	5							1	5	3	14	1	5	12	54			1	5
VIII-IX	56	11	19	5	9	1	*	2	*			2	4	8	14	5	9	20	36	2	4		
X-XIII	129	17	13	17	13			1	1			4	3	10	8	10	8	66	51	4	3		
XIV-XXII	470	114	24	40	8	16	3	9	2			7	2	11	2	10	2	263	56				
XXIII-XXIV	43	16	37	5	12	10	23	6	14														

*Less than one percent.

Our third set of attributes pertaining to end-scrapers concerned the specific areas of the flakes selected for retouching. These areas were: (1) only the shorter edge, (2) the shorter edge and two adjacent sides, (3) all edges, (4) all or part of the dorsal surface, and (5) any combination of these five edge, side, and surface areas. These attributes were plotted to see if they were significant in regard to time and space, and the results were combined with the other two sets of attributes of end-scrapers. When these three sets of attributes—chipping techniques, types of flakes used, and areas selected for retouching—are studied as a whole, there are some ninety possible groupings. However, only fourteen actual combinations of the three sets of attributes proved to be valid. These were: (1) crude prismatic flakes with one or both ends worked by percussion; (2) large flat flakes with one end worked by rough or controlled percussion; (3) large flat flakes with one end, the sides, and one surface worked by rough or controlled percussion; (4) nodules worked by rough percussion (incomplete fragments); (5) nodules worked by rough percussion along the edge of more than one plane; (6) nodules with a domed upper surface worked on all edges by rough percussion; (7) nodules with a flat upper surface worked on all edges by rough percussion; (8) small nodules worked on all edges and one surface by controlled percussion or by pressure; (9) flakes with a concave cutting edge worked by rough or controlled percussion; (10) thin flakes with the short end retouched by pressure-flaking; (11) snapped blades with one end retouched; (12) small, ovoid, plano-convex flakes with all edges and one surface retouched; (13) thin flakes with all edges retouched; and (14) snapped blades with all edges retouched.

The geometrical forms of the end-scrapers—ovoid, domed, discoidal, keeled, and so on—were then taken into consideration, and the trial types were further redefined. Using the fourteen trial types that seemed to have satisfactory significance in time for Coxcatlan Cave, we decided at this point to test further and to interdigitate the end-scraper materials from the various zones of other excavated sites. The fourteen trial types still seemed to hold as we added new material, but we began to suspect that three of them, all of which involved various kinds of small, flat flakes showing three different forms of pressure-retouching, might be grouped together. These three trial types, however, were found only in levels with ceramics, so we began to analyze the end-scrapers from sites with ceramics to test the types further. The result was that the minor variations in the shape of the three trial types of small, flat flakes had about the same distribution in time, and

the three groups could justifiably be combined as a single type. The resulting twelve types of end-scrapers may be seen in Table 6, which gives the distribution of the scrapers throughout the sequential layers of the stratified sites. Table 7 shows the distribution of end-scrapers from the single-period and surface-component material.

It is very apparent from Tables 6 and 7 that the twelve types of end-scrapers provide significant trends throughout our various levels. Even on the basis of these limited data, it would be possible to divide the Tehuacan sequence into a number of tentative periods, which would, of course, have to be tested against trends shown by the other types of artifacts. This, in effect, is what we eventually did, and the next few paragraphs will briefly summarize the trends exhibited by the twelve types of end-scrapers as they occurred throughout the sequence finally established on the basis of our total complex of artifact types.

The earliest type of end-scraper—a crude, keeled scraper—was dominant in the Ajuereado levels and barely lasted into the subsequent El Riego phase. A companion type—the crude, ovoid, plano-convex end-scraper—also appeared in Ajuereado times, but it persisted with some degree of significance into the Abejas phase. Long, crude, flat-flake end-scrapers ran through the whole sequence and were a little more popular in the earlier periods than in the later ones. Scraper-planes were rare in the earliest Ajuereado phase but became dominant in El Riego and Coxcatlan levels and showed some degree of popularity up to historic times. Multifaceted scraper-planes, however, existed only in the El Riego phase. The type we call gouges originated in the El Riego phase and reached its greatest popularity in Coxcatlan and Abejas times, after which it seems to die out. Crude discoidal end-scrapers had a similar origin and were most popular over approximately the same span of time, but they continued to be used with a fairly high degree of frequency throughout the later periods of our sequence. Thin-flake end-scrapers first appeared in El Riego times, gradually increased in popularity into Santa Maria and Palo Blanco times, and then lost some of their popularity during the Venta Salada phase. End-of-blade scrapers originated in Abejas times, reached their greatest popularity in the Ajalpan and Santa Maria phases, and lasted into the Palo Blanco and Venta Salada phases. Small, finely chipped, ovoid, plano-convex end-scrapers originated during the Ajalpan phase, when they also were most popular, and gradually died out during the other ceramic periods. Small, finely retouched, flat-topped end-scrapers appeared first in Ajalpan levels, but they

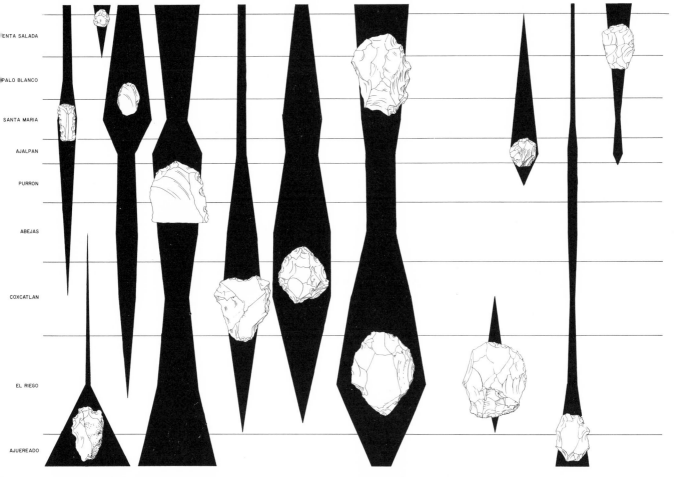

Fig. 14. Distribution of end-scraper types in the Tehuacan cultural sequence.

reached their greatest popularity during the Venta Salada phase. The final type—small thumbnail or discoidal end-scrapers—appeared only in components of the Venta Salada phase. Thus, our end-scraper types—or the combination of types, or the frequency percentages of these types—mark off each phase of our sequence extremely well (see Fig. 14).

Leaving aside the typology for a moment, certain inferences can be made about the use and function of the different types of end-scrapers. Both the crude ovoid and the crude keeled types from the Ajuereado phase could very well have been put into large wooden handles to be used as scrapers, and one of the keeled scrapers actually had some gum on its side, indicating that it had been hafted. End-scrapers may have continued to have been hafted throughout the sequence, but hafting seems to have become popular again only with end-of-blade scrapers starting in the Abejas phase. Besides the end-of-blade scrapers, the three small finely retouched types of end-scrapers of the last four ceramic

phases could also have been hafted in wood or bone handles. We found one end-of-blade scraper still in position in a fragment of wood, and we uncovered a small fragment of a rib bone containing a broken piece of flint which could have been part of a small, finely retouched end-scraper. The scraper-planes, crude discoidal scrapers, and many of the gouges popular in the Archaic phases—El Riego, Coxcatlan, and Abejas—would have been very difficult to haft and were probably held in the hand and used in the manner of a wood plane. The scrapers made from large, flat flakes, which persisted throughout the sequence, may also have been used without a handle.

Both the earlier and the later small, haftable end-scrapers certainly were used for scraping skins, and we found pieces of leather associated with them during excavation. Although scraper-planes and crude discoidal scrapers could have been used on skins, they were apparently used more often for pulping plants. We found some dried vegetable material on the cutting

33

edge of one small discoidal scraper, and one of the large scraper-planes had a highly polished ventral surface. I doubt that this degree of polish would have resulted from scraping relatively soft skins, but it could have come from planing relatively hard fibrous materials. The gouges, although they could have been used on skins and plants, may have been used in woodworking. We found many fragments of wood that had been planed with an object which had a concave cutting edge like that of the gouges.

The typology of end-scrapers, then, not only denotes changes in ideas about style and about the different types of scrapers preferred during particular periods, but it also gives us a glimpse into how and why scrapers were used, and this in turn reflects to some degree other cultural and subsistence activities.

End-Scrapers—*Type Descriptions*

Crude, Keeled End-Scrapers

Fig. 15
74 specimens; 64 excavated, 10 collected.
Dimensions in cm.: length (27 specimens), 1.8–5.4, average, 3.7; width (52 specimens), 1.5–3.5, average 2.5; thickness (55 specimens), 0.9–2.4, average, 1.4.

These end-scrapers range from a teardrop-shaped or ovoid outline to an almost rectangular outline. The retouched narrow end, or cutting edge, varies from slightly convex to almost pointed. The opposite narrow end may range from concave to convex, and the lateral edges are either nearly straight or slightly convex. The relatively flat ventral surface is marked by a single flake scar and usually shows a slight convexity at the bulb of percussion, as well as a slight tendency toward convexity on other parts of the surface. A central ridge, or keel, with relatively steep slopes usually runs the length of the dorsal surface. The convex, retouched narrow end is also relatively steep and gives the tool a snub-nosed appearance. The opposite end, or base, varies considerably and is sometimes steep and sometimes slopes gradually toward the edge.

Manufacturers of this type of scraper probably used a long, narrow, thick prismatic flake struck from an irregular core without a prepared striking platform. They then sharpened the dorsal surface of one narrow end—usually the end farthest from the bulb of percussion—by controlled or direct percussion-flaking; one very late example, however, may have been fashioned by pressure-flaking. This retouching produced the relatively steep convex cutting edge. Slightly over half of these end-scrapers have had a few percussion blows struck against the long narrow edges, which made the

sloping dorsal surface even steeper and further accentuated the medial ridge.

I presently know of excavated scrapers of this type from only three regions of Mexico: eastern Tamaulipas, Hidalgo (in Tecolote Cave), and the Tehuacan Valley. In the latter area they appeared in Ajuereado and El Riego horizons and were more popular in the earlier period. In the Sierra de Tamaulipas four of the ten scrapers classified as snub-nosed end-scrapers (see Mac-Neish 1958: Fig. 26, nos. 6, 8) are of this type, and three of these came from the Lerma levels of 8000 to 7000 B.C. In the Hidalgo excavations of Cynthia Irwin-Williams they also are found in the earlier levels.

Crude, Ovoid, Plano-Convex End-Scrapers

Fig. 15
127 specimens; 74 excavated, 53 collected.
Dimensions in cm.: length (48 specimens), 2.8–8.1, average, 4.2; width (55 specimens), 2.6–5.8, average, 3.6; thickness (67 specimens), 0.6–2.6, average, 1.4.

These scrapers are roughly ovoid or tear-drop-shaped in outline, and they have one or two definitely convex cutting edges. About a third of the sample have both narrow ends chipped so that they are neatly convex, and both ends could have been used for scraping. There seems to be no significant temporal difference between those with one end and those with both ends sharpened by chipping. Ventral surfaces are relatively flat or slightly concave, except for the bulb of percussion. Dorsal surfaces are convex, with relatively gently sloping sides leading to the cutting edges and relatively flattened central portions, but most of these scrapers still have a snub-nosed appearance at the cutting edge.

These end-scrapers were made from long, narrow, relatively thick, flat flakes. Scars from percussion-flaking on the dorsal surface show that flakes were removed from the lateral edges toward the center. The scars of about half the specimens do not extend as far as the center, leaving relatively flat, unflaked central areas. One or both narrow ends are usually more carefully worked and have slightly steeper surfaces and more definitely convex cutting edges.

These scrapers are common in early horizons in eastern Mexico from Chiapas to Tamaulipas. In the Santa Marta Cave in Chiapas they are found in the Santa Marta complex; in the Tehuacan region they appear principally in the preceramic components, although a few were uncovered in later levels; in Queretaro and Hidalgo they date from about the same time period as in the Tehuacan Valley. In the Sierra de Tamaulipas they appear mainly in the Lerma horizon.

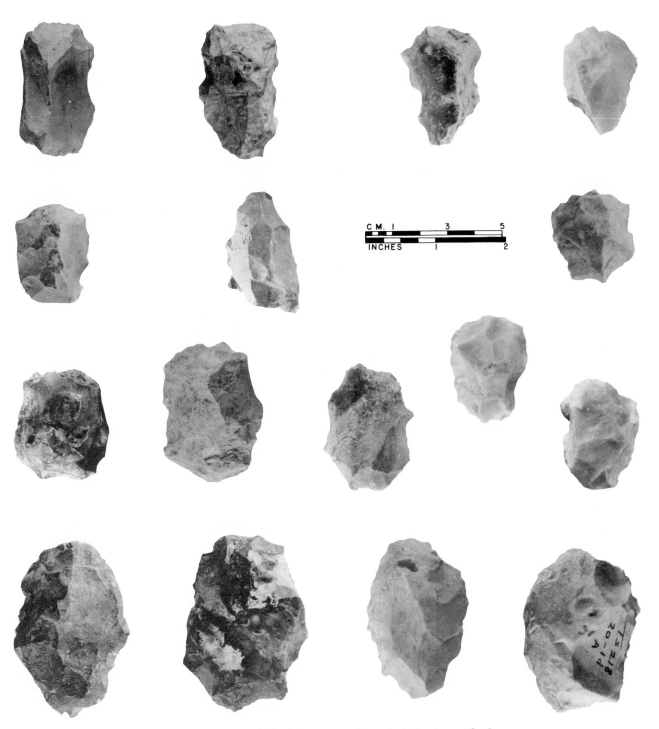

Fig. 15. End-scrapers. *Rows 1, 2:* Crude keeled scrapers. *Rows 3, 4:* Crude ovoid, plano-convex scrapers.

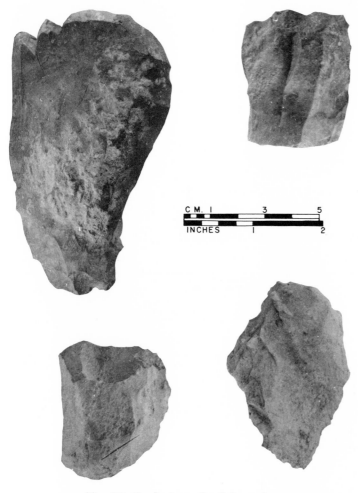

CM. I   3   5
INCHES   I   2

Fig. 16. Crude, long, flat-flake end-scrapers.

Crude, Long, Flat-Flake End-Scrapers

Fig. 16

398 specimens; 294 excavated, 104 collected.

Dimensions in cm.: length (139 specimens), 1.1–10.3, average, 4.6; width (164 specimens), 1.9–8.8, average, 4.0; thickness (264 specimens), 0.7–3.0, average, 1.1.

The shape of this type of scraper is difficult to describe. End-scrapers of this type generally are longer than they are wide and have one convex shorter edge, but the sides, base, and general outline show extensive variations. Ventral surfaces are usually relatively flat, as are most portions of the dorsal surfaces. However, the cutting edges are usually very steep and relatively thick.

These scrapers were made from large, elongated, thick, flat flakes. A narrow end of the flakes, usually the one farthest from the bulb of percussion, was formed into the steep convex cutting edge by controlled per-

cussion, or more often, by crude percussion-flaking. The dorsal surface was not worked further, and usually the lateral edges were not further sharpened, although about fifteen examples had received a few rough percussion blows along the lateral edges.

This extremely general type of scraper is found throughout the Tehuacan sequence and was slightly more popular in the earlier periods. As far as its geographical range is concerned, it probably was used (though it is usually not recorded) in all periods in all parts of Mesoamerica.

Scraper Planes

Figs. 17, 18

1,092 specimens; 164 domed planes excavated, 178 domed planes collected; 183 flat-topped planes excavated, 126 flat-topped planes collected; 265 fragments excavated, 176 fragments collected.

Dimensions in cm. of domed planes: length (112 specimens), 3.2–9.8, average, 5.6; width (125 specimens), 3.4–11.9, average, 4.7; thickness (149 specimens), 1.8–8.0, average, 3.6. Flat-topped planes: length (125 specimens), 2.0–11.2, average, 5.4; width (119 specimens), 3.6–13.1, average, 7.2; thickness (147 specimens), 1.4–6.0, average, 2.5.

Scraper-planes range in outline from round to oval or even teardrop-shaped. Generally speaking, the domed planes are more rounded than the flat-topped variety. All the planes have flat ventral surfaces, but they show considerable range in the form of the dorsal surface, which varies from almost pointed to flat. Regardless of the form of the dorsal surface, scraper-planes are quite thick.

Most examples appear to have been made from large nodules, pebbles, or ellipsoidal cores that had been broken in half, often by one strong percussion blow. The newly created surface became the ventral surface of the newly formed scraper, as well as the striking platform for the removal of flakes—usually by percussion blows—from the lateral edges of the dorsal surface. Thus one of the functions of these so-called scraper-planes was to serve as cores for obtaining long, narrow flakes. There is little doubt, however, that these tools also served as scrapers. For instance, controlled-percussion flakes were also removed from the dorsal edges of the majority of our sample in order to sharpen them; the bases of four specimens are polished from use; and plant fibers had adhered to the cutting edges of two specimens.

Those scrapers which retained a peaked dorsal surface are classified as domed. However, about half of our sample had been further fashioned into flat-topped

Fig. 17. Scraper-planes, domed variety.

Fig. 18. Scraper-planes. *Left, top to bottom,* flat-topped variety. *Right, top to bottom,* different surfaces of a multi-faceted scraper-plane.

38

scraper-planes. This was accomplished by removing the domed surface with one or more percussion blows struck sideways against the more pointed end of the original nodule. In our original analysis, as well as in the analysis of materials from both Chiapas and Tamaulipas, the flat-topped and domed scraper-planes were considered to be different types. However, in the very large sample from Tehuacan there does not seem to be any significant temporal difference between the two. Therefore, we have consolidated them into one type, although for comparative purposes Tables 6 and 7 give statistics for both varieties separately.

Scraper-planes are found throughout the Tehuacan sequence, but they were most popular during El Riego and Coxcatlan times. In Chiapas, they were used only in the preceramic period, while in Tamaulipas their greatest popularity occurred in the Infiernillo phase. However, in much of central Mesoamerica their temporal distribution is similar to that of Tehuacan. North of Mesoamerica they seem to be more prevalent in the western United States than in the eastern Woodlands, and they have been considered diagnostic of the Desert Culture. However, scraper-planes are also found in British Columbia, the Yukon, and Alaska, far north of the so-called Desert Culture area. Scraper-planes are also found in western Montana in association with the Cordilleran tradition, which is commonly considered to be older than the Desert Culture tradition.

Multifaceted Scraper-Planes

Fig. 18

169 specimens; 81 excavated, 88 collected.

Dimensions in cm.: length (47 specimens), 1.6–13.1, average, 5.2; width (50 specimens), 2.9–12.7, average, 5.8; thickness (52 specimens), 1.6–13.1, average, 4.1.

Multifaceted scraper-planes vary in outline from almost round to an uneven oval. One end is usually definitely convex, and occasionally the other is squared off at the striking platform to produce another cutting edge on a different plane. Generally speaking, all scraper-planes have at least one flat ventral surface and a convex, steep-sided, or domed surface. Since the scraper-planes described here have been retouched on more than one surface, they characteristically have one or more domed surfaces and more than one flat surface, and therefore they are categorized as multifaceted.

These scrapers appear to have been made from spheroidal or ellipsoidal percussion-chipped cores or bifaces that had been broken in half. The newly created surface was used as a striking platform to remove flakes by percussion from the adjacent steeply sloping surfaces. Wide scars indicate that the flakes removed were

quite large and that the broken-faceted nodules must therefore have served as cores for obtaining flakes. However, about three quarters of our sample gave evidence not only of the removal of large flakes, but also of the removal of many tiny flakes—a technique that could produce an especially sharp cutting or scraping edge. Multifaceted scraper-planes were fashioned from ordinary scraper-planes by breaking off a large section to make a new flat or ventral surface. Another series of flakes was removed to sharpen an edge of the new surface. This process produced scrapers with two cutting edges on different planes. Three examples had yet another scraping surface prepared in a similar way, and twenty-two, in addition to the scraping surface, had one or more bifacially worked sinuous edges formed by flakes having been removed while the edge was being used for chopping; flakes had been removed by percussion as well to form the chopping edge prior to its use. Hence, some of these scrapers were not only multifaceted but also had multiple uses.

In the Tehuacan Valley this type of scraper seems to be confined to the El Riego phase. In Tamaulipas the type appeared in the Infiernillo phase of about the same time period. I have also seen multifaceted scraper-planes in collections of Cochise materials from Arizona, although they were not specifically classified as such.

Gouges

Fig. 19

198 specimens; 132 excavated, 66 collected.

Dimensions in cm.: length (77 specimens), 2.1–8.0, average, 4.3; width (97 specimens), 1.8–6.9, average, 3.5; thickness (119 specimens), 0.6–3.2, average, 1.6.

Gouges have a somewhat indeterminate outline and range from rough isosceles triangles to an elongated form with a tendency toward cuboidism. One end has usually been retouched to make it concave. The ventral surface is relatively flat. Gouges are usually thick, with steep sides and flat central surfaces on the dorsal side.

Gouges were made from long, flat flakes. About half of our sample are scarred from rough percussion blows along the lateral edges, and most specimens have a narrow end made concave by two or three percussion blows. These ends have been sharpened and made even more concave by well-controlled percussion-chipping at the cutting edges.

Gouges are found as far south as Chiapas, where they appear in the Santa Marta complex. In the Tehuacan region they appear mainly in the El Riego, Coxcatlan, and Abejas horizons, but they lasted through ceramic times. From the Tehuacan region to Texas they seem

Thin-Flake End-Scrapers

Fig. 20

224 specimens; 178 excavated, 46 collected.

Dimensions in cm.: length (77 specimens), 1.9–7.7, average, 3.6; width (77 specimens), 1.2–5.6, average 3.0; thickness (161 specimens), 0.4–4.2, average, 1.0.

These end-scrapers are irregularly shaped flakes that are generally a little longer than they are wide and are uniformly thin. One narrow convex end is chipped on the dorsal surface to form a thin cutting edge.

These scrapers were fashioned from long, thin, flint flakes and have a narrow edge—opposite the striking platform in about one third of the examples—sharpened for cutting. This thin cutting edge is never more than 0.4 cm. thick. The cutting edge was retouched by controlled percussion in about a fourth of the sample; the rest were chipped by pressure-flaking or simply from use.

In the Tehuacan region thin-flake end-scrapers originated in the El Riego phase and are a minority type in the preceramic levels. They became an important type in the Santa Maria and Palo Blanco phases, and were still fairly prevalent in the Venta Salada phase. It is difficult to plot geographical distribution for such a generalized type of scraper.

Crude Discoidal Scrapers

Fig. 21

360 specimens; 242 excavated, 118 collected.

Dimensions in cm.: length (158 specimens), 1.5–8.8, average, 4.1; width (181 specimens), 1.8–6.8, average, 3.8; thickness (233 specimens), 1.3–3.3, average, 1.4.

CM. 1   3   5
INCHES 1   2

Fig. 19. Gouges.

to have an almost unbroken distribution via Queretaro, Hidalgo, San Luis Potosi, Tamaulipas, and Nuevo Leon. In general, gouges existed in the period from about 6000 B.C. to the beginning of the Christian era.

Fig. 20. Thin-flake end-scrapers.

Fig. 21. Crude discoidal scrapers.

Crude discoidal scrapers are rather small tools, roughly oval to round in outline. They have flat ventral surfaces and steep dorsal sides leading either to a domed or flattened central dorsal portion.

Discoidal scrapers were made from small, very thick flakes. One flat surface served as a striking platform, and flakes were removed all around the edge by percussion or controlled-percussion techniques. The sides on which the flake scars appear are usually very steep, and the scars often extend to the center of the dorsal surface, giving it a domed appearance. Occasionally, on the flatter, wider flakes, the retouching did not produce a dome, and part of the original flat surface of the flake remains intact.

Crude discoidal scrapers were used in the Tehuacan region from the El Riego phase throughout the sequence and were most popular in the Archaic periods. In Tamaulipas and Chiapas they seem to have a more limited range, from roughly 6000 to 2000 B.C. Discoidal scrapers appear to be a common type in Mesoamerica, and they extend into the Desert Culture area in western North America.

End-of-Blade Scrapers

Fig. 22
162 specimens; 48 excavated, 114 collected.
Dimensions in cm.: length (22 specimens), 1.9–6.9, average,

2.4; width (28 specimens), 0.8–4.2, average, 1.9; thickness (30 specimens), 0.3–1.1, average, 0.5.

End-of-blade scrapers are roughly rectangular in outline, and one of the narrower ends—usually the end opposite the striking platform—is very slightly convex. Ventral surfaces are flat. One to four parallel ridges run the length of the dorsal surfaces.

End-of-blade scrapers were manufactured from flint or obsidian blades struck from polyhedral cores. Most of the excavated specimens are obsidian, but the few preceramic examples are flint. The ends opposite the

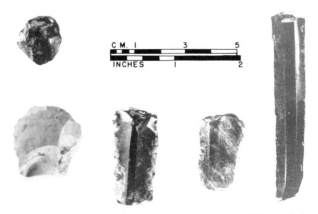

Fig. 22. Finely chipped end-scrapers. *Upper and lower left,* thumbnail scrapers; *center and right,* end-of-blade scrapers.

41

Fig. 23. Fine flat-topped end-scrapers.

striking platforms of nearly all the specimens were carefully sharpened by pressure-flaking to form a convex cutting edge, and the striking platforms had been snapped off. Several of these specimens displayed further pressure-retouching along the lateral edges, and two also had both of the narrower ends retouched. Only two specimens retained their striking platforms and had a straight cutting edge.

In the Tehuacan region end-of-blade scrapers first appeared in Archaic levels. They reached maximum popularity in the late Formative Santa Maria phase, but persisted until historic times. In the Valley of Mexico they are found throughout the ceramic phases, but are most popular in late Formative times. In Chiapas end-of-blade scrapers appear in the Santa Marta complex, but in Tamaulipas, this type of scraper was not uncovered in preceramic levels. These limited data indicate that end-of-blade scrapers diffused in Mexico toward the northeast.

Fine, Flat-Topped End-Scrapers

Fig. 23

43 specimens; 30 excavated, 13 collected.

Dimensions in cm. of 16 specimens: length (11 specimens only), 2.2–6.0, average, 3.8; width, 2.2–4.3, average, 3.2; thickness, 0.5–1.4, average, 0.8.

These scrapers range from an oval or tear-drop shape to isosceles triangles, with the former shapes predominant. Ventral surfaces and the tops of the dorsal surfaces are both flat.

These scrapers were made from elongated flat flakes. The lateral edges have been retouched by pressure-flaking, which is usually not straight, and the sides are

therefore only slightly convex. The end farthest from the bulb of percussion also has been retouched by slightly steeper pressure-flaking to make a convex cutting edge. For the most part, this fine pressure-flaking has not affected or scarred the flat central area of the dorsal surface.

This type of end-scraper originated in the Formative period of the Tehuacan sequence, but it did not become popular until Classic and Postclassic times. The type seems equivalent to Tolstoy's well-made, end-of-blade scrapers, which have a similar distribution in the Valley of Mexico. The flat-flake type found in Tamaulipas seems to be related; it also reached its greatest popularity in Postclassic times.

Fine Ovoid, Plano-Convex End-Scrapers

Fig. 24

81 specimens; 39 excavated, 42 collected.

Dimensions in cm.: length (23 specimens), 1.8–3.5, average, 2.8; width (22 specimens), 1.9–3.6, average, 2.4; thickness (26 specimens), 0.7–1.6, average, 1.1.

Roughly oval in outline, these small end-scrapers tend to have slightly flattened basal ends. In cross section they are plano-convex, with a flat ventral surface and a hemispherical dorsal surface. They were made from small, thick flakes, round to oval in outline. Dorsal surfaces have been retouched by controlled percussion-flaking so that they have a bulbous appearance. The cutting edge and adjacent edges have been steeply sharpened by pressure-flaking.

These end-scrapers appear first in their greatest frequency in early Formative levels and last into Postclassic times, but they decrease in popularity over this span. Similar scrapers are recorded for the Classic pe-

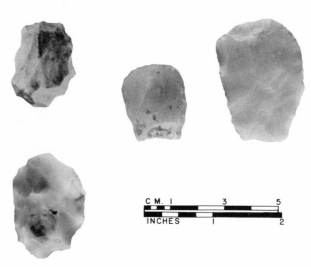

Fig. 24. Fine ovoid, plano-convex end-scrapers.

riod at Uaxactun. The "small oval scrapers" found by Tolstoy in the Valley of Mexico seem to be of the same type; these were most popular in the early Zacatenco and early Arbolillo levels which are characteristic of the Formative period in this region. Similar types of end-scrapers appear much earlier north of Mesoamerica.

Thumbnail End-Scrapers
Fig. 22
14 specimens; 5 excavated, 9 collected.
Dimensions in cm. of 2 specimens: length, 1.7 and 2.8; width, 1.9 and 2.8; thickness, 0.5 and 0.9.

These scrapers have the outline of a thumbnail and are flat ventrally. The central areas of the dorsal surfaces are either flat or very slightly convex. Two specimens were made from small broken portions of blades, and the others were made from small, flat flakes. All dorsal edges have been pressure-retouched.

Thumbnail end-scrapers were found only in Postclassic levels in the Tehuacan Valley. In Tamaulipas they appeared in levels of about the same period. North of Mesoamerica thumbnail scrapers appeared much earlier and in much larger proportions.

REFERENCES

BUTLER, B. R.
1961   *The Old Cordilleran Culture in the Pacific Northwest*. Idaho State College Museum, Occasional Papers, No. 5. Pocatello, Idaho.

EKHOLM, GORDON F.
1944   *Excavations at Tampico and Panuco in the Huasteca, Mexico*. AMNH-AP, Vol. 38.

HAURY, EMIL W., *et al.*
1950   *The Stratigraphy and Archaeology of Ventana Cave, Arizona*. Tucson: University of Arizona Press.

JENNINGS, JESSE D.
1957   *Danger Cave*. Memoirs of the Society for American Archaeology, No. 14. Salt Lake City, Utah.

KIDDER, ALFRED V.
1947   *The Artifacts of Uaxactun, Guatemala*. CIW, Publication No. 576.

MacNEISH, RICHARD S.
1958   *Preliminary Archaeological Investigations in the Sierra de Tamaulipas, Mexico*. APS-T, Vol. 48, Part 6.
1964   "Archaeological Excavation, Comparisons, and Speculations." *Investigations in the Southwest Yukon*. Papers of the Robert S. Peabody Foundation for Archaeology, Vol. 6. Andover, Massachusetts.

MacNEISH, RICHARD S., AND F. A. PETERSON
1962   *The Santa Marta Rock Shelter, Ocozocoautla, Chiapas, Mexico*. Papers of the New World Archaeological Foundation, No. 14. Provo, Utah.

SAYLES, E.B., AND ERNST ANTEVS
1941   *The Cochise Culture*. Medallion Papers, No. 22. Globe, Arizona.

SUHM, DEE ANN, A. D. KRIEGER, AND E. B. JELKS
1954   *An Introductory Handbook of Texas Archaeology*. TAS-B, Vol. 25.

TOLSTOY, PAUL
——   "Stone, Bone, and Antler Tools of Central Mexico from Preclassic to Aztec Times." To be published in *Handbook of Middle American Indians*. Austin: University of Texas Press.

VAILLANT, GEORGE C.
1930   *Excavations at Zacatenco*. AMNH-AP, Vol. 32, Part 1.

CHAPTER 3

Laterally Worked Unifaces

O F ALL the nonceramic artifacts, laterally worked unifaces were the least satisfactory in terms of defining types to serve as time markers. These kinds of tools seem to be neither as sensitive nor as susceptible to cultural change as the other chipped- and ground-stone tools, but the possibility keeps plaguing me that perhaps our system of analysis was inadequate for the task of determining what their significant changes were. Because of this, many of the unifacial artifacts described below must be thought of as trial types and not as final types.

All tools termed "unifaces" have, of course, only one modified surface, and one or both lateral edges are worked in some manner. Burins not formed from bifacial artifacts are one type belonging to this class and are here defined as long, flat flakes or blades which have had a spall removed from one side by a burin blow —that is, a blow aimed in the direction of the flake's or blade's longitudinal axis but struck against the narrow end in such a manner as to remove a spall from the adjacent longer side. The long edge from which the "burin spall" has been removed is left with a deep, sharp concavity, positioned just below the striking platform, which can be used for incising or for cutting in a gougelike way. Our unifacial burin sample consists of five specimens from the Ajuereado and El Riego levels and three others from surface collections. This sample, of course, is woefully inadequate, particularly when comparative data indicate that the five excavated specimens represent two different burin types.

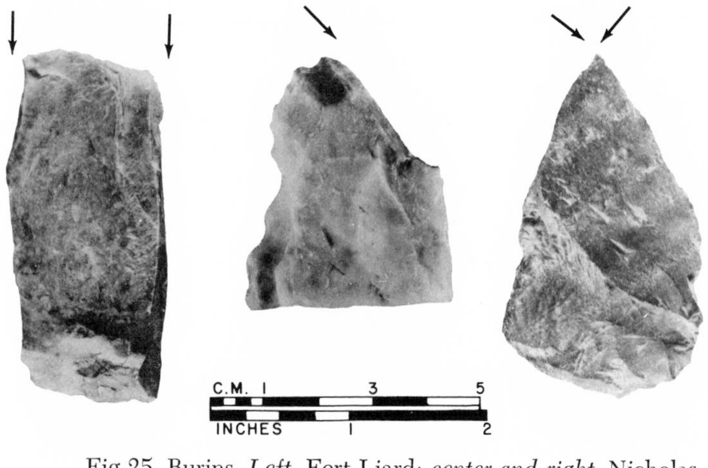

Related to burins are flake gravers, which may have been used in a similar way but which were made in a different manner. Flake gravers are fashioned by retouching unifacially one end of a flake so that it has a point or teatlike projection. These tools were found throughout the Tehuacan sequence in gradually diminishing numbers, and therefore they do have some temporal signifiance.

Spokeshave-like tools have a distribution somewhat similar to that of flake gravers, but proportionately more of these unifacial artifacts come from preceramic levels. These tools are rather long and have been chipped along one lateral edge of the dorsal surface in such a manner that the other edge is deeply concave and notched.

Our other eight categories of unifaces are more difficult to classify and should be considered as trial types. All the tools in these categories are retouched or utilized flakes or side-scrapers. Study revealed that thick flakes with a longer edge or edges that had been marked or retouched were more popular in earlier periods than were thin flakes with similar features. For this reason, we originally divided the side-scrapers into two trial types based on their thickness or thinness. Further plot-

Fig.25. Burins. *Left,* Fort Liard; *center and right,* Nicholas angled.

Fig. 26. Flake gravers.

ting of attributes disclosed that flakes with two edges marked or retouched were more popular earlier than flakes with only one edge so defined. In this manner, our reshufflings of groups according to attributes uncovered four fairly satisfactory trial types. Additional examination of these artifacts revealed that some of the lateral edges were intentionally retouched and had long, uniform flake scars, whereas the edges of others were nicked, with unevenly spaced scars of different lengths. The latter scars we considered to be evidence of wear from use, rather than evidence of intentional retouching. Finally then, on the basis of whether the worked edges had been retouched on purpose or were merely nicked from use, our four groups of flakes were further subdivided into eight trial types. The actual reshuffling of the artifacts revealed that five groups out of the eight had some temporal significance.

Thin flakes with two edges scarred only from use, for instance, appeared in significant numbers in Ajuereado times, although they extended into the Abejas phase. Thick flakes with two retouched edges lasted into Abejas times, and thick flakes with two utilized edges also extended into that phase and appeared again in Palo Blanco times. Thin flakes with one edge utilized were found throughout the sequence in diminishing

amounts. The fifth group also appeared throughout the sequence; it included such diverse trial types as thin flakes with two edges retouched; thick flakes with one edge either retouched or worked; and thin flakes with one edge retouched. After much debate, we decided that since this last group of laterally worked flakes or side-scrapers was so extensive and so diverse, it would be clearer and more useful to present all eight trial types separately.

In the following pages, each of the eleven types of unifaces is described and illustrated. Tables 8 and 9 show the temporal distribution of the unifaces found in our excavated and surface sites. I hope future analysts are able to make more "chronological" sense from this information than appears here.

Laterally Worked Unifaces

Nicholas Angled Burin*

Fig. 25

5 specimens; 3 excavated, 2 collected.

Dimensions in cm. of 5 specimens: length, 2.8–6.0, average,

* This burin type is named after Nicholas Coe, who, at the age of five years, was the first to find and recognize a burin in the Tehuacan Valley.

45

4.3; width, 2.1–3.3, average, 2.6; thickness, 0.7–1.4, average, 1.1.

These burins were made from flat unifacial flakes. The longer edges of the flakes were retouched, possibly to shape them for further use. Spalls struck from the longer edge of the center specimen in Fig. 25 have left scars that form an obtuse angle with the retouched edge. A second burin blow removed part of the retouching from the specimen shown at the right.

In the Tehuacan region these burins come from the Ajuereado and El Riego horizons. The only other burins of this type from Mexico seem to be those found with extinct animals in Cynthia Irwin-Williams' excavations in the Valsequillo basin near Puebla. Some of the Texas burins listed by Jeremiah Epstein, others from Five Mile Rapids in Oregon, and Flint Creek burins of the northern Yukon are similar, as are the flake burins of north-

east Asia. I suspect, therefore, that the Mexican burins had an Asian origin.

Fort Liard Burins

Fig. 25
3 specimens; 2 excavated, 1 collected.
Dimensions in cm. of 3 specimens: length, 6.0, 5.2, 2.1; width, 2.8, 1.5, 1.1; thickness, 0.8, 1.1, 0.4.

Fort Liard burins are manufactured from long, flat, rectangular flakes. One of the two examples from excavation had burin blows struck on both ends, removing spalls from both sides. The other two specimens had a single spall removed from one side.

These burins were found in early El Riego levels in the Tehuacan Valley, but Irwin-Williams found some with extinct animals in the Valsequillo basin. Others have been recorded from the western United States,

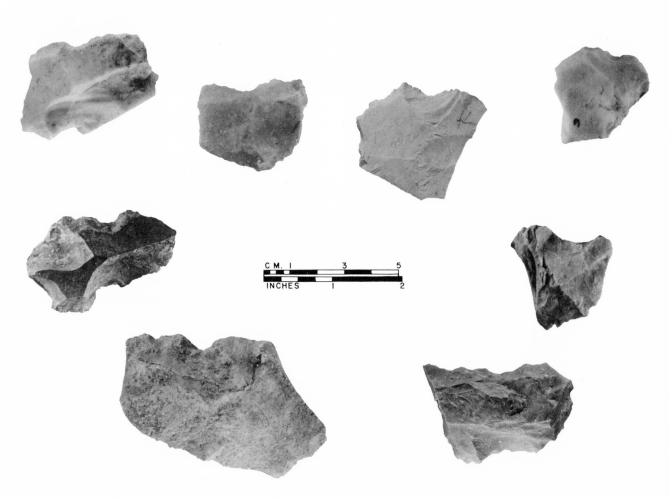

Fig. 27. Spokeshave-like tools.

western Canada, Alaska, and Siberia. These burins may also have an Asian origin.

Flake Gravers

Fig. 26

195 specimens; 85 excavated, 110 collected.

Dimensions in cm. of 14 specimens with smooth edges: length, 2.1–5.3, average, 4.1; width, 1.9–5.5, average, 3.0; thickness, 0.7–1.8, average, 1.2. Specimens with serrated edges: length (27 specimens), 1.9–8.2, average, 3.7; width (26 specimens), 1.8–5.3; average, 3.2; thickness (27 specimens), 0.6–1.9, average, 1.8.

Flake gravers are made from flat flakes, many of which have been struck from blocky cores. Ventral surfaces are flat except for the bulb of percussion. Dorsal surfaces show a few flake scars, usually running in the general direction of the longitudinal axis. Generally speaking, flake gravers are longer than they are wide, but their form depends on the kinds of flakes from which they were made. One of the shorter ends usually has been retouched by pressure-flaking to form a small, teatlike point. A majority of the specimens have been chipped unifacially, but both surfaces of eight specimens have been chipped. The latter specimens are chipped on the right edge of the ventral surface and the left edge of the dorsal surface, or vice versa, and display a beveled edge in profile. About twenty specimens were finely retouched along the dorsal edges adjacent to the graver point. Others were laterally retouched by percussion-flaking, and this resulted in irregularly serrated edges leading up to the graver point.

Flake gravers are found throughout the Tehuacan sequence, but they tend to be slightly more prevalent in the earliest horizon, Ajuereado. They also are common throughout the sequence in Queretaro. None were noted in the excavations in Chiapas, and in Tamaulipas they were found only in the Lerma horizon. In the Great Plains of the United States they appear with Folsom points, and they also appear in early horizons in the Southwest.

Spokeshave-like Tools

Fig. 27

190 specimens; 135 excavated, 55 collected.

Dimensions in cm. of specimens with smooth edges: length (27 specimens), 1.5–5.9, average, 3.2; width (28 specimens), 2.1–6.7, average, 3.9; thickness (28 specimens), 0.6–2.5, average, 1.3; concavity width (29 specimens), 0.7–3.2, average, 1.3; concavity depth (29 specimens), 0.2–0.7, average, 0.3. Specimens with serrated edges: length (42 specimens), 1.8–6.5, average, 3.2; width (43 specimens), 1.9–8.0, average, 3.8; thickness (43 speci-

mens), 0.8–2.0, average, 1.2; concavity width (42 specimens), 0.4–2.5, average, 0.6, concavity depth (43 specimens), 0.1–0.5, average 0.3.

These unifaces are made from elongated flat flakes, most of which were struck from blocky cores. Ventral surfaces are flat except for the bulb of percussion, and dorsal surfaces show a few rough flaking scars. Most of these specimens were pressure-retouched along one lateral edge of the dorsal surface, which made a part of the edge sharply concave. The concavity is usually quite deep in proportion to its width, and frequently the inner part of the notch shows evidence of having been utilized. Sixteen examples have been retouched and notched on both lateral dorsal edges. There are two varieties, one with serrated edges and the other with smooth edges.

These unifaces are found throughout the Tehuacan sequence, but they were slightly more popular in preceramic times and the Ajalpan phase than in the later periods. Similar tools have not been noted for most of Mexico, but they are found throughout the sequence in Tamaulipas.

Thin Flakes, Two Edges Utilized

Fig. 28

127 specimens; 17 excavated, 110 collected.

Fig. 28. Thin flakes, two edges utilized.

Fig. 29. Thick flakes, two edges retouched or utilized.

Dimensions in cm. of 13 specimens: length, 2.5–6.0, average, 4.2; width 2.5–3.7, average, 3.2; thickness, 0.7–1.2, average 1.0.

These unifaces are elongated, very flat flakes with smooth ventral surfaces that are usually marked by a bulb of percussion. Dorsal surfaces display one or two flake scars. Both lateral edges have been used for sawing, cutting, or scraping.

Although this extremely simple type of artifact is known from many sites in North America, it surprisingly enough seems to have some chronological significance in the Tehuacan Valley. It appears in significant numbers in the Ajuereado horizon and seems to last into El Riego times, but it is unknown in later periods.

Thick Flakes, Two Edges Retouched

Fig. 29

39 specimens; 26 excavated, 13 collected.

Dimensions in cm. of 14 specimens: length, 4.7–6.8, average, 5.7; width, 6.6–10.4, average, 8.2; thickness, 1.5–1.7, average, 1.6.

These long, relatively thick flakes, with six exceptions, have been struck from cuboid cores. Ventral surfaces are flat, except for the bulb of percussion, and dorsal surfaces show a few long, longitudinal flake scars. Both lateral edges have been retouched dorsally by percussion or by pressure-flaking.

Although these crude side-scrapers are widespread in the New World, they do seem to have some temporal

Fig. 30. Thin flakes, one edge utilized.

significance in the Tehuacan Valley, in spite of a small sample. Almost all examples come from the three earliest phases—Ajuereado, El Riego, and Coxcatlan—of the Tehuacan sequence.

Thick Flakes, Two Edges Utilized

Fig. 29

87 specimens; 50 excavated, 37 collected.

Dimensions in cm. of 16 specimens: length, 3.6–7.5, average, 5.2; width, 6.0–9.2, average, 7.5; thickness, 1.3–2.2, average, 1.8.

These elongated thick flakes have flat ventral surfaces and dorsal surfaces scarred by percussion-flaking. The two lateral edges of the dorsal surface have been nicked, probably from use. Flakes like these are found almost everywhere in the world.

Thin Flakes, One Edge Utilized

Fig. 30

727 specimens; 321 excavated, 406 collected.

Dimensions in cm. of 16 specimens: length, 3.1–4.7, average, 3.9; width, 1.8–3.3, average, 2.6; thickness, 0.6–1.1, average, 0.9.

Fig. 31. Thick flakes, one edge retouched. *Lower left,* a thick flake with one edge utilized.

49

Fig. 32. Thin flakes, two edges retouched.

Along one lateral edge of these thin flakes there is evidence of retouching resulting from use. This extremely generalized tool is found throughout the Tehuacan sequence and exists throughout North America.

Thick Flakes, One Edge Retouched

Fig. 31

208 specimens; 168 excavated, 40 collected.

Dimensions in cm. of 13 specimens with smooth edges: length, 3.4–5.9, average, 4.6; width, 4.3–9.0, average, 6.9; thickness, 1.3–2.0, average, 1.7. Of 9 specimens with serrated edges: length, 3.9–5.8, average, 5.2; width, 3.9–9.3, average, 6.1; thickness, 0.5–2.9, average, 1.7.

These slightly elongated flakes were struck from many different kinds of cores. Their ventral surfaces are flat, and the dorsal surfaces display a few flake scars. One lateral edge of the dorsal surface has been intentionally retouched, probably by percussion-flaking, although some of the retouching is fine enough to have been produced by pressure. There are two varieties, one with serrated edges and one with smooth edges.

This is a common type of side-scraper throughout North America, and in the Tehuacan sequence it appears in all periods. It is slightly more popular in the Ajuereado phase than in any other, which may or may not be significant.

Thin Flakes, Two Edges Retouched

Fig. 32

106 specimens; 59 excavated, 47 collected.

Dimensions in cm. of 15 specimens: length, 1.9–4.8, average, 3.1; width, 2.9–6.0, average, 4.1; thickness (8 specimens), 0.6–1.3, average, 0.9.

These thin, flat flakes have relatively smooth ventral surfaces and dorsal surfaces that were scarred by one or two percussion blows. Two of the edges were retouched on the dorsal surface by fine pressure-flaking. Some specimens were retouched on opposite long edges, and eight with a pointed appearance were retouched on adjacent long edges. The edges of a few specimens from El Riego levels were slightly more serrated than the edges of others.

These unifaces are common throughout North America and appear throughout the Tehuacan sequence.

Thin Flakes, One Edge Retouched

Fig. 33

905 specimens; 774 excavated, 131 collected.

Dimensions in cm. of 47 specimens with smooth edges: length, 2.5–5.1, average, 3.4; width, 2.1–4.7, average, 3.6; thickness, 0.6–1.7, average, 1.1. Specimens with serrated edges: length (30 specimens), 1.5–5.0, average, 3.2; width (27 specimens), 1.6–6.0, average, 3.8; thickness (32 specimens), 0.5–1.9, average, 1.0.

Fig. 33. Thin flakes, one edge retouched.

These tools are variously shaped thin flakes struck from a variety of core types. Ventral surfaces are flat and dorsal surfaces may show evidence of pressure-flaking. One of the longer edges has been pressure-retouched on the dorsal surface, which sometimes produced a serrated edge.

Thin unifaces of this type are one of the most common artifacts in North America. They appear in the Tehuacan Valley in all horizons; although very numerous in even the earliest period, they seem to increase in popularity in the later periods of the sequence.

Thick Flakes, One Edge Utilized

Fig. 31

277 specimens; 160 excavated, 117 collected.

Dimensions in cm. of 35 specimens: length, 3.2–8.0, average, 5.4; width, 1.2–6.6, average, 4.4; thickness, 1.6–2.3, average, 1.9.

These unifaces are elongated thick flakes, and one of the longer edges is nicked along its dorsal surface. These rather irregular markings probably indicate that the edge has been used but was not intentionally retouched. Utilized flakes such as these are found almost universally.

REFERENCES

ALEXANDER, HERBERT L.
1963 "The Levi Site: A Paleo-Indian Campsite in Central Texas." *Am. Ant.*, 28:510–28.

BONCH-OSMOLOVSKY, G., AND V. GROMOV
1936 "The Paleolithic in the Union of Soviet Socialist Republics." *International Geological Congress, XVIth Session, 1933*. Washington.

CRESSMAN, LUTHER S.
1960 *Cultural Sequences at The Dalles, Oregon.* APS-T, Vol. 50, Part 10.

EPSTEIN, JEREMIAH F.
1960 "Burins from Texas." *Am. Ant.*, 26:93–97.

GROMOV, V. I.
1945 "Twenty-five Years of the Quaternary of the U.S.S.R." *AJS*, Vol. 243.

HAURY, EMIL W., *et al.*
1950 *The Stratigraphy and Archaeology of Ventana Cave, Arizona.* Tucson: University of Arizona Press.

JENNINGS, JESSE D.
1957 *Danger Cave.* Memoirs of the Society for American Archaeology, No. 14. Salt Lake City, Utah.

KIDDER, ALFRED V.
1947 *The Artifacts of Uaxactun, Guatemala.* CIW, Publication No. 576.

LORENZO, JOSÉ LUIS
1961 "Un Buril de la Cultura Precerámica de Teopisca, Chiapas." *Homenaje a Pablo Martínez del Río.* INAH, Mexico.

MACNEISH, RICHARD S.
1958 *Preliminary Archaeological Investigations in the Sierra de Tamaulipas, Mexico.* APS-T, Vol. 48, Part 6.

1959 "Men out of Asia: As Seen from the Northwest Yukon." *Anthropological Papers of the University of Alaska*, 7:41–59. Fairbanks.

1964 "Archaeological Excavation, Comparisons, and Speculations." *Investigations in the Southwest Yukon.* Papers of the Robert S. Peabody Foundation for Archaeology. Andover, Massachusetts.

MACNEISH, RICHARD S., AND F. A. PETERSON
1962 *The Santa Marta Rock Shelter, Ocozocoautla, Chiapas, Mexico.* Papers of the New World Archaeological Foundation, No. 14. Provo, Utah.

ROBERTS, FRANK H. H.
1935 *A Folsom Complex.* Smithsonian Miscellaneous Collections, Vol. 94, No. 4. Washington.

VAILLANT, GEORGE C.
1930 *Excavations at Zacatenco.* AMNH-AP, Vol. 32, Part 1.

YOSHIZAKI, M.
1959 *Tachikawa Preceramic Industries in South Hokkaido.* Hokkaido Municipal Museum Research Bulletin, No. 6. Tokyo.

CHAPTER 4

Projectile Points

PROJECTILE points turned out to be among the best time markers for the Tehuacan sequence. Our final analysis was based upon a large sample of about 1,200 specimens from excavation and about 600 specimens from surface collections. Preliminary classification, based on some 840 specimens—or about half our final sample—was begun during the winter of 1962, while excavations were still in process. The methods we followed in classifying the projectile points differed somewhat from the procedures followed in analyzing the other chipped-stone artifacts, because some classification of Mesoamerican points already existed, and the materials from Tehuacan could be compared with previously established archaeological types. The stratified Santa Marta Cave in Chiapas had yielded thirty-nine points for classification, and the large sample of projectile points from the state of Tamaulipas included more than 2,500 examples—1,176 from the Sierra de Tamaulipas, about 800 from excavation in the Sierra Madre, and about 600 from surface collections or minor tests in the northern coastal area. Thus our preliminary task was to compare the sizable sample of projectile points from the Tehuacan Valley with the types already established on the basis of adequate samples from two other regions of Mexico.

Almost as soon as the Tehuacan specimens were laid out on the laboratory tables, we could see that many of them were extremely similar to the materials from Tamaulipas and Chiapas. We immediately identified among our examples nineteen of the types found in the other two regions. These included Lerma, Plainview, Abasolo, Tortugas, Flacco, Gary, Nogales, Catan, Palmillas, Matamoros, Almagre, Ensor, Morhiss, Teotihuacan, Tula, Harrell, Starr, Fresno, and San Lorenzo projectile points. When the temporal distribution of these types from Tehuacan, Chiapas, and Tamaulipas was checked, it became clear that they were roughly

contemporaneous in each of the three areas. Certainly, on a cursory level, these particular projectile points seemed to be time markers for a wide area of eastern Mexico.

Our Tehuacan sample contained as well two types—Shumla and Agate Basin—similar to previously classified types from Texas in both form and temporal distribution. The identification of these twenty-one types, then, left us with a residue of about one hundred projectile points which differed sufficiently from previously described types from either Chiapas, Tamaulipas, or Texas so that they could not be considered variants of any of these types.

We grouped the residual points into eight general categories with distinctive forms and distinctive temporal positions. The earliest of these was a long, narrow, concave-based type, found only in Zones XV–XXII of of Coxcatlan Cave, which we called El Riego. A second type, found only in Zones X–XVI of Coxcatlan Cave, had a triangular body with a straight stem and was eventually named La Mina. A leaf-shaped type with serrated edges came from Coxcatlan Zones VIII–XI and was later designated Pelona. A side-notched type called Abejas was also found in the earlier levels of Coxcatlan Cave.

In later levels and associated with pottery were four other distinctive types of projectile points. One of them was similar in outline to a Lerma point but was generally smaller in size, it was not diamond-shaped in cross section as Lerma points usually are, and it was found only with Formative ceramics rather than in early horizons—with, in fact, a long gap between the latest recorded Lerma point and the earliest of the similar smaller points. We separated these particular projectile points into a new classification termed Zacatenco. Roughly contemporaneous with Zacatenco points, but lasting into the late Formative period, was a small, stemmed point with prominent shoulder barbs which was unlike any known projectile point from Texas, Chiapas, or Tamaulipas. We called these Salado points, and the type became an important time marker for the Tehuacan sequence.

In the latest horizon of the Tehuacan Valley, a large, neatly made, side-notched projectile point made its appearance. In general form the type was somewhat like a Harrell point, but examples of it were much longer than the Harrell points described for Texas or Tamaulipas, and they seemed to be confined specifically to central Mexico. This type, initially named Ajalpan, was ultimately classified as Texcoco. A final type of projectile point which we called Tehuacan appeared only with Classic and Postclassic ceramics. It was large and carefully fashioned, with a wide, expanding stem and rather poorly defined corner notches.

Late in the spring of 1962, after our tentative classification of projectile points had been made, two events caused us to re-examine our preliminary groupings. First, we received a manuscript from Paul Tolstoy, in which he illustrated and classified 397 projectile points from various excavations in the Valley of Mexico. The points he described were, for the most part, similar to the ones with which we were working; his analysis helped as well to connect, at least geographically, the series from Tamaulipas with the materials from Tehuacan. His manuscript caused us to alter the name of our Ajalpan type to his previously defined Texcoco type, and it heightened our hunch that something was wrong with our Gary classification. The second and perhaps even more important event was the sharing of information with Cynthia Irwin-Williams, who was working in northern Puebla and who had found some 800 projectile points in two excavations undertaken in Queretaro and northern Hidalgo. As we began to discuss and compare projectile points with her, we were forced to sharpen our postulates concerning them, and some of these terms and concepts I shall now briefly review.

The following definition served to separate projectile points from all other artifacts: a projectile point is a bifacially chipped tool, usually longer than it is wide and generally symmetrical, with sharp edges at the pointed end and specialized chipping at the other end· to facilitate hafting. This definition, it was felt, emphasized the morphological aspects of projectile points and minimized functional considerations.

As noted previously, typology is an archaeological device with which changing concepts can be marked off in space and time. To determine types, one starts with individual features or attributes of artifacts, then isolates the diagnostic features or modes, then groups and combines the modes to evolve types. This concept of mode (Rouse 1939) is basic to this method of achieving a type.

At its simplest, a mode is a specific feature of an artifact which, in contrast to other more generalized features, has temporal significance. It is determined in the first instance by comparing and contrasting all possible attributes of artifacts from various stratigraphic levels. In the case of projectile points, it is necessary to examine the size; the kinds of stems, bases, and tangs; the chipping techniques employed; and many other features. There are several hundred possible combinations of attributes that could be considered in studying these particular artifacts. When projectile points are examined from level after level and from various sites, it becomes apparent that certain of these features are found only in certain periods and only in certain places. These specific features which have significance in time and space are modes.

We had, for instance, a class of triangular points with contracting stems, percussion-flaked bodies, and retouched edges. These features of this particular kind of point, individually or in combination, appeared throughout much of our total sequence; hence they had spatial importance but little significance in time. As a group, these points had been typed by others as Gary points. When we re-examined these projectile points after our methodological concepts had been tightened, it became clear that the feature of size had modal significance, because the smaller Gary-like points appeared only in the later periods of our sequence. On the basis of this modal characteristic of small size and four additional features, we broke our general class into two types, Gary points and Garyitos—that is, little Gary points.

The larger Gary points were re-examined, first with regard to their bases. It turned out that the points with more rounded bases came from early time levels, although a few lasted into later levels; that the points with squared bases came only from middle periods; and that points with pointed bases were more popular in later periods. Here again was a feature which had definite temporal significance and was therefore a mode.

Next we examined the projectile points' shoulders and shoulder tangs. Appearing throughout the sequence were Gary-like points with weak shoulders and no shoulder tangs. Early in the sequence there were some specimens with pointed shoulders and rather weak tangs. These were followed by points with very long, straight shoulder tangs or barbs; and these, in turn, were followed by others with hooked shoulder barbs. With four more modes within the general Gary class

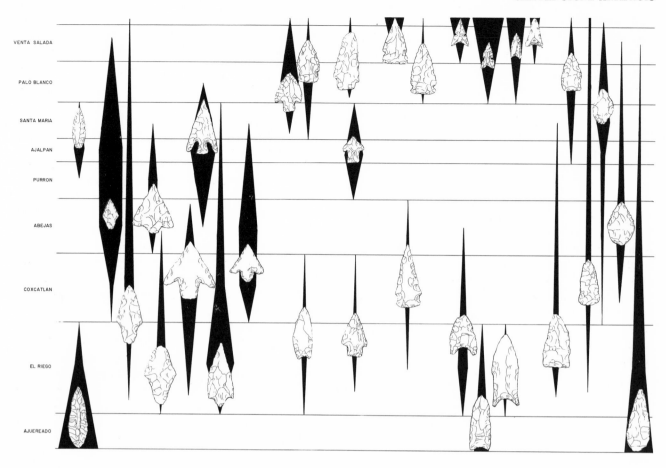

Fig. 34. Distribution of projectile-point types in the Tehuacan cultural sequence.

thus differentiated. we began to seek model clusters which we hoped would provide exclusive types. As it turned out, large points with contracting stems, rounded bases, and weak shoulders appeared throughout much of the sequence. These became the San Nicolas type. Large points with contracting stems and prominent shoulders appeared only in the early part of the sequence and were eventually divided into the Trinidad and Hidalgo types—the latter type appeared earlier and had long stems in proportion to short bodies, whereas Trinidad points appeared a little later and had the opposite proportions. Large points with very prominent barbs and squared bases were found only in the middle of our sequence and were eventually termed Tilapa points. Following these in time were two small Gary-like varieties with pointed bases and slightly different barbs or tangs which we called Coxcatlan and Garyito points.

As is obvious from the above examples, then, a projectile point possesses a number of features which may be combined into one or more modes. A projectile point

type may represent a combination of two or three significant features or modes and may include as well a number of minor attributes which help to differentiate it from other types of projectile points, but which are not significant as time markers.

In the winter of 1963, with our concepts and general methodology re-examined and revised, we began our final classification of projectile points. Our comparative materials encompassed some 4,000 examples, including types from Chiapas, Tamaulipas, and Texas; Paul Tolstoy's analysis of the Valley of Mexico points; and Cynthia Irwin-Williams' work in Queretaro and Hidalgo. These comparative data made it easier to observe the evolution of particular types of points, to see when one type diminished and another increased, or when established types disappeared and new types appeared. Our Tehuacan sample of some 1,800 projectile points, out of which thirty-two types emerged, provided adequate material to mark out our total archaeological sequence (see Fig. 34 and Tables 10 and 11). Since most of these projectile points came from excavated levels which could be dated, we were able as well to gather information about the origin and diffusion of many of the thirty-two types of points. Finally, as Fig. 34 illustrates, a series of types of projectile points clustered together at specific time periods, and this became one of the bases for defining our several archaeological phases.

The earliest phase, Ajuereado, was characterized by Lerma, Plainview, and Abasolo projectile points. The latter two types carried on into the second phase, El Riego, and were joined by a host of new types, including El Riego, Flacco, Tortugas, Agate Basin, La Mina, Hidalgo, Trinidad, Nogales, and, toward the end of the phase, San Nicolas and Tilapa points. In the next cultural phase, Coxcatlan, the Abasolo, Trinidad, Nogales, Tilapa, and San Nicolas points continued in significant proportions, but the phase was more typically characterized by yet another complex of points, which included the Abejas, Almagre, and Coxcatlan types. Pelona and Garyito points were also found in this horizon but are more representative of the subsequent phase, Abejas. The earlier Tilapa, San Nicolas, Almagre, and Coxcatlan points also appeared in significant numbers in Abejas components. The early ceramic phase of Ajalpan saw the rise of the Shumla and Catan types, which had appeared in insignificant amounts previously, as well as the first occurrence of the Salado and Zacatenco types. Garyito, Coxcatlan, and San Nicolas points also continued in use. In the following Santa Maria phase most of these types continued to be used, along with the new Matamoros, Palmillas, and Tehuacan types. The Palo Blanco phase witnessed the disappearance of many of the early types, with the exception of San Nicolas and Catan points. The Matamoros, Palmillas, and Tehuacan types, which had originated in the Santa Maria phase, now reached their greatest popularity, and four new types—Ensor, Morhiss, Teotihuacan, and Tula—came into existence. Both Teotihuacan and Tula points became more popular in the final Venta Salada phase of the Tehuacan sequence, during which Texcoco, Harrell, and Starr points were introduced.

In this volume projectile points are discussed from a morphological point of view in order to establish typology and chronology. In later volumes of the Tehuacan series, these artifacts will be considered with other aspects of the Tehuacan Valley's material culture in an attempt to reconstruct a way of life typical for each of the various cultural periods. Although the details belong to another volume, a few of the interpretations which relate to projectile points should be of interest here.

The large size of the projectile points found in early levels in association with dart mainshafts and wooden fragments of foreshafts indicate that large spear or dart points precede arrowpoints. The fact that small projectile points and arrowshafts are found in later levels supports this hypothesis. In terms of the Tehuacan materials, there is no evidence that the bow and arrow was used before the time of Christ.

Our materials also contain discernable information about hafting techniques. From the Ajuereado through the Coxcatlan phase, projectile points seem to have been attached to shafts by one of two methods. Either the stems of projectile points were inserted into slots and secured by string wrapped round and round both shaft and stem, or stemless projectile points were inserted into slots and held in place by string wrapped tightly around the shaft so that the forward part of the shaft clamped firmly against the projectile point. Beginning in the Abejas phase and lasting to the Conquest, a different binding technique seems to have been employed. Projectile points were still inserted in slots in shafts or foreshafts, but they were now held fast by bindings that first encircled the shaft below the projectile point and then were brought up to crisscross parts of the shaft and parts of the point. This method helped prevent the projectile point from slipping out of place during the moment of forward thrust.

We also were able to make a few observations about the degree of penetration of the projectile points. The early points tended to be thick and relatively narrow. This meant that they had to be hurled or inserted with considerable force in order to penetrate an animal; but once they penetrated, they tended to stay embedded.

Fig. 35. Lerma points.

With the rise of Coxcatlan points, projectile points became very much thinner and sharper. Such a point would penetrate easily, but it would tend to work its way out just as easily, and so leave an animal cut and bleeding. The earlier points, then, were efficient because of their shocking power, and the later points were efficient because they bled and weakened the prey so that it could be trailed and eventually captured. Later points attached to arrows had yet other advantages, arising from the increased force of propulsion the bow made possible and from the factor of reduced weight which arrows provided. Being able to carry a number of arrows with relative ease meant that a hunter could shoot more projectile points into a single quarry, and using a bow instead of a lance shaft favorably altered the speed with which he could repeat the attack. In these later periods, the light-weight, rapid-fire advantages provided by the bow and arrow were just as important in warfare as they were in the chase.

Projectile Points—*Type Descriptions*

Lerma Points

Fig. 35

33 specimens; 20 excavated, 13 collected.

Dimensions in cm.: length (7 specimens), 4.0 to over 6.5, average, 5.3; width (18 specimens), 1.5–2.7, average, 2.2; thickness (14 specimens), 0.7–1.4, average, 1.3.

These points in outline resemble a laurel leaf. They show a slight tendency to be widest just below the midpoint. The bases are not quite so pointed as the tips, and the bases of several specimens are almost rounded. All but two examples tend to be diamond-shaped in cross section.

Lerma points are generally fashioned almost entirely by percussion-flaking. However, two points from the surface, shown at the right-hand side of Fig. 35, and two fragments from excavation (not illustrated) display not only crude percussion-flaking scars radiating more or less from the midpoint, but also scars from controlled percussion-flaking at right angles to the edges. The edges of these specimens are slightly serrated. About half the Lerma points from excavation have crudely ground bases, with the ground portion extending upward from 1.0 to 3.0 cm. The bases of the others show evidence of percussion-flaking only.

At the time of writing, Lerma points have been reported in Mexico not only from Tehuacan but also from the Lerma culture in Tamaulipas (MacNeish 1958, p. 62), from the excavation of the Iztapan mammoth in the Federal District (Aveleyra 1956), in the earliest zone of the San Nicolas rock shelter in Queretaro (C. Irwin-

Fig. 36. Abasolo points.

Williams, personal communication), and in the early San Baltasar remains in northern Puebla. The same type is also reported from Texas (Suhm, Krieger, and Jelks 1954), and some of the early San Dieguito points from southern California (Rogers 1939) seem to be similar. Lerma points seem to have been in existence in

Mexico before 7000 B.C. They may have lasted somewhat longer in Texas than they did in Mexico. The Lerma points from Texas, however, appear to be slightly larger and flatter.

Comparisons with assemblages to the south of Mexico reveal that this type of projectile point is one of the earliest recorded. It appears in El Jobo in Venezuela (Cruxent and Rouse 1956), in Ecuador (Mayer-Oakes and Bell 1960), in Peru (Tschopik 1946), and in Chile (Bird 1943). North of Mexico, it is mainly distributed in the western portion of the continent, and the type closely resembles the Cascade point from the earliest horizons of Oregon (Cressman 1960), Washington (Daugherty 1956), Idaho (Butler 1961), and British Columbia (Borden 1960). These in turn are generally similar to those in the Yukon (MacNeish 1964), in the Northwest Territories of Canada (MacNeish 1963), and Alaska (Campbell 1959). As H. M. Wormington (1957) and others have pointed out, this double-pointed laurel-leaf-shaped projectile point is one of the few early American traits to be found in the northeastern Asian Paleolithic. Is it not possible that the Lerma point is a derivative of Paleolithic Asian prototypes which diffused into the New World via the Rocky Mountains and later traveled into South America?

Abasolo Points

Fig. 36

69 specimens; 41 excavated, 28 collected.

Dimensions in cm.: length (13 specimens), 3.8–7.4, average, 5.3; width (36 specimens), 2.2–4.2, average, 2.9; thickness (40 specimens), 0.6–1.4, average, 1.1.

Abasolo points have the outline of a tear drop, with rounded bases, slightly convex sides, and tapering tips. The broadest portion of the projectile point is just above the base, where it blends into the sides. The bases are often thinned. Only six specimens from excavation were in any way complete, and even fewer specimens from the surface collections were unbroken, so much of this description derives from basal portions of incomplete specimens.

These artifacts have been roughed out by percussion-flaking, which usually converges toward the center. A commonly expressed hypothesis is that Abasolos are projectile-point blanks, and this idea has some merit. Most of the edges near the tips display pressure-flaking scars, and over half of the complete specimens have been retouched in such a manner as to make the tips beveled in cross section. The basal sections of about a fourth of the specimens have been chipped by percussion, although the chipping was not pronounced, and all of these showed evidence of pressure-retouching.

In the Tehuacan region and in most other Mexican sites Abasolo points are found throughout the excavated sequences. Points having the same general form are also widespread throughout North America, and so it is difficult to discuss specific relationships.

Plainview Points

Fig. 37

9 specimens; 5 excavated, 4 collected.

Dimensions in cm. of 6 specimens: length (one specimen only), 5.9; width, 2.2–2.6, average, 2.5; thickness, 0.6–1.3, average, 0.9; average depth of basal concavity, 0.25; average width of basal concavity, 1.4.

Five of the nine Plainview specimens are basal fragments; therefore statements about form are estimates at best. It would seem that these points had roughly parallel sides, abrupt tips, and shallow concave bases. They may have been roughed out originally by percussion-chipping, and our four complete specimens show evidence of the use of this technique. However, four of the specimens from excavation also are marked by parallel ripple-flaking, and one example displays collateral flaking, possibly achieved by controlled percussion-flaking. All but the crudest point show attempts at basal thinning by percussion, and all examples have ground lateral basal edges. Three of the five excavated points also have ground basal concavities.

Plainview points have been reported from Nuevo Leon, Tamaulipas, and Puebla. Their over-all distribution, of course, ranges from Mexico well into Alaska. The Tehuacan specimens seem to have lasted from the late Ajuereado period to the Coxcatlan period. In Texas

Fig. 37. Plainview points.

Fig. 38. El Riego points. The specimen in the upper center has a reworked tip.

and the Great Plains these points may be even older. They seem to have appeared later in Canada and Alaska than in the Southwest. One can speculate that the Plainview type was developed in the western United States from other early concave-based points. Later the type probably spread both northward and southward and was usually confined to a grassland environment.

El Riego Points

Fig. 38

18 specimens; 10 excavated, 8 collected.

Dimensions in cm.: length (3 complete specimens), 5.0–10.8, average, 8.1; width (11 specimens), 2.4–3.5, average, 3.0; thickness (11 specimens), 0.7–1.4, average, 0.9; depth of basal concavity (10 specimens), 0.2–0.7, average, 0.47; width of basal concavity (10 specimens), 1.0–2.7, average, 1.5.

El Riego projectile points are long and lanceolate with deep, concave bases. They have relatively long bodies with parallel or slightly concave sides, and long, tapering tips with slightly convex edges. They are made primarily by percussion-flaking, and the edges and bases are retouched either by pressure-flaking or by very well-controlled percussion flint-knapping. The bases are usually thinned by percussion blows, and nine of them have been ground. Ten specimens also have ground basal lateral edges. Two specimens, after having been broken, were reworked to form blunted tips.

So far El Riego points have been found only in the Tehuacan Valley, and there they are representative of the El Riego phase. In the Big Bend region of Texas a variety of Plainview point called Golondrina is similar.

The general form of this type of projectile point suggests that it was derived from other early concave-based points, which include Plainview, Meserve, Folsom, Clovis, and others. It is also interesting to note resemblances between the El Riego points and the so-called Eastern Fluted types. I consider this similarity to be an example of cultural convergence.

Flacco Points

Fig. 39

36 specimens; 23 excavated, 13 collected.

Dimensions in cm.: length (23 specimens), 3.2–5.7, average, 4.2; width (28 specimens), 1.8–3.3, average, 2.8; thickness (30 specimens), 0.6–1.3, average, 0.9; depth of basal concavity (30 specimens), 0.3–0.9, average, 0.6.

In rough outline Flacco points are isoceles triangles with deep concave bases. However, eleven of our sample have only slightly tapering bodies, and ten have abruptly sloping tips, which give them a triangular-pentagonal outline. All have deep concave bases. Particularly distinctive are the almost spurlike or barblike projections at the junction of the base and sides.

Although these points may have been chipped originally by percussion, only about half of our examples display crude flake scars on the surfaces of their bodies. All

58

Fig. 39. Flacco points.

Flacco points appeared in the Tehuacan region in the El Riego phase. They were found in the lower levels of Tecolote Cave in Hidalgo, in the middle levels of the San Nicolas Cave in Queretaro, in southern Tamaulipas, and in surface collections in the Valley of Mexico. This type seems to be absent from southern and western Mexico, Texas, and the Southwest. Its early occurrence in Tehuacan and Hidalgo suggests a central Mexican origin. However, both in this region and in northern Mexico the type seems to last as late as 2000 B.C. Flacco points were probably derived from the El Riego type.

Fig. 40. Nogales points.

edges show evidence of fine retouching, by either controlled percussion or pressure-flaking, that usually converges toward the center of the body surface. Most specimens have ground lateral basal edges. The bases usually have been retouched to form a deep concavity or, in five cases, almost a V-shaped notch; and seven examples show long basal thinning scars.

59

Nogales Points

Fig. 40

49 specimens; 20 excavated, 29 collected.

Dimensions in cm.: length (9 specimens), 3.5–6.7, average, 5.0; width (30 specimens), 2.1–5.1, average, 3.3; thickness (37 specimens), 0.6–1.4, average, 1.1.

Nogales points in outline resemble long isosceles triangles with slightly convex bases. Most of them are made only by percussion-chipping and are therefore often called quarry blanks. Only five of our excavated examples had edges retouched by pressure-flaking, but at least half of them had bases thinned by one to five percussion blows. Since such thinning would greatly facilitate hafting, I believe these tools were used as large projectile points or as small knives and not as quarry blanks. The tips of five specimens have also been retouched so that in cross sections they have a beveled appearance.

This type of projectile point is widespread in the New World from about 8000 B.C. to historic times.

Tortugas Points

Fig. 41

28 specimens; 9 excavated, 19 collected.

Dimensions in cm. of 13 specimens: length (7 specimens only), 4.5–7.6, average, 5.5; width 2.2–4.7, average, 3.1; thickness, 0.6–1.3, average 1.0.

In outline Tortugas points are long isosceles triangles with straight to slightly concave bases. They were chipped into triangular form by percussion-flaking, and then all edges were retouched. The tips of over half the sample have been beveled. The bases of eight excavated points have been thinned by one to five percussion blows, but all the specimens had carefully retouched bases. Although none had ground bases, the lateral edges of a few points were ground from 1.0 to 3.5 cm. up from the base.

Besides the Tehuacan Valley, Tortugas points are found in the Santa Marta Cave in Chiapas, the lowest zone of the Tecolote Cave in Hidalgo, in Tamaulipas, and over much of Texas. Although they have also been found in the Valley of Mexico, they seem to be rare in northwestern and western Mexico. Tortugas points appear earliest in Chiapas, Puebla, and Hidalgo and later, about 4000 and 3000 B.C. respectively, in Tamaulipas and Texas, which may indicate that this type was invented in southern Mexico and then spread north and eastward. In northern Mexico, Tortugas points lasted into historic times, but in southern Mexico they disappeared by 500 B.C.

Although Tortugas points may have originally been

Fig. 41. Tortugas points.

developed from types such as Abasolo, they seem also to have been influenced by concepts regarding basal thinning and grinding.

Hidalgo Points

Fig. 42

14 specimens; 10 excavated, 4 collected.

Dimensions in cm.: length (3 specimens), 3.8–5.9, average,

Fig. 42. Hidalgo points.

where they may last until 1000 B.C. Hidalgo points are related to Gary points, and in central Mexico they seem to be an early variant.

Trinidad Points

Fig. 43
60 specimens; 57 excavated, 3 collected.
Dimensions in cm.: length (20 specimens), 3.7–6.5, average,

Fig. 43. Trinidad points.

4.8; width (5 specimens), 2.6–3.3, average, 3.0; thickness (12 specimens), 0.6–1.0, average, 0.8; stem length (9 specimens), 1.5–3.8, average, 2.7; stem width (10 specimens), 1.5–2.7, average, 2.0.

Hidalgo points have small, almost equilateral triangular bodies and contracting stems that are as long as or longer than their bodies. There is a narrow right-angled shoulder between the stem and the body. Most specimens have percussion-shaped bodies and retouched edges. The stems of eight points from excavation had ground lateral edges.

Hidalgo points are found in most of Mexico and in Texas and the Southwest. They first appeared in the El Riego phase in the Tehuacan Valley. They are very numerous in Hidalgo in the lowest level of Tecolote Cave, where they are estimated to date about 7000 B.C. Elsewhere they cannot be dated earlier than about 4000 B.C. This chronology suggests a central Mexican origin. In this area they seem to die out by 4000 B.C., but else-

longer than the stems, are roughly the shape of isosceles triangles and have slightly convex edges. The shoulders are usually marked with fairly prominent short barbs, although the shoulders of a few specimens are defined by merely the right-angled junction of stem and body. Most of these points were flaked initially by percussion-chipping and were thinned and formed into final shape by percussion-chipping or pressure-retouching. Only a few examples have ground stems.

Trinidad points appear over much of North America, Mexico, and Central America. They extend in time from about 7000 B.C. to A.D. 1000. They seem to occur slightly earlier in Mexico than in the United States. Trinidad points perhaps developed out of a type similar to an Almagre or a Gypsum Cave point.

La Mina Points

Fig. 44

16 specimens; 11 excavated, 5 collected.

Dimensions in cm.: length (5 specimens), 4.1 to over 5.1, average, 4.8; width (14 specimens), 2.1–3.1, average, 2.8; thickness (15 specimens), 0.6–1.0, average, 0.8; stem length (15 specimens), 1.3–1.7, average, 1.5; stem width (15 specimens), 1.3–2.3, average, 1.9.

La Mina points have short, straight-sided stems with straight to slightly convex bases. The stem is usually a little more than half the width of the base of the body and is separated from it by a sharp shoulder at right angles to the main axis. The body, which is two to three times as long as the stem, forms an isosceles triangle with very slightly convex edges.

These projectile points were made from small triangular blanks formed by percussion-flaking. A blow was struck on each surface near the corner to make a rough stem. Finally all edges and the stem were retouched on both surfaces by pressure-flaking to provide a good cutting edge and to give the point its final shape. Only three stems show any evidence of grinding.

La Mina points are found in Puebla, the Valley of Mexico, Hidalgo, Queretaro, and southwest Tamaulipas. In the Tehuacan region they are found in components of the El Riego and Coxcatlan phases. In Hidalgo and Queretaro they date from 5000 to 3000 B.C., and in Tamaulipas from 2000 to 1000 B.C. These dates suggest a southern Mexico origin. La Mina points seem to be related to the Carrollton type from Texas and are possibly ancestral to Morhiss points.

Agate Basin Points

Fig. 45

27 specimens; 16 excavated, 11 collected.

Dimensions in cm.: length (2 specimens), 5.4 to over 8.0;

Fig. 44. La Mina points.

4.9; width (20 specimens), 2.1–5.6, average, 3.0; thickness (60 specimens), 0.4–1.1, average, 0.8; stem length (42 specimens), 0.6–2.5, average, 1.6; stem width (48 specimens), 1.1–2.4, average, 1.7.

Trinidad points have relatively short, wide, contracting stems with convex bases. Their bodies, which are

These long, narrow, lanceolate points are widest near the midpoint. They have straight to slightly concave bases. In cross section they are usually quite thin. Although they may have been percussion-chipped originally, most surfaces display evidence of controlled percussion-flaking, in the form of rough collateral flaking. Almost all have ground basal and lateral edges.

Similar points are found from Tehuacan to Alaska (see Wormington 1957). In the United States, this type is found within a range of 8000 to 4000 or 3000 B.C. In the Tehuacan Valley, Agate Basin points are confined to the El Riego and Coxcatlan phases. They seem unrelated to other points in the Tehuacan Valley, but they are in the Yuma tradition, which connects such types as Scottsbluff, Eden, Angostura, Milnesand, and others.

San Nicolas Points

Fig. 46

63 specimens; 45 excavated, 18 collected.

Dimensions in cm.: length (10 specimens), 4.2 to over 6.1, average, 5.4; width (21 specimens), 2.0 to over 3.6, average, 3.2; thickness (27 specimens), 0.5 to over 1.2, average, 0.8; stem length (28 specimens), 0.7 to over 2.9, average, 1.9; stem width (33 specimens), 1.1 to over 2.7, average, 1.8.

These long, narrow projectile points have short, wide, contracting stems and convex or almost pointed bases. The shoulder where the stem joins the body is not well marked; at most, there is a short step roughly at right angles to the main axis. The straight or very slightly convex edges of the long, narrow bodies taper to points. The body surfaces generally have been percussion-flaked, and the edges in some cases are retouched. Stems, however, are usually more carefully pressure-flaked. The stems of a few points, all from earlier levels, have been ground.

San Nicolas points are found over most of Mexico and much of the United States and Canada. Their time range generally extends from about 5500 B.C. to historic times, with their greatest popularity occurring about 1000 B.C. The type was probably derived from early Gary-like points.

Abejas Points

Fig. 47

12 specimens; 8 excavated, 4 collected.

Dimensions in cm.: length (estimated), 6.0; width (6 specimens), 2.5–3.6, average, 3.0; thickness (8 specimens), 0.7–1.1, average, 1.0; notch depth (8 specimens), 1.0–3.0, average, 1.5; notch width (8 specimens), 0.7–1.3, average, 0.9.

Fig. 45. Agate Basin points.

width (14 specimens), 1.7 to over 3.8, average, 2.4; thickness (17 specimens), 0.6–1.0, average, 0.8; basal width (14 specimens), 1.4–2.3, average, 1.7.

Fig. 46. San Nicolas points.

These long, narrow, triangular points have slightly convex bases and wide, shallow, side notches. Their maximum width is at the base. They were chipped by percussion from relatively thick flakes, and then they were notched by single percussion blows struck on opposite surfaces. Their bases have been reasonably well retouched to form a sharp cutting edge, and the sides and tips have been steeply pressure-flaked bifacially.

So far, this type has been reported only from the Tehuacan Valley, where examples were found in components of the El Riego, Coxcatlan, and Abejas phases. These points are perhaps ancestral to the Ensor types in the Tehuacan area. They are vaguely similar to some of the longer Cochise points from northwestern Mexico and may have been derived directly or indirectly from that source.

Tilapa Points

Fig. 48

73 specimens; 66 excavated, 7 collected.

Dimensions in cm.: length (5 specimens), 3.5–5.1, average, 4.1; width (13 specimens), 3.6–5.5, average, 4.8; thickness (34 specimens), 0.5–1.0, average, 0.7; stem length (22 specimens), 0.7–2.2, average, 1.5; stem width (30 specimens), 1.8–2.7, average, 2.1.

These short, stubby points have relatively short, wide, and slightly contracting stems with straight to slightly convex bases. Their bodies are often wider than they are long and are very much wider than the stems. The

Fig. 47. Abejas points.

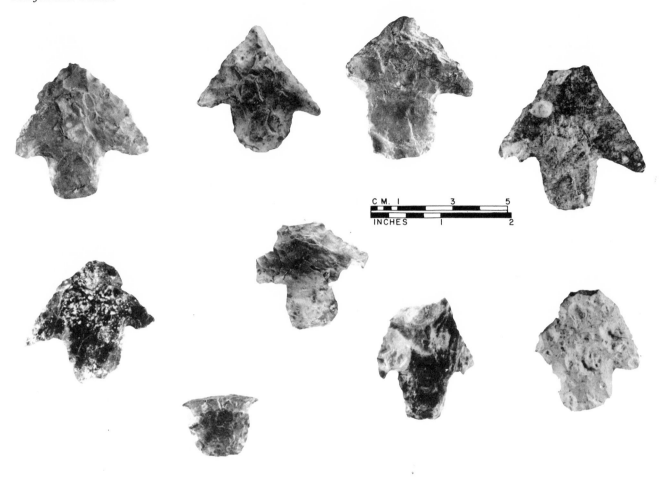

Fig. 48. Tilapa points.

huge barbs at the junction of body and stem are perhaps the most distinctive feature of Tilapa points. The long and contracting barbed shoulders usually slope toward the base at a forty-five-degree angle to the longitudinal axis.

Tilapa points were made from equilateral, triangular, bifacial blanks formed by percussion-chipping. Percussion blows struck at two corners of the blank removed large triangular flakes, leaving a rough corner-notched point. Pressure-flaking applied at the edges shaped a contracting stem and prominent shoulder barbs. The edges of the body were similarly pressure-retouched, often in such a manner as to give them an almost serrated appearance. The stem of one excavated specimen still had gum adhering to it, indicating that it had been hafted, possibly in a wide, flat foreshaft, and was held in place by gum and string.

So far Tilapa points have been reported only from the Tehuacan Valley and the San Nicolas Cave in Quere-

taro. The type existed from about 5500 to 3600 B.C. It is probably a development from the Trinidad type and perhaps is transitional to the Coxcatlan type.

Coxcatlan Points

Fig. 49

160 specimens; 155 excavated, 5 collected.

Dimensions in cm.: length (63 specimens), 2.5–5.6, average, 3.3; width (79 specimens), 2.0–4.7, average, 3.4; thickness (151 specimens), 0.4–0.9, average, 0.6; stem length (100 specimens), 0.6–1.4, average, 1.0; stem width (100 specimens), 0.5–2.0, average, 1.3.

Coxcatlan points generally are very thin and small and have been made with careful, delicate precision. They have triangular bodies, tapering tips, and straight to slightly concave lateral edges, which are often finely serrated. The short, contracting stems are slightly longer than they are wide and have definitely convex edges, which make the bases very convex or pointed. The most

65

often making the point wider than it is long. The base of the barb is always slightly concave—and this gives the barb a hooklike appearance.

Coxcatlan points were made from thin flakes which were probably removed from cores by percussion blows. The flakes appear to have been further thinned and shaped by some suitable technique. All edges were retouched by very fine pressure-flaking. Steep pressure-flaking applied to the body edges of about half the specimens gives them a finely serrated appearance.

At the time of writing, these points are known only from Oaxaca, the Tehuacan Valley, the Valley of Mexico, Hidalgo, and Queretaro. In the Tehuacan region, Coxcatlan points begin very strongly in the Coxcatlan phase, and they last into Ajalpan times. They seem to be a central Mexican specialty and perhaps were derived from Tilapa points. This type probably contributes to the ancestry of the Garyito type.

Almagre Points

Fig. 50

27 specimens; 25 excavated, 2 collected.

Dimensions in cm.: length (3 specimens), 4.7 to over 5.7, average, 5.1; width (11 specimens), 3.1–4.3, average, 3.6; thickness (19 specimens), 0.4–1.1, average, 0.6; stem length (14 specimens), 0.3–1.6, average, 0.8; stem width (14 specimens), 1.3–3.0, average, 2.0.

These projectile points have wide, triangular bodies and poorly defined, short, wide, convex to pointed stems. In many cases the stem is little more than a "bump" in the middle of the base. Almagre points are made of thin, flat flakes which have a few percussion scars on their surfaces. These scars generally point toward the center of the body, but they give the appearance of radiating away from the center. The edges are usually very neatly retouched bifacially.

Almagre points are found in Chiapas, Puebla, Hidalgo, Queretaro, Tamaulipas, and western Mexico. They also appear in Texas, where they are very common in the Big Bend region. In Tamaulipas, Texas, and Tehuacan these points may be as old as 5500 B.C.; in western Mexico, Chiapas, and perhaps in the Southwest of the United States, they may have appeared before 7000 B.C. They seem to be an early variant of the Gary point, and are closely related to, or perhaps are the same as, Gypsum Cave points (Harrington 1933).

Garyito Points

Fig. 51

99 specimens; 76 excavated, 23 collected.

Dimensions in cm.: length (30 specimens), 2.2–4.6, average, 2.9; width (38 specimens), 1.7–3.0, average, 2.4; thick-

Fig. 49. Coxcatlan points.

distinctive feature of the type, however, is its shoulder. Coxcatlan shoulder barbs are very pronounced and extend laterally at right angles to the longitudinal axis,

66

Fig. 50. Almagre points.

ness (73 specimens), 0.4–1.0, average 0.6; stem length (30 specimens), 0.5–1.7, average, 1.0; stem width (30 specimens), 0.8–1.9, average 1.1.

Triangular bodies with straight to very slightly convex edges, contracting stems with convex edges, and straight to convex or almost pointed bases are characteristics of Garyito points. In these features the points are very much like Coxcatlan points, but the bodies of Garyito points are not as wide as those of the Coxcatlan type and the shoulder barbs are very different. Garyito barbs are short and contracting, with straight basal and frontal edges, and the basal edges are usually at right angles to the longitudinal axis.

These points were made from small, thin, obsidian or flint flakes struck from cores by a series of percussion blows. Over half of the sample had been pressure-flaked along the edges bifacially, to round them into their final form. The rest, however, were more skillfully worked, in the manner of Coxcatlan points, by either controlled percussion or fine retouching.

Garyito projectile points have been found in Oaxaca, Puebla, the Valley of Mexico, Hidalgo, and Queretaro. They range from the Coxcatlan to the Palo Blanco phase in the Tehuacan Valley, and were most popular in the Ajalpan period. Garyito points are like Gary points except for their smallness, and they seem to have been derived from the Coxcatlan and Trinidad types.

Shumla Points

Fig. 52
61 specimens; 34 excavated, 27 collected.

Fig. 51. Garyito points.

67

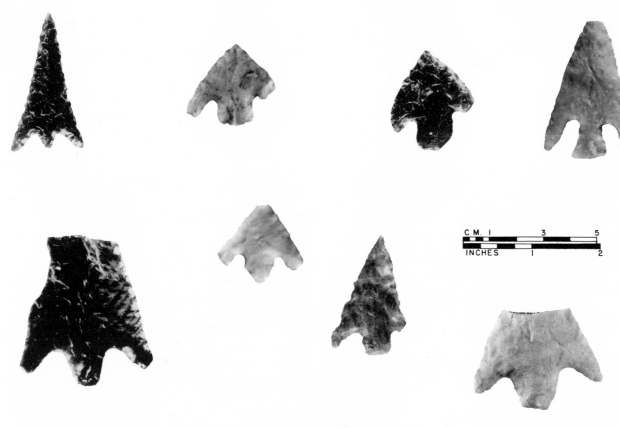

Fig. 52. Shumla points.

Dimensions in cm.: length (17 specimens), 2.3–10.0, average, 4.8; width (29 specimens), 2.2–5.1, average, 3.3; thickness (50 specimens), 0.5–1.0, average, 0.6; stem length (32 specimens), 0.5–1.5, average, 1.0; stem width (32 specimens), 0.7–1.9, average, 1.5.

There is considerable variation in the geometric form of the Shumla points found in the Tehuacan region. Characteristically, Shumla points have long downward-pointing shoulder barbs made by basal notching. The outer edges of the barbs are straight to convex, and the inner edges are straight to slightly convex. The short stems are usually just slightly longer than the barbs, although a few specimens have barbs that are longer than the stems. The stems vary from very slightly expanding to extremely contracting, and bases range from slightly convex to pointed. Bodies usually have slightly convex or straight sides which blend into a tapering tip. Body forms, however, range from equilateral to long narrow triangles.

Although points of this category from Texas also show considerable variation, the Shumla points from Tehuacan (and I might add, from the Valley of Mexico)

Fig. 53. Catan points.

68

Fig. 54. Pelona points.

show an even greater range. Some of the specimens from Tehuacan are shorter and wider and have smaller and more pointed or contracting stems than those found in Texas. On the basis of this spacially significant modal characteristic, there would be some justification in establishing a new Mexican type, or at least a subtype. However, these southern variants are not numerous and they gradate into the more formal Texas type. Furthermore, all the points seem to have the same temporal position. Therefore, for the moment, I consider them all to be of the same type.

Most of the Shumla points from Tehuacan were made from long, thin obsidian or flint flakes. The flakes were shaped by controlled percussion-flaking, which often resulted in diagonal ripple or collateral flaking. Edges were then retouched. Barbs were formed by basal notching accomplished by skillfully placed percussion blows struck on opposite surfaces near the base. Although the notch between barb and stem was not further worked, the rest of the barb and stem were retouched.

Shumla points extend from Texas to northern Ta-maulipas, Nuevo Leon, San Luis Potosi, Queretaro, Hidalgo, Puebla, and Oaxaca. For some unknown reason the type appears to be absent from southern Tamaulipas and the Vera Cruz area. Shumla points appeared in the Big Bend region of Texas and in adjacent Coahuila by at least 7000 B.C., and this early date suggests that the points were invented in that area and spread southward into the plateau of central Mexico, where they became a dominant type during the Formative period. In the Tehuacan excavations the earliest Shumla points were found in Coxcatlan components, and the type lasted into Santa Maria times.

The fact that the earlier forms of Shumla points have contracting stems and shoulder barbs suggests a connection with the Gary type and also that these points evolved from various concepts of style associated with points belonging to the Gary tradition, such as Trinidad, Coxcatlan, El Riego, and so forth.

Catan Points

Fig. 53

31 specimens, 22 excavated, 9 collected.

Dimensions in cm.: length (10 specimens), 2.9–4.4, average, 3.8; width (14 specimens), 1.5–2.7, average, 2.2; thickness (17 specimens),0.4–0.9, average, 0.7

Catan points are small and tear-drop-shaped. They have convex bases which blend into bodies with convex edges. The tips are relatively abrupt. They are manufactured mainly from flat flakes by percussion-flaking. Three examples are almost unifacial, and a few have crudely retouched edges near the tips.

This rather small, generalized projectile point is found from Oaxaca to Alaska. It may have come into use in the Tehuacan Valley in the Abejas phase or even earlier, but it reached its greatest popularity in ceramic times. Catan points probably developed from the Abasolo type.

Pelona Points

Fig. 54

34 specimens; 29 excavated, 5 collected.

Dimensions in cm.: length (12 specimens), 3.4–5.7, average, 4.5; width (21 specimens), 2.4–3.8, average, 2.8; thickness (27 specimens), 0.5–1.0, average, 0.7.

These short, wide, lenticular to tear-drop-shaped projectile points have pointed or very convex bases. They are widest at the midpoint. Usually the edges from the midpoint to the tip are serrated and contrast with the smooth edges of the basal half.

Pelona points were formed from oval blanks made by percussion-chipping. One end of the blank was pressure-flaked to make a rounded or pointed base; this process also thinned the base, which would have facilitated hafting. Well-controlled percussion-flaking or rough pressure-flaking applied to the upper half of the edges formed rough serrations. Finally, the tip was pressure-retouched to produce a tapering point.

Pelona points appear in the Tehuacan Valley, the Valley of Mexico, Hidalgo, Queretaro, northwest Mexico, and the southwestern United States. In the Tehuacan region the type may have originated in the Coxcatlan phase, but it reached its maximum popularity during the Abejas phase. Pelona points seem to have died out by the time of Christ. In Hidalgo and Queretaro, Pelona points came into use at about the same time they appeared in Tehuacan, but they died out sooner. However, the few Pelona specimens reported from the Red Band layer of the Ventana Cave in Arizona apparently are earlier than any found in Mexico. This suggests an origin in the Southwest of the United States and a diffusion through western Mexico into central Mexico.

Pelona points may be a specialized type which

Fig. 55. Zacatenco points.

evolved from the earlier and more general Abasolo type. It appears to resemble and perhaps parallel the Desmuke points of Texas and northeast Mexico.

Zacatenco Points

Fig. 55

16 specimens; 7 excavated, 9 collected.

Dimensions in cm.: length (6 specimens), 3.7–4.1, average, 3.9; width (12 specimens), 1.3–2.1, average, 1.6; thickness (13 specimens), 0.6–1.2, average, 0.8.

These short lenticular projectile points have pointed bases and tips. They are widest just below the midpoint. They were made from long, narrow, flat or prismatic flakes, usually of obsidian. Their edges display rough collateral ripple-flaking scars. The technique used to retouch the edges makes the points hexagonal or diamond-shaped in cross section. Over half of the sample have ground basal lateral edges.

So far these projectile points have been found only with remains of the Formative period in the Valley of Mexico, the Tehuacan Valley, and elsewhere in Puebla.

The geometric form of the Zacatenco point suggests that it was derived from the Lerma point. However, Lerma points had ceased to be produced a long time before Zacatenco points were first made. Such a gap in time suggests that perhaps Zacatenco points may have been a re-invention that happened to encompass concepts associated with the extinct Lerma type.

Salado Points

Fig. 56

39 specimens; 22 excavated, 17 collected.

Dimensions in cm.: length (13 specimens), 2.4–4.7, average, 3.3; width (13 specimens), 1.6–3.0, average, 2.4; thickness (21 specimens), 0.5–0.8, average, 0.6; stem length (21 specimens), 0.6–1.3, average, 0.9; stem width (24 specimens), 1.0–1.5, average, 1.2.

Salado points have short, narrow, straight stems with straight to convex bases. The triangular bodies of the majority of the sample are equilateral, but a few are somewhat more elongated. They have short barbs with concave inner edges and straight to slightly convex outer edges. The barbs slope downward at about a forty-five-degree angle from the main axis of the point.

These projectiles were formed from flint or obsidian

Fig. 57. Palmillas points.

Fig. 56. Salado points.

flakes by percussion-chipping, and all edges were neatly retouched. The barbs were also made by pressure-flaking, and the bases have been thinned both by percussion and by retouching.

71

Salado points are found in Formative components of the Valley of Mexico and the Tehuacan Valley. They look rather like Garyito points with straight squared stems.

Palmillas Points

Fig. 57

24 specimens; 15 excavated, 9 collected.

Dimensions in cm.: length (11 specimens), 3.8–5.7, average, 4.5; width (20 specimens), 2.1–4.0, average, 2.9; thickness (20 specimens), 0.5–1.0, average, 0.6; stem length (19 specimens), 0.7–1.5, average, 1.1, stem width (20 specimens), 1.1–2.6, average, 1.4.

These corner-notched points have expanding stems with convex bases. The long, triangular bodies have convex edges and tapering tips. The shoulder barbs point downward at about a forty-five-degree angle from the main axis of the projectile point.

The long triangular blanks from which these points were fashioned may have been made by percussion-chipping. The surfaces and edges were reworked by a suitable pressure or percussion technique. The corner notches seem to have been made by single percussion blows struck on opposite surfaces, but the barbs and stems have been further retouched.

In most of Mexico, Palmillas points are found from late Formative to historic times. The same type or a related type is widespread in the United States, where it probably appeared earlier than in Mexico. The type therefore may have spread southward into Mexico.

Matamoros Points

Fig. 58

21 specimens; 9 excavated, 12 collected.

Dimensions in cm.: length (8 specimens), 3.2–4.4, average, 3.7; width (12 specimens), 2.1–2.7, average, 2.3; thickness (17 specimens), 0.4–1.0, average, 0.7.

These small stemless projectile points usually are the shape of isosceles triangles with convex edges and straight to concave bases. In cross section they are lenticular and are thick in relation to their width. They were crudely made by percussion-flaking. The edges of some of the specimens were retouched by pressure-flaking.

Matamoros points are found from Chiapas northward to Oaxaca, Puebla, the Valley of Mexico, San Luis Potosi, Tamaulipas, and into Texas. In southern Mexico and in Texas they first appear after about 500 B.C., but in Tamaulipas they may go back as far as 2000 B.C. This suggests a northeastern Mexican origin.

These projectile points seem to be diminutive examples of the earlier Tortugas and Nogales types.

Fig. 58. Matamoros points.

Tehuacan Points

Fig. 59

77 specimens; 13 excavated, 64 collected.

Dimensions in cm.: length (6 specimens), 3.1 to over 5.0, average, 4.2; width (30 specimens), 2.0–3.3, average, 2.7; thickness (32 specimens), 0.4–1.0, average, 0.8; stem length (30 specimens), 0.7–1.2, average, 1.1; stem width (29 specimens), 1.5–3.1, average, 2.2.

Tehuacan points are characterized by short, broad, expanding stems with straight to slightly convex bases. The long and rather narrow triangular bodies have slightly convex edges. Shoulders are narrow and just barely mark off the stem, which is only slightly less wide than the body.

Tehuacan points apparently were made from long, thin flakes removed from cores by percussion blows. Other percussion blows were applied bifacially to the end of the flake, to produce corner notches. All edges were pressure-retouched, and the surfaces were further thinned by an appropriate flaking technique. Impressions left on gum adhering to the base of a Tehuacan point from El Riego Cave indicate that the stems of these points were inserted in the slots of foreshafts and were bound into place by string wrapped in crisscross fashion.

Tehuacan points have been found in Oaxaca, Puebla, and the Valley of Mexico. In both the Tehuacan region and the Valley of Mexico they were dominant in the Classic period, but they lasted into Postclassic times. The fact that a few of these projectile points from Tehuacan are also found in late Formative components suggests a southern Mexican origin.

Superficially Tehuacan points resemble the Lange points found in Texas, but there is a considerable geographical and temporal gap between the two types. Lange points are generally very much older than Tehuacan points. Also, neither Lange nor Tehuacan points are found in the extensive sample of projectile points recorded from Tamaulipas in northeastern Mexico. For these reasons, I believe that the two types are an example of convergent evolution, and that the Tehuacan type is neither a late survivor nor a descendant of the Lange type from Texas.

Ensor Points

Fig. 60
21 specimens; 4 excavated, 17 collected.
Dimensions in cm. of 12 specimens: length (9 specimens only), 4.2 to over 9.0, average 5.6; width, 1.6–2.9, aver-

Fig. 60. Ensor points.

Fig. 59. Tehuacan points.

73

Fig. 61. Morhiss points.

Fig. 62. Teotihuacan points.

age, 2.5; thickness, 0.5–0.9, average, 0.7; notch depth, 0.2–0.5, average, 0.3; notch width, 0.4–0.7, average, 0.5.

These long, narrow projectile points have tapering tips, slightly convex bodies, deep, narrow side notches, and convex bases. The widest portion of the projectile point is just above the notches. Ensor points are thin and have been very neatly chipped. Surfaces show signs of few of the original rough percussion blows and usually are marked by rough collateral flaking. The edges and notches have been finished by pressure-flaking.

Ensor points were common in Mexico during the Classic period, although in a few regions they are found in both late Formative and Postclassic sites. The earliest

74

Ensor points come from Archaic sites in the southeastern United States. However, these points appear somewhat later in Texas and the Southwest, and they are found only in Classic and Postclassic components in the Tehuacan Valley. I suspect that they diffused from the southeast of the United States into Mexico.

Morhiss Points

Fig. 61

18 specimens; 3 excavated, 15 collected.

Dimensions in cm.: length (6 specimens), 3.9–7.3, average, 5.6; width (9 specimens), 1.8–2.9, average, 2.6; thickness (11 specimens), 0.4–0.8, average, 0.6; stem length (11 specimens), 0.8–1.7, average, 1.1; stem width (12 specimens), 1.3–2.1, average, 1.7.

Morhiss projectile points have short, wide stems, poorly defined shoulders, and narrow triangular bodies with straight to slightly convex edges. The stems tend to taper very slightly toward either slightly convex or slightly concave bases.

These points were made from thin flakes initially shaped and thinned by percussion-flaking. About half of the specimens seem to have been corner-notched by bifacial percussion blows. The other half may have been similarly notched, but the retouching in the notch has obscured any evidence of percussion-chipping. Even the notches of specimens showing evidence of primary percussion-chipping have been finely retouched. The bases of the stems were also thinned by percussion before the edges were retouched. In fact, all edges and considerable portions of the bodies have been finely retouched.

Morhiss points have an unbroken distribution throughout eastern Mexico from Oaxaca northward; they also appear in Texas. In the Tehuacan Valley and southern Mexico they are found principally in Classic and Postclassic components, but in Tamaulipas they first appear in Formative times. In Texas, however, Morhiss points originated at least by 2000 B.C., suggesting a southward diffusion of the type. They probably were ultimately derived from such early stemmed types as Scottsbluff and Eden.

Teotihuacan Points

Fig. 62

38 specimens; 13 excavated, 25 collected.

Dimensions in cm.: length (23 specimens), 1.7–4.2, average, 2.9; width (29 specimens), 1.0–1.7, average, 1.3; thickness (29 specimens), 0.2–0.6, average, 0.3; side-notch depth (27 specimens), 0.05–0.15, average, 0.1; side-notch width (27 specimens), 0.1–0.8, average, 0.25.

Fig. 63. Tula points.

These small, narrow, triangular points have small side notches usually located a bit above the base. The bases range from slightly concave to distinctly notched. The projectile points are made from small prismatic blades struck from polyhedral cores, usually of obsidian. They

75

Fig. 64. Texcoco points.

have been shaped by pressure-flaking along the edges.

Teotihuacan points seem to be confined to Mesoamerica, although a few examples from northwest Mexico and from the Southwest of the United States appear to be of this type. In Mexico these points seem to have first appeared in the Classic period, about the time of Christ, and they were most popular in Postclassic times. They were obviously derived from the same set of concepts as Harrell points, which in turn may have entered Mexico from the Southwest of the United States.

Tula Points

Fig. 63

24 specimens; 7 excavated, 17 collected.

Dimensions in cm. of 15 specimens: length 1.8–3.3, average, 2.5; width 0.7–1.9, average, 1.2; thickness, 0.15–0.4, average, 0.2.

These small, fine, stemless, isosceles-triangular points have straight to slightly convex sides and straight to deeply concave bases. They are made from prismatic blades, usually of obsidian, which have been retouched bifacially along the edges.

Tula points have been found in most of Mesoamerica in Classic and Postclassic periods, but unlike their companion type, the Teotihuacan point, they have not been found in Tamaulipas. They are closely related to Starr and Cameron points as well. They appear to have origi-

nated in Mesoamerica, based in part on concepts involved in Starr, Fresno, and other types, which may have spread into Mexico from the north.

Texcoco Points

Fig. 64

42 specimens; 4 excavated, 38 collected.

Dimensions in cm.: length (12 specimens), 2.5–5.9, average, 4.3; width (27 specimens), 1.8–3.2, average, 2.5; thickness (31 specimens), 0.4–0.8, average, 0.5; notch depth (25 specimens), 0.2–0.6, average, 0.3; notch width (25 specimens), 0.4–0.8, average, 0.5.

Texcoco projectile points are large, thin, triangular points with side notches. The body edges are slightly convex, and the bases range from slightly convex to slightly concave, the former being a little more popular. The deep and rather narrow notches are positioned some distance up the sides from the base, which gives the basal portion below the notches a rectangular appearance.

These points were made from thin, long flakes whose edges have been finely retouched. The surfaces are also finely worked, and it is difficult to determine whether by pressure-flaking or by very well-controlled percussion-chipping. The neat side notches were made by pressure-flaking.

Texcoco points are found only in Postclassic horizons

CM. 1   3   5
INCHES   1   2

Fig. 65. Harrell points.

in the Valley of Mexico, Puebla, and Oaxaca. They probably were locally derived in central Mexico from the Ensor and Harrell types.

Harrell Points

Fig. 65

37 specimens; 4 excavated, 33 collected.

Dimensions in cm.: length (20 specimens), 1.7–3.1, average, 2.4; width (24 specimens), 1.0–2.1, average, 1.5; thickness (26 specimens), 0.2–0.5, average, 0.3; notch depth (26 specimens), 0.05–0.3, average 0.1; notch width (27 specimens), 0.05–0.5, average, 0.2.

These small, delicate, triangular arrowpoints have fine side notches and bases that range from very slightly convex to deeply concave or occasionally notched. They are made from small, thin flakes that have been delicately pressure-retouched along the edges. Eight specimens not only have retouched edges but delicately worked surfaces as well.

Harrell points are found throughout North America. They do not appear in Tehuacan and the Valley of Mexico until Postclassic times, and they seem to have spread into Mexico from the north. They are related to other types of arrowpoints in North America, and they may ultimately have been derived from the small triangular arrowpoints of the Arctic Small Tool tradition, which spread into the New World from northeast Asia.

Starr Points

Fig. 66

13 specimens; 4 excavated, 9 collected.

Dimensions in cm. of 5 specimens: length (4 specimens only), 1.6–3.0, average, 2.3; width, 1.6–2.9, average, 2.1; thickness, 0.4–0.7, average, 0.5.

Starr points are small, stemless, triangular arrowpoints with concave bases and straight to slightly concave edges. They are made from small, flat flakes whose edges have been finely retouched .

Starr points are found from Alaska to Mexico. In Mesoamerica they are associated with Postclassic times, although they spread from Asia into the New World about 3000 B.C.

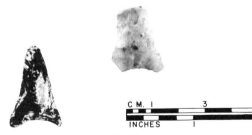

CM. 1   3   5
INCHES   1   2

Fig. 66. Starr points.

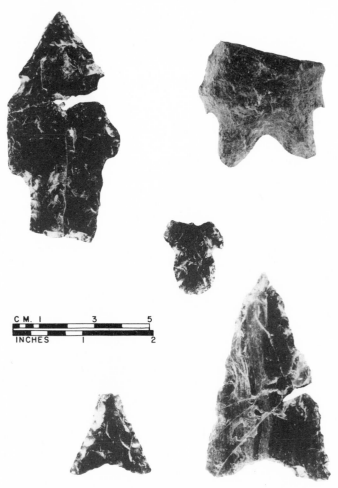

Fig. 67. Aberrant points. *Upper left,* Scottsbluff point; *upper right,* Pedernales point; *center,* Stunning point; *bottom row,* triangular points.

Aberrant Projectile Points

Scottsbluff Point

Fig. 67
1 specimen from Zone XVIII, Tc 50
Dimensions in cm.: length, 8.1; width, 4.1; thickness, 0.9; stem length, about 2.3; stem width, about 2.6.

This large obsidian point has a wide, straight stem and a straight base. The shoulders are squared, but are only a little wider than the stem. The lower half of the body has straight parallel sides, and the upper portion terminates rather abruptly in a tip that was reworked, probably after the original tip had been broken. The basal edges of the stem are heavily ground, and the lower half of the body and the stem have crude ripple-flaked surfaces and retouched edges. Irregular flake scars cover most of the reworked tip.

78

This specimen was uncovered in an El Riego component.

Pedernales Point

Fig. 67
1 specimen from Level 3–4, Tc 35w
Dimensions in cm.: width, 4.6; thickness, 0.9; stem length, 1.7; stem width, 3.6.

This basal fragment of a large spear point has a wide, short, straight stem with a deeply notched base. The shoulders are not well defined, and the body edges were probably convex. Most of the body surfaces show evidence of rough percussion-flaking, but the edges are retouched, and the sides and base of the stem have been ground. This specimen was found in a component of the Coxcatlan phase. Similar points occur in Texas and northern Mexico from 4000 B.C. to A.D. 1000.

Stunning Point

Fig. 67
1 specimen from Zone H, Ts 204
Dimensions in cm.: length, 2.8; width, 2.3; thickness, 0.6; stem length, 1.9; stem width, 1.6.

This small obsidian fragment has a long rounded stem, rather sharp shoulders, and a truncated body with a blunted tip. This point came from an Ajalpan component.

Triangular Points

Fig. 67
3 specimens; 2 excavated, 1 collected
Dimensions in cm. of 2 specimens: length, 3.3 and 7.5; width, 3.0 and 4.6; thickness, 0.7 and 0.8.

These triangular points have slightly concave or convex sides and V-shaped bases. The edges and surfaces show pressure-flaking scars. They were found in levels of the Santa Maria phase and may be vaguely related to the Matamoros or Tortugas types, although they are much more neatly chipped and have V-shaped bases.

Fresno Points

Fig. 68
6 specimens collected
Dimensions in cm. of 2 specimens: length, 2.3 and 3.1; width, 1.4 and 1.8; thickness, 0.3 and 0.4.

These narrow triangular points have convex edges and straight to concave bases. They were made from thin flakes, which have been pressure-retouched. Fresno points are a common type in most of North America and are usually associated with late time periods. The type probably diffused from northeastern Siberia about

3000 b.c. I suspect that the Tehuacan surface examples are from the Venta Salada phase.

San Lorenzo Points

Fig. 68
5 specimens collected
Dimensions in cm. of 3 specimens: length, 2.4–3.5; width, 1.4–1.8; thickness, about 0.5.

These small, narrow projectile points have corner notches, expanding stems, and slightly convex bases. They were manufactured from small flakes, which were retouched. These points are found in the Tehuacan region, the Valley of Mexico, and southwest Tamaulipas, and they may be related to the Scallorn type of Texas. Our surface examples may have come from the Venta Salada phase.

Corner-Notched Flake Point

Fig. 68

This point, from the surface, is made from a concave-convex flake that was pressure-flaked along the edges. It has shallow corner notches near its convex base. It is 5.1 cm. long, 2.3 cm. wide, and 0.7 cm. thick. As a colleague said, "It looks as though it was made by the village idiot."

Pentagonal Point

Fig. 68

One pentagonal point was obviously aberrant. It is made from a fairly thick flake and has finely retouched edges. It is about 3.8 cm. long and 2.5 cm. wide.

Stemmed Point

Fig. 68

This thin plano-convex flake has been retouched to a point at one end. The other end has been pressure-flaked to form a wide rounded stem. It is 2.8 cm. long and 1.7 cm. wide.

Fig. 68. Aberrant points. *Row 1:* Fresno points. *Rows 2, 3:* San Lorenzo points. *Row 4:* Corner-notched flake point; stemmed point; pentagonal point.

REFERENCES

Alexander, Herbert L.
  1963 "The Levi Site: A Paleo-Indian Campsite in Central Texas." *Am. Ant.*, 28:510–28.
Aveleyra Arroyo de Anda, Luis
  1951 "Reconocimiento Arqueológico en la Zona de la Presa Internacional Falcón, Tamaulipas y Texas." *RMEA*, 12:31–59. Mexico.
  1956 "The Second Mammoth and Associated Artifacts at Santa Isabel Iztapan, Mexico." *Am. Ant.*, 22:12–28.

Aveleyra Arroyo de Anda, Luis, and
  Manuel Maldonado-Koerdell
  1953 "Association of Artifacts with Mammoth in the Valley of Mexico." *Am. Ant.*, 18:332–40.
Bird, Junius B.
  1943 *Excavations in Northern Chile.* AMNH-AP, Vol. 38, No. 4.
Borden, C. E.
  1960 "DjRi 3, An Early Site in Fraser Canyon, British Columbia." *Contributions to Anthropology, 1957.*

National Museum of Canada, Bulletin No. 162. Ottawa.

BULLEN, R. P., AND W. W. PLOWDEN
1963 "Preceramic Archaic Sites in the Highlands of Honduras." *Am. Ant.*, 28:382–85.

BUTLER, B. R.
1961 *The Old Cordilleran Culture in the Pacific Northwest.* Idaho State College Museum, Occasional Papers, No. 5. Pocatello, Idaho.

CAMPBELL, JOHN M.
1959 "The Kayuk Complex of Arctic Alaska." *Am. Ant.*, 25:94–105.

CASON, JOE E.
1952 "Report on Archaeological Salvage in Falcon Reservoir, Season of 1952." *TAPS-B*, 23:218–59.

CRESSMAN, LUTHER S.
1960 *Cultural Sequences at The Dalles, Oregon.* APS-T, Vol. 50, Part 10.

CRUXENT, J. M., AND IRVING ROUSE
1956 "A Lithic Industry of Paleo-Indian Type in Venezuela." *Am. Ant.*, 22:172–79.

DAUGHERTY, RICHARD D.
1956 "Archaeology of the Lind Coulee Site, Washington." *APS-P*, 100:223–78.

EPSTEIN, JEREMIAH F.
1961 "The San Isidro and Puntita Negra Sites: Evidence of Early Man Horizons is Nuevo Leon, Mexico." *Homenaje a Pablo Martínez del Río*, pp. 71–74. INAH.

FAY, GEORGE E.
1956 "Peralta Complex—A Sonoran Variant of the Cochise Culture." *Science*, 124:1029.

HARRINGTON, M.R.
1933 *Gypsum Cave, Nevada.* Southwest Museum Papers, No. 8. Los Angeles.

HAURY, EMIL W., *et al.*
1950 *The Stratigraphy and Archaeology of Ventana Cave, Arizona.* Tucson: University of Arizona Press.

HEIZER, ROBERT F.
1951 "Preliminary Report on the Leonard Rockshelter Site, Pershing County, Nevada." *Am. Ant.*, 17:89–98.

HIBBEN, FRANK C.
1941 *Evidences of Early Occupation in Sandia Cave, New Mexico, and Other Sites in the Sandia-Manzano Region.* Smithsonian Miscellaneous Collections, Vol. 99, No. 23. Washington.

JENNINGS, JESSE D.
1957 *Danger Cave.* SAA-M No. 14. Salt Lake City.

JOHNSON, L.
1964 *The Devil's Mouth Site.* University of Texas, Department of Anthropology, Archaeological Series, No. 6. Austin.

KAPLAN, LAWRENCE, AND R.S. MACNEISH
1960 *Prehistoric Bean Remains from Caves in the Ocampo Region of Tamaulipas, Mexico.* BML, Vol. 19, No. 2.

KAUFFMAN DOIG, FEDERICO
1963 *Tres Etapas Pre-Chavin.* Lima.

KIDDER, ALFRED V.
1947 *The Artifacts of Uaxactun, Guatemala.* CIW, Publication No. 576.

KRIEGER, ALEX D.
1946 "Artifacts from the Plainview Bison Bed." *Bulletin of the Geological Society of America*, No. 58, pp. 927–54.

LANNING, E. P., AND E. A. HAMMEL
1961 "Early Lithic Industries of Western South America." *Am. Ant.*, 27:139–54.

MACNEISH, RICHARD S.
1948 "The Pre-Pottery Faulkner Site of Southern Illinois." *Am. Ant.*, 13:232–43.
1958 *Preliminary Archaeological Investigations in the Sierra de Tamaulipas, Mexico.* APS-T, Vol. 48, Part 6.
1963 "The Early Peopling of the New World." *Early Man in the Western American Arctic: A Symposium.* Anthropological Papers of the University of Alaska, Vol. 10, No. 2. Fairbanks.
1964 "Archaeological Excavation, Comparisons, and Speculations." *Investigations in the Southwest Yukon.* Papers of the Robert S. Peabody Foundation for Archaeology, Vol. 6. Andover, Massachusetts.

MACNEISH, RICHARD S., AND F. A. PETERSON
1962 *The Santa Marta Rock Shelter, Ocozocoautla, Chiapas, Mexico.* Papers of the New World Archaeological Foundation, No. 14. Provo, Utah.

MAYER-OAKES, WILLIAM J., AND R. E. BELL
1960 "An Early Man Site Found in Highland Ecuador." *Science*, 131:1805–06. Washington.

MEDVEDEV, G. I.
1964 "The Place of the Culture of Verknolenskaia Gora in the Archaeological Sequence of the Baikal Region." *Am. Ant.*, 29:461–66.

OKLADNIKOV, A. P. AND I. A. NEKRASOV
1959 "New Traces of an Inland Neolithic Culture in the Chukotsk Peninsula." *Am. Ant.*, 25:247–56.

ROGERS, MALCOLM. J.
1939 *Early Lithic Industries of the Lower Basin of the Colorado River and Adjacent Desert Areas.* San Diego Museum Papers, No. 3. San Diego.

ROUSE, IRVING
1939 *Prehistory in Haiti.* Yale University Publications in Anthropology, No. 21. New Haven.

SUHM, DEE ANN, A. D. KRIEGER, AND E. B. JELKS
1954 *An Introductory Handbook of Texas Archaeology.* TAS-B, Vol. 25.

TERRA, HELMUT DE
1949 "Early Man in Mexico." *Tepexpan Man.* Viking

Fund Publications in Anthropology, No. 11. New York.

TOLSTOY, PAUL
—— "Stone, Bone, and Antler Tools of Central Mexico from Preclassic to Aztec Times." To be published in *Handbook of Middle American Indians*. Austin: University of Texas Press.

TSCHOPIK, HARRY, JR.
1946   "Some Notes on Rock Shelter Sites near Huancayo, Peru." *Am. Ant.*, 12:73–80.

VAILLANT, GEORGE C.
1930   *Excavations at Zacatenco*. AMNH-AP, Vol. 32, Part 1.

WORMINGTON, H. M.
1957   *Ancient Man in North America*, 4th ed. Denver Museum of Natural History, Popular Series, No. 4. Denver, Colorado.

CHAPTER 5

Other Bifaces

IN THIS chapter we shall discuss such bifacially chipped artifacts as drills, choppers, knives, disks, and artifact burins. When we began our study of this group of tools, we were immediately able to separate the burins made from bifacial artifacts and the square-based drills from all the other bifaces. The rest of the group fell into two basic morphological classes: thick bifaces with one or more battered edges, or choppers; and relatively thin bifaces with sharp edges, or knives.

As we worked with the thin bifaces, or knives, it seemed that only two sets of attributes—geometrical form and chipping techniques—were temporally sensitive. As it turned out, our first sorting into trial types on the basis of forms and techniques stood up under further testing and proved to be adequate. The earliest knives were ovoid bifaces fashioned by percussion or by poorly controlled pressure-flaking. They lasted from the El Riego phase to historic times. Square-based knives extended over the same span, but so few of them were found in levels attributable to the El Riego, Palo Blanco, and Venta Salada phases that it is more correct to say that square-based knives are representative of the Coxcatlan through the Santa Maria phase. Large, crude knifelike disks were prevalent principally in the Abejas, Ajalpan, and Santa Maria phases. Smaller, more neatly made, knifelike disks are time markers for only the Abejas and Ajalpan phases, although a few were found in Santa Maria levels. Neatly chipped, thin knives, usually with a tear-drop or leaf-like outline, appeared first in the Ajalpan phase and increased numerically in each successive period. The few half-moon-shaped bifaces, or side-blades, were confined to late Palo Blanco times and the Venta Salada phase.

The thicker bifaces with battered edges, which could have served both as choppers and as cores, were not quite so sensitive temporally. Once a type appeared, it tended to persist throughout the sequence. The various types did come into existence at different times, however, and they did show a percentile shift in popularity. The earliest and crudest slab chopper was confined chiefly to preceramic periods and was most popular in Ajuereado times. Flake choppers and blocky-core choppers persisted throughout the whole sequence; however, the blocky-core choppers appear in about the same proportion in all horizons, whereas the flake choppers are popular early and gradually decrease in importance. Spherical, battered pebbles that could have served not only as cores and choppers but also as hammers first appear in El Riego times and practically disappear by the end of the Ajalpan phase. The ellipsoidal choppers or cores with only one or two battered sections along their edges and the discoidal choppers with edges battered all the way around extend from the El Riego through the Venta Salada phase. The ellipsoidal choppers, however, are most popular in El Riego times and then decrease in importance; whereas the discoidal choppers are more popular later, from Coxcatlan through Santa Maria times. Pebble choppers do not appear in significant numbers until the Coxcatlan and Abejas phases, and after the Abejas phase they persist only as an insignificant minority type. The bifacial knives and chopper-cores, then, are fairly acceptable time markers, despite the fact that they persist in large numbers over long periods of time. The burins and drills, although represented by inadequate samples and restricted to early horizons, also appear to be acceptable time markers.

Bifacial Artifacts—*Type Descriptions*

Slab Choppers

Fig. 69
92 specimens; 46 excavated, 46 collected.
Dimensions in cm.: length (31 specimens), 4.9–11.6, aver-

Fig. 69. Slab choppers.

Fig. 70. Flake choppers.

age, 8.0; width (37 specimens), 3.8–16.2, average, 8.9; thickness (41 specimens), 1.1–4.5, average, 3.3.

Slab choppers are fashioned from rather long, flat slabs of relatively soft stone, usually shale or limestone. In fact, these choppers are sometimes referred to as "the more attractive pieces of roof-fall." In many cases, one surface of the original rock, boulder, or piece of roof-fall is still apparent. Although slab choppers do not have a well-defined form, most of them are longer than they are wide and are relatively thin with two nearly flat surfaces. Usually one of the longer edges has been modified by percussion blows or by actual battering while the tool was being used as a chopper. In other words, slab choppers are flat slabs which, with little or no modification, were used as choppers.

In the Tehuacan excavations slab choppers appear in significant numbers only in the Ajuereado horizon, but they last as a minority type into El Riego, Coxcatlan, and Abejas times. Although they have relatively good temporal significance for the Tehuacan Valley, they are of such a crude and general nature that it is difficult to plot any wider distribution.

Flake Choppers

Fig. 70
220 specimens; 162 excavated, 58 collected.
Dimensions in cm.: length (113 specimens), 2.9–7.5, average, 4.8; width (145 specimens), 3.2–12.7, average, 5.4; thickness (162 specimens), 1.1–4.0, average, 2.6.

Flake choppers are made from large, thin chalcedony or flint flakes. Both surfaces usually are marked by long scars from percussion blows. The form is determined by the shape of the flake, but most of the choppers are longer than they are wide and are relatively thin. The bifacial chipping is usually along one of the longer edges and consists of four or five percussion blows on both surfaces. Usually the chipped edge has also been battered by use. In many ways flake choppers resemble large flake scrapers that have been battered along one edge.

In the Tehuacan excavations this kind of chopper is prominent in preceramic horizons and is most popular during the Ajuereado phase. It is found, however, as a minority type in the later ceramic horizons. Flake choppers are found with Santa Marta remains in Chiapas and with Lerma, Nogales, and Infiernillo remains in Tamaulipas. The relatively generalized features make it difficult to plot extensive relationships; in North America generally, flake choppers are a fairly widespread tool found in many horizons.

Blocky-Core Choppers

Fig. 71
523 specimens; 303 excavated, 220 collected.

Because of their rough appearance, it is hard to describe a characteristic shape for these choppers. They tend to be quadrangular and are usually as thick as they are wide or long. They are too irregular for exact measurement and range from 3 to 12 cm. in length, width, and thickness. Blocky-core choppers were made by chipping flint nodules with a series of percussion blows. The flakes removed by these blows must have been quite large and could have been used to make other kinds of artifacts. Most blocky-core choppers have a number of angular, roughly scarred surfaces. Although these crude objects may have served primarily as cores, at least a third of our specimens were also battered at the junction of different planes and thus gave direct evidence of having been used as choppers. There seems to be no difference in the temporal distribution of the battered and unbattered specimens.

This very general and widespread type of chopper is found throughout the Tehuacan sequence. It has a rather peculiar distribution in that sequence, however, in that it is more popular in the two earliest phases, Ajuereado and El Riego, and again in the latest two phases, Palo Blanco and Venta Salada.

Spherical Battered Pebbles

Fig. 71
75 specimens; 31 excavated, 44 collected.

These spherical choppers were made from river pebbles. Their outer surfaces have been battered and scarred both by percussion blows and as a result of their having been used as hammers or battering implements. Their diameters range from about 6 to 11 cm.

Artifacts similar to these are found over much of North America, and in the Tehuacan region they appear rather sparsely throughout the entire sequence. Spherical battered pebbles are often referred to as and classified with pebble hammers.

Ellipsoidal Choppers

Fig. 72
167 specimens; 116 excavated, 51 collected.
Dimensions in cm.: length (73 specimens), 2.7–8.1, average, 4.8; width (91 specimens), 3.0–11.1, average, 6.0; thickness (95 specimens), 1.9–4.6, average, 2.9.

These choppers vary in outline from lenticular to almost round, with the most common form ellipsoidal. They are generally quite thick in proportion to their width. They are made of chert or flint, and both sur-

Fig. 71. Blocky-core choppers; *bottom row*, spherical battered pebbles.

Fig. 72. Ellipsoidal choppers.

faces have been chipped by a series of percussion blows. The blows tended to be more controlled near the edges, and the scars more or less radiate out from the central, thickest portion of the chopper. Sixty-seven of the excavated sample were battered along one of the longer cutting edges, twenty-one were battered along two longer edges, and all edges of the remainder were battered. When all edges are battered, the choppers become altered to a more discoidal-shaped variant.

This type first appears in the Tehuacan sequence in the El Riego phase, and it reaches its maximum popularity at that time. After that, it represents a minor fraction of the total choppers found, but it continues to be found throughout the sequence. This type of chopper —reported as a "nodule chopper"—was common in the Santa Marta phase of Chiapas. It also is a prominent feature of the Chalco complex in the Valley of Mexico. In eastern Mexico and the western United States, it is diagnostic of the Desert Culture and is actually most prevalent in Cochise sites. In northeastern Mexico, it is less common and is found in large proportions only in the Infiernillo phase. In the Sierra de Tamaulipas, it occurs throughout the sequence but is a major type only in the Lerma horizon. Some of the more discoidal variants among the Tehuacan sample, however, closely resemble the large chipped disks so common in the Nogales and La Perra horizons of the Sierra de Tamaulipas, although the latter are much more finely fashioned and the battering occurs uniformly all around the circumference. Farther east, in the United States, ellipsoidal choppers are rare.

Discoidal-Core Choppers

Fig. 73
305 specimens; 219 excavated, 86 collected.

These choppers range from almost spherical to discoidal. Surfaces are covered with scars from percussion blows, and many specimens look as though they were exhausted cores. Eighty-eight of our excavated sample, however, do show evidence of battering along one edge, and thus some of them, though they may also have served as cores, definitely did serve as choppers. The specimens with battered edges tend to be thicker and less spherical than the others, but the temporal distribution of the two varieties seems to be the same. The diameter of the choppers ranges from about 3 to 6 cm.

In the Tehuacan Valley this type is found in the two earliest phases, but it becomes prominent in Coxcatlan times and continues popular into the Venta Salada phase. As a type, discoidal-core choppers are relatively widespread in North America. However, there is a thin, discoidal variant with battered edges that shows a much

Fig. 73. Discoidal-core choppers.

more limited geographical range. A few examples were found in the Tehuacan region. So far as I know these variants do not appear in Chiapas, western Mexico, or the Valley of Mexico, but they are prominent in the Ocampo, Nogales, La Perra, and Abasolo horizons in Tamaulipas in northeastern Mexico. They are also found in preceramic sites in Texas.

Pebble Choppers

Fig. 74

80 specimens; 43 excavated, 37 collected.

Dimensions in cm. of 36 specimens: length (35 specimens only), 3.3–8.7, average, 5.6; width, 4.3–12.0, average, 6.6; thickness, 1.7–5.2, average, 3.3.

Pebble choppers vary in shape from ellipsoidal to roughly triangular, with the former shape more common. They are relatively thin in proportion to their width. All of our specimens have been made from river pebbles or boulders, and part of the original cortex of the pebble or boulder is still intact. The edges, however, have been thinned and sharpened by a series of rude percussion blows. All edges of about half of the specimens are so fashioned; the remainder of the specimens have only a part of the edge retouched, leaving the rest of the edge with the cortex of the pebble showing. The percussion-fashioned edges also show evidence of battering, usually along one of the longer edges. However, one specimen has been sharpened to a point, and the pointed end is battered as well. Two other variants are more discoidal in outline.

Pebble choppers are rare in all horizons in the Tehuacan Valley except Coxcatlan and Abejas. Only one battered nodule from the Santa Marta Cave in Chiapas even vaguely resembles this type, and examples are rare in Tamaulipas. A few specimens from the Infiernillo phase are somewhat similar, but they may be unfinished bifacial choppers rather than pebble choppers. Pebble choppers are, however, a prominent feature of the Desert Culture, and they appear earlier in the western United States than they do in Mexico, suggesting a diffusion from that area. Although the concepts involved in this type are not complex and re-invention is possible, pebble choppers from early horizons do have an unbroken distribution from western North America into eastern Asia.

Artifact Burins

Fig. 75

5 specimens; 1 excavated, 4 collected.

Dimensions in cm. of 5 specimens: length, 2.5–4.7, average,

Fig. 74. Pebble choppers.

3.4; width, 2.3–3.7, average, 2.9; thickness, 0.6–1.5, average, 0.8.

The five artifact burins were made from projectile points or bifaces that had been snapped in two. The broken surface had been used as a striking platform, and a blow against it removed a burin spall from one of the edges.

The only excavated artifact burin from Tehuacan was from an Abejas component, but the presence of a burin of this type in the jaw of a mammoth found by Juan Armenta in Puebla makes me suspect that this type might eventually be uncovered in earlier time levels in the Tehuacan Valley. Similar tools appear in early horizons in western North America.

Square-Based Drills

Fig. 75
4 specimens; 3 excavated, 1 collected.

Three of the square-based bifacial drills are fragments, and this description is based upon the single complete specimen. It has a square, bifacially chipped base, and from the middle of the opposite side extends a long, tapering, bifacially chipped drill point. The base is 3.3 cm. wide and about 3.2 cm. long; the point has a maximum width of about 1.2 cm. and is about 2.8 cm. long. The maximum thickness is about 1.0 cm.

In the Tehuacan Valley square-based bifacial drills were found in components of the Formative period, and the surface example perhaps is from the Classic period. In the Valley of Mexico, Tolstoy notes that similar drills are found in Formative and Classic times. In North America, these drills appear much earlier, particularly those associated with the Archaic cultures of the eastern United States.

Thin, Crude, Ovoid Bifaces

Fig. 75
116 specimens; 72 excavated, 44 collected.
Dimensions in cm.: length (27 specimens), 2.9–8.5, average, 5.4; width (43 specimens), 2.5–6.0, average, 3.8; thickness (60 specimens), 0.7–2.4, average, 1.2.

These bifaces vary from an oval to a tear-drop-shaped outline. They are made from large, rather thin flakes that have been percussion-chipped into form. Usually a series of percussion blows were struck against their surfaces to thin them, leaving large, rough scars. Slightly better-controlled blows struck at the edges rounded them into shape. One end of a few specimens, possibly the base, has been thinned by two percussion blows struck in the direction of the longitudinal axis.

Crude ovoid bifaces are an extremely general type

of artifact, found in most horizons throughout the New World. In the Tehuacan Valley bifaces of this type were found fairly consistently in all horizons except the earliest. Whether this absence is due to a cultural difference or to an inadequate sample cannot be determined.

Thin, Crude, Square-Based Bifaces

Fig. 76

59 specimens; 41 excavated, 18 collected.

Dimensions in cm.: length (15 specimens), 3.7–6.0, average, 4.9; width (20 specimens), 2.3–6.0, average, 4.6; thickness (30 specimens), 0.7–1.9, average, 0.8.

These bifaces, like the ovoid type, are also made from large, relatively thin, percussion-chipped flakes. Again the edges tend to be more carefully worked than the centers. Shapes vary from roughly square to the outline of isosceles triangles. Controlled percussion-flaking worked on relatively square bases has resulted in their being thinned, perhaps to facilitate hafting.

In the Tehuacan sequence these knives do not appear in significant numbers until the Coxcatlan phase, and they carry through as a significant type until the end of the Santa Maria phase. Again, in terms of a wider distribution pattern, square-based bifaces are a fairly common type over much of North America. However, in Mexico these particular knives are absent from

Fig. 75. Various bifaces. *Top row:* two artifact burins and a square-based drill; *beneath scale,* thin, crude, ovoid bifaces.

Fig. 76. Thin, crude, square-based bifaces.

Fig. 77. Large and small bifacial disks; *bottom row*, thin, fine bifaces.

the Santa Marta phase in Chiapas. In Tamaulipas, they appear throughout the sequence, reaching their greatest popularity during preceramic times.

Large Bifacial Disks

Fig. 77
33 specimens; 20 excavated, 13 collected.
Dimensions in cm.: length (17 specimens), 3.0–5.8, average,

4.1; width (18 specimens), 2.8–5.5, average, 3.9; thickness (19 specimens), 0.9–2.0, average, 1.3.

These large disks are relatively thin. They have been made from thin flakes, and their surfaces show evidence of a few rough percussion blows. They have, however, been rounded into form by rather carefully controlled percussion-flaking at the edges. They were probably used as crude knives.

In the Tehuacan sequence, large disks are found in significant numbers in three horizons: Coxcatlan, Abejas, and Ajalpan. They are not found in Chiapas, and in Tamaulipas they appear mainly in the Nogales, La Perra, and Almagre horizons. They also seem to be absent from the Cochise cultures of western Mexico and the Southwest of the United States.

Small Bifacial Disks

Fig. 77.
19 specimens; 12 excavated, 7 collected.
Dimensions in cm. of 8 specimens: length, 2.3–2.9, average, 2.6; width, 2.5–2.7, average, 2.5; thickness, 0.9–1.2, average, 1.0.

These disks are much like the larger bifacial disks, except that they are smaller and more delicately chipped. They have been made from thin flakes of flint, and usually only the edges show scars from well-controlled percussion-chipping. They probably were used as crude knives.

In the Tehuacan Valley small bifacial disks appear only in the Ajalpan and Santa Maria phases. In Tamaulipas they are found throughout ceramic horizons from Laguna to Los Angeles. From my limited knowledge of other artifact sequences in Mexico, it would seem that small bifacial disks are probably confined to ceramic horizons.

Thin Fine Bifaces

Fig. 77
20 specimens; 17 excavated, 3 collected.
Dimensions in cm.: length (one specimen), 7.3, but broken fragments indicate that most were considerably larger; width (4 specimens), 3.2–5.4, average, 4.4; thickness (9 specimens), 0.3–1.2, average, 0.8.

These bifaces vary in outline from tear-drop-shaped to lanceolate. They have been made from thin flakes that were further thinned by controlled percussion-flaking. However, in the final stage of manufacture they have been pressure-flaked not only along their edges but also across their surfaces. The pressure-flaking on the surfaces is often of the ripple-flake variety.

This again is an extremely general type of knife or

Fig. 78. Half-moon side-blades.

dagger in North America. However, in Mexico and in the Tehuacan Valley in particular, thin bifaces appear only with ceramic remains.

Half-Moon Side-Blades
Fig. 78
7 specimens; 3 excavated, 4 collected.

Dimensions in cm. of 3 specimens: length, 5.3–6.6, average, 5.5; width, 2.7–3.6, average, 3.3; thickness, 0.7–1.2, average, 0.9.

These half-moon-shaped bifaces were made from thin flakes roughed into form by percussion-flaking. The edges were pressure-flaked to sharpen them for cutting. Often the convex longer edge is more finely retouched than the straight edge.

Two of the excavated specimens from Tehuacan come from the Venta Salada phase, and the other comes from a very late Palo Blanco component. The four surface specimens were associated with remains of the Venta Salada phase. Although I have seen knives of this type in Mexican archaeological collections, I know of none that has been found in excavation. This type of biface is common in the plains of the United States and Canada, and it is diagnostic of late horizons in Arctic North America. Whether the Mexican knives are related to those found farther north cannot be determined on the basis of present evidence.

REFERENCES

ALEXANDER, HERBERT L.
  1963 "The Levi Site: A Paleo-Indian Campsite in Central Texas." *Am. Ant.*, 28:510–28.

EPSTEIN, JEREMIAH F.
  1960 "Burins from Texas." *Am. Ant.*, 26:93–97.

FAY, GEORGE E.
  1956 "Peralta Complex—A Sonoran Variant of the Cochise Culture." *Science*, 124:1029.

HARRINGTON, M. R.
  1933 *Gypsum Cave, Nevada.* Southwest Museum Papers, No. 8. Los Angeles.

MacNEISH, RICHARD S.
  1958 *Preliminary Archaeological Investigations in the Sierra de Tamaulipas, Mexico.* APS-T, Vol. 48, Part 6.

MacNEISH, RICHARD S., AND F. A. PETERSON
  1962 *The Santa Marta Rock Shelter, Ocozocoautla, Chiapas, Mexico.* Papers of the New World Archaeological Foundation, No. 14. Provo, Utah.

SUHM, DEE ANN, A.D. KRIEGER, AND E. B. JELKS
  1954 *An Introductory Handbook of Texas Archaeology.* TAS-B, Vol. 25.

TERRA, HELMUT DE
  1949 "Early Man in Mexico." *Tepexpan Man.* Viking Fund Publications in Anthropology, No. 11. New York.

TOLSTOY, PAUL
  —— "Stone, Bone, and Antler Tools of Central Mexico from Preclassic to Aztec Times." To be published in *Handbook of Middle American Indians.* Austin: University of Texas Press.

CHAPTER 6

Flint-Knapping Techniques

I N THE preceding chapters various flint-knapping features and techniques have been noted as factors to be considered alone and in combination when establishing typology for chipped-stone artifacts. I should like here to discuss flint-knapping further and from a more general point of view, for I believe that definite changes in chipping techniques are discernible within the long cultural sequence uncovered in the Tehuacan Valley.

My first observation concerns major shifts in the general methods used by the ancient craftsmen to form tools from their flint and obsidian materials. On a very gross level, chipped-stone tools were manufactured in three ways: directly from flakes, directly from blades, or indirectly from flakes, blades, and chunky fragments of flint and obsidian by the application of bifacial retouching. As may be seen in Table 14, making tools directly from flakes is the most popular method for the

Ajuereado and El Riego phases, and then it is gradually displaced by other techniques during the rest of the sequence. Bifacial tools, although present in the earliest horizons, do not become dominant until late Coxcatlan and Abejas times. Indirect bifacial flint-knapping continues as the dominant technique until the end of the Santa Maria phase, after which it declines in popularity. Blades and tools made from blades are manufactured from Ajuereado to Santa Maria times, but they suddenly increase in popularity and become the predominant type of stone tool used in the Venta Salada phase.

A second generalization I should like to make about flint-knapping concerns the relative use of crude percussion-chipping techniques as opposed to pressure-flaking or well-controlled percussion-flaking. As Table 14 shows, percussion-chipping is extensively used in the earliest horizons, but its popularity gradually de-

Table 14. Distribution of Flint-Knapping Characteristics in the Tehuacan Cultural Sequence

| | | | Kinds of Flakes | | | | Kinds of Tools | | | | | | Kinds of Flaking | | | |
| | | | unprepared striking platforms | | prepared striking platforms | | flake tools | | bifacial tools | | blade tools | | crude percussion | | pressure or controlled percussion | |
Period	Total Flakes Studied	Total Tools Studied	No.	Percent	No.	Percent	No.	Percent	No.	Percent	No.	Percent	No.	Percent	No.	Percent
Venta Salada	55	807	11	20	44	80	181	22	145	18	481	60	401	49	406	51
Palo Blanco	455	1083	173	38	282	62	432	40	232	21	419	39	707	65	376	35
Santa Maria	216	874	81	39	125	61	292	33	361	42	221	25	625	71	249	29
Ajalpan	610	555	289	47	321	53	131	23	366	65	58	12	423	76	132	24
Purron		7					2		1		4		5		2	
Abejas	424	1079	149	35	275	65	377	35	538	50	164	15	763	72	316	28
Coxcatlan	276	1007	98	38	178	62	451	45	427	42	129	13	756	75	251	25
El Riego	1030	2491	498	48	532	52	1623	65	619	25	249	10	2041	82	450	18
Ajuereado	95	155	62	65	33	35	113	73	25	16	17	11	136	88	19	12

creases during the rest of the sequence. On the other hand, finer flaking increases only very slightly up to the penultimate Palo Blanco phase, and then in the final Venta Salada phase, it is as popular as the crude work.

A third observation concerns the presence or absence of a prepared striking platform on the finished tool. Although all the chipped-stone materials were taken into consideration, my conclusions are based primarily on a separate study made of a smaller, representative sample selected from the various levels of Coxcatlan Cave and the open Ajalpan site. Only in the Ajuereado phase were flakes without prepared striking platforms dominant over those with prepared platforms (see Table 14). By El Riego times, flakes with prepared striking platforms were in the majority and remained so throughout the rest of the sequence. Although we never attempted to chart the data systematically, we also examined various objects from the same levels as the flakes that could have served as cores. Cores with and without prepared striking platforms seemed to be present in proportions similar to the proportions of the two kinds of flakes.

A fourth observation concerns polyhedral cores and the blades removed from them (see Chapter 1). Crude polyhedral cores, usually of flint, were dominant in the preceramic horizons, and finely fashioned obsidian nuclei were popular in ceramic horizons. Also, crude polyhedral cores without prepared striking platforms were the only type used in Ajuereado times, but by the El Riego phase the same type of core with a prepared striking platform was more popular. In the Coxcatlan and Abejas phases, crude cylindrical polyhedral cores joined the other two nuclei as basic materials for deriving blades. Skillfully made fine cores, often of obsidian and usually without prepared platforms, also made their appearance in the Abejas phase. This type of core continued to be manufactured, together with the older cruder cores, throughout the ceramic sequences. However, it was the finely made nuclei with prepared striking platforms, the bitapered fine nuclei, and the fine nuclei with ground striking platforms which, in that order, were most popular during the ceramic periods.

With the above observations as a preface, I would now like to outline the flint-knapping techniques typical during each of the successive cultural periods of the Tehuacan sequence. I shall attempt to take into account all the available information and all the artifactual materials which have a bearing on flint-knapping, such as, the proportion of flakes to cores found in the various occupational floors; the number of hammerstones found; the presence or absence of antler flakers or ham-

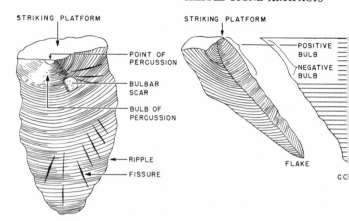

Fig. 79. Diagram of a flake; after Oakley 1957, courtesy of University of Chicago Press.

mers; the incidence of bones which could have been used to work flint; the spatial distribution of chipped-stone materials from stratified floors or open sites, and so forth. I shall add as well my own impressions, and a few guesses.

The Ajuereado phase is characterized by the predominance of tools derived from flakes (Fig. 79). These tools were usually struck from blocky cores without prepared striking platforms. However, a few flake tools were also struck from cores (probably blocky ones) which had prepared striking platforms, and although these were a minority in terms of the total number of flakes produced, they were more numerous than either bifaces or blades. The blades of this period probably were struck from conical cores without prepared striking platforms. It is my general impression that all of the above kinds of tools were manufactured by direct-percussion techniques using a hammerstone (Fig. 80). The bifacial tools, although also generally made by percussion-chipping, usually were fashioned from an originally fairly thick flint blank or from a very thick flake. The technique for making burins seems to have been understood at this period too, but it was little used.

Tools derived from flakes were also characteristic of the subsequent El Riego phase, but a number of technical changes had occurred. The majority of the flakes now came from cores with prepared striking platforms, and so did the majority of the numerically fewer crude blades. I further suspect that the percussion blows administered to the cores were as often struck with an implement softer than stone, such as an antler hammer, as with a pebble hammer. Some blades and flakes may also have been scaled off by indirect percussion (Fig. 81). Although bifaces were still being made by percussion, they now show considerable fine retouching, perhaps accomplished with an antler flaker. When making

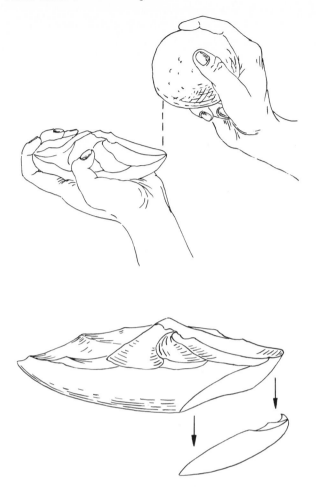

Fig. 80. Percussion-chipping technique; after Holmes 1919.

projectile points, the El Riego people chose thick flakes which they worked bifacially.

The flake and blade trends originating in the El Riego period continued into the Coxcatlan phase. The most noticeable difference at this period is that bifaces have become as numerous as flake tools. Projectile points are now even more delicately and skillfully worked, and pointed blades and flakes seem to have been struck from cylindrical cores by indirect percussion.

These same trends continue into the Abejas phase, although the production of flakes and crude blades has begun to decrease as bifacial tools become even more numerous. Something new is found in Abejas levels, however; for well-made obsidian nuclei without prepared striking platforms begin to appear, along with the resultant finer blades. I also would guess that indirect percussion was now used as frequently as direct percussion.

The flint-knapping techniques of the Purron phase would appear to be similar to those of Abejas times, but

this is only surmised on scanty evidence from a woefully inadequate sample.

Conclusive changes in flint-knapping, however, emerge in the Ajalpan phase. Flake production is at its lowest ebb. The flakes which are found seem to have been struck from cores with prepared striking platforms. Bifacial tools made initially by percussion and then retouched are still dominant, but fine blades are now replacing crude blades. Even so, blade-making is not very popular. The most noticeable thing about the few fine blades found in Ajalpan zones is that they are made by at least three different techniques. The older method of turning out fine blades by percussion exerted against nuclei with unprepared platforms is of course still used. However, some fine blades are now fashioned from hemiconical or bullet-shaped cores with prepared striking platforms. Others are removed from bitapered cores, both ends of which served as striking platforms. Probably these two newer types of blades were manufactured by the billet technique, using a tool softer than stone. In this period too, smaller end-scrapers and fine, delicately fashioned, bifacial knives begin to be made by pressure-flaking (Fig. 82).

In the Santa Maria phase most of the older flint-knapping techniques continue in use, although flakes made from cores with unprepared platforms are now

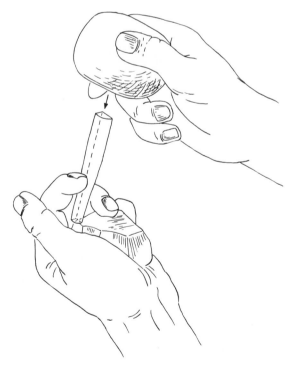

Fig. 81. Indirect percussion-chipping technique; after Holmes 1919.

95

rare, and fine blades have become more common at the expense of the bifaces. Blade-makers of the Santa Maria phase commonly used bitapered polyhedral cores, from which they struck long pointed blades. New in this period is the fashion of snapping the tips and striking platforms off fine blades and then retouching the edges, so that they could be set into handles and used as side-blades.

In the Palo Blanco phase the fine-blade industry yields more tools than either the flake or bifacial industries. In this period, too, the technique of making blades from cores with ground striking platforms by impulsive pressure is first used (Fig. 83). Some projectile points are made from blades. The rectangular side-blades of this period are also made from blades.

The Venta Salada phase is mainly characterized by the culmination of the various trends in flint-knapping which began in earlier horizons. For instance, blades made from nuclei with ground striking platforms are now very popular, as are projectile points and side-blades made from snapped blades. Bifaces shaped by percussion, tools made from flakes, flake-making in general, and some of the older techniques for making fine blades are all in the process of disappearing. Large projectile points fashioned by percussion and by fine flaking are giving way to smaller projectile points, often made by retouching thin flakes. In fact, in this last period percussion techniques were little used, except, of course, to produce the initial flakes for later reworking.

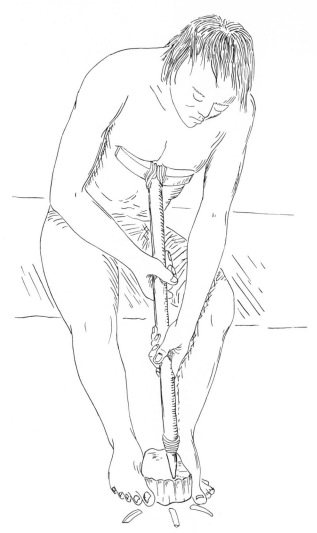

Fig. 83. Impulsive pressure-flaking technique; after Holmes 1919.

Scrapers of this period are uniformly smaller and more delicately made, and the larger bifacial knives are also more finely fashioned. Half-moon bifaces (side-blades) are manufactured for the first time.

Besides the studies of Epstein (1964) and Tolstoy (in press), both of whom used materials from ceramic horizons in the Valley of Mexico, few comparative data are available regarding the flint-knapping techniques used in prehistoric times in Mesoamerica. Some of the changes in flint-knapping noted by these two authors parallel those occurring in the ceramic horizons of Tehuacan. But, obviously, more studies from more areas in Mesoamerica, covering longer periods of time, are badly needed. After all, flint-knapping is just as much a cultural activity as making pots, or building a temple, or marrying a very "cross" cousin!

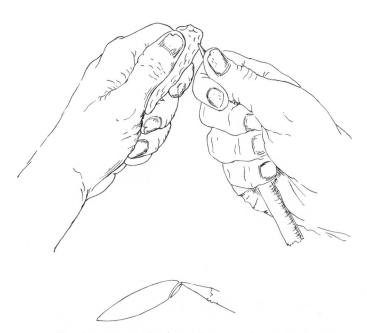

Fig. 82. Pressure-flaking technique; after Holmes 1919.

REFERENCES

EPSTEIN, JEREMIAH F.
1964 "Towards the Systematic Description of Chipped Stone." *XXXV Congreso Internacional de Americanistas, Mexico, 1962,* I:155–69. Mexico.

HARRINGTON, M. R.
1933 *Gypsum Cave, Nevada.* Southwest Museum Papers, No. 8. Los Angeles.

HOLMES, WILLIAM H.
1919 *Handbook of Aboriginal American Antiquities.* BAE-B, No. 60.

OAKLEY, KENNETH P.
1957 *Man the Tool-maker.* Chicago: University of Chicago Press.

TOLSTOY, PAUL
——— "Stone, Bone, and Antler Tools of Central Mexico from Preclassic to Aztec Times." To be published in *Handbook of Middle American Indians.* Austin: University of Texas Press.

PART II: GROUND-STONE ARTIFACTS

CHAPTER 7

Food-Preparation Artifacts

MESOAMERICAN archaeological reports usually describe artifacts used in preparing food in a rather cursory fashion—thereby relegating many of the ground-stone tools to a position of minor importance. Although vessels used to prepare food may indeed have changed little over the ages, we decided to test this negative assumption. We therefore set about establishing trial types of food-preparation artifacts, using the materials excavated from Coxcatlan Cave. Fortunately, these initial types needed little refining as we integrated the materials from the other excavated sites—so none of us succumbed to injured backs from shuffling about the 2,000 or so heavy stone specimens that made up our sample. We were pleasantly surprised to find that these ground-stone artifacts—pestles, mortars, stone bowls, metates, milling stones, mullers, and manos—were very sensitive indicators of cultural change.

We classified the pestles first; these we defined as elongated stone objects with one end flattened by a rotary grinding or pecking motion, either intentionally or through use. It is generally assumed that such objects were used to grind nuts, seeds, berries, and the like in various types of mortars. There is, however, a school of thought which proposes that some of these objects were used as floor polishers or smoothers. We learned from Florence Müller of the Teotihuacan Project that she had tested this idea by having her plastering crew attempt to use pestles to smooth plaster. They found that the pestles did not work at all.

We uncovered forty-five pestles during excavations in the Tehuacan Valley. Once these were laid out according to the level in which they were found, they immediately could be separated into eight basic categories, based primarily on geometric form. In terms of general temporal significance, long, conical pestles and

rectangular and cylindrical ones appear early in our sequence. The cuboid type are found in late preceramic times and last through the Palo Blanco phase. The rise of bell-shaped and flat-iron pestles is confined to the Ajalpan and Santa Maria phases. Truncated cone-shaped pestles first appear in the Ajalpan phase and last to the Venta Salada phase. The large thumbtack-shaped pestles, or "floor smoothers," are found only in the Venta Salada phase.

Mortars, which are defined as stones having one concave surface marked by pecking or rotary grinding, were classified into three types. Tecomate mortars were confined to the El Riego phase. Flat-bottomed mortars with flaring rims also were found mainly in El Riego levels, although one appeared in the Santa Maria period. Hemispherical mortars were discovered in both the El Riego and Coxcatlan phases.

The stone bowls used in preparing food were similar to the mortars in general form, but all were less than 2.5 cm. thick and none showed evidence of interior working. Also, food had definitely been burned in the interior of a bowl from Coxcatlan Cave. Tecomate-shaped stone bowls appear only in the Coxcatlan and Abejas phases, and hemispherical bowls are found in these two phases and in the Ajalpan and Santa Maria phases as well. Bowls with flaring rims were confined to the Abejas horizon.

Manos and mullers and fragments of both were very numerous in our excavations. Manos are stones used in metates with a back-and-forth motion, whereas mullers were used in milling stones with a rotary motion. It is often difficult to tell these two grinders apart, but separation was facilitated by using a microscope to distinguish the direction of the grinding. Ovoid mullers and ovoid manos appear throughout our sequence from the El Riego phase on, although they were rare in the Palo

101

Table 15. Mortars, Pestles, and Stone Bowls from Excavated Components according to Phase

	AJUE-READO		EL RIEGO															COXCAT-LAN						ABEJAS						AJALPAN								SANTA MARIA												PALO BLANCO				VENTA SALADA					
	Tc 50, XXIII	Tc 35w, 6	Tc 50, XXII	Tc 50, XXI	Tc 50, XX	Tc 50, XIX	Tc 307, H	Tc 50, XVIII	Tc 50, XVII	Tc 272, R	Tc 50, XVI	Tc 35w, 5	Ts 51, DE	Tc 307, G	Tc 50, XV	Tc 50, XIV	Ts 381w, pit	Tc 50, XIII	Tc 50, XII	Tc 35w, 4	Tc 254, E	Tc 50, XI	Tc 272, N	Tc 50, X	Tc 307, B	Ts 51, C	Tc 50, IX	Ts 381e, house	Tc 50, VIII	Ts 204, H	Ts 204, G	Ts 204, G1	Ts 204, F	Ts 368, K3	Ts 204C, pit	Ts 368, K2	Ts 368, J	Ts 368, H	Ts 368, G	Ts 368, F	Ts 368, E	Ts 367, D1	Ts 367, C	Ts 368, B	Ts 368w, B1	Ts 218-6, G	Ts 218-10, C2	Ts 218-10, C	Tc 50, VII	Tc 307, A	Ts 218-10, A	Tc 35e, E	Tc 35e, D	Tc 35w, 3	Tc 50, II	Tc 35w, 2	Ts 368e, A	Ts 367, A	Tr 65, A
Thumbtack pestles																																																											2
Effigy bowls																																																									1	1?	
Flat-iron pestles																																									1		2	2															
Truncated-cone pestles																														1															1				1							1			
Bell-shaped pestles																														1	2		1				1						1	1					1							1		
Flaring-rim bowls																												1																														
Hemispherical bowls																				1				1					1													1			1													
Cuboid pestles																										1		1			1	1	1																							3		
Tecomate bowls																		1					1														2																					
Long, rectangular pestles													1	2		1	1																													1					1								
Hemispherical mortars					2								2	1	1		1	2	1	3																																							
Conical pestles													1			1	1	2	2													1																				2							
Flaring-rim mortars											1			1			2	1																																		1							
Cylindrical pestles	1												2		1	1		1	2																																								
Tecomate mortars		1		1									1				1																																							1			
Bowl fragments													1	1			1															1	1	2				3	1				1	1	1	2	1	2	4		3				1			1	
Mortar fragments		2	1			1	4	5	1	2	3	5	5	6	4	1		1	4	2									1														1						1	1	1							1	
TOTAL MORTARS, PESTLES, BOWLS	1	1	2	1	1	3	1	7	8	1	8	5	10	7	12	12	1	2	5	5	1	1	1	1	1	1	1	6	1	2	6	2	2	1	1	2	2	1	1	4	3	1	1	2	1	2	2	4	1	2	6	1	3	1	2	1	1	2	2

Table 16. Mortars, Pestles, and Stone Bowls from Surface Sites according to Possible Phase

	EL RIEGO			ABEJAS	SANTA MARIA	PALO BLANCO WITH VENTA SALADA REMAINS					PALO BLANCO OR VENTA SALADA			VENTA SALADA WITH PALO BLANCO REMAINS								VENTA SALADA			MULTI-COMPONENT SITES							UNCLASSIFIED		TOTAL
	Ts 387	Ts 388	Ts 381w	Ts 381e	Tr 25	Ts 67	Tr 229	Ts 205	Tr 180	Tr 121	Tr 301	Tr 234	Tr 227	Tr 210	Tr 240	Tr 306	Tr 64	Tr 276	Tr 33	Tr 122	Ts 339	Tr 247	Tr 228	Ts 82	Tr 187	Ts 327	Tr 337	Tr 125	Tr 1	Tc 39	Ts 204	Ts 367	Ts 204E	Ts 368	Tr 358	Tc 7	Tr 218	Tr 352	TOTAL
Thumbtack pestles						1													1																		1		2
Effigy bowls					1														1																		1		3
Flat-iron pestles																	1																				1		2
Truncated-cone pestles																	1				1			1					1										4
Bell-shaped pestles																		1												1	1	1							5
Flaring-rim bowls																														1									1
Hemispherical bowls				1											1	1										1					1								5
Cuboid pestles						1						2																			1								4
Tecomate bowls																										1													1
Long, rectangular pestles																																					1		1
Hemispherical mortars																																						1	1
Conical pestles					1				1												1		1	1															5
Flaring-rim mortars																																							0
Cylindrical pestles	1							1	1		1	1	1				1														1	1							9
Tecomate mortars																																							0
Bowl fragments			3																												2								5
Mortar fragments	1	1	1																												1				1				5
TOTAL MORTARS, PESTLES, BOWLS	1	1	2	4	1	1	1	1	1	1	1	2	1	1	1	1	1	1	1	2	1	1	1	1	1	1	1	1	1	4	1	2	1	1	1	1	5	2	53

Blanco and Venta Salada horizons. Spherical and oblong manos mainly come from the Coxcatlan, Abejas, Ajalpan, and Santa Maria phases, although a few doubtful examples are from our two final phases. Long manos that are lenticular in cross section are found in the Abejas, Ajalpan, and Santa Maria phases, whereas long manos that are triangular in cross section appear from Ajalpan times to the Spanish conquest. Although our sample is very small, cylindrical manos are found from the Santa Maria to the Venta Salada horizon, and cuboid and stave-shaped manos come from Palo Blanco and Venta Salada times. The "dog-bone" type is found only in the Venta Salada phase.

Changes in muller and mano types often parallel changes in milling-stone and metate types, and these changes are probably functionally interrelated. Metates and milling stones are, of course, the large stones in which the smaller manos and mullers were used, and sometimes both grinding agents were used in the same receptacle. Ovoid manos and mullers were probably used in boulder metate–milling stones, and all three have the same temporal distribution from the El Riego to the Venta Salada phase. Trough metates and oblong manos are found principally from El Riego to Ajalpan times. Large, ovoid, plano-convex metates and long manos are found from the Abejas phase to the Conquest, while lipped-saucer, lipped-oblong, and basin-shaped metates appear in significant proportions only in the Santa Maria and Ajalpan horizons. Large rectangular metates with feet come from the Palo Blanco and Venta Salada phases.

Although many of the changes in the various types of ground-stone tools may be stylistic variations and reflect cultural compulsions, some are probably connected with changing uses. The early mortars and pestles of preceramic times may have been used to grind or pound vegetal materials, as well as paint, while the later pestle types may have been used to grind chili in clay *molcajetes*. Early manos and metates may also have been used to pulverize vegetal materials. The oblong manos and trough metates, as well as the later lipped saucer-shaped metates and smaller manos, may have been used to grind corn for gruel. All the later types were probably used to make *nixtamal*. Regardless of their varying uses, however, their forms were very significantly different in various periods, which allows these artifacts to be excellent marker types.

Pestles—*Type Descriptions*

Cylindrical Pestles

Fig. 84

17 specimens; 8 excavated, 9 collected.

Dimensions in cm. of one specimen: length, 11.9; width (4 specimens), 4.5–7.0, average, 5.5; thickness, 4.2; diameter, 4.5.

All specimens are made of basalt and were pecked into cylindrical form. The ends have been ground as well as pecked. A few scratches on the ends of two specimens reveal that they have been ground in a circular motion.

Cylindrical pestles first appear in the Tehuacan sequence late in the Ajuereado period and last through the El Riego phase. I have no record of pestles of this type having been found elsewhere in Mexico, although the type is common in Archaic cultures of the eastern United States.

Conical Pestles

Fig. 84

15 specimens, 10 excavated, 5 collected.

Dimensions in cm. of 4 specimens: length, 9.1–23.1, average, 14.6; maximum diameter, 5.3–6.3, average, 6.2; minimum diameter (5 specimens), 3.0–4.6, average, 4.0.

These pestles are long cones with slightly convex bases and relatively pointed tips. Of the excavated pestles three were made of basalt and seven from hard river pebbles. The pestles were first pecked into form and then the basal portions were apparently ground with a rotary motion. The tips also bear evidence of hammering and further pecking.

In the Tehuacan Valley conical pestles first appear in the El Riego phase. However, one was found in an Ajalpan level and two in a Palo Blanco level, indicating a fairly extensive duration in time. The only similar pestles reported from Mexico were found by Paul Tolstoy in the Valley of Mexico.

Long Rectangular Pestles

Fig. 84

8 specimens; 7 excavated, 1 collected.

Dimensions in cm. of 6 specimens: width, 6.3–7.5, average, 6.6; thickness, 3.6–4.7, average, 4.3; length (2 specimens only), 11.9 and 14.6.

These pestles are long and roughly rectangular in outline, and they are oblong to rectangular in cross section. They were made from rectangular river pebbles, and the little work required to square their ends was accomplished by pecking. The long sides were further squared by either chipping or rough pecking. Both ends of these pestles usually show evidence of pecking and grinding in a circular motion. A flattened surface of a pestle from Zone XVI of Coxcatlan Cave had been used as an anvil.

Fig. 84. Pestles. *Upper row*, long rectangular, cylindrical, and conical; *lower right*, cuboid.

These pestles appear mainly in the El Riego phase. Similar pestles are unknown from the rest of Mexico.

Cuboid Pestles

Fig. 84

12 specimens; 8 excavated, 4 collected.

Dimensions in cm.: width (6 specimens), 5.4–8.2, average, 6.7; length (4 specimens), 7.0–10.1, average, 8.5; thickness (5 specimens), 5.0–7.0, average, 6.1.

Three pestles from excavated sites are made of basalt and five from river pebbles. The four sides have been pecked flat, and this makes the pestles roughly square in cross section. In outline they range from square to very slightly rectangular. The slightly convex ends have been pecked and ground in a circular motion. They are generally quite small in size, and as one of my colleagues remarked, "They fit the hand very nicely."

Cuboid pestles first appear in the Coxcatlan phase of the Tehuacan sequence, and they carry through until Venta Salada times. Although they have not been described for other parts of Mexico, Florence Müller informs me that they are also found at Teotihuacan.

Flat-Iron Pestles

Fig. 85

7 specimens; 5 excavated, 2 collected.

Dimensions in cm. of one specimen: length of base, 8.5; width, 6.2; thickness, 2.5.

These uniquely shaped pestles have ovoid, flattened bases, above which a large handle loops from one end to the other, making them resemble small flat-irons. They are made of basalt and were pecked into form. The convex, ovoid base, however, displays evidence of polishing, as does the middle part of the handle. The polishing, of course, may have resulted from use.

Flat-iron pestles are found only in the Formative periods of the Tehuacan sequence. Tolstoy has reported finding them in the Classic period in the Valley of Mexico.

Bell-Shaped Pestles

Fig. 86

12 specimens; 7 excavated, 5 collected.

Dimensions in cm.: length (5 specimens), 6.6–10.0, average, 8.0; width (7 specimens), 4.8–7.4, average, 6.2; thickness (4 specimens), 4.3–5.5, average, 4.9.

Four pestles from excavation are made of basalt and three from sandstone pebbles. They are roughly conical in shape, with slightly convex bases. Just above the base a rather deep groove ground around the conical body gives it a bell-shaped form. Although the groove and

Fig. 85. Flat-iron pestle or smoother, three views.

105

Fig. 86. Truncated-cone and bell-shaped pestles.

base have been ground, the rest of the pestle has been shaped by pecking.

In the Tehuacan Valley, bell-shaped pestles come only from the Formative periods, but in the Valley of Mexico they are found in both Formative and Classic periods.

Truncated-Cone Pestles

Fig. 86

8 specimens; 4 excavated, 4 collected.

Dimensions in cm. of 3 specimens: maximum diameter, 4.1–4.7, average, 4.4; minimum diameter, 3.7–4.1, average, 3.9.

One excavated pestle is made of basalt and the others from excavation are made from hard pebbles. They resemble small, wide, truncated cones, with flattened bases and flattened tips. The conical walls, which may have been pecked into form initially, show considerable evidence of grinding. The tips of two pestles show evi-

dence of both grinding and pecking, but the tips of two others show evidence only of pecking. The basal portions of the four from excavation show evidence of grinding in a circular motion.

In the Tehuacan Valley these pestles first appear in the Formative period, and they last into the Postclassic period. Tolstoy records them for Formative and Classic periods in the Valley of Mexico.

Thumbtack Pestles or "Polishers"

Fig. 87

4 specimens; 2 excavated, 2 collected.

Dimensions in cm. of 2 specimens: diameter of disk, 12.0 and 14.0; thickness of disk, 2.4 and 2.6; diameter of handle, 4.8 and 5.2; length of handle (one specimen), 5.0.

The two excavated pestles are made of basalt and volcanic tufa. Each has a dish-shaped base, from which protrudes a short conical handle. All areas except the flat basal portions have been pecked into form. The base has not only been pecked, but has been ground completely flat as well.

Thumbtack pestles are found only in the Postclassic period in the Tehuacan Valley, but similar ones have been reported from both Classic and Postclassic periods in the Valley of Mexico.

Mullers and Manos—*Type Descriptions*

Ovoid Mullers

Fig. 88

181 specimens; 174 excavated, 7 collected.

Dimensions in cm. of 38 specimens: length, 6.6–16.8, average, 9.4; width, 6.4–10.9, average, 7.6; thickness (41 specimens), 3.1–6.6, average, 4.3.

Ovoid mullers, which were used with a circular motion in milling stones, are made from river pebbles, and the ancient valley peoples had a tendency to select ones of sandstone. These pebbles, ovoid in cross section, are relatively wide and flat, and they vary in outline from almost rectangular to round. Ovoid mullers, in fact, actually were not manufactured at all; rather they are just "used" pebbles. The marks from use usually consist of circular scratchings on one or both flat surfaces. Although many of our sample were broken, seventy-five complete specimens had circular scratches on two surfaces and eighteen were scratched on only one surface. Some fifteen of our sample had peck marks on one narrow end—indicating that they were also used as hammerstones—and three other specimens had peck marks on both ends.

Ovoid mullers are found throughout the Tehuacan se-

Fig. 87. Thumbtack pestles or smoothers; *left*, two views of the same specimen.

quence, as they are throughout the sequences in Chiapas, the Valley of Mexico, and Tamaulipas. Farther west and north they are one of the diagnostic traits of the Desert Culture.

Ovoid Manos

Fig. 89

92 specimens; 85 excavated, 7 collected.

Dimensions in cm.: length (29 specimens), 6.8–13.8, average, 10.1; width (39 specimens), 5.0–10.5, average, 6.5; thickness (40 specimens), 4.1–7.7, average, 5.1.

Ovoid manos are extremely similar to ovoid mullers in size and form. They are roughly oval to round in outline and usually have two relatively flattened surfaces. Like the mullers, they are made from river pebbles. The flattened surfaces, however, have been scratched with a back-and-forth motion, indicating that they were used in some type of metate. Almost all the manos in our sample had been used on two surfaces. There was some attempt—crude though it may have been—to make some of them more rectangular in form; over half the specimens had been chipped or pecked on the two narrower ends, and on sixteen others the pecking continued around the sides.

Ovoid manos are not found in the Tehuacan Valley until late El Riego times, and they reach their greatest popularity in the Coxcatlan, Abejas, and Ajalpan phases. They are also found in Tamaulipas in the Nogales, Ocampo, and La Perra cultural phases. Unfortunately, most Mesoamerican sources usually group ovoid manos with ovoid mullers, and so I am unable to discuss distribution further for this area. However, in the Southwest of the United States and in western Mexico, ovoid manos are prevalent in all but the earliest stages of these sequences—that is, in all but the Sulphur Springs phase. In this respect the distribution of ovoid manos in the Desert Culture area of North America and in the Tehuacan Valley is quite similar.

Spherical Manos

Fig. 89

35 specimens; 22 excavated, 13 collected.

Dimensions in cm. of 14 specimens: diameter, 6.4–20.6, average, 10.5; width, 4.0–9.0, average, 7.0.

These manos were fashioned from selected spherical river cobbles, usually of sandstone, which were relatively small in diameter, generally about 10 cm. A small portion of the surface has been flattened by a back-and-forth grinding motion.

Spherical manos first appear in the Coxcatlan phase in the Tehuacan sequence, and they last through the

Fig. 88. Ovoid mullers.

CM. 1   3   5
INCHES   1   2

Fig. 89. Spherical and ovoid manos.

Fig. 90. Oblong manos.

Venta Salada phase. They are similar to the pebble manos found in both Tamaulipas and Chiapas. The manos from Chiapas antedate those from Tehuacan, having been in use between 7000 and 6000 B.C.

Oblong Manos

Fig. 90

75 specimens; 41 excavated, 34 collected.

Dimensions in cm. of 13 specimens: length, 9.3–15.3, average, 11.8; width, 6.2–10.1, average, 7.7; thickness (12 specimens), 3.6–7.1, average, 4.7.

These short, oblong manos were made from relatively flat, ovoid pebbles. Both ends have been flattened by percussion blows or by pecking. The longer sides of eight examples have also been straightened by pecking. Both surfaces of twenty-one excavated specimens have been ground with a back-and-forth motion. One of these specimens has been ground on both surfaces but at two slightly different angles, giving it a roughly hexagonal cross section. Six of the manos from excavation are ground on a single side; the remaining specimens were too fragmentary to determine whether they were ground on one surface or two.

Oblong manos originated in the Coxcatlan phase in the Tehuacan Valley; they appear with some prevalence from that period through the Santa Maria phase and appear again in Venta Salada times. Two oblong manos appearing in the La Perra horizon of Tamaulipas are similar, as is one from the Santa Marta Cave in Chiapas. Helmut de Terra classified a number of similar objects found on the surface as belonging to the so-called Chalco complex of the Valley of Mexico. He also uncovered an oblong mano in the excavation of the Chicoloapan site.

Long, Sub-Rectangular Manos, Lenticular in Cross Section

Fig. 91

122 specimens; 38 excavated, 84 collected.

Dimensions in cm. of 10 specimens: length (2 specimens only), 16.9 and 21.3; width, 6.9–10.5, average, 8.4; thickness, 3.7–6.7, average, 5.8.

Most of these manos were made from long granitic or sandstone pebbles. They are widest at the midpoint, and the long, slightly convex sides taper toward the narrow, convex ends. In transverse cross section they are lenticular, since they taper toward both sides as well as toward both ends. They were originally pecked into shape, and then the convex surfaces were ground, probably both intentionally and through use. Although most of our specimens are fragments, they indicate that

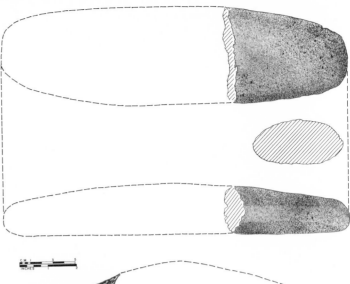

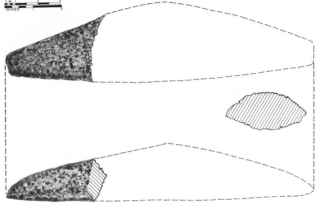

Fig. 91. Long, sub-rectangular manos, lenticular in cross section.

the manos must have been long enough to have been used with two hands.

Three examples of this type of mano came from Abejas levels, but they are the most common type in the two Formative phases of Ajalpan and Santa Maria. They also are found in the Formative and Classic periods in the Huasteca, and Tolstoy records them at Tlatilco in the Valley of Mexico.

Long, Sub-Rectangular Manos, Triangular in Cross Section

Fig. 92

90 specimens; 32 excavated, 58 collected.

Dimensions in cm. of 10 specimens: length (2 specimens only), 18.2 and 37.0; width, 5.7–9.5, average, 8.1; thickness, 4.4–5.9, average, 5.2.

111

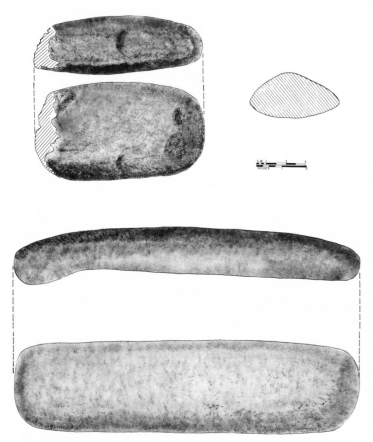

Fig. 92. Long, sub-rectangular manos, triangular in cross section.

In general outline these manos are much like the previous type, with long, slightly convex sides and short, slightly convex ends. In cross section, however, they have a very different form, triangular instead of lenticular. One surface, usually the most highly polished, is almost completely flat; the other two surfaces vary from slightly convex to polished flat and give the mano its prismatic form. One unusual specimen has a knob at one end. Although most of our sample are fragments, the manos appear to have been long enough and big enough to have been used with two hands. About half of the sample are made of volcanic tufa and the others of either sandstone or granite.

In the Tehuacan Valley these manos first appear in the Formative periods and last to Postclassic times. They seem to be absent from northern Mexico, and Tolstoy records them as coming only from the Formative period in the Valley of Mexico.

Long Cylindrical Manos

Fig. 93

24 specimens; 6 excavated, 18 collected.

Dimensions in cm. of 6 specimens: length, 9.8–14.7, average, 12.0; width, 5.5–8.0, average, 7.0; thickness, 5.0–7.5, average, 6.1.

Four manos from excavation are made of volcanic tufa, and two of a hard granite-like green stone. They have been ground into shape. The long, cylindrical bodies taper very slightly toward both flattened ends. Some specimens show slightly more polish on the two opposite surfaces, while others are more evenly polished all the way round.

One cylindrical mano was found in a very late Formative level, one came from a Classic level, and the others found in the Tehuacan Valley were of Postclassic origin. Tamaulipas is the only other region I know of in Mexico where similar manos have been found; there they appear in the late Formative and Classic periods.

Cuboid Manos

Fig. 94

73 specimens; 21 excavated, 52 collected.

Dimensions in cm.: length (9 specimens), 5.0–23.8, average, 11.0; width (7 specimens), 6.7–8.0, average, 7.3; thickness (8 specimens), 3.7–7.6, average, 5.1.

All but four of the manos from excavation are made of volcanic tufa. In outline the manos are roughly rectangular, although they taper slightly near the ends; in cross section most of them are rectangular. The four sides and the ends have been ground. Usually the two wider sides show more polish than the other surfaces. There seem to be two varieties of cuboid manos as far as length is concerned, but we have not separated them into two types because their temporal distribution is the same. The relatively short variety (about 15 cm. long) could have been used with one hand; the other kind is much longer and would have been used with two hands.

In the Tehuacan Valley cuboid manos appear in the Classic and Postclassic periods. They have a similar distribution in the Valley of Mexico, but in Tamaulipas they are found only in Postclassic components.

Stave-Shaped Manos

Fig. 93

10 specimens; 5 excavated, 5 collected.

Dimensions in cm. of 3 specimens: length, 8.2–18.0, average, 14.5; width, 7.3–10.5, average, 8.4; thickness, 3.0–4.6, average, 3.8.

Stave-shaped manos are rectangular both in outline and in cross section. One surface is relatively flat and the other slightly convex, giving the manos a stave-shaped appearance. The convex surface usually is more

Fig. 93. Long cylindrical manos, *top and center;* fragments are slightly less than half full length. *Bottom,* a stave-shaped mano.

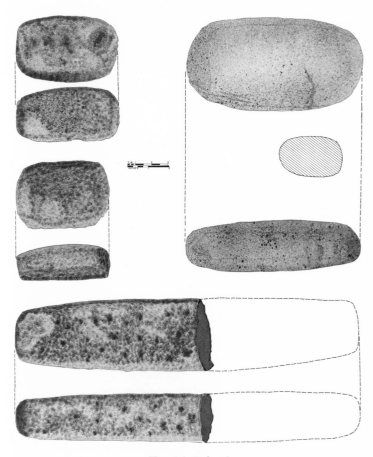

Fig. 94. Cuboid manos.

highly polished than the other surfaces. All but one of our sample were made of volcanic tufa; the exception was of sandstone. All were ground into shape.

Stave-shaped manos were found in very late Classic and Postclassic levels in the Tehuacan Valley. I do not know of similar manos being found in other parts of Mexico, although Tolstoy recorded a Postclassic "polisher" with a similar form from the Valley of Mexico. Whether or not this is the same as the Tehuacan type, I am unable to determine.

Dog-Bone Manos

Fig. 95

12 specimens; 4 excavated, 8 collected.

Dimensions in cm. of 3 specimens: width, 6.5–8.0, average, 7.4; thickness, 4.5–7.3, average, 6.0.

Dog-bone manos are made of volcanic tufa. They are long and narrow, with flattened ends, and tend to be ovoid in cross section. They are widest at the midpoint and taper very slightly toward each end; slight ridges at each end give the whole mano the general shape of a tibia. They have been ground into form, and the rather

114

knobby ends may result from their having been used in metates that were too narrow. Two hands would be needed to grind with these manos.

Although dog-bone manos are found only in Postclassic components in the Tehuacan Valley, similar ones from Classic times have been found in the Valley of Mexico and in Sinaloa.

Mortars and Stone Bowls—*Type Descriptions*

Tecomate Mortars

Fig. 96

5 specimens excavated.

Dimensions in cm.: diameter (4 specimens), 14.0–16.0, average, 15.0; wall thickness (3 specimens), 3.9–4.9, average, 4.2.

Two tecomates are made of volcanic tufa, and the others are of basalt, sandstone, and quartz. There seems to be no uniformity in the material chosen for these large vessels, although our sample is too small to be representative. These mortars appear to have been cut and pecked into their general form and then very roughly ground. The interiors seem to be more highly polished and ground than the exteriors. Judging from

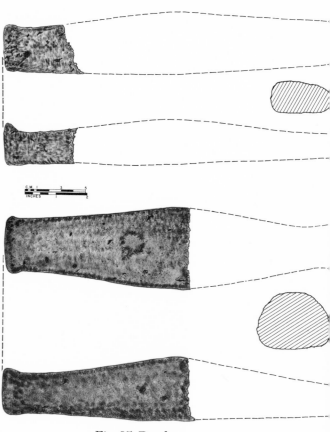

Fig. 95. Dog-bone manos.

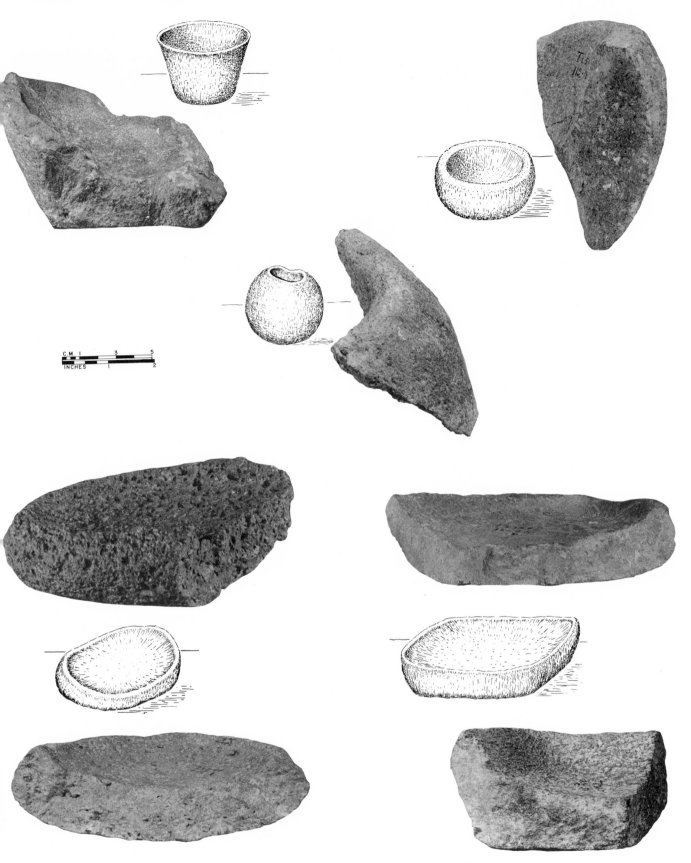

Fig. 96. Mortars and metates. *Upper left,* flat-bottomed mortar with flaring rim; *upper right,* hemispherical mortar. *Center,* tecomate mortar. *Lower left,* saucer-shaped lipped metate (2 fragments); *lower right,* oblong lipped metate (2 fragments).

they were over 25 cm. high. They have small mouths and large globular or spherical bodies. Interiors are roughly conical in shape and the bottoms of the interiors show evidence of pecking.

Tecomate mortars are found in the Tehuacan Valley mainly in the El Riego phase. Some of the "ollas de piedra" found in the Sierra de Tamaulipas are extremely similar, but their mouths are usually not so constricted.

Hemispherical Mortars

Fig. 96

14 specimens; 13 excavated, 1 collected.

Dimensions in cm. of 9 specimens: diameter, 10.0–44.0, average, 18.0; wall thickness, 3.2–6.3, average, 4.2; height (one specimen only), 9.5.

Eight specimens are made of volcanic tufa and the rest from various kinds of granitic or sandstone boulders. These mortars are hemispherical in form, and the lip portion is very much thinner than the rounded bottoms. Exteriors have been roughly gouged or pecked, while the interiors are uniformly ground. Interiors also show evidence of some pecking, along with further grinding in a circular motion.

In the Tehuacan Valley hemispherical mortars appear in the El Riego and Coxcatlan horizons. In Tamaulipas they are present in the La Perra and Nogales phases, while in northern Tamaulipas they occur in the Repelo, Abasolo, and Catan complexes. Some of the stone bowls from the Formative stage at Ocos, Guatemala, and the Valley of Mexico resemble the Tehuacan type, but it is difficult to determine whether they are actually bowls or mortars.

Flat-Bottomed Mortars with Flaring Rims

Fig. 96

6 specimens excavated.

Dimensions in cm.: diameter (3 specimens), 10.0–14.0, average, 13.0; basal diameter (1 specimen), 10.0; wall height (4 specimens), 6.9–12.4, average, 9.4; wall thickness (3 specimens), 2.7–3.2, average, 3.0.

Three specimens are made of volcanic tufa and three are probably of limestone. The mortars have small flat bottoms and rather low, tapering, flaring rims with almost pointed lips. The exteriors have been shaped by pecking and gouging and the interiors by grinding. The bottoms of the interiors display circular grinding scars, and one specimen is covered inside with red paint.

Five of these mortars were found in levels of the El Riego phase, but one was found in a Palo Blanco zone of the East Niche of El Riego Cave. Similar mortars have not yet been recorded from other parts of Mexico.

Fig. 97. Stone bowls. Two fragments of effigy bowls; tecomate bowl; bowl with flaring rim.

the diameter and general slope of their mouths—all our specimens are fragments—the vessels must have been extremely large and cumbersome. I would guess that

116

Fig. 98. Boulder metate—milling stone.

Stone-Bowl Tecomates

Fig. 97

5 specimens; 4 excavated, 1 collected.

Dimensions in cm.: diameter (one specimen), 26.0; wall thickness near lip (2 specimens), 1.8 and 3.6; wall fragment height (one specimen), 10.2.

Most stone-bowl tecomates are made of volcanic tufa. Body exteriors have been gouged and pecked, and the interiors and lips have been ground, although they may have been pecked initially as well as ground. These tecomates appear to have had spherical or elliptical bodies with small mouths. The walls are quite thin, and the lips are pointed and slope inward. In some ways they resemble tecomate mortars, but their walls are much thinner, and their interiors are more roughly spherical and much larger. One specimen had burnt food adhering to the interior.

Two of the excavated specimens date from the Coxcatlan phase and two from the Abejas phase. Stone-bowl tecomates have not been recorded from other parts of Mexico besides the Tehuacan Valley.

Hemispherical Stone Bowls

10 specimens; 5 excavated, 5 collected.

Dimensions in cm. of one nearly complete specimen: maximum diameter, 24.0; basal diameter, 22.0; maximum thickness, 2.5; height, 7.5.

These stone bowls, of marble, limestone, or volcanic tufa, have been finely ground into hemispherical form. The walls are very thin, and there is no evidence of scratching or marks from use, which suggests that the bowls were used as receptacles. Some stone bowls from the surface collections have flat bottoms but are otherwise similar.

Hemispherical bowls are found in the Tehuacan sequence from Coxcatlan to Palo Blanco times. Michael D. Coe has recorded them for Ocos, Guatemala, and I have been told they appear in Chiapa de Corzo I. Tolstoy notes hemispherical stone bowls from Tlaltilco, and they are characteristic of other sites of the Formative period in the Valley of Mexico.

Stone Bowls with Flaring Rims

Fig. 97

2 specimens; 1 excavated, 1 collected.

Dimensions in cm. of one specimen: rim diameter, 24.0; basal diameter, 16.0; rim height, about 8.0; maximum thickness at base, 2.4.

Both specimens have been ground into form from hard basalt. They have flat bases and low rims that flare outward. The specimen from the surface has a narrow groove around the inner edge of its rim, but there is no evidence of grinding or pecking in the interior of this bowl. The specimen from excavation had burned car-

117

bon adhering to the inner wall, which suggests strongly that these stone bowls were used as cooking vessels.

The excavated bowl came from an Abejas component, and the other bowl was found on the surface of the Ajalpan site.

Effigy Bowls

Fig. 97

5 specimens; 2 excavated, 3 collected.

Dimensions in cm. of one specimen: length, about 15.0; width, about 13.5; wall height, about 3.5; maximum thickness, about 2.6.

These specimens are fragments that had been finely ground into their original shape from granitic stone. One of the more complete surface specimens was half-moon in outline and had a low evenly notched lip. Another fragment, from excavation, was part of a bowl that must have had at least two flanges which protruded from the exterior sides and which possibly represented parts of the body of some animal or fish. The other three fragments were from small bowls, all of which had notched lips and incisions on small areas of their interiors.

Two specimens found in situ came from Venta Salada levels, but the specimens from the surface may be from earlier periods. This type of stone effigy vessel is fairly common in the Valley of Mexico, and is also known from coastal Vera Cruz. The bowls' greatest distribution, however, seems to be in northwestern Mexico, and they are a common feature of the Hohokam culture of the Southwest.

Metates—*Type Descriptions*

Boulder Metate–Milling Stones

Fig. 98

304 specimens; 256 excavated, 48 collected.

Dimensions in cm. of one complete specimen: length, 31.4; width, about 28.0; maximum thickness, 4.4; thickness in center of ground portion, 2.3.

In studying these materials we tried at first to follow the archaeological classification used in the Southwest of the United States, which is based on a distinction between slab and block. It soon became apparent that such a classification was not going to be very helpful in analyzing our materials. Of our 256 specimens from excavation, 157 were slabs of rock-fall or broken river boulders. In the Southwest these would have been classified as either slab or block, but many of our Tehuacan Valley specimens were definitely made of river boulders. Only fourteen excavated specimens appeared to have been made from slabs of rock or from cave rock-

fall, and four of these are over two inches thick, which would exclude them from the slab category of the Southwest. Interestingly enough, nine of the fourteen come from El Riego Cave, which has no river boulders near it. Therefore, as far as the Tehuacan Valley is concerned, the distinction made in the Southwest between slab and block does not seem valid. It may be said then, that the majority of boulder metate–milling stones in the Tehuacan Valley were made from large river boulders, and also that the majority have been slightly ground on one surface with a rotary motion. Only twenty-five excavated specimens had been ground on two surfaces. Other than this circular grinding which resulted from use, there is no evidence of intentional shaping of these stones.

Boulder metate–milling stones are found from El Riego to historic times in the Tehuacan Valley. Although they are not usually recorded from other archaeological sequences in Mexico, I believe that if they were, they would be equally as common.

Boulder Trough Metates

Fig. 99

22 specimens; 12 excavated, 10 collected.

Dimensions in cm. of 2 specimens: length, over 25.0; width, 23.0; thickness, 5.4 and 7.3; maximum depth of ground surface, 1.8 and 4.5.

These metates are made from relatively flat, oval river boulders. One surface is deeply concave and was ground with a back-and-forth motion, probably with a mano held in one hand.

This type of metate is found in the Tehuacan Valley from El Riego to Ajalpan times. Three were found in very much later horizons, but I believe them to be evidence of aboriginal digging. One of the specimens which Helmut de Terra illustrates for the Chalco complex is similar, and so is a small fragment from Chicoloapan. One of the specimens found in the Santa Marta Cave in Chiapas seems to be of this type. In Tamaulipas such metates are common in the Nogales, La Perra, and Ocampo phases. In northwestern Mexico and the United States Southwest, they are found in the Chiricahua periods and become dominant during San Pedro times.

Ovoid Plano-Convex Metates

Fig. 99

167 specimens; 66 excavated, 101 collected.

Dimensions in cm. of excavated and surface specimens from Ts 204: length of one nearly complete specimen, 39.5; width (6 specimens), 10.2–23.6, average, 17.2; thickness (30 specimens), 2.6–8.0, average, 5.5; maximum con-

Fig. 99. Metates. Ovoid plano-convex metate; boulder trough metate; basin-shaped metate.

119

cavity (13 specimens), 0.2–1.2, average, 0.7; maximum edge thickness (7 specimens), 2.3–3.1.

About half of these metates are made of volcanic tufa and the rest either from large sandstone or granitic boulders. Ventral edges have been pecked and ground so that they are convex. Dorsal surfaces were originally pecked almost flat, but back-and-forth grinding resulting from use has made the dorsal surfaces of some examples very slightly concave. The edges between the dorsal and ventral surfaces usually are sharp and are almost pointed in cross section. Since most of the excavated specimens are fragmentary, the whole outline is difficult to determine, but it would seem to be generally oval. Fortunately some complete specimens collected from the surface at the Ajalpan site (Ts 204) reveal that these metates were indeed ovoid in outline. All of the complete examples are extremely large and would require the use of a two-handed mano.

In the Tehuacan region ovoid plano-convex metates first appear in Abejas levels, and they are very prominent in the Ajalpan phase. Their popularity continues to the Conquest.

Saucer-Shaped Lipped Metates

Fig. 96

33 specimens; 19 excavated, 14 collected.

Dimensions in cm. of 13 specimens: thickness (14 specimens), 1.6–6.4, average, 3.3; lip height, 0.2–1.8, average, 0.8; maximum lip thickness, 1.4–4.0, average, 2.0.

The majority of the metates from excavation are made of volcanic tufa, and the others are made of sandstone. They are relatively small and vary in outline from round to oval. Although they may have been pecked into form initially, most of them display grinding marks on all surfaces. Scratches on interiors, however, indicate that most of the interior grinding was accomplished with a back-and-forth motion, and there are only occasional circular scratches. Paint adheres to the interiors of a number of these metates. The bottoms vary from almost flat to very slightly convex. The markedly convex lateral edges fall sharply away to a deeply concave dorsal surface, outlining and encircling the dorsal grinding surface with a sharp ridge.

This type of metate appears only with Formative remains in the Tehuacan Valley; it reaches its greatest popularity in the Ajalpan phase. Tolstoy has recorded similar metates from the Formative period in the Valley of Mexico.

Oblong Lipped Metates

Fig. 96

38 specimens; 17 excavated, 21 collected.

Dimensions in cm. of 7 specimens: thickness, 1.8–5.9, average, 3.3; lip height, 0.3–3.3, average, 1.1; maximum lip thickness, 0.8–3.6; average, 2.1.

Ten metates from excavation are made of volcanic tufa and seven of sandstone. Their surfaces show little evidence of pecking; they seem to have been formed by grinding and abrading. In outline they are roughly oblong—that is, they have two short, straight ends and two long sides connected by rounded corners. Ventral surfaces, or bases, are flat. Very convex lateral edges fall away to relatively flat or slightly concave dorsal grinding surfaces. The scratches from use on the dorsal side are back-and-forth in direction, and the grinding surface is outlined by a fairly prominent ridge. Although not as large as the ovoid plano-convex metates, this type of metate is bigger than the saucer-shaped lipped metates.

Although oblong lipped metates are found in the early Formative Ajalpan phase, they seem to reach their greatest popularity in the Tehuacan Valley during middle or late Formative times, and one specimen is from an early Classic component. This temporal distribution matches that of the Valley of Mexico, where Tolstoy found these metates to be most popular at the Tlaltilco site.

Basin-Shaped Metates

Fig. 99

38 specimens; 13 excavated, 25 collected.

Dimensions in cm.: thickness (4 specimens), 4.1–6.8, average, 5.6; depth (3 specimens), 0.1–1.3, average, 0.8.

Basin-shaped metates all seem to be made of granite or well-consolidated sandstone. They are oval in outline and have been ground into form. They are relatively thick in comparison to their length and width. Bases are quite convex and gradually blend into convex sides, which in turn blend into elongated, concave dorsal surfaces. Although all surfaces show evidence of some grinding, the interiors are much more finely ground and sometimes are almost polished. These metates are not overly wide, and probably a one-handed mano would have been used with them.

In the Tehuacan Valley basin-shaped metates appear in the Santa Maria phase. In the Valley of Mexico they are found in middle and late Formative periods, but Tolstoy also noted that they are found at Teotihuacan, presumably in the Classic period.

Rectangular Tripod Metates

147 specimens; 41 excavated, 106 collected.

Dimensions in cm.: average length, 67; average width, 75. Length of 12 legs, 6.6–15.0, average, 10.0; width of 15 legs, 6.3–13.3, average, 7.8; thickness of 13 legs, 3.3–8.0, average, 4.3. Maximum thickness of working area (13 specimens), 2.9–5.0, average, 3.9; specimens too fragmentary to measure area used for grinding.

These metates are made of volcanic tufa. They are rectangular in outline, with very slightly concave dorsal surfaces. The sides are more or less straight and at right angles to the dorsal grinding surface. Both dorsal and ventral surfaces have been pecked into shape. Ventral surfaces are very slightly convex and rest on three prominent feet. The feet are roughly triangular in outline, although some of our examples are badly worn. In earlier periods the feet tended to be ovoid in cross section, and they became more rectangular later. A single foot centered at one end of the metate is larger and taller than the two feet at the opposite end, which gives the grinding surface a downward slope. Tripod metates are extremely large, and two-handed manos would be used with them.

Tripod metates are first found in the Classic Palo Blanco phase of the Tehuacan sequence but become dominant in the Postclassic Venta Salada phase. This is the type of metate commonly used in the Tehuacan Valley today. In the Valley of Mexico, footed metates first appeared somewhat earlier, in late Formative times, but they reached their greatest popularity in the Postclassic period.

REFERENCES

COE, MICHAEL D.
1961 *La Victoria: An Early Site on the Pacific Coast of Guatemala.* PMAE-P, Vol. 53.

EKHOLM, GORDON F.
1942 *Excavations at Guasave, Sinaloa, Mexico.* AMNH-AP, Vol. 38.

GLADWIN, H. S., *et al.*
1937 *Excavations at Snaketown: Material Culture.* Medallion Papers, No. 25. Globe, Arizona.

JENNINGS, JESSE D.
1957 *Danger Cave.* SAA-M, No. 14. Salt Lake City.

MACNEISH, RICHARD S.
1954 *An Early Archaeological Site near Panuco, Vera Cruz.* APS-T, Vol. 44, Part 5.
1958 *Preliminary Archaeological Investigations in the Sierra de Tamaulipas, Mexico.* APS-T, Vol. 48, Part 6.

MACNEISH, RICHARD S., AND F. A. PETERSON
1962 *The Santa Marta Rock Shelter, Ocozocoautla, Chiapas, Mexico.* Papers of the New World Archaeological Foundation, No. 14, Provo, Utah.

MEDELLIN ZENIL, ALFONSO
1960 *Cerámicas del Totonacapan.* Universidad Veracruzana. Jalapa, Vera Cruz.

SAYLES, E. B., AND ERNST ANTEVS
1941 *The Cochise Culture.* Medallion Papers, No. 22. Globe, Arizona.

TERRA, HELMUT DE
1949 "Early Man in Mexico." *Tepexpan Man.* Viking Fund Publications in Anthropology, No. 11. New York.

TOLSTOY, PAUL
—— "Stone, Bone, and Antler Tools of Central Mexico from Preclassic to Aztec Times." To be published in *Handbook of Middle American Indians.* Austin: University of Texas Press.

VAILLANT, GEORGE C.
1930 *Excavations at Zacatenco.* AMNH-AP, Vol. 32, Part 1.

CHAPTER 8

Artifacts for Other Purposes

A WIDE variety of ground-stone artifacts are included in this chapter. Most of these artifacts were sufficiently different from one another in form and use to be separated almost immediately into distinct classes. The majority of these groups had temporal significance, but since samples were small, the types we established should be considered as trial types only. Before being accepted as valid, they should be tested and compared with larger samples from stratigraphic excavations.

The materials are described in three categories, based on how they were used. The first group includes tools used for grinding and abrading; the second, tools used percussively; and the third, objects that in some way were ornamental.

The earliest type of abrading tool is a hammerstone. It is found principally in the El Riego, Coxcatlan, and Abejas phases. Small paint dishes were first used in the El Riego phase; they appear thereafter throughout the sequence. Anvil stones and polishing pebbles are found in late preceramic horizons and in most of the ceramic phases. Paint palettes, for grinding vegetal and mineral pigments, and rubbed pebbles appear first in late preceramic levels and then continue until the Conquest. Abrader saws originate in Ajalpan times, and they continue in use through the rest of the sequence. Ground-stone disks seem to be confined to the Palo Blanco phase. The one whetstone excavated was found in a Venta Salada component.

As for the tools used percussively, pebble hammer-

Table 19. Tools for Grinding and Abrading from Excavated Components according to Phase

	EL RIEGO	COXCATLAN	ABEJAS	AJALPAN	SANTA MARIA	PALO BLANCO	VENTA SALADA	TOTAL
Rectangular whetstone							1	1
Ground-stone disks						1		1
Abrader saws				3, 1, 2	1, 2, 1 3	1 3, 1, 1	1, 1	21
Slab paint palettes			1 1 1	6 15 7 1, 5 4	1 1 3, 2 1 2, 1, 2 6	2	3, 1	66
Rubbed pebbles			1, 1	2, 1, 1 1	1, 2, 1 1, 1 2	1 1 1	6	24
Polishing pebbles			1 1 1	7 4, 2, 1 1 1	3, 1, 2 1 1 1 4, 1	1, 1, 1	2 5, 2	45
Anvil stones		2	1 1	1 1	1, 1			8
Abrader hammerstones	1 4 2 1	2 1	1 1	1	1	1	1 1	18
Small paint dishes		1		1, 1, 1		1 1		6
TOTAL	1 4 3 1	2 2 1	3 2 4 1 2	14 27 7 4 1 1 2 10 5	1 2 3 2 6 1 2 1 3 2 2 4 5 2 13 1 1	3 7 2 2 1 1 1 1	2 8 1 2 4 7	190

Column headers under each phase (left to right):
- EL RIEGO: Tc 50, XVIII; Tc 50, XVI; Tc 50, XV; Tc 50, XIV
- COXCATLAN: Tc 50, XIII; Tc 50, XI; Tc 307, C
- ABEJAS: Tc 50, X; Tc 50, IX; Tc 50, VIII; Ts 381e, house; Tc 272, L
- AJALPAN: Ts 204, H; Ts 204, G; Ts 204, G¹; Ts 204, F; Ts 204, F¹; Ts 204, E; Ts 368, K³; Ts 368, K²; Ts 368, K
- SANTA MARIA: Ts 368, J; Ts 368e, I; Ts 368e, H; Ts 368e, F; Ts 368e, E; Ts 367, D²; Ts 367, D¹; Ts 367, C; Ts 368e, D; Tc 272, I; Ts 368e, C²; Ts 368e, C¹; Ts 368e, C; Ts 368e, B; Ts 218-10, C; Ts 218-10, B; Tc 50, VII
- PALO BLANCO: Ts 218-6, A; Ts 218-10, A; Tc 272, F; Tc 272, C; Tc 50, V; Tc 50, IV; Ts 35w, 3-4; Tc 35e, E
- VENTA SALADA: Tc 35e, C; Tc 35e, B; Tc 50, II; Tc 35e, A; Ts 367, A; Tr 62, A

Table 20. Tools for Grinding and Abrading from Surface Sites according to Possible Phase

	SANTA MARIA	PALO BLANCO		PALO BLANCO WITH VENTA SALADA REMAINS					PALO BLANCO OR VENTA SALADA							VENTA SALADA WITH PALO BLANCO REMAINS															VENTA SALADA					MULTI-COMPONENT SITES								UNCLASSIFIED			TOTAL
	Tr 212	Tr 73	Tr 291	Tr 302	Tr 207	Tr 153	Tr 301	Tr 322	Tr 304	Tr 280	Tr 196	Tr 198	Tr 193	Tr 305	Tr 240	Tr 306	Tr 328	Tr 23	Tr 324	Tr 276	Tr 350	Tr 319	Tr 244	Tr 216	Tr 357	Tr 230	Tr 184	Tr 187	Tr 42	Tr 56	Tr 88	Tr 327	Tr 323	Tr 337	Tr 91	Tr 204c	Tr 204E	Tr 204	Tr 367	Tr 223	Tr 368	Tr 218	Tr 218B	Tr 349	Ts 352	Ts 312	TOTAL
Rectangular whetstone																						1																									1
Ground-stone disks								2										1					1														1	2	1	1					2	1	12
Abrader saws							1		1												1									1																	4
Slab paint palettes												1					1			1										1				1			1	1	10		1					1	19
Rubbed pebbles																															1																1
Polishing pebbles		1	1	1	1	1	2			1	2		3	1	1	1			1	1				1	1		1	2	3			1	1					13	1								42
Anvil stones																																				13			1								14
Abrader hammerstones																										1																3	1				5
Small paint dishes	1																																		1				1					1			4
TOTAL	1	1	1	1	1	1	3	2	1	1	2	1	3	1	1	1	1	1	1	2	1	1	1	1	1	1	1	2	3	2	1	1	1	1	1	13	2	16	14	1	1	3	1	1	2	2	102

stones are found throughout the sequence; adzes seem to be confined to the Ajalpan and Santa Maria horizons; square-polled celts appear from the Ajalpan through the Venta Salada phase; and pointed-poll celts extend from the Santa Maria phase to the Conquest. A single full-grooved maul was found at a Palo Blanco site. Rectangular grooved barkbeaters were found in both Palo Blanco and Venta Salada horizons, and one club barkbeater was collected from the surface at a Venta Salada site. Two trapezoidal hoelike tools came from a surface and an excavated Venta Salada component.

Ground-stone ornaments had a more limited time range. Discoidal beads, which were the earliest type, were first made in the Abejas phase and lasted to the Conquest. Spherical beads were found throughout ceramic times. Our so-called atlatl weights, which may instead have been ornaments, appeared in the Ajalpan and Santa Maria phases. Stone pendants, earplugs, and labrets may have lasted from the Ajalpan phase to the Conquest.

Tools Used for Grinding and Abrading— *Trial Types*

Abrader Hammerstones

Fig. 100

23 specimens; 18 excavated, 5 collected.

Dimensions in cm.: length (10 specimens), 2.3–15.2, aver-age, 7.3; width (15 specimens), 1.1–4.2, average, 2.0; thickness (16 specimens), 0.5–2.5, average, 1.4.

Long, narrow pieces of schist, sandstone, or other sedimentary rock were selected for these tools. The long, narrow edges or the elongated surfaces of hammerstones show some evidence of rubbing or abrading. Twelve examples display fine pecking on one end and four examples are finely pecked on both ends.

Abrader hammerstones are found most frequently in the El Riego phase, but they last into Coxcatlan and Abejas times. Three were found from still later periods, but the incidence is insignificant. Abrader hammerstones have not, as far as I know, been reported for other areas of Mesoamerica.

Small Paint Dishes

Fig. 101

10 specimens; 6 excavated, 4 collected.

Dimensions in cm. of 4 specimens: length, 8.2–10.2, aver-age, 9.3; width (3 specimens only), 5.1–9.3; average, 7.6; depth, 0.5–1.1, average, 0.6.

Three of the excavated dishes used for grinding paints were made from quite small ovoid pebbles, and two were made of volcanic tufa. The sixth example was a fragment, the exterior edges of which had been roughly pecked to give a circular outline, and one surface was deeply ground and pecked to make it concave. Paint

Fig. 100. Abrader hammerstones, actual size.

These river pebbles have been polished through use so that a part of their surface has a high shine. Seven examples from Formative components had red paint on them, and two from the Classic had been used so often that one surface was worn flat.

From the Abejas phase onward, polishing pebbles appear throughout the Tehuacan sequence. They are also found throughout the Valley of Mexico sequence.

Anvil Stones

Fig. 103

22 specimens; 8 excavated, 14 collected.

Dimensions in cm. of 3 specimens: length, 5.2–8.9, average, 6.4; width, 4.9–6.4, average, 5.5; thickness (6 specimens), 1.1–5.3, average, 3.2.

Anvil stones are made from relatively flat pebbles. A small area of one of the flattened surfaces has been pecked. The flattened surfaces of an oblong mano, a cuboid mano, a polishing pebble, and a rectangular pestle had been used as anvils.

Anvil stones were found from Coxcatlan to Palo Blanco times in the Tehuacan Valley. This type is widespread over much of North America and usually is found over longer time spans.

Rubbed Pebbles

25 specimens; 24 excavated, 1 collected.

Dimensions in cm. of 12 specimens: length (11 specimens only), 4.8–11, average, 6.4; width, 4.0–8.1, average, 6.3; thickness, 2.6–5.9, average, 4.5.

Rubbed pebbles are small ovoid pebbles. Usually a small area on one side of the pebble has been ground or rubbed to produce a concave surface. Although they re-

still adhered to the concave surfaces of three specimens.

Small paint dishes were first made in the El Riego phase of the Tehuacan sequence, and they continued in use through the Palo Blanco phase. They are a common vessel throughout Mexico.

Polishing Pebbles

Figs. 102, 103

87 specimens; 45 excavated, 42 collected.

Dimensions in cm.: length (13 specimens), 1.6–9.9, average, 5.5; width (17 specimens), 1.1–8.2, average, 4.4; thickness (18 specimens), 0.8–5.5, average, 3.1.

Fig. 101. Small paint dish, actual size.

124

semble ovoid mullers or manos, rubbed pebbles differ in that they were not the grinding agent but rather the stone on which a grinding tool was used.

So far in Mesoamerica, rubbed pebbles have been recorded only from the Tehuacan Valley. They appear from Abejas to Venta Salada times.

Slab Paint Pallettes

Fig. 104
85 specimens; 66 excavated, 19 collected.

Paint pallettes are shallow slabs of sedimentary rock, usually limestone or sandstone, one small flattened portion of which has been ground. They usually contain hematite paint. The grinding is so shallow that it might go unnoticed if the vestiges of paint did not attract attention; however, under a microscope the grinding is visible.

Our specimens are so fragmentary that no true dimensions can be given. None of the fragments is over 3.0 cm. thick, and the average thickness is 1.7 cm. Lengths range from 6.6 to 8.9 cm. and average 7.7 cm. The fragments range in width from 3.6 to 8.9 cm. and average 7.0 cm.

Three paint pallettes are from the Abejas phase, and others appeared throughout the rest of the Tehuacan sequence. Paint pallettes have been excavated throughout most of North America.

Abrader Saws

Fig. 105
25 specimens; 21 excavated, 4 collected.

Fig. 102. Polishing pebble, two views, actual size.

Fig. 103. Anvil stones, actual size. The specimen on the left is a polishing pebble also used as an anvil.

125

Fig. 104. Slab paint palette, actual size.

Dimensions in cm. of 7 specimens: length (6 specimens only), 4.8–11.9, average, 7.8; width, 3.2–10.5, average, 4.9; thickness, 0.8–3.7, average, 1.5.

Abrader saws are made from relatively flat slabs of slate, shale, sandstone, or jadeite. They show evidence of rubbing or grinding along one edge, which is probably the result of their having been used with a sawlike motion in some kind of groove.

Abrader saws first appear in the Ajalpan phase of the Tehuacan sequence and continue through the Venta Salada period. They have a similar span elsewhere in central Mesoamerica.

Ground-Stone Disks

Fig. 106

13 specimens; 1 excavated, 12 collected.
Dimensions in cm.: diameter (5 specimens), 4.2–13, average, 7.0; thickness (8 specimens), 1.0–2.3, average, 1.5.

Ground-stone disks are made from flat slabs of sandstone, shale, or mica schist. They look as though the flat surfaces were first smoothed somewhat, and then the edges were ground until the slab assumed a circular, disklike appearance. The circular edges, which vary from almost flat to very definitely rounded, look worn. The disks perhaps were used in a grinding process.

The only disk found in excavation in the Tehuacan Valley came from a Palo Blanco site. Similar specimens have not been recorded from other parts of Mexico.

Rectangular Whetstones

2 specimens; 1 excavated, 1 collected.

The whetstone from excavation was made from a flat pebble. Its edges were ground smooth, which gave it a

rectangular outline, 8.4 cm. long and 3.3 cm. wide. Its surface had been ground, or abraded against, until the stone was about 1.6 cm. thick. It came from the Venta Salada level of Las Canoas site.

Tools Used Percussively—*Trial Types*

Pebble Hammerstones

374 specimens; 363 excavated, 11 collected.
Dimensions in cm.: length (48 specimens), 3.2–15.8, average, 7.6; width (55 specimens), 1.9–9.7, average, 5.3; thickness (57 specimens), 1.2–8.3, average, 4.2.

Fig. 105. Abrader saws, actual size. The lower specimen is also shown in profile.

126

Table 21. Tools for Chopping or Beating from Excavated Components according to Phase

	AJUEREADO		EL RIEGO																COXCATLAN			ABEJAS		PURRON		AJALPAN											SANTA MARIA																					PALO BLANCO								VENTA SALADA									TOTAL
	Tc 50 XXIII	Tc 35w, 6	Tc 50, XXII	Tc 50, XXI	Tc 255, C	Tc 50, XX	Tc 50, XIX	Tc 307, H	Tc 50, XVIII	Tc 50, XVII	Tc 272, R	Tc 50, XVI	Tc 35w, 5	Ts 51, DE	Tc 307, F	Tc 50, XV	Tc 50, XIV	Tc 381w, pit	Tc 50, XIII	Tc 50, XI	Tc 307, C	Tc 50, X	Tc 50, IX	Tc 272, K	Tc 272, K'	Ts 204, H	Ts 272, J	Ts 204, G	Ts 204, G'	Ts 204, F	Ts 204, F'	Ts 204, E	Ts 368e, K²	Ts 368e, K'	Ts 368e, K	Ts 368e, J	Ts 368e, I	Ts 368e, G	Ts 368e, F	Ts 368e, E	Ts 367, D²	Ts 367, D'	Ts 367, C	Ts 368e, D	Ts 272, I	Ts 368e, C²	Ts 368e, C'	Ts 272, H	Ts 368e, C	Ts 368w, D	Ts 272, G	Ts 368e, B	Ts 204, A	Ts 218-6, G	Ts 218-11, C	Ts 218-10, C	Tc 50, VII	Ts 218-6, A	Ts 218-10, A	Tc 272, F	Tc 50, VI	Tc 272, C	Tc 254, B	Tc 50, V	Tc 35e, E	Tc 35e, C	Tc 35e, B	Tc 50, II	Tc 35w, 2	Tc 35w, 1	Tc 35e, A	Ts 367, A	Tc 62, A	Tc 65, A	
Club barkbeater																																																																													
Full-grooved maul																																																																											
Trapezoidal hoe																																																																				1							1
Rectangular grooved barkbeaters																																																																		1						1			2
Pointed-poll celt																																																					1		2		1									1						1			5
Square-poll celt																										1	1		1														1	1				1										1																1	8
Celt fragments																										2				1													2					1	1		1					3	1	1															13
Square-poll adzes																											1																	1																														2
Pebble hammerstones	1	1	2	2	3	1	1	1	12	3	4	18	1	10	1	9	4	10	5	1	1	1	1	1	1	44		31	10	20	11	7	2	12	6	8	8	5	3	9	4	1	4	5	2	3	1	2	1	2	2	3	2	1	6	19	2	5	3	1	1	1	1	1	5	2	3	1	2	2	1		6	2	363
TOTAL	1	1	2	2	3	1	1	1	12	3	4	18	1	10	1	9	4	10	5	1	1	1	1	1	1	44	3	33	10	20	11	8	2	13	6	8	8	5	3	9	4	1	7	7	2	3	1	2	1	2	2	4	2	1	6	19	2	5	6	1	1	2	1	1	5	3	3	1	4	2	1	1	7	2	394

Fig. 106. Ground-stone disks, actual size.

Either river pebbles or hard cobble stones were used as hammerstones. There is a slight tendency for the smaller ones to appear early in the sequence and for the larger ones to be found with ceramics, but the tendency is not sufficiently great to justify subdividing the group into two types. Since the aborigines apparently picked up random pebbles when they needed a hammer, there is considerable variation in the shape of these artifacts. The most common forms are ellipsoidal or egg-shaped, but elongated, spherical, discoidal, and elongate-cuboid forms also are found. The majority show evidence of pecking from use on one of the narrow edges; about a fifth of the sample are pecked on both narrow ends, and a minority are pecked on two ends and the sides. Three specimens were pecked on one end and on two sides; two on both ends and one side, and another on one end and one side. These three variants were found with Formative remains.

Pebble hammerstones are found throughout the Tehuacan sequence, and they are widespread in the New World.

Square-Poll Adzes

Fig. 107

9 specimens; 2 excavated, 7 collected.

Dimensions in cm. of 5 specimens: length, 5.4–12.2, average, 9.1; width (8 specimens), 2.3–6.0, average, 4.4; thickness, 1.2–3.7, average, 2.3.

Four of the adzes are made of gray granite and five of a hard greenstone. All have been ground and polished into shape, after first having been sawed with a blade. They are rectangular in cross section, and have a flat

127

Table 22. Tools for Chopping or Beating from Surface Sites according to Possible Phase

	SANTA MARIA	PALO BLANCO			PALO BLANCO WITH VENTA SADADA REMAINS						PALO BLANCO OR VENTA SALADA														VENTA SALADA WITH PALO BLANCO REMAINS															VENTA SALADA			MULTI-COMPONENT SITES					UNCLASSIFIED		TOTAL
	Ts 67	Tr 73	Tr 73B	Tr 16	Tr 229	Tr 205	Tr 173	Tr 301	Tr 106	Tr 102	Tr 304	Tr 30	Tr 196	Tr 198	Tr 199	Tr 308	Tr 135	Tr 287	Tr 178	Tr 192	Tr 283	Tr 293	Tr 278	Tr 210	Tr 324	Tr 167	Tr 151	Tr 120	Tr 244	Tr 216	Tr 357	Tr 245	Tr 339	Tr 289	Tr 288	Tr 285	Tr 294	Tr 187	Tr 78	Tr 191	Tr 337	Tr 91	Tr 204	Tr 367	Tr 218	Tr 218A	Tr 218B	Tr 352	Tr 298	
Club barkbeater																																	1																		1
Full-grooved maul																			1																															1
Trapezoid hoe							1																																											1
Rectangular grooved barkbeaters																																																1		1
Pointed-poll celt		1					1							2										2									1									1	1		1	3		1		14
Square-poll celt	1	1	1		2		1			2	1						2				2	1			1							1		1		1						1	1	1	1		1			23
Celt fragments		2	1				1		1	2	1		2										2	1	1										2		1	1	2					6	3	1	1			31
Square-poll adzes		1									1	1																							1	1										1			1	7
Pebble hammerstones		1								1	1				1			1		1	1				1													1	1	1										11
TOTAL	1	5	2	1	2	2	2	2	2	2	2	2	1	2	1	2	1	3	1	1	4	1	1	2	1	1	1	1	1	1	2	2	1	1	1	1	1	1	2	1	1	1	8	2	8	1	2	1	2	90

ventral surface and a convex dorsal surface which slopes sharply toward one end to form a cutting edge. Seven of the sample are rectangular in outline, and two examples are slightly wider at the cutting edge than at the poll.

The two adzes from excavation came from the Formative periods, Ajalpan and Santa Maria, but some of the surface examples may be from the Classic period.

Fig. 107. Square-poll adz, actual size.

Tolstoy records square-poll adzes only in Classic times in the Valley of Mexico.

Square-Polled Celts

Fig. 108

31 specimens; 8 excavated, 23 collected.

Dimensions in cm.: length (2 specimens), less than 8.2 to more than 9.5; width (4 specimens), 1.8–7.0, average, 4.3; thickness (5 specimens), 0.7–2.4, average, 1.6.

Five square-polled celts from excavation were made of greenstone and the other three of dark granite. In cross section these celts are rectangular, and they were shaped by grinding. The bases or polls are square or very slightly convex, and they are at right angles to the sides and surfaces. The widest part of the tool is the cutting edge, although it is only slightly wider than the base. The surfaces are very slightly convex, except where they slope sharply toward the cutting edge. The angle of the slope leading to the cutting edge is identical on each side.

In the Tehuacan region, square-polled celts first appear in Formative levels and last through Postclassic times. They have a similar distribution in the Valley of Mexico.

Pointed-Poll Celts

Fig. 108

19 specimens; 5 excavated, 14 collected.

Dimensions in cm. of 3 specimens: length (one specimen

Fig. 108. Celts, actual size. *Upper and lower left,* square-poll celts, front and side views; *upper right,* celt fragment, two views; *lower right,* pointed-poll celt, two views.

not much longer than it is wide, and a wide, shallow groove has been ground around its middle.

The maul was found on the surface of a Palo Blanco site. Tolstoy notes a similar maul from El Arbolillo 2 in the Valley of Mexico.

Rectangular Grooved Barkbeaters

Figs. 110, 135
3 specimens; 2 excavated, 1 collected.
Dimensions in cm. of 2 specimens: length, 9.5 and 7.5; width, 7.5 and 4.5; thickness, 2.7 and 3.8.

The two excavated barkbeaters are made of volcanic tufa. Both are oblong in outline and roughly rectangular in cross section. A deep, wide groove runs around the circumference of the smaller specimen, and a deep, less wide groove runs around the sides and distal end of the larger specimen. The larger beater was found with its

Fig. 109. Full-grooved maul, actual size.

Fig. 110. Rectangular grooved barkbeater, two views, actual size. See also Fig. 135.

only), slightly over 14.2; width, 4.8–7.7; thickness, 3.0–4.5.

All the pointed-poll celts in our sample are made from hard greenstone and have been ground into shape. They are roughly triangular in outline, with a pointed—or almost pointed—poll. In cross section they range from round to oval. Both wider surfaces are convex, and these slope gradually to the cutting edge.

Pointed-poll celts are found in the Tehuacan region from late Formative times through the Postclassic period. In the Valley of Mexico they seem to appear earlier but otherwise have approximately the same temporal distribution.

Full-Grooved Maul

Fig. 109
1 specimen collected from Tr 287.
Dimensions in cm.: length, 9.1; width, 8.6; thickness, 8.4.

The maul is made of basalt. It is roughly circular in cross section and has ground, slightly convex ends. It is

130

racket-shaped wooden handle fitted into this groove (see Fig. 135 and p. 157 for illustration and description). This specimen has ten parallel longitudinal incisions on one surface, and the smaller beater (Fig. 110) has seven parallel incisions on one surface; the opposite surfaces are unmarked. The barkbeater from the surface has eight parallel grooves on each of its flat surfaces.

As is the case in much of Mesoamerica, the Tehuacan grooved barkbeaters are from Classic and Postclassic components.

Club Barkbeater

Fig. 111
1 specimen collected from Tr 120.

The club-shaped barkbeater was abraded or ground into form from hard gray stone. The distal end is oblong in both outline and cross section and is about 14.2 cm. long, 5.5 cm. wide, and 4.8 cm. thick. The two narrower sides each have a series of parallel grooves—fourteen on one side and sixteen on the other—about 0.1 cm. wide and deep, about 0.2 cm. apart, and about 13.5 cm. long. The incised portion of the barkbeater merges into a tapering, nearly cylindrical handle, about 12.5 cm. long and ranging from 2.5 to 5.0 cm. in diameter.

This unique specimen came from the surface of a Venta Salada site in the Tehuacan Valley. Stone club barkbeaters are of unknown archaeological age in both Mexico and Southeast Asia. However, since they are sufficiently complex in form and are associated with an intricate method of making barkcloth, some kind of genetic connection is possible. Unfortunately, the necessary evidence for making such a connection is still lacking.

Trapezoidal Hoes

Fig. 112
2 specimens; 1 excavated, 1 collected.
Dimensions in cm. of one specimen: length, 11.4; width at narrow end, 5.8; width at cutting edge, 10.0; thickness, 1.6.

The specimen from excavation is a hoelike object made from a flat piece of sandstone. The edges were flaked to give it a trapezoidal form, and then the wider end was ground on both sides to give it a sharp cutting edge. The specimen from the surface is fragmentary.

The excavated specimen was found in a Postclassic component. In the Valley of Mexico, Tolstoy records trapezoidal hoes for both Classic and Postclassic periods.

Fig. 111. Club barkbeater, two views.

131

Fig. 112. Trapezoidal hoes.

Ornaments—*Trial Types*

Discoidal Beads

Fig. 113
46 specimens; 26 excavated, 20 collected.
Dimensions in cm.: diameter (5 specimens), 0.7–1.6; thickness (6 specimens), 0.1–0.6.

The discoidal beads are made of jadeite, gray stone, or obsidian. Probably a long thin cylinder was ground into shape and sawed into a number of disks. A hole was then ground in the center of each disk. Four of the holes appear to have been made with a hand drill, but a bead from Zone F of Ts 204 could have been drilled with a bow drill.

132

Table 23. Ornaments from Excavated Components according to Phase

	ABEJAS	AJALPAN										SANTA MARIA														PALO BLANCO	VENTA SALADA							TOTAL
	Tc 50, VIII	Ts 204, H	Ts 204, G	Ts 204, G^1	Ts 204, F	Ts 204, F^1	Ts 368, K^3	Ts 368, K^2	Ts 368, K^1	Ts 368, J	Ts 368, I	Ts 368, G	Ts 368, F	Ts 368, E	Ts 367, D^2	Ts 367, D^1	Ts 367, C	Ts 368e, C^1	Ts 368e, C	Ts 368e, B	Tc 218-11, F	Ts 368e, B^1	Ts 204, A	Ts 218-10, C	Tc 35w, 3-4	Tc 35e, C	Tc 35w, 3	Tc 50, II	Tc 35w, 2	Tc 35w, 1	Ts 368, A	Tc 35e, A	
Labrets																	1	1		1													3
Polished minerals															1	2	1																4
Ear plugs				2	1	1			1			1	1	1		1	1		1				1								1	1	14
Discoidal beads	1				2									10							1			2				4	1	3		2	26
Spherical beads								1																	2	1	1						5
Pendants		1	2	1	1	1	1	1	1						1	2			1			1							1		1		16
Atlatl weights										1	1																						2
TOTAL	1	1	2	3	4	2	1	2	2	1	1	1	1	11	2	5	3	1	2	1	1	1	1	2	2	1	1	4	2	3	2	3	70

Discoidal beads are found from late preceramic times to the Spanish Conquest, both in the Tehuacan region and in much of Mesoamerica.

Spherical Beads

Fig. 113
8 specimens; 5 excavated, 3 collected.

Two of the excavated beads are made of jade, two of white stone, and one of gray stone. One specimen may have been ground initially to form a sphere, but the other four appear to have been thick disks cut from a cylinder and then ground into spherical form. Before they were ground, they were pierced, perhaps with a bow drill. They range from 0.4 to 1.1 cm. in diameter.

In the Tehuacan Valley, as well as in the rest of Mexico, spherical beads first appear in late Formative times and last to the Conquest.

Atlatl Weights

Fig. 114
2 specimens excavated.

The first of these specimens, illustrated at the left of Fig. 114 is of gray steatite. It has been drilled longitudinally by a tubular bit about 1.2 cm. in diameter. The relative straightness of the hole, which is drilled less than half way through, suggests that a bow drill was used. This specimen is approximately hour-glass

Table 24. Ornaments from Surface Sites according to Possible Phase

	PALO BLANCO	PALO BLANCO OR VENTA SALADA	PALO BLANCO WITH VENTA SALADA REMAINS	VENTA SALADA WITH PALO BLANCO REMAINS			VENTA SALADA			MULTI-COMPONENT SITES				TOTAL
	Tr 77	Tr 301	Tr 117	Tr 52	Tr 211	Tr 43	Tr 289	Tr 323	Tr 179	Tr 142	Tr 204	Tr 367	Tr 218B	Tr 204 E	
Labrets		1								1	1	2			5
Polished minerals															0
Ear plugs:															
tubular											2				2
flat														1	1
Discoidal beads	1		1		1	1	3			12	1				20
Spherical beads										1	1	1			3
Pendants			1	1			1				7	1	1		12
Atlatl weights															0
TOTAL	1	1	2	1	1	2	3	1	1	12	10	5	1	2	43

shaped, and the outer surface is highly polished. The fragment measures 5.5 cm. long and 3.9 cm. wide.

The other specimen, shown at the right in the illustration, could conceivably have been used as an atlatl

133

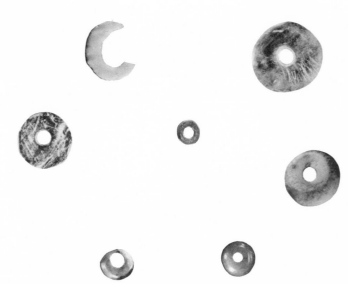

weight. It is a fragment of a natural stony deposit, such as forms on reeds or sticks in heavily mineralized water. Its longitudinal trough-like depression appears to be a mold of the object about which it grew, but one end of the depression has been slightly modified. In length the piece measures 5.6 cm.; its maximum width is 3.6 cm.

These stone objects were uncovered in deposits of the Ajalpan and Santa Maria phases of the Tehuacan sequence. I know of no similar types in Mesoamerica. They are reminiscent of atlatl weights from Archaic cultures of the eastern United States.

Pendants

Figs. 115, 116

28 specimens; 16 excavated, 12 collected.

Dimensions in cm.: length (5 specimens), 1.8–6.0, average, 4.0; width (7 specimens), 0.5–2.8, average, 1.8; thickness (8 specimens), 0.1–1.4, average, 0.7.

Fig. 113. Discoidal and spherical beads, actual size.

Fig. 114. Atlatl weights, actual size. *Left,* three views of an unfinished weight; *right,* two views of a second specimen.

Fig. 116. Effigy pendants, actual size.

Fig. 115. Stone pendants, actual size.

The pendants are made of jadeite, gray stone, or white stone. They were first sawed into shape and then ground or polished. The flat pendants are either rectangular, oblong, or oval, except for one oddly shaped specimen with a large hump along one side (Fig. 115). All of these pendants have a hole in one end, usually made with a bow drill, and some of them have a second hole beside or beneath the first one.

Four examples, however, are rather special (Fig. 116). One extremely small specimen has been cut in the outline of a bird, with a hole through the bird's head. Two others are in roughly human form, with horizontal grooves separating the head from the body and the body from the legs. One of these pendants has three partially drilled holes to represent the eyes and mouth, and the other has a horizontal hole drilled from one edge to the other, almost literally from ear to ear. This

135

hole also seems to have been made with a bow drill. The fourth unique pendant is a small animal head of jadeite. A hole for suspension is drilled through the back of the head from opposite sides. Under pointed doglike ears and a creased, rather bulbous forehead are two large conical drillings for eyes. A large blunted muzzle is marked with two nostrils and a wide, partially open mouth. The boxer-like appearance of this head suggests that the animal represented is a dog.

In the Tehuacan Valley stone pendants were first manufactured in the early Formative Ajalpan phase, and they continued to be made through the Postclassic Venta Salada phase. In the rest of Mexico, they appear to cover a similar time span. All the effigy pendants from Tehuacan are from Formative components.

Earplugs

Fig. 117

17 specimens; 14 excavated, 3 collected.

Dimensions in cm.: length (3 specimens), 0.8–3.5; diameter (2 specimens), 3.2; wall thickness (5 specimens), 0.1–0.4.

The earplug specimens are fragments, and it is difficult to discern their original form. However, they seem to have been roughly spool-shaped. The earlier examples, which were usually made of pottery, were larger and wider than later ones. The latest example is flatter than the others, and is very constricted at the central part of the spool. The stone earplugs were ground from jadeite, obsidian, and a hard brown stone.

Earplugs are found from Formative to Postclassic times in Mesoamerica, including the Tehuacan Valley.

Labrets

Fig. 117

8 specimens; 3 excavated, 5 collected.

Dimensions in cm. of 4 specimens: length, 1.0–2.4, average, 2.1; diameter of rim, 1.2–2.1, average, 1.6. Basal length of one specimen only, 2.5—but the others must have been longer.

Two labrets are made of obsidian, two of onyx, and the others of jadeite. They have usually been ground into the shape of small stove-pipe hats—or perhaps "high hats" would be a better description—with cylindrical bodies and thin ovoid rims to catch the inner lip.

The labrets found in excavation came from Santa Maria components. Others have not been recorded for Mesoamerica.

Miscellaneous Objects

Throughout the sequence, we found small fragments of hematite, and some of this had been ground. From Ajalpan times on, fragments of yellow ochre were found.

Fig. 117. Ear plugs and labrets, actual size. *Row 1:* early ear plugs, made of pottery; *rows 2,3:* later ear plugs. *Row 4:* labrets, end and side views.

At Coatepec, in Zone C, a large cylinder of ground galena was uncovered, and at Quachilco, in Test 10, Zone A, we excavated a piece of ground copper. A cylindrical object of stone with a high content of copper was found in Zone A of the Coatepec Site. A small slab of polished onyx was uncovered in Zone C of the East Niche of El Riego Cave.

A fragment of stone on which was carved a large geometric glyph came from the surface of Tr 117, a Palo Blanco site. Three stone balls, about 6 to 10 cm. in diameter, were collected from Tr 302, Tr 208, and Tr 199, all Palo Blanco sites. Some stone statues of animals or deities had been found previously in the Tehuacan Valley, but their provenience is unknown.

REFERENCES

COE, MICHAEL D.
   1961   *La Victoria: An Early Site on the Pacific Coast of Guatemala.* PMAE-P, Vol. 53.

MacNEISH, RICHARD S.
   1954   *An Early Archaeological Site near Panuco, Vera Cruz.* APS-T, Vol. 44, Part 5.
   1958   *Preliminary Archaeological Investigations in the Sierra de Tamaulipas, Mexico.* APS-T, Vol. 48, Part 6.

TOLSTOY, PAUL
   1963   "Cultural Parallels between Southeast Asia and Mesoamerica in the Manufacture of Bark Cloth." *Transactions of the New York Academy of Science,* Series II, 25:646–62.
   ——   "Stone, Bone, and Antler Tools of Central Mexico from Preclassic to Aztec Times." To be published in *Handbook of Middle American Indians.* Austin: University of Texas Press.

VAILLANT, GEORGE C.
   1930   *Excavations at Zacatenco.* AMNH-AP, Vol. 32, Part 1.

PART III: OTHER CLASSES OF ARTIFACTS

CHAPTER 9

Bone, Antler, Shell, and Copper Artifacts

Only a few bone, antler, shell, and copper artifacts were found in the Tehuacan excavations. For descriptive purposes, I have divided these artifacts into a series of trial types and have plotted their distribution throughout our various components. When better comparative data are available from larger samples found in good archaeological context, perhaps some of these trial groups may become valid final types. In any event, I hope the data and illustrations presented in this chapter will be useful to those undertaking classification in the future.

Bone Artifacts—*Trial Types*

Split-Bone Awls

Fig. 118
30 specimens excavated.

These awls were made from split long bones of animals. One end of the split bone was ground to a point. The basal portions on all but two specimens are broken, and therefore some of the sample could be fragments of other types of awls. The two more complete examples have rounded bases. All the specimens are from 5.0 to over 7.0 cm. long, 1.0 cm. wide, and 0.5 cm. thick.

Split-bone awls appear in the Tehuacan sequence from El Riego times on; they were a common tool in the New World.

Deer-Tibia Awls

Fig. 118
2 specimens excavated.

These awls are made from split pieces of deer tibiae which retain the proximal ends. The splintered end has been ground to a point. One complete example is 17.1 cm. long, the shaft is about 0.8 cm. thick, and the maximum width at the proximal end is 2.8 cm.

In the Tehuacan Valley these awls are found in the El Riego horizon.

Proximal-End Metapodial Awls

Fig. 118
4 specimens excavated.

These awls are made from deer metapodials with proximal ends attached. A sliver of the shank has been polished to a point. They range from 8.0 to 12.6 cm. long, from 1.2 to 1.8 cm. in maximum width of shank, and from 0.8 to 1.4 cm. in maximum thickness of shank.

The awls are found from El Riego to historic times in the Tehuacan Valley, and they appear throughout the sequence in the Valley of Mexico.

Distal-End Metapodial or Metatarsal Awls

Fig. 118
16 specimens excavated.

To make these awls, the distal ends of deer metapodials or metatarsals were sliced along the shank at an obtuse angle to the main axis and were then polished to a point. The one complete example is 11.7 cm. long, 2.5 cm. wide, and 1.5 cm. thick.

Distal-end awls are found mainly in the Formative periods of the Tehuacan sequence, although a few are from Classic and Postclassic components. They appear only in the Formative period in the Valley of Mexico.

Antler-Base Hammers

Fig. 119
3 specimens excavated.

The hammers are made from the proximal portions of deer antlers. The head of the hammer was formed by whittling the antler to a dull point a few inches above the base. The handle was formerly the base of the antler,

Table 25. Bone Tools from Excavated Components according to Phase

Column groups by phase: **AJUEREADO** (Tc 50, XXIII); **EL RIEGO** (Tc 50, XIX – XIV); **COXCATLAN** (Tc 50, XIII – XI); **ABEJAS** (Tc 50, X – VIII); **PURRON** (Tc 272, K); **AJALPAN** (Ts 204, H – Ts 368e, J); **SANTA MARIA** (Ts 368e, I – Tc 50, VII); **PALO BLANCO** (Ts 218-10, A – Tc 35e, D); **VENTA SALADA** (Tc 35e, C – Ts 367, A).

	Tc 50, XXIII	Tc 50, XIX	Tc 50, XVIII	Tc 50, XVI	Tc 50, XV	Tc 50, XIV	Tc 50, XIII	Tc 50, XII	Tc 35w, 4	Tc 50, XI	Tc 50, X	Tc 50, IX	Tc 50, VIII	Tc 272, K	Ts 204, H	Ts 204, G	Ts 204, G[1]	Ts 204, F	Ts 204, F[1]	Ts 204, E	Ts 368e, K[2]	Ts 368e, J	Ts 368e, I	Ts 368e, G	Ts 368e, F	Ts 367, D[2]	Ts 367, D[1]	Ts 367, C	Ts 272, H	Ts 368w, D	Ts 368e, B	Ts 218-10, C[1]	Ts 218-6, D	Tc 50, VII	Ts 218-10, A	Tc 50, V	Tc 50, IV	Tc 35e, D	Tc 35e, C	Tc 35e, B	Tc 35w, 3	Tc 50, II	Tc 35w, 2	Tc 368e, A	Tc 35e, A	Ts 367, A	TOTAL
Effigy pendant																																							1								1
Long-bone handle																																	1														1
Sliced human fibula																													1																		1
Puma-tooth pendant																												1																			1
Polished fibulas																										1?					1																2
Human cranium disks																						1													1												2
Polished mammoth or mastodon tusk																				1																											1
Rib weaving tools or spatulas															1								2																					1			4
Rib pendants																					1																	1									2
Drilled scapula																					1																										1
Bird-bone beads														1							1	1									1								1							1	6
Metapodial or metatarsal awls, distal ends															1	2					1		1	1	1		1	1		1	1	1	1		2									1			16
Cut or split antler tips								1	1																																						2
Flat bone needles							1								1	1		1											1																1		6
Metapodial awls, proximal ends			1											1																										1				1			4
Round antler needles								4			1									2			1	1	1			1							1									1			13
Pentagonal plaque					1																																										1
Antler-tine flakers					1							1		1						1														1	1												6
Deer tibia awls			1	1																																											2
Antler-base hammers		1			1															1																											3
Split-bone awls				1	1	3	1				1	1	1	1	1			2			1	2									1			3	1		1		1	1	2	1		1	1	1	30
Worked antlers or bones	1					3									1	1													1						4	1				2						2	16
TOTAL	1	1	2	1	3	12	2	1	1	4	2	1	1	1	3	4	3	8	3	2	2	3	4	1	2	2	3	3	1	2	1	2	2	4	9	1	2	2	3	3	2	2	1	3	2	3	121

to which a small part of the skull adheres. The dull point at the head had been further blunted from use as a hammer. One specimen is 3.4 cm. long, and the horn is about 0.7 cm. in diameter. The other complete example is 5.5 cm. long, 3.5 wide, and 1.9 cm. thick.

In the Tehuacan Valley, antler-base hammers appear from El Riego to Ajalpan times.

Antler-Tine Flakers

Fig. 119
6 specimens excavated.

These specimens are single-prong deer antlers whose tips have been used for flaking. Four specimens consist of the whole prong with part of the skull adhering. Four of the specimens have been charred near the tip, probably to make them harder. The length of the four complete specimens ranges from 8.9 to 18.1 cm. and averages 13.2 cm.

In the Tehuacan Valley antler-tine flakers are found from the early preceramic El Riego phase through the Postclassic Venta Salada phase. In the Valley of Mexico they are found from the early Formative through the Postclassic period.

Round Antler or Bone Needles

Fig. 120
13 fragments excavated.

These fragments of needles are made from slivers of bone or antler. They have been polished so that they have a circular cross section and a long tapering point. The longest fragment measures 10.8 cm., and the smallest complete example is 5.5 cm. long. The needles range from 0.3 to 0.7 cm. in maximum diameter. Three of the more complete specimens had eyes slotted through them, and one had a bored eye. One needle had a groove carved around it.

Fig. 118. Awls, actual size. *Row 1:* split-bone awl; distal-end metatarsal awl. *Row 2:* distal-end metapodial awl; proximal-end metapodial awl; deer-tibia awl.

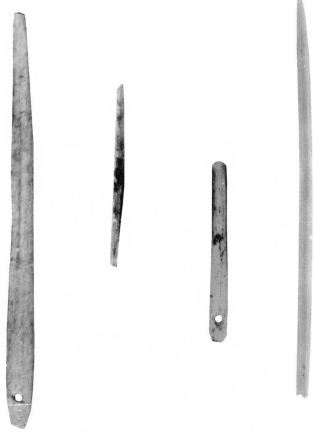

Fig. 120. Bone and antler needles, actual size. The left-hand specimen is round; the others are flat.

Fig. 119. Antler-tine flakers and two views of an antler-base hammer. Actual size.

Round needles are found throughout the Tehuacan sequence beginning with the El Riego phase. They also appear throughout the Valley of Mexico sequence.

Flat Bone Needles

Fig. 120
6 specimens excavated.

The fragments of four needles are small slivers of flat bone. They have been polished, and a hole has been drilled through one end. The more complete examples are from 7.0 to 11.3 cm. long, 0.5 to 0.9 cm. wide, and about 0.3 cm. thick.

They appear from Coxcatlan through Venta Salada times in the Tehuacan sequence.

Cut and Split Antler Tips

Fig. 121
2 specimens excavated.

144

Pentagonal Plaque

Fig. 122

This single piece of split long bone has been cut and polished into a boat-shaped outline. It is 5.1 cm. long, 2.1 cm. wide, and about 0.4 cm. thick. The wider end has several shallow parallel grooves across it. It was found in Zone XV of Coxcatlan Cave, an El Riego component.

Bird-Bone Beads

6 specimens excavated.

Tubular sections, from 0.5 to 1.0 cm. in diameter, which had been sawn from the leg bones of birds, were polished for use as beads. They appear in the Ajalpan, Santa Maria, Palo Blanco, and Venta Salada horizons.

Weaving Tools or Spatulas of Rib Bone

Fig. 122
4 specimens excavated.

These four fragments were cut from deer ribs. Each has a flat polished end that has been ground to a rounded tip. They are between 0.3 and 0.5 cm. thick,

Fig. 121. *Row 1:* cut (*left*) and split (*right*) antler tips. *Row 2:* fragment of scapula with a drilled hole; a piece of worked antler. Actual sizes.

One tip cut from a deer antler was found in Zone 4 of the West Niche of El Riego Cave. The other antler tip was from Zone XII of Coxcatlan Cave; both components are of the Coxcatlan phase. The latter specimen came from a tip that had been split longitudinally in half; all its edges were then ground. Both specimens had small worked areas at the tips.

Fig. 122. Weaving tool or spatula of rib bone; bone plaque; handle made of long bone. Actual size.

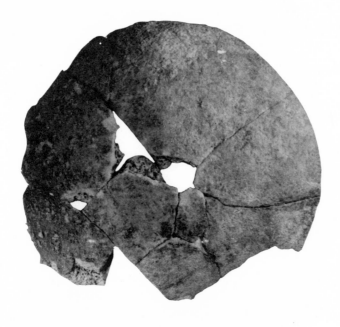

Puma Canine Pendant

A small fragment of a puma canine is highly polished and may have been used as a pendant or bead. It was found in a Santa Maria component.

Long-Bone Handle

Fig. 122

A highly polished long-bone fragment was encircled by two grooves of different widths spaced about 1.0 cm. apart. It must have been over 5.0 cm. long originally and over 2.0 cm. in diameter. It may have been used as a handle. This artifact is from a Santa Maria component.

Human Cranium Disks

Fig. 123
2 specimens excavated.

Two disks cut from human skulls were found in Ajalpan and Palo Blanco components. The more complete example is about 8.5 cm. in diameter.

Rib Pendants

Fig. 124
2 specimens excavated.

One small piece of rib bone cut into trapezoidal form had a narrow groove cut across the middle and another cut across one end. It had been polished so that the edges were sharp. It is 4.0 cm. long, 1.4 cm. wide, and 0.9 cm. thick at the center. This pendant came from a Palo Blanco component. Another small fragment of rib bone was found in an Ajalpan component, and it too was probably used as a pendant.

Effigy Pendant

Fig. 124

This small piece of bone, 4.1 cm. long and about 0.6 in diameter, had been ground into cylindrical form, and

Fig. 123. Disk cut from a human cranium, outer and inner sides, actual size.

have a maximum width of from 1.0 to 2.1 cm., and were probably longer than 9.0 cm.

These tools come from Ajalpan, Santa Maria, and Venta Salada components. In the Valley of Mexico the "spatulas" reported by Tolstoy appear throughout the sequence.

Fig. 124. Rib-bone and effigy pendants, actual size.

146

then each end was polished to a dull point. The lower two-thirds of the pendant is encircled by a series of ten parallel grooves spaced about 0.2 cm. apart. A hole has been hand-drilled through the topmost groove from side to side. At the top of the pendant another hole was bow-drilled at right angles to the first hole. A small human face was etched on the flattened area between the two holes. This effigy pendant is from an early Venta Salada component.

Other Bone or Ivory Objects

A piece of mammoth or mastadon ivory that had been intentionally polished by man was found in Zone F¹ of Ts 204; a piece of scapula with a drilled hole (Fig. 121) came from Zone F of Ts 204; a cut and polished fragment of fibula was found in Zone C¹ of Test 10 of Ts 218, and a similar fragment came from Zone D² of Ts 367. A sliced or grooved piece of human fibula was found in Zone C of Ts 367.

Among sixteen other pieces of worked antler or bone, three cut long bones were found in Zone XIV of Tc 50 and two in Zone B of Tc 35e; two pieces of polished bone came from Zone A of Ts 367; four grooved fragments of long bones came from Zone A of Test 10 of Ts 218, and there were single pieces of worked antler (Fig. 121) or bone in Zone XXIII of Tc 50, Zone H of Ts 204,

Zone G of Ts 204, Zone D² of Ts 367, and Zone IV of Tc 50.

Two pieces of mammoth tusk uncovered in Zone C of Ts 204 were highly polished but gave no evidence of having been worked by human hands.

Shell Artifacts

Shells, except for snail shells, were relatively rare in the Tehuacan sites, and shell artifacts were rarer still. Small, pierced marginella beads uncovered with Burial 2 of Zone XIV of Coxcatlan Cave are the earliest shell artifacts that we found. They date from the latter part of the El Riego phase. Three small discoidal shell beads came from a late level of the West Niche of El Riego Cave. Small discoidal or ovoid pendants made of fresh-water shells were found in various levels of the Ajalpan, Santa Maria, and Venta Salada phases, as well as at two surface sites. A piece of pierced columella was uncovered in a late Santa Maria component, and from earlier components of the same period came two fragments of oliva shells that were pierced at one end to form tinklers. Fragments of worked conch and mollusk shells were found in the refuse and on the surface, but their original purpose was not discernible.

All other identifiable shell artifacts came from the surface. These include two shell tinklers, a notched mol-

Table 26. Shell Artifacts from Excavated and Surface Components

	EL RIEGO	AJALPAN				SANTA MARIA			VENTA SALADA	SURFACE SITES																										TOTAL
	Tc 50, XIV	Ts 204, H	Ts 204, G	Ts 204, G¹	Ts 204, F	Ts 367, D¹	Ts 367, C	Ts 218-6, D	Tc 35w, 1	Ts 204	Ts 323	Ts 316	Ts 297	Ts 294	Ts 310	Ts 218	Ts 75	Ts 184	Ts 276	Ts 323	Ts 362	Ts 155	Ts 197	Ts 209	Ts 221	Ts 231	Ts 287	Ts 330	Ts 301	Ts 339	Ts 343	Ts 344	Ts 345	Ts 358	
Worked fragments:																																			
conch						1																1	1	1	1	1	1	1	1	2	1	2	1	1	16
mollusk		2	1	2		2			1								2	1	1	1	2	1													16
Columella spherical beads						?										2																			2
Columella crescent																	1																		1
Columella disk																1																			1
Discoidal beads									3																										3
Notched mollusk pendants									1									1																	2
Columella pendant							1																												1
Oliva tinklers						1	1			1	1																								4
Mollusk pendants		1		1		1		1	1	1	1																								7
Marginella beads	31																																		31
TOTAL	31	2	2	2	1	2	4	2	6	1	1	1	1	1	1	1	1	4	1	1	1	2	2	1	1	1	1	1	1	1	2	1	2	1	84

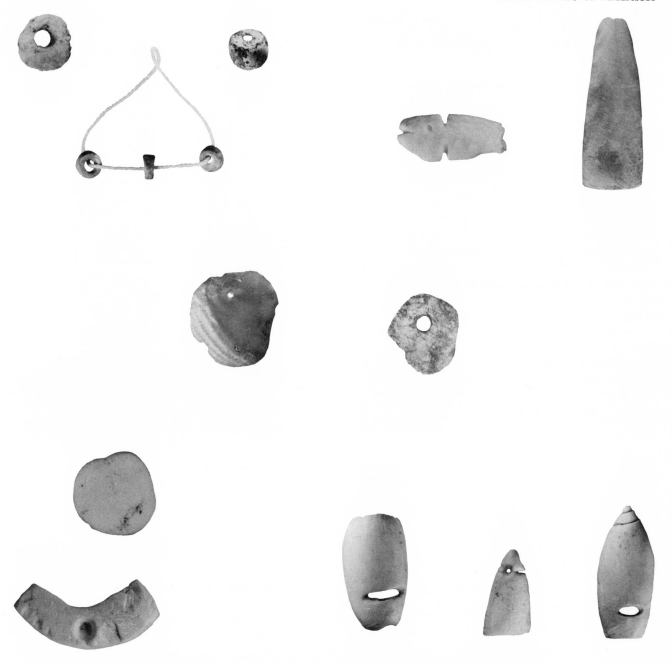

Fig. 125. Shell artifacts, actual size. *Upper left*, 2 large beads of columella and 3 small discoidal beads; *upper right*, fish-shaped and trapezoidal pendants; *center*, fresh-water shell pendants; *lower left*, a columella disk and a half-pierced piece of columella; *lower right*, olive-shell tinklers.

lusk shell pendant in the shape of a fish, a trapezoidal pendant about 4.7 cm. long and 1.7 cm. wide; a disk 2.0 cm. in diameter cut from a columella; two spherical columella beads about 1.0 cm. in diameter, and a crescent-shaped piece about 3.0 cm. long cut from a conch shell.

Table 26 shows the occurrence of shell artifacts in both excavated and surface components. Some of the artifacts are illustrated in Fig. 125.

Copper Artifacts

Although copper stains appeared on a number of bones from the Venta Salada levels of El Riego Cave, and even though private collectors showed us copper coils and bells reputedly from the Tehuacan Valley, we found only one copper artifact in survey and one in excavation.

The larger copper artifact, found during survey, came from Ts 56 and dates from the Venta Salada phase. It is a copper bell made by the lost-wax technique (Fig. 126). The bell is roughly pear-shaped and has a long slit in its base. The cylindrical head is about 1.0 cm. in diameter and is topped by a small looped handle. The bell is 5.5 cm. long and has a maximum diameter of 2.8 cm.

The other artifact, found in Level 1 of Tr 65, the ancient Coxcatlan village, is also of the Venta Salada period. This is a smaller but similar bell, made by the same technique (Fig. 126). It is about 3.5 cm. long and is decorated by thin zig-zag strips of copper welded on opposite surfaces.

Fig. 126. Two copper bells, actual size.

REFERENCES

EKHOLM, GEORGE F.

1944 *Excavations at Tampico and Panuco in the Huasteca, Mexico.* AMNH-AP, Vol. 38.

MacNEISH, RICHARD S.

1954 *An Early Archaeological Site near Panuco, Vera Cruz.* APS-T, Vol. 44, Part 5.

1958 *Preliminary Archaeological Investigations in the Sierra de Tamaulipas, Mexico.* APS-T, Vol. 48, Part 6.

TOLSTOY, PAUL

—— "Stone, Bone, and Antler Tools of Central Mexico from Preclassic to Aztec Times." To be published in *Handbook of Middle American Indians.* Austin: University of Texas Press.

CHAPTER 10

Wooden and Other Vegetal Artifacts

WE FOUND in excavation 228 artifacts or fragments of artifacts made from wood or some other vegetal material, such as cane or gourd. I shall describe these tools as trial types in the following pages. There were in addition some 149 pieces of wood from excavation which showed evidence of human workmanship. Although these pieces could hardly be called artifacts, they do merit brief description.

Fifty-nine of these wooden objects are small sticks, between 0.5 and 6.0 cm. in diameter, with the bark shaved off or stripped away. An additional seventy-eight sticks had been whittled or cut. About a third of these stubs were cut or broken into various lengths by means of an encircling groove. Of course, some of these worked objects may have been parts of wooden artifacts which are now so fragmentary that we cannot recognize them for what they were, or some may have been wooden tools that were never completed.

Besides these shaved and whittled objects, there are twelve fragments which I refer to as "worked logs." They range from 3.5 to 8.7 cm. in diameter, and from 21.2 to 55.0 cm. long. Nine of the smaller ones had been sharpened to a dull point, but perhaps this was a by-product of the method employed to remove them from the original tree or large branch. Each of these logs had been struck a series of hefty blows with some kind of heavy implement, such as an adz, celt, or chopper. The blows had been struck in the same direction around the whole circumference, making one end of the log almost pointed. Apparently, when the encircling chopping had almost cut through, the desired piece of wood was broken off, and in this way the end of the log, although tapering, was blunted. Two of the twelve logs are longer and heavier than the others but had been cut in a similar manner. One of the twelve from a later Palo Blanco level (Zone B of Tc 35e) had been cut in a different

fashion: a series of blows had been struck on one side of this log at an oblique angle to the main axis until the log was cut three-quarters of the way through. Then the opposite side was chopped in a similar manner until severing was completed. We see, then, in our sequence of wood fragments, an evolution from the beaver-like method of cutting—perhaps with an adz—to the lumberjack style of felling—perhaps with an ax.

Wooden Artifacts—*Trial Types*

Pointed Sticks

Fig. 127
26 specimens excavated.

The pointed sticks seem to be of three varieties. The first group consists of split or flattened sticks that have been whittled and then polished to a relatively dull point. They are about 0.8 cm. thick and 1.0 to 2.0 cm. wide. All are broken off at the end opposite the point, so that their original lengths are unknown, but they must have measured more than 5.0 cm. The sticks in the second group are usually less than 1.0 cm. in diameter and are longer than 6.0 cm. They have long, tapering sharp points. The sticks in the third group are larger, between 1.0 and 2.5 cm. in diameter; the longest specimen measures 35.0 cm. They also have tapering, sharp points, but two of the largest sticks also have flattened, pounded ends. The first two varieties are found from the El Riego phase on, but the latter type appears only in late Palo Blanco and Venta Salada levels.

Atlatl

1 specimen excavated.

One wooden atlatl was excavated. It is 1.9 cm. wide, 1.7 cm. thick, and was relatively long. Both ends have been broken off, so it can only be surmised that it was longer than 37.0 cm. Half of the length of the stick has been flattened and is smooth and polished. The final third of this flattened portion has a rounded groove down the middle about 0.3 cm. deep and 0.7 cm. wide. This groove expands slightly toward the broken end, and the proximal end of a dart shaft would fit into it. The groove may have been terminated originally by some sort of spur to catch the base of the dart shaft. The specimen was found in a component of the Coxcatlan phase.

Atlatl Foreshafts

8 specimens excavated.

The bark has been stripped off these short straight sticks, and their surfaces have been smoothed. They

Table 27. Wood and Vegetal Artifacts from Excavated Components according to Phase

	EL RIEGO			COXCATLAN				ABEJAS				AJALPAN		SANTA MARIA				PALO BLANCO										VENTA SALADA								TOTAL
	Tc 50, XVI	Tc 50, XV	Tc 50, XIV	Tc 50, XIII	Tc 50, XII	Tc 254, E	Tc 50, XI	Tc 254, D	Tc 50, IX	Tc 50, VIII	Tc 272, L	Tc 272, J	Tc 254, C	Tc 272, I	Tc 272, H	Tc 272, G	Tc 50, VII	Tc 272, F	Tc 50, VI	Tc 272, E	Tc 272, D	Tc 272, C	Tc 272, A	Tc 50, V	Tc 254, B	Tc 50, IV	Tc 35e, D	Tc 35e, C	Tc 50, III	Tc 35e, B	Tc 50, II	Tc 35w, 2	Tc 35w, 1	Tc 50, I	Tc 35e, A	
Haft with flake																														1						1
Decorated comb																																	1			1
Cane fire tongs																														1						1
Carved paddle																													1							1
Ciruela-seed tinkler																												1								1
Whittled plug																												1								1
Painted wood																												1			1					2
Racket handle for barkbeater																												1								1
Cane arrow mainshaft fragments:																																			
distal ends																												1	1							2
proximal ends																										1								1		2
Rectangular loom sticks																									1											1
Spine needle																									1			1		1						3
Combs of tied sticks																											1	2		1						4
Cane tubes																				1																1
Threaded needle																								1												1
Fire-making tools:																																				
hearths																								1				1		1						3
drills																								1				1							1	3
Pounded sticks														1					3							1	1	1		1						8
Cut cane												1		1	1	19	1	6	1	5	1			4		3		2	22		1	2		2	2	74
Atlatl mainshaft fragments, distal ends										1																									1	2
Carved nuts or seeds										1					1											1		3		1						7
Cut slabs									1									1	2						2			1								7
Digging sticks						1		2	1								1							1	1	2				4						13
Atlatl foreshaft fragments:																																				
blunted ends					1	1		1					1						1							1		1								7
pointed ends								1																												1
Snare parts					1			1	1									1						1	1									1		7
Atlatl					1																															1
Cut or pierced gourds					2		1		3	4		2			1		1	2							1	2		2	3	1	7	2	1	2	1	38
Spine pins	1																1									1							1			4
Pointed sticks:																																				
flat				1									1											1	2						2					7
large																										1				2	2			2		7
small	1			1				1	1	1			1												1	1				2				2		12
Polished or cut fragments:																																				
cut logs or stakes											2							4	1									1					2	2		12
cut sticks				1				4	5	8							1	3	2						4	22		4	18	2				2	2	78
polished sticks	2	1	2	1	1		1	4		2							1							2	2	1	2	1	17	9	6			2	2	59
TOTAL	4	2	2	3	7	1	7	11	12	17	3	3	3	1	2	20	7	15	10	10	1	1	2	9	10	31	4	22	63	27	22	3	4	9	17	375

Fig. 127. Pointed sticks, actual size. *Left,* polished round variety; *right,* flat variety.

measure from 16.7 to 27.1 cm. long and from 1.0 to 1.6 cm. wide. The proximal ends of six specimens are tapering but blunted; however, one of the earliest specimens has an almost pointed proximal end. The distal end of the latter specimen is whittled and blunted, and a groove encircles it about 4.0 cm. from the tip. The proximal ends of all the specimens are somewhat polished from use and are scarred from being inside a cane mainshaft. The distal ends of three specimens are broken off, and one specimen lacks the blunted end. The latter, however, has a slot covered with gum in the distal end. Two of the more complete examples also have slotted distal ends. One of these has an incised design consisting of three long, thin rectangles that parallel the main axis of the shaft. They are separated from each other by two parallel encircling lines about 0.5 cm. apart.

The atlatl foreshafts were found in levels dating from the Coxcatlan phase to Venta Salada times. I suspect they will be found in earlier horizons in future investigations.

Fig. 128. Parts of snares, actual size. The right-hand specimen is a trigger.

Snares

Fig. 128
7 specimens excavated.

Seven fragments that came from levels dating from the Coxcatlan to the Venta Salada phase could be interpreted as being parts of snares. Five of these are broken sticks ranging from 7.5 to 46.0 cm. long. They are also relatively thin, ranging from 0.5 to 1.0 cm. in diameter. These five fragments have one worked end; the ends of two specimens are merely smoothed, and the ends of the other three are encircled by grooves. A piece of string is tied into the groove of one specimen by a square knot, and the other end of the string is frayed and broken. The two remaining fragments are short pieces, 6.5 and 8.1 cm. long, which have been cut off at both ends. They also have one grooved end. These specimens, I believe, were triggers for snare traps, and the previous five examples may have been parts of spring snares.

Digging Sticks

Fig. 129
13 specimens excavated.

The digging tools are made from long, fairly thick sticks ranging from 1.3 to 3.4 cm. in diameter. They have been whittled to a point at one end (one example was pointed on both ends), and the point has been burned and ground. Three of the sample not only had ground and burnt ends, but the ends had a dull luster as well which could be interpreted as dirt-polish. Three of the more complete sticks were 50.0, 74.4, and 89.8 cm. long. It is significant that digging sticks are found from the Coxcatlan through the Venta Salada phases— the same time range as domesticated corn.

Cut Slabs

7 specimens excavated.

Seven slabs of wood about 1.0 cm. thick were apparently riven from pieces of logs and then cut so they would have straight edges. The only complete example found is roughly rectangular in form and measures 20.3 cm. long and 6.7 cm. wide. It, like the others, has smoothed surfaces and ground edges. Perhaps the other, more fragmentary pieces originally had a similar form. They appear from Abejas to Venta Salada times.

Pounded Sticks

Fig. 130
8 specimens excavated.

These sticks are without bark, and one end has been

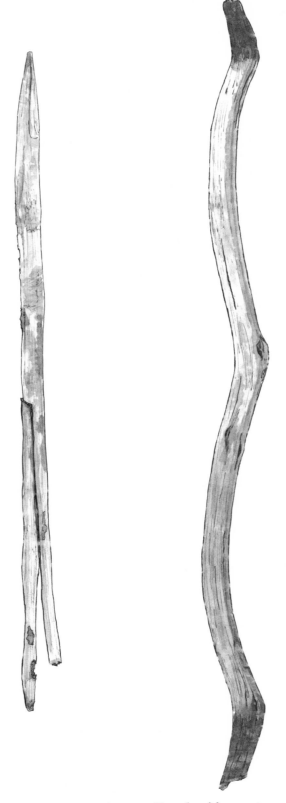

Fig. 129. Digging sticks. Actual lengths of fragments are 74 cm. and 89 cm.

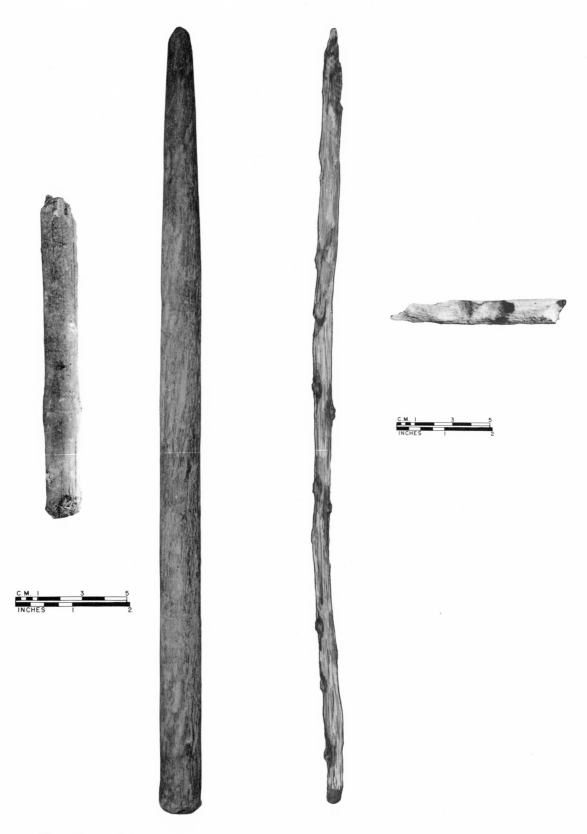

Fig. 130. Pounded sticks.

Fig. 131. Bit and hearth for making fire.

Fig. 132. Threaded wooden needle; spine pins; needle and thread made from a single agave leaf. Actual size.

frayed by pounding. The range from 14.0 to 78.0 cm. long and 1.2 to 2.4 cm. in diameter. One of the four examples with both ends intact has a point dulled by polishing, and the ends of the others have been sharpened. These pounded sticks are found from Santa Maria through Venta Salada times.

Fire-Making Equipment

Fig. 131
6 specimens excavated.

Three of the specimens are sticks more than 25.0 cm. long and are about 1.0 cm. in diameter. They each have a blunted, burned and polished, or well-worn end. I believe that these three sticks served as drill bits.

The other specimens are made from softer pieces of wood that are flat on one side. In the flat sides there are several charred ground holes about 1.5 cm. in diameter. These I consider to be hearths for the drills.

All the specimens were found in Palo Blanco or Venta Salada components.

Threaded Needle

Fig. 132
1 specimen excavated.

This needle came from a Palo Blanco component. Both tips are missing, but the needle must have been longer than 7.0 cm. It has a maximum width of 0.3 cm. and a maximum thickness of 0.15 cm. About an equal distance from each end, a slot 0.6 cm. long and 0.07 cm. wide had been cut through from one surface. A piece of two-ply, S-twist cord of soft bast fiber was still positioned in this slot.

Combs of Tied Sticks

Fig. 133
3 fragments excavated.

These fragments are each composed of a series of small sticks tied together. The sticks are about 0.2 cm. in diameter and about 8.0 cm. long; some are double-pointed, and all of them may have been so originally. One fragment is bundled together and tied with a maguey strand, as can be seen in the illustration. The other example illustrated is held together by two-ply, Z-twist cord twined in an over-two, under-one pattern.

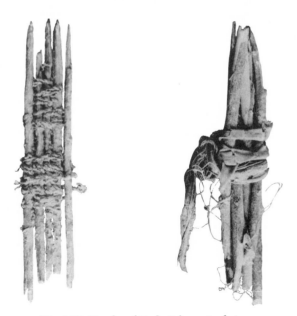

Fig. 133. Combs of tied sticks, actual size.

155

These thin rectangular plaques are about 0.8 cm. thick, between 16.7 and 26.0 cm. long, and 5.0 to 5.5 cm. wide. After they were sliced longitudinally from a large

Fig. 134. Loom stick, actual size.

The specimens come from late Palo Blanco and Venta Salada levels. Whether they were actually combs is open to question. However, they could very well have been used as weaving combs or tamping implements.

Rectangular Loom Sticks

Fig. 134
3 specimens excavated.

156

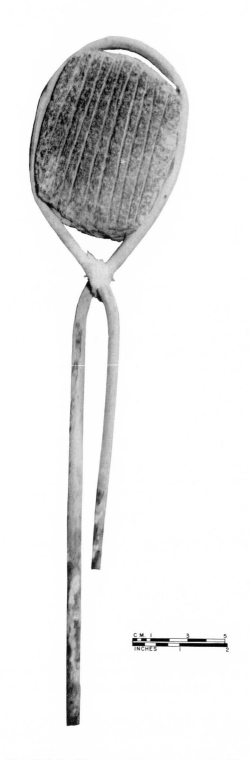

Fig. 135. Barkbeater with racket-type handle.

log, their surfaces were smoothed and their edges rounded, and a hole was hand-drilled through the edge midway along one side. On the smallest example the edge opposite the hole has considerable polish, which I believe is the result of its having been used to push or tamp down weft threads inside a loom. These objects could also have served as large pendants. All three were excavated from Palo Blanco and Venta Salada levels.

Racket Handle of Barkbeater

Fig. 135
1 specimen excavated.

The stone head of this barkbeater is described with the ground-stone tools in Chapter 8. The description here will be confined to the perishable parts of the tool, which was found in an early Venta Salada component.

The handle was made from a piece of vine or a stick about 1.0 cm. in diameter and about 80.0 cm. long. Initially, the middle of the stick—probably after the wood had been soaked and slightly weakened by whittling—was placed against the distal end of the stone beater, in a groove that runs around three sides of it. The two ends of the stick were then bent together to force the central section into the groove along the sides of the stone head. The ends were crossed over at the proximal end of the head and secured with a strand of barkcloth tied in a square knot. Thus the head was firmly held by the loop made from the bent stick. The two ends extending beyond the loop were each about 24.0 cm. long. These were bent so that they were parallel to each other and to the longitudinal axis of the head. Impressions and wear on the handle indicate that a small stick, about 12.0 cm. long and about 1.0 cm. in diameter, had been inserted vertically between the parallel ends of the handles, with one end even with the ends of the handle. The three sticks were lashed together by encircling strands at two points, just back from the ends of the inserted stick. This portion of the implement became the handgrip.

In Tolstoy's terminology this tool would be a racket or "Java-Celebes" type of barkbeater. Quite frankly, in spite of my prejudice against flights of fancy regarding prehistoric trans-Pacific contacts, the resemblance between this barkbeater from Tehuacan and those of the Celebes is truly remarkable. It is extremely difficult to believe that this complex tool was invented independently in both areas.

Painted Wood

Fig. 136
2 specimens excavated.

Fig. 136. Painted stick, two views, actual size. This specimen was covered with a red stain; the darker patches in the photograph are resin, not pigment.

Fig. 137. Whittled plug, actual size.

One stick shows the remains of reddish paint, and another slab of wood has yellow ochre stains. Both are from Venta Salada components.

Whittled Plug

Fig. 137
1 specimen excavated.

This small, short, solid cylinder is made of relatively soft wood. It is 4.1 cm. long and about 3.3 cm. in diameter. One end has been whittled down slightly all the way around. The workman who found it, as a joke, inserted it in a gourd water bottle as a plug. I suspect his assumption about its original use is correct. It was excavated from a Venta Salada level of the East Niche of El Riego Cave.

Carved Paddle

Fig. 138
1 specimen excavated.

In an early Venta Salada component of El Riego Cave, we found a wooden paddle shaped like a meat cleaver. It is about 1.5 cm. thick, its maximum length is 29.8 cm., and the widest part of its blade is 8.3 cm. The handle is about 10.0 cm. long, has a rounded end, and measures about 3.0 cm. across the widest part. It extends from the narrower end of the paddle blade. The paddle was whittled from a slab of pine wood, and its edges were ground. The lower side and end of the blade are relatively sharp, and the other edges are squared or flat. This object could have been a weaving tool, or it may have been used to stir soup, but the original finder immediately used it to paddle his digging partner.

Handle Containing a Flint Chip

Fig. 139
1 specimen excavated.

This artifact, a handle with a flint chip inserted in its side, was made from a long straight stick 2.5 cm. in

158

Fig. 138. Carved paddle.

diameter and probably considerably over 15.0 cm. long. The distal end of the stick had been sawed, and about 1.0 cm. from this end, a deep groove about 7.5 cm. long and 1.5 cm. wide has been sliced into the stick's side. A flat, roughly rectangular flake of flint, 7.0 cm. long, 5.0 cm. wide, and 1.0 cm. thick, is still in place in the groove. The outer edge of this flake is sharp, but shows little or no evidence of work or use. The flake is held in place by a series of agave fibers wrapped around the end of the flake and the stick, at an acute angle to the main axis of the stick. The fibers, the part of the flake in the groove, and the surface of the stick next to the groove are covered with a heavy coating of pine pitch.

This implement, from Level 1 of the West Niche of El Riego Cave, a Venta Salada zone, could have been used as a small ax or chopper. If the flake alone had been found, I doubt very much whether anyone would have guessed how it had been used or how it had been attached to the wooden haft.

Artifacts of Vegetal Substances—*Trial Types*

Spine Pins

Fig. 132

4 specimens excavated.

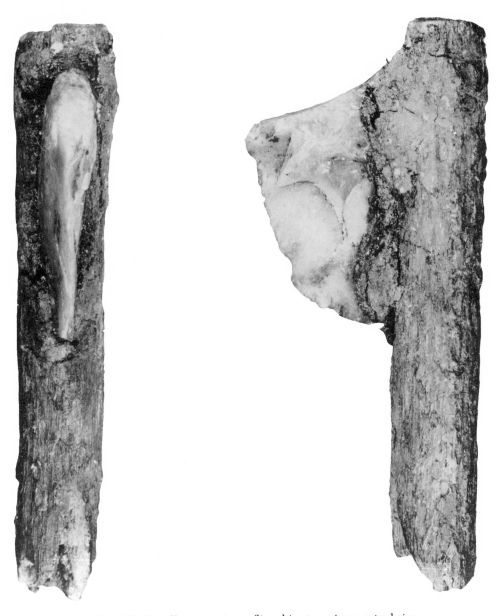

Fig. 139. Handle containing a flint chip, two views, actual size.

Although cactus and agave spines are found throughout the Tehuacan sequence and the ancient valley people could have used them in some way, only four spines from excavation show definite evidence of human workmanship. One spine from a late El Riego component has slice marks across its broken end and gum adheres to this broken end. One spine from a Santa Maria component has a ball of gum on one end. Two spines from later levels each have thin adhering agave strands wrapped around one end. All the spine pins are about 6.0 cm. long. This trial type seems to range from El Riego times to the Spanish Conquest.

Cut or Pierced Gourds

38 specimens excavated.

From Coxcatlan times on, cut or pierced fragments of gourds were found. Two large fragments from late levels of the East Niche of El Riego Cave were obviously parts of water bottles. The ends of these gourds had been cut off to make constricted mouths. Two holes were hand-drilled near the mouth of each gourd for the insertion of string to make a handle. Whether the earlier gourd fragments were from water bottles is questionable.

Carved Nuts or Seeds

Fig. 140
7 specimens excavated.

A small fragment of an *Acrocomia mexicana* seed has marks cut into it. Another seed of the same species has been cut at one end and hollowed out; then three small holes were bored around a cut slit. These seeds are from Venta Salada zones of the East Niche of El Riego Cave. Three halves of avocado seeds (*Persea* sp.) have faces carved on the rounded surfaces—that is, two circular holes for eyes cut above a longer slit for the mouth. Two of these come from a Venta Salada level of the same

Fig. 141. Cane tube, *left*, cut at both ends. Three cane "cigarettes," *center and right*, with one charred end. Actual size.

cave, and the other was from a Palo Blanco component of the cave. The remaining two specimens are *Jatropha* seeds and have similar faces cut in them. One was found in Zone VII of Coxcatlan Cave, a Santa Maria component, and the other is from Zone VIII, an Abejas floor.

Atlatl Mainshaft Distal Ends

2 fragments excavated.

Two pieces of *carrizo* (cane), about 1.5 cm. in diameter, were found with one end worked and the other broken off. The longer fragment is about 86.0 cm., and the unbroken end has been roughened by a series of small cuts. The interior of the cane near the cut reveals evidence of wear in the form of rubbing. This rubbing was probably caused by the insertion of a cylindrical or conical object, such as an atlatl foreshaft. The shorter fragment has also been cut at one end and shows scars from interior rubbing. Also, an area about 1.5 cm. wide has been scraped back from the cut end, and both gum and string fibers still adhere to this section. The string probably was originally wrapped around the whole scraped area. In the Southwest of the United States and in southwest Tamaulipas string wrapping appears at the distal ends of atlatl dart mainshafts, and probably served as reinforcement to keep the foreshaft from

Fig. 140. Carved avocado, jatropha, and acrocomia seeds, actual size.

160

Fig. 142. Cane arrowshaft, perhaps a bunt, actual size.

splitting the cane. One of the specimens from Tehuacan came from an Abejas level, and the other from a Venta Salada component. I suspect a more adequate sample would reveal that atlatl mainshafts were common throughout the sequence.

Cut Cane

Fig. 141
74 specimens excavated.

These pieces of *carrizo* or cane, from Ajalpan to Venta Salada levels, have been cut off at one end by an encircling groove. They range from 3.2 cm. to a meter in length. The end opposite the cut one is usually broken or frayed. There are, however, six pieces—one each from Zones I, II, and III from Coxcatlan Cave, one from Zone B of the East Niche of El Riego Cave, and one each from Zones E and F of Purron Cave—which are shorter, about 2.0 to 6.0 cm. long. The ends opposite the cut ends of these specimens are burned. They look very much like the "cane cigarettes" of the Southwest of the United States and of Tamaulipas.

Cane Tubes

Fig. 141
4 specimens excavated.

Four pieces of cane were cut at both ends by encircling grooves to form tubes. They range from 2.5 to 9.9 cm. in length and from 0.7 to 1.6 cm. in diameter. They come from Palo Blanco and Venta Salada components.

Spine Needle

Fig. 132
1 specimen excavated.

An agave leaf (11.2 cm. long) had a chewed basal end, and the chewed fibers have been wound into two-ply, Z-twist string of S-twist yarns. The string is about 7.0 cm. long and is connected with the unmodified spine at the tip of the leaf—thereby making a weaving needle with the thread attached. It came from a Palo Blanco component.

Cane Arrow Mainshafts

Fig. 142
4 fragments excavated.

All four cane fragments have one end broken off, but the largest specimen is still 41.0 cm. long. They range from 0.5 to 1.0 cm. in diameter. Two specimens are proximal-end fragments and were found in late Palo Blanco levels. The earlier of these has a V-shaped notch, and the other has a U-shaped notch, with an area just above the notch scraped to hold winds of string.

The two specimens found in Venta Salada levels are distal ends. A notch 1.5 cm. deep has been cut in one of the specimens. Gum still adheres to the interior of this notch, and the exterior surface has been scraped to hold string. String and leather thongs still cover the end of the other specimen (illustrated), and the notch for the arrowpoint cannot be seen. Perhaps this particular Postclassic specimen is an arrow bunt.

Ciruela Seed Tinkler

Fig. 143
1 specimen excavated.

A ciruela-seed tinkler came from a Venta Salada level of the East Niche of El Riego Cave. The seed had been cut in half, and a hole was drilled through the flat surface. A fine two-ply, Z-twist cord of maguey fiber was inserted through the hole; it was looped and made fast inside the seed shell by a square knot. I believe the loop once held some object to rattle inside the seed, since the inner part of the loop is frayed. The other end of the string, which protruded out of the seed, was attached to a larger string which was probably the selvage edge of a piece of fabric.

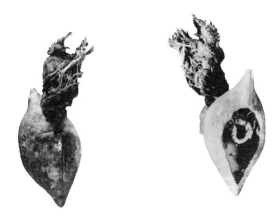

Fig. 143. Ciruela seed tinkler, two views, actual size.

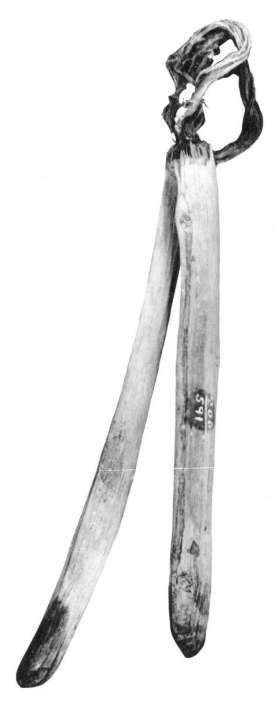

Fig. 144. Split-cane tongs, actual size.

Fire Tongs

Fig. 144

1 specimen excavated.

The tongs were made from a piece of split cane, about 1.4 cm. in diameter and about 15.0 cm. long. The cane was folded in half, so that the split surfaces were on the inside facing each other. A piece of cotton string has been tied in an overhand knot at the fold, perhaps to

serve as a loop to hang up the tongs. Both ends of the split cane are blunted and charred on the inside. As one workman commented, the tongs would not be very useful with a big fire, but would serve very well to pick tortillas out of hot ashes. This seems to be a supportable guess—though we found no tortilla remains. The tongs came from a Venta Salada level.

Decorated Comb

Fig. 145

1 specimen excavated.

Half a comb came from Zone A of the East Niche of El Riego Cave. A plaque about 7.0 cm. long, 3.5 cm. wide, and 0.6 cm. thick, made from wet agave fibers, served as the base for this double-edged comb. Long (4.5 cm.), thin (0.1 cm.), tapering wooden teeth, with a maximum width of 0.3 cm., were stuck into the two longer edges of the plaque. The teeth extended into the plaque about 1.7 cm., and extended out from the edges about 2.8 cm. They were set with their thin edges outward and their flattened surfaces facing each other. Originally there probably were about forty-four teeth on each side of the plaque. The center tooth was perpendicular to the main axis of the plaque, while the teeth on either side of it sloped very slightly away from the middle, so that the teeth at the end of the plaque were almost 30 degrees from perpendicular, and the comb had a fanlike appearance.

The plaque was made firm by a thin layer of asphalt or gum. A painted design was repeated on both surfaces of the plaque. This decoration seems to consist of a small half-moon, about 2.5 cm. in diameter, painted in yellow and black and centered at the edge of one of the longer sides. Fanning out from the moon are a series of rectangles, end to end. They represent, I think, conventionalized feathers. They are painted alternately almost black and a light crimson. Against the black hair of an Indian woman, this decorated comb would have been quite striking. The style and colors are similar to designs in the Borgia Codex.

Fig. 145. Decorated comb, actual size.

REFERENCES

Cosgrove, C. B.
1947 *Caves of the Upper Gila and Hueco Areas in New Mexico and Texas.* PMAE-P, Vol. 24, No. 2.

Kidder, Alfred V., and S. J. Guernsey
1919 *Archaeological Exploration in Northeastern Arizona.* BAE-B, No. 65.

Loud, L. L., and M. R. Harrington
1929 *Lovelock Cave.* UCPAAE, Vol. 25, No. 1.

MacNeish, Richard S.
1958 *Preliminary Archaeological Investigations in the Sierra de Tamaulipas, Mexico.* APS-T, Vol. 48, Part 6.

Martin, Paul S., *et al.*
1952 *Mogollon Cultural Continuity and Change.* Fieldiana: Anthropology, Vol. 40. Chicago: Natural History Museum.

Tolstoy, Paul
1963 "Cultural Parallels between Southeast Asia and Mesoamerica in the Manufacture of Bark Cloth." *Transactions of the New York Academy of Science,* Series II, 25:646–62.

—— "Stone, Bone, and Antler Tools of Central Mexico from Preclassic to Aztec Times." To be published in *Handbook of Middle American Indians.* Austin: University of Texas Press.

CHAPTER 11

Baskets and Petates

Baskets

DURING excavations, forty-six baskets or fragments of baskets were uncovered, and one impression of a section of a basket was found in clay. Since twenty-eight of these specimens were associated with the burials in Zone XIV of Coxcatlan Cave, the sample for the other fifteen zones of that cave are skimpy, to say the least. Nevertheless, in spite of the limited sample, the trial types of baskets do seem to show definite trends in our sequence from the El Riego phase through the Venta Salada phase.

The sequence of basketry begins with dish-pan-shaped baskets made of bundle-foundation coils held together by noninterlocking stitches, and these were found in levels of the El Riego phase. They were followed later in the El Riego phase and in early Coxcatlan times by coiled baskets with bundle foundations linked either by twining or more commonly by interlocking stitches. One coiled basket was found in late Coxcatlan times whose bundle foundation was held together by both interlocking and split stitching. From the Abejas phase to the Conquest, coiled baskets with split stitching to link the bundle foundations are found. Although our sample is very inadequate, it would appear that in the Tehuacan sequence there is a development in coiled basketry from those sewn with noninterlocking stitches to those sewn with split stitches. From the Ajalpan or Santa Maria phase on, twilled baskets, molded-grass baskets, and wicker baskets are added to the sequence.

This evolution of basketry is very different from that found in the Southwest and Great Basin areas of the United States and in southern Tamaulipas in Mexico. In the Southwest and Great Basin areas, twined basketry appears earliest and is followed by coiled bundle-foundation basketry with stitching and still later by twilled and wicker baskets. In Tamaulipas, the earliest baskets were coiled with a stick foundation and had Fuegian wound loops and interlocking stitches. They were followed by twilled baskets and finally by split-stitch and twined coiled basketry. I cannot help but wonder if perhaps there were three early centers of basket-making, with diffusion taking place later among these areas. Is it not possible that the Tehuacan Valley (or at least Mesoamerica) is the place of origin of the coiled basket with bundle foundation and ultimately of the coiled basket with bundle foundation linked by split stitching? Is it not possible that the Mexican coiled, split-stitch basketry later diffused northward

Table 28. Baskets from Excavated Components according to Phase

	EL RIEGO			COXCATLAN		ABEJAS	AJALPAN	SANTA MARIA	PALO BLANCO					VENTA SALADA				TOTAL
	Tc 50, XVI	Tc 50, XV	Tc 50, XIV	Tc 50, XIII	Tc 50, XI	Tc 50, VIII	Tc 272, J	Ts 367, C	Tc 50, VI	Tc 272, E	Tc 272, D	Tc 272, C	Tc 254, B	Tc 35e, C	Tc 50, III	Tc 53e, B	Tc 50, II	TOTAL
Wicker																	1	1
Molded Grass									1							1		2
Twilled								*		1	1				1			3
Coiled bundle foundation:																		
split stitched						1	1		2			1	1	1		1		8
interlocking and split stitched					1													1
interlocking stitched			9	1														10
twined			1															1
noninterlocking stitched	1	1	18															20
TOTAL	1	1	28	1	1	1	1	*	3	1	1	1	1	1	1	2	1	46

*Impression in clay.

to Tamaulipas and the western United States? Perhaps, too, the locally developed twilled basketry of Tamaulipas diffused to the western United States, as well as southward in Mesoamerica. The twined basketry of the western United States might have spread first to the Tehuacan region and then later to Tamaulipas. At present, the data are so meager that we can only speculate, but it is hoped that future investigations will test these hypotheses and arrive at well-documented answers to the questions raised here.

Baskets—*Trial Types*

Coiled Bundle-Foundation Baskets, Noninterlocking Stitching

20 specimens excavated, 18 of which were associated with Burials 2–6, Zone XIV, Tc 50.

All but two of these baskets had wide mouths and conoidal bottoms and were shaped like inverted Chinese coolie hats. All the specimens are fragmentary and many were crushed, but they seem to have ranged in diameter from about 25.0 to 60.0 cm., and in height from about 15.0 to 25.0 cm. The two exceptions were examples found with Burials 2 and 3. These were hemispherical in form and were about 20.0 cm. in diameter and from 8.0 to 10.0 cm. high.

The coiled bundles vary in diameter from 0.3 to 0.6 cm., with the most common diameter being about 0.5 cm. The coils seem to be made of four to ten stalks of grass.

The noninterlocking stitches range from 0.15 to 0.3 cm. wide, and they are spaced from 0.4 to 0.8 cm. apart. In all but three examples, the stitching runs from lower left to upper right. The thread is grass or agave fibers.

In the Tehuacan region this type of basket is confined to the El Riego horizon. It appears in the Southwest of the United States much later, with ceramics, and is also found in the Big Bend area of Texas.

Coiled Bundle-Foundation Basket, *Twine Stitching*

Fig. 146
1 specimen from Burial 3, Zone XIV, Tc 50.

This basket was roughly cylindrical and was about 20.0 cm. in diameter and 15.0 cm. high. It has a coiled

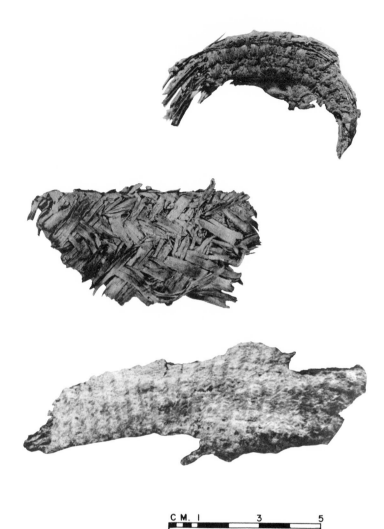

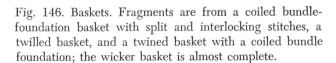

Fig. 146. Baskets. Fragments are from a coiled bundle-foundation basket with split and interlocking stitches, a twilled basket, and a twined basket with a coiled bundle foundation; the wicker basket is almost complete.

165

bundle foundation composed of grass stalks. The coils are about 0.2 cm. in diameter and are linked together by two stitches each about 0.1 cm. wide. The stitches had been Z-twisted—that is, twisted in a counterclockwise direction—around and through each bundle; they were spaced about 0.4 cm. apart.

This specimen was found with Burial 3 in Zone XIV of Coxcatlan Cave, a late El Riego component. The head from the burial was contained in the basket. The only analogous basket types I know of come from the early levels of Danger Cave in Utah.

Coiled Bundle-Foundation Baskets, Interlocking Stitching

10 specimens excavated.

These baskets seem to have been wide-mouthed (from 20.0 to 30.0 cm. in diameter) and shallow (about 15.0 cm. high) and to have had conoidal bottoms. The coils are composed of bundles of grass from 0.3 to 0.5 cm. in diameter. The stitches that interlock the coils are about 0.2 cm. wide. They proceed from lower right to upper left and are between 0.4 and 0.6 cm. apart. These baskets were found in the El Riego and Coxcatlan horizons in the Tehuacan Valley. Baskets of this type have been found with later remains in the Big Bend region of Texas, and in the Southwest.

Coiled Bundle-Foundation Basket, Interlocking and Split Stitching

1 specimen from Zone XI, Tc 50.

The fragments of this basket indicate that it probably was shaped like a Chinese coolie's hat. The coils of grass stalks are about 0.5 cm. in diameter. Linking the coils are strands of grass between 0.2 and 0.4 cm. wide. They are roughly at right angles to the coils and link them together both by interlocking stitches and by being sewn through the split portion of another stitch. The stitches are close together (about 0.3 cm. apart), and there seems to be no regular pattern in the use of split stitches or interlocking stitches. This specimen is from the Coxcatlan phase.

Coiled Bundle-Foundation Baskets, Split Stitching

Figs. 146, 147
8 specimens excavated.

These baskets have relatively flat bottoms and flaring walls, except the earliest one, which is in the form of a coolie hat. They range from at least 10.0 cm. to over 30.0 cm. in diameter and are from 5.0 to 10.0 cm. high.

The coils of grass stalks range from 0.5 to 1.0 cm. in diameter. The coils are linked by stitches from 0.3 to

0.6 cm. wide, and each of these stitches is inserted through a split in the stitch that precedes it. One large specimen is exceptional in not having a wholly coiled bottom; instead a series of strips 2.0 cm. wide and about 6.5 cm. long radiate from the center of its flat bottom and are sewn into the coils that complete the bottom of the basket (Fig. 147).

This type of basket first appears in Abejas times and lasts to the historic period. It is the common type of basket in much of North America, where it seems to appear later than our first Tehuacan examples.

Twilled Baskets

Fig. 146
3 specimens excavated; 1 clay impression uncovered.

Although the three specimens consist only of small rim fragments, I would guess that these baskets were roughly cylindrical in form and measured from 15.0 to 20.0 cm. in diameter. Palm strands, from 0.5 to 1.5 cm. wide, are woven in a two-over-two, two-under-two pattern. The twill weave is at a 45-degree angle to the rim of the vessel, and the strands are folded over and linked into the weaving and end just below the rim.

Twilled basketry first appeared in the Santa Maria period in the Tehuacan Valley, and today it is the popular type in the region. The type appears elsewhere in North America, and occurs earliest in southwest Tamaulipas, where twilled basketry was found with remains of the Ocampo phase of before 3000 B.C.

Wicker Basket

Fig. 146
1 specimen from Zone B, Tc 35e.

This small basket is roughly cylindrical and is about 10.0 cm. in diameter and 7.0 cm. high. The ribs of the basket consist of sixteen flat sticks about 0.6 to 0.8 cm. wide, 0.2 cm. thick, and over 20.0 cm. long. These were arranged so that their midpoints crossed one another and so that the ends radiated out from the center at evenly spaced intervals. Then strands of agave about 0.3 cm. wide were woven through the sticks, first above one stick and then below the next and so on until a bottom about 9.0 cm. in diameter was formed. The ribs were then bent upward at right angles to the bottom to make the sides. The horizontal weaving of strands continued, with the pattern changed to one strand over two ribs on the outside and under one rib on the inside, until the top of the ribs was reached. The final strand was then bent down inside the other horizontal weavings.

This specimen was found in a Venta Salada com-

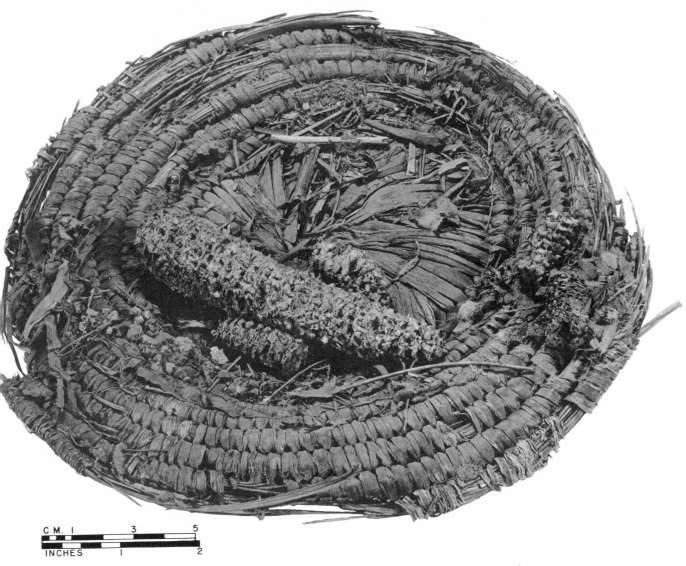

Fig. 147. Bottom of a split-stitched coiled bundle-foundation basket, showing unusual construction.

ponent at Tehuacan, and the type has not yet been un-covered in other archaeological sites in Mexico.

Molded Grass Basket-like Object

2 specimens excavated.

One basket-like bed of grass was about 30 by 20 cm. and the other was about 60 by 30 cm. Both were about 10 cm. thick. To make these beds, a shallow pit was dug in the floor of the cave. Stalks of grass complete with roots were placed in the pit so that the tassels were in the center and the roots at the edge. The ends of the stalks or roots were woven over one, under one; the

tasseled ends were pressure-matted together to form a crude basket-like bed.

One molded grass bed appeared in a Palo Blanco context; the other was found in a Venta Salada zone.

Petates

Nine fragments of woven mats or petates were un-covered in excavation, all in Palo Blanco or Venta Salada levels, and a piece of clay bearing the impres-sion of a twilled mat (or basket?) was found in an Ajal-pan component (Ts 368, Zone K). All but one of these specimens were twilled in a two-over-two pattern. The

167

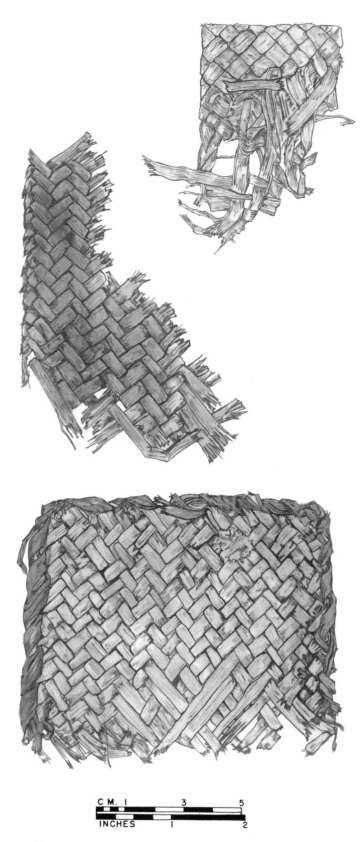

exception is a fragment from Zone D of Purron Cave, a Palo Blanco component, which seems to be the end of a mat or band 4.4 cm. wide (Fig. 148). The piece was made from strips of palm leaves or corn leaves about 0.5 cm. wide in a one-over-one checker weave. The weave is at a 45-degree angle to the side of the mat. The edges are made by folding over strips and weaving them back into the mat at a 90-degree angle to the initial weaving. Ends of strands are merely overlapped with the beginning of new strands.

Of the twilled examples, all woven in a two-over-two, two-under-two pattern, four are made from palm leaves and four from agave leaves. The strips range from 0.3 to 1.2 cm. wide. Two specimens and the clay impression represent only the central portions of mats (or baskets?); six examples, however, have preserved selvages. On four specimens the selvage was made by folding over a strip at a 90-degree angle, and then ending the weave 2.0 to 3.0 cm. below the fold (Fig. 148). New strands start at the fold, overlapping the old ones briefly, then continuing as single strands. One large fragment indicates that the mats were at least 30 cm. long or wide. These four fragments are from one Palo Blanco level (Tc 254, Zone B) and two Venta Salada levels (Tc 35e, Zone C, one specimen; Zone B, two specimens). The twilled fragments without selvages are from the Venta Salada period (Tc 35e, Zone C; Tc 50, Zone III).

The other variety of twilled petate has a different type of selvage. Here the edge of the mat is made by bringing a strand woven in the two-over-two fashion up to the edge, folding it at a 90-degree angle, then continuing to twill weave it. When the weave was completed, two strands of agave were twined through the weave at its edge (Fig. 148). One fragment is from a mat more than 30 cm. long; the other mat was narrow (11 cm.) and relatively short. These two specimens are from Venta Salada components (Tc 35e, Zones B and C).

Fig. 148. Petates. Checker-weave fragment; twilled fragment with strips folded at selvage; twilled fragment with a sewn selvage.

REFERENCES

COSGROVE, C. B.
1947   *Caves of the Upper Gila and Hueco Areas in New Mexico and Texas.* PMAE-P, Vol. 24, No. 2.

JENNINGS, JESSE D.
1957   *Danger Cave.* SAA-M, No. 14.

KIDDER, ALFRED V., AND S. J. GUERNSEY
1919   *Archaeological Exploration in Northeastern Arizona.* BAE-B, No. 65.

LOUD, L. L., AND M. R. HARRINGTON
1929   *Lovelock Cave.* UCPAAE, Vol. 25, No. 1.

MACNEISH, RICHARD S.
1958   *Preliminary Archaeological Investigations in the Sierra de Tamaulipas, Mexico.* APS-T, Vol. 48, Part 6.

CHAPTER 12

Bark Cloth, Cordage, Knots, and Sandals

Bark Cloth

FIFTY-FIVE pieces or artifacts of bark cloth were excavated principally from levels that could be assigned to Classic or Postclassic periods. A few fibers from Zone X of Coxcatlan Cave, an Abejas component, may have been bark cloth. I suspect, however, that these early examples represent accidental usage of bark for purposes other than making cloth.

To make bark cloth, pieces of bark apparently were stripped from the tree known locally as *amate* (*Ficus* sp.). The six wads of bark that we found stuck to the bottom of a plaster-lined basin in Zone C of the East Niche of El Riego Cave would seem to indicate that the next step was soaking. A barkbeater found in the same level—considered together with the flattened appearance of the excavated specimens of bark cloth—may indicate that the bark was beaten while still wet. The beaten fibers have a thin, meshlike quality, somewhat like cheesecloth or mosquito netting, which could only mean that they were used as cloth and not as paper.

Thirty-three of the specimens found in the refuse were narrow strips, ranging from about 2.0 to 12.0 cm. wide and from 3.0 to 17.0 cm. long. The largest specimen, which we referred to as a blanket, was found covering most of Burial 1 in Zone VI of Coxcatlan Cave. Although we never attempted to unfold it completely because of its fragility, this blanket is certainly more than a meter long and is at least half a meter wide. Another piece of bark cloth from the same level is smaller, about 10.0 by 10.0 cm., and it was dyed black.

A piece of bark cloth 12.0 cm. long and about 10.0 cm. wide had been folded or pleated into four equal layers, making a strip with the dimensions 12.0 by 2.5 cm. This four-layer strip has been doubled over unequally, so that one portion is shorter than the other, to form a rectangle measuring 7.0 by 2.5 cm. A second and quite narrow strip of bark cloth is tied around the doubled-over strip about 2.0 cm. below the crosswise fold. It is tied in a square knot. See Fig. 149.

Four strips of bark cloth about 1.0 cm. wide were each knotted in an overhand knot, and two examples consisted of similarly knotted pieces tied together with

Fig. 149. Bark cloth. A rectangular pad tied with a narrow strip; a square-knotted specimen; and a miniature sandal.

Table 29. Bark Cloth from Excavated Components according to Phase

	ABEJAS Tc 50, X	PALO BLANCO Tc 50, VI	Tc 272, F	Tc 50, V	Tc 50, IV	Tc 35e, E	Tc 35e, D	VENTA SALADA Tc 35e, C	Tc 50, III	Tc 35e, B	Tc 50, II	Tc 50, I	TOTAL
Handle for blade											1		1
Two pieces tied with square knot					1						1		2
Loops with square knots								1	1	3			5
Piece folded into rectangle											1		1
Single sandals									2				2
Strips tied in overhand knots						1					3		4
Sandals tied in pairs					2						2		4
Two knotted strips tied together		1									1		2
Piece dyed black		1											1
Blanket		1											1
Fragments	1?	8	1		4			7	2	2	5	2	33
TOTAL	1?	11	1	1	6	1	1	8	5	2	13	6	56

string. Five strips of cloth, each about 10.0 cm. long by approximately 1.5 cm. wide, were made into loops by tying their ends together in square knots. These loops may have been parts of sandals. Another specimen consisted of two strips tied together with a square knot (Fig. 149).

A strip of bark cloth approximately 1.0 cm. wide was wrapped compactly around one end of a small obsidian blade to make a handle. See above, p. 25, and Fig. 10.

The most unusual bark cloth articles found were miniature sandals (Fig. 149). We uncovered a total of six in various Classic and Postclassic levels of Coxcatlan Cave. Two sandals were found singly and the other four in pairs. Each pair was held together by a single thread tied in a square knot. The sandals were made in two parts. The soles were fashioned by folding strips of cloth 3.0 to 4.0 cm. wide and 10.0 to 30.0 cm. long in half or in quarters to make small rectangles 5.0 to 7.0 cm. long. The ankle loops were made by tying the ends of small strips together with square knots The strips measure about 10.0 by 1.5 cm. The ankle loops were loosely sewn to the rectangular soles by a thread of bark cloth about 0.3 cm. wide. This thread went from the knot in the ankle loop down through one back corner of the rectangular sole, then lengthwise down under the sole to the front corner on the same side, then up through the sole and up and through the front of the ankle loop, and then back down through the same corner, across under the front end of the sole and up through the other

front corner, then through the front of the ankle strap and back down through the same corner. It then ran lengthwise from the front corner to the back corner along the same side, came up through the corner, and was tied with a square knot into the back of the ankle loop.

These tiny sandals do not appear to have been used as footwear, even by infants, and they are unique for the archaeological record. After a considerable period of unusual silence and lack of comment when the sandals were being excavated, one of our urbane workmen, when I was alone with him, confided that the Indian *brujas*, or witches, hung such sandals in their caves as offerings. This statement has an air of authenticity, for Frederick A. Peterson found strips of bark cloth stained with dried blood, burnt copal, and modern candle wax in a "witches' cave" near Ajalpan, which he explored during the archaeological reconnaisance.

Cordage

The 662 pieces of cordage found in excavation date from the El Riego phase to the Venta Salada phase of the Tehuacan sequence. However, only the Palo Blanco and Venta Salada horizons were represented by adequate samples. The El Riego phase yielded fifty-eight specimens and the Santa Maria phase fifteen examples, with the periods between yielding but a few pieces of cordage or none. The larger sample from the later horizons is partly owing to the fact that about a third of the cordage had been used in the manufacture of textiles, and the Palo Blanco and Venta Salada components together contained eighty-four pieces of fabric, with two to four different strands of yarn in each specimen. The rest of the cordage fell into two categories: bundles of cotton containing many small bits of yarn and short, well-worn pieces of string or yarn which occurred randomly throughout the refuse. The latter specimens were usually found along with agave or leaf strands, some with and some without knots. Proportionately, the agave and leaf strands were double the amount of cordage, and in the preceramic levels this material was from four to six times more numerous than cordage. A few strips of leather also were uncovered, but they were mainly from late levels.

In attempting to classify the cordage into types having temporal significance, various categories had to be considered, each of which had several different attributes. We had hoped to arrive at a number of different attribute clusters which would be time markers, but the attributes failed to cluster satisfactorily, and eventually we were forced to choose single-attribute categories which seemed to be diagnostic. As Table 30

Table 30. Cordage from Excavated Components according to Phase

Phase groupings — EL RIEGO: Tc 50, XVI / Tc 50, XV / Tc 50, XIV. COXCATLAN: Tc 50, XII / Tc 254, E / Tc 50, XI. ABEJAS: Tc 254, D / Tc 50, IX / Tc 50, VIII. AJALPAN: Tc 272, J / Ts 204, F¹. SANTA MARIA: Ts 367, C / Tc 272, G / Tc 50, VII. PALO BLANCO: Tc 50, VI / Tc 272, A(B) / Tc 272, C / Tc 50, V / Tc 254, C¹ / Tc 254, B / Tc 50, IV / Tc 35e, E / Tc 35e, D. VENTA SALADA: Tc 35e, C / Tc 50, III / Tc 35e, B / Tc 50, II / Tc 50, I / Tc 35e, A.

	50,XVI	50,XV	50,XIV	50,XII	254,E	50,XI	254,D	50,IX	50,VIII	272,J	204,F¹	367,C	272,G	50,VII	50,VI	272,A(B)	272,C	50,V	254,C¹	254,B	50,IV	35e,E	35e,D	35e,C	50,III	35e,B	50,II	50,I	35e,A	TOTAL VARIETIES	TOTAL TYPES
Human hair yarn, Z-twist																								2		1			2	5	5
6-ply coarse rope, Z-twist																	1							1						2	2
Cotton cord:																															
2-ply S-twist																	10						1	3	10			4	4	32	
2-ply Z-twist																1	3	1	1	2			6						1	15	47
Corn-leaf (husk) cord, 2-ply, Z-twist										1														3	2	1				7	7
3-ply coarse cord, Z-twist, bast fiber										1							1				1			2	1					6	6
Braid																							1	2						3	3
4-ply cotton rope, Z-twist										1																				1	1
Cotton yarn:																															
S-twist																	2		2					2					1	7	
Z-twist							?				1			6	4		8	5	6	20	20			40	38	50	35	15	82	330	337
Coarse yarn:																															
Z-twist, thin bast fiber															1															1	
Z-twist, thick bast fiber					1			1											2					2		1				7	
S-twist, fine hard (agave) fiber							3	1						1	1															6	14
2-ply coarse cord:																															
Z-twist, fine bast fiber		5	1								*	*		1	2			1												10	
S-twist, fine bast fiber		2			?						*	*		2	4		1	1		4	1			1	2		1			19	
S-twist, thick bast fiber		2	1			3									12			1		2	3			1	1					26	
Z-twist, thick hard (agave) fiber			*					1	1							2	2	6	1		3		1	2	3	2		1	3	28	
Z-twist, fine hard (agave) fiber		1	16			1	1	1	1		*	*		1	2			6		10	4	1	11	13	6	15	13	10	9	122	
S-twist, fine hard (agave) fiber	1	1	6								*	*		1																9	214
4-ply coarse rope:																															
S-twist, fine bast fiber		2																												2	
Z-twist, thick bast fiber		1	7																					1						9	
Z-twist, fine hard (agave) fiber							1								1			1												3	
Z-twist, thick hard (agave) fiber	2	1	9	1																										13	27
TOTAL	6	12	40	1	3	3	4	3	3	1		1		14	27	3	6	36	8	24	33	3	43	68	56	81	51	31	102	663	663

*Clay impressions of cords.

demonstrates, individual attributes in some cases were as sensitive in establishing trends as attribute clusters.

The basic material from which yarns were composed is an illustration of this. Our archaeological yarns were made from cotton, corn leaves, human hair, hard fibers, and soft bast fibers. Hard fibers came from at least two agave species, which were impossible to tell apart because the strands were badly mutilated during the process of manufacture. Soft blast fibers were made from kapok, cotton, roots, *Agave ferox*, *Ficus* sp., or tillandsia leaves—all of which in their twisted forms are difficult to distinguish. When these yarns were studied in terms of temporal trends, there were some obvious temporal differences, as the accompanying tabulation shows.

	Hard Fiber	Soft Bast	Cotton	Corn Leaf	Human Hair
Venta Salada	78	14	285	6	5
Palo Blanco	53	38	92		
Santa Maria	3	4	7	1	
Ajalpan			1		
Abejas	9	1	?		
Purron					
Coxcatlan	3	4			
El Riego	37	21			
Total	183	82	385	7	5

Throughout the sequence hard and soft fibers decrease in over-all importance, with the soft fibers decreasing proportionately more than the hard fibers during the last two phases. Cotton fibers first appear in the Ajalpan (or perhaps late Abejas) phase, and increase very rapidly. Corn fibers are first used in the Santa Maria phase, and human hair fibers first appear in the Venta Salada phase, but neither fiber is found in very significant amounts.

The size of the yarn is, of course, closely connected with the materials used, and after considerable measuring and manipulating and expanding and contracting of categories, we finally settled on two broad classes: (1) Fine yarns, less than two millimeters in diameter, with a twist not longer than four millimeters, and composed of from two to ten strands of hard, soft, or hair fibers, or from five to thirty strands of cotton; and (2) thick yarns—that is, all yarns which were larger and contained more strands than the first category. In terms of trends, the finer yarns increased steadily in popularity throughout the sequence and became predominant from Santa Maria times on. The thicker yarns, while almost as numerous as the finer ones in the El Riego and Coxcatlan phases, decreased rapidly in popularity in later periods. Although the use of cotton and human-hair fibers increased with the growing use of fine yarns, there was little correlation between yarn size and trends in the use of hard and soft fibers, even though fine yarns made of hard fibers showed a gradual, but not significant, increase.

The next feature considered was the direction of the twist used to make the basic yarn. There are two possibilities: (1) clockwise, or right twist, or S-twist, and (2) counterclockwise, or left twist, or Z-twist. I prefer to use the terms "S-twist" and "Z-twist." Analysis revealed no single unilinear trend for either. For example, Z-twisting was predominate in the El Riego levels, was about as popular as S-twisting in Santa Maria times, and then became predominate again in the later levels. There was, therefore, in later levels a significant increase in Z-twisting, fine yarns, and cotton fiber, but any other combination of attributes showed little significance.

In contrast, the number of yarns used to manufacture the final string, cord, or rope proved to have very sig-

nificant temporal trends, as the accompanying tabulation shows. Four-ply rope is dominant early, but quickly gives way to two-ply cord, which is found throughout the sequence. One-ply cord or yarn first appears in the Coxcatlan horizon, and then increases in use throughout the rest of the sequence. Three-ply rope and braid appears first in the Santa Maria phase and lasts until the Conquest. Six-ply cord or rope is found first in the Palo Blanco horizon and also lasts to the Conquest.

The kinds of materials used for string or rope and the number of yarns in the cordage were, then, the most sensitive attributes of cordage in the Tehuacan sequence. The yarn size and the twist of the yarn changed considerably less throughout our sequence, although there was a tendency for cords to become finer and for Z-twisting to increase. We therefore attempted to correlate our two more sensitive sets of attributes to obtain significant clusters of attributes sensitive to cultural change. Yarn size and direction of twist correlated with these clusters, but most other attributes became instead variations within the types. As more data become available, our final types may need modification. In the meantime, on the basis of present materials, they are reasonably acceptable cordage time markers for the Tehuacan Valley, in spite of the fact that our sample is limited, especially in the middle periods of the sequence.

The earliest cordage type is four-ply coarse rope. It is found mainly in the El Riego phase, but it lasts into the Coxcatlan phase and thereafter becomes insignificant. The next type, two-ply coarse cord, first appeared in the El Riego phase and lasts to the Conquest, although it decreases in importance throughout our sequence. Coarse yarns appear mainly in late preceramic times, but they last into the ceramic period. Four-ply cotton rope and coarse braid appear in ceramic times only. Coarse three-ply cord and cotton yarn were also uncovered throughout the ceramic periods, and the latter type increased steadily in popularity. Cotton cord and coarse six-ply rope appear only in components of the last two periods, and human-hair yarn is a product of the final period.

In terms of cultural inferences, cotton Z-twist yarn had obviously been made on a spindle, and it was twirled in the same way as it is today in the Tehuacan region. Although early examples of spindle whorls were not found in excavation, I believe that all this cotton yarn was made with whorls, and that some kind of spindle whorl had therefore been in existence since Ajalpan times.

All the other string seems to have been hand-made, and the ancient Tehuacaneros seemed to care little whether they twisted it clockwise or counterclockwise,

	4-Ply	2-Ply	1-Ply	3-Ply	6-Ply
Venta Salada	1	111	271	4	1
Palo Blanco	2	106	71	3	1
Santa Maria	1	6	7	1	
Ajalpan			1		
Abejas		5	5		
Purron					
Coxcatlan	2	4	1		
El Riego	22	36			
Total	28	268	356	8	2

or whether they used twists of cotton, hair, corn leaves, or hard or soft fibers. This contrasts with the Southwest of the United States, where these factors show definite trends in time and are connected with whether or not the rolling is accomplished with the right or left hand, with an up or down motion, and on the right or left thigh. It was the end product that seemed to be important to the peoples of the Tehuacan Valley. "What is the yarn, cord, or rope to be used for?" must have been their first question. Our archaeological record gives the following answers: cotton yarn seems to have been used for blankets; four-ply coarse cord for binding or for carrying ropes; braid for ankle loops of sandals; two-ply coarse cord for twine blankets, nets, and so forth; cotton cord for sandals or clothing; four-ply cotton cord for sandal straps; and human hair for inclusion in medicine bundles. Thus changes in cordage types (except perhaps for the use of the spindle whorl) do not reflect changes in cordage techniques but rather changes in cordage usage. Further, as more kinds of fabrics were used, more kinds of cordage types came into existence.

Two stumbling blocks prevent extensive extra-areal comparisons of cordage types and trends. One is the lack of cordage data for Mesoamerica, and the other is the dissimilarity of the extensive data from the Southwest. Certain similarities do exist, however. For example, Z-twist cotton yarn made with a spindle whorl appears late everywhere, and two-ply coarse cord is common throughout the few sequences we do have. On the other hand, the trend from Z-twist to S-twist, using either hard or bast yarns, which is typical of the Mogollon region and other parts of the Southwest, and also of southern Tamaulipas, is barely discernible in the Tehuacan sequence. If the Tehuacan cordage sequence is typical of Mesoamerica, then it further points out the cultural differences which exist between this area and the greater Southwest.

Cordage—*Type Descriptions*

Four-Ply Coarse Rope

Fig. 150*a, b*
27 specimens excavated.

The most common yarns used in four-ply coarse rope are relatively thick (3 to 5 mm. in diameter) and very tightly Z-twisted (4 mm. long). The yarn made of maguey contains over ten strands, and the bast-fiber yarn has even more strands. The Z-twisted yarns have been S-twisted into cords, and then two cords have been Z-twisted into rope 6 to 11 mm. in diameter, with the twist about 8 to 12 mm. long. Rope made from finer

S-twisted yarns about 1 mm. in diameter is a variation of this type. Hard-fiber four-ply yarns have been Z-twisted to make a single rope. S-twisted rope of soft bast fibers is made of S-twisted yarns that are Z-twisted into cord. Most of the four-ply coarse rope is found in El Riego horizons, but the technique seems to last until Coxcatlan times, and a few isolated examples are found in later periods.

Two-Ply Coarse Cord

Figs. 150*c–h*, 151
214 specimens excavated.

Two-ply coarse cord appears throughout the sequence in steadily decreasing total sample proportions. About 160 specimens are made from fine rather than thick hard- or bast-fiber yarns from 5.0 to 2.0 mm. in diameter. Most of the early examples of fine yarns are tightly S-twisted with a twist from 1 to 5 mm. long. However, twenty-eight Z-twisted fine-yarn specimens also appear throughout the sequence, of which nineteen are of bast fibers and nine of hard. Ten S-twisted fine bast-fiber yarns have been twisted lightly in the opposite direction to make two-ply cord, never more than 2 mm. in diameter. A lesser number of specimens were made from thicker yarns, 2 to 4 mm. in diameter, of both hard and bast fibers that were either S- or Z-twisted; the yarns were twisted in the opposite direction to make cord 4 to 10 mm. in diameter.

Coarse Yarn

Fig. 150*i*
14 specimens excavated.

A few coarse yarns were found from the Coxcatlan phase throughout the remainder of the sequence. The hard-fiber yarns are about 1 to 2 mm. in diameter and are S-twisted. The bast-fiber examples range from less than 1 mm. to 5 mm. and are Z-twisted.

Cotton Yarn

Fig. 150*j*
At least 337 specimens excavated.

Cotton yarns appear in increasing amounts from Ajalpan times on, although there was one possible example from an Abejas level, and some cotton fibers were found in levels of both the Coxcatlan and El Riego phases. Cotton yarns are very fine, measuring from 0.5 to 1.0 mm. in diameter. They have been spun with a Z-twist by the use of a spindle whorl, with the exception of seven S-twisted examples—six from the Palo Blanco phase and one from the Venta Salada phase. A few

174

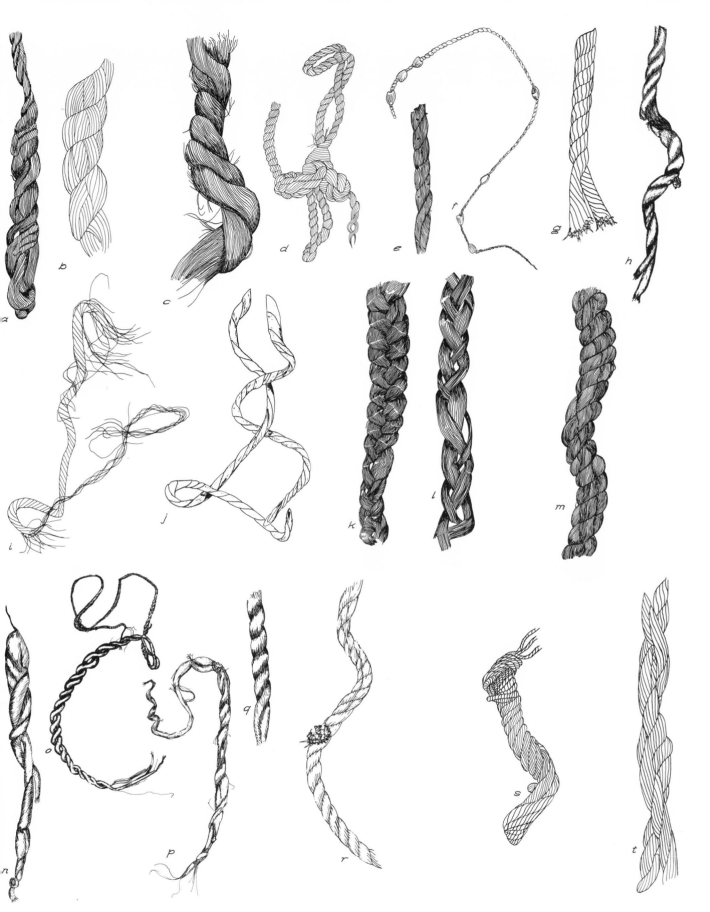

Fig. 150. Cordage. Drawings not made to same scale. *Row 1: a, b,* 4-ply coarse rope; *c, d, e,* 2-ply coarse cord; *f,* necklace of small seeds on fine 2-ply hard-fiber cord; *g, h,* 2-ply coarse cord. *Row 2: i,* coarse yarn of fine hard fiber, *j,* cotton yarn; *k, l,* braid; *m,* 3-ply coarse cord. *Row 3: n, o, p, q,* cotton cord; *r,* 4-ply cotton rope; *s, t,* 6-ply coarse rope.

of the later specimens are relatively uneven in diameter and may possibly have been rolled by hand.

Braid

Figs. 150*k*, *l*; 153
3 specimens excavated.

One braided rope from a Palo Blanco level of El Riego Cave is made of three thick S-twisted hard-fiber yarns; it was used as a sandal ankle strap. Two pieces of braid, from a Venta Salada level of the same cave, are each made of three stalks of grass; one of the braids forms a coil.

3-Ply Coarse Cord

Figs. 150*m*, 151
6 specimens excavated.

The examples of three-ply cord were found in Santa Maria, Palo Blanco, and Venta Salada levels. All are made from thick S-twisted maguey yarns 3 to 10 mm. in diameter. These in turn have been Z-twisted into heavy cord often 15 mm. in diameter.

Corn Cord

Fig. 151
7 specimens excavated.

The examples of corn leaves or husks that have been made into cord are from Santa Maria through Palo Blanco levels. In all cases the leaves or husks were first S-twisted to make a crude yarn 3 to 9 mm. in diameter, and then two yarns were Z-twisted to make cord. Five specimens have square knots tied at one end, and ropes with cobs attached could have been hung up for drying.

Fig. 151. Cordage, actual size. *Left*, 3-ply, Z-twist coarse cord of maguey fiber. The other specimens are examples of 2-ply, Z-twist cord of various fibers and corn leaves.

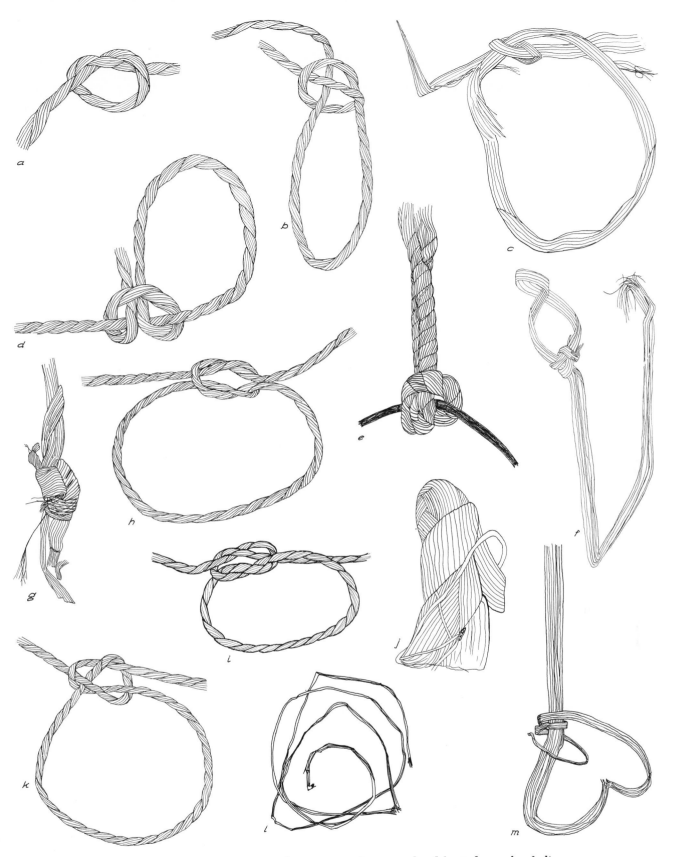

Fig. 152. Knots. Drawings not made to same scale. *a*, overhand knot; *b*, overhand slip knot; *c*, overhand slip knot in fiber strand; *d*, two half hitches making a loop; *e*, two half hitches joining cord to stalk; *f*, two half hitches forming a loop in an agave strand; *g*, square knot in maguey strands; *h*, square knot making a loop; *i*, granny knot making a loop *j*, coil of fibrous maguey; *k*, bowline knot making a loop; *l*, coiled maguey strand; *m*, loop made by a coil.

Cotton Cord

Fig. 150n–q

47 specimens excavated.

This type of cotton cord was found only in Palo Blanco or Venta Salada levels. The fine yarns are less than a millimeter in diameter and appear to be made with a spindle whorl, even though many are S-twisted. Two yarns apparently were twisted by hand in the direction opposite the yarn twist to make cords. Thirty-two of the cords are S-twisted.

6-Ply Coarse Rope

Fig. 150s–t

2 specimens excavated.

Two pieces of rope, one each from a Palo Blanco and a Venta Salada level, are six-ply. Both are made from fine bast-fiber yarn that was Z-twisted by hand. Two yarns in turn have been S-twisted into cord, and three cords have been Z-twisted to make rope about 3 mm. in diameter.

Human-Hair Yarn

5 specimens excavated.

Five human-hair yarns were found in Venta Salada levels. They are about 2 mm. in diameter and have been Z-twisted by hand. Two of them look like small brushes. One of our workmen told us that present-day "witches" keep tufts of human hair in their medicine bundles.

Knots

One of the final artifact studies of the Tehuacan project was concerned with 347 knots and coils. We divided the specimens into a series of classes—presented below —so that we would not be bound by any typological entanglements. The distribution of the classes of knots is shown in Table 31.

Overhand Knots

Figs. 152, 153

59 specimens excavated.

Simple overhand knots were made in a wide variety of materials. Thirty-three knots were tied in hard agave fibers and one in a bark strip. What their original purpose was is unknown, although two examples, both from a Palo Blanco level of San Marcos Cave, may have been parts of slip-loop snares. Ten overhand knots were tied in softer bast fibers or in pieces of chewed and softened maguey. Perhaps here the function of the overhand knot was to keep the fibers from separating. This also could be true of the single piece of knotted bark cloth. It might have been the purpose of the overhand knots in two Z-twisted cotton yarns and in the Z-twist agave yarn example, and it might explain as well the overhand knots in the three pieces of two-ply, Z-twist cord of soft yarns; two pieces of two-ply, Z-twist string made from hard yarn; two pieces of two-ply, S-twist cotton string, and the one piece of two-ply, S-twist string of soft yarn. The three bundles of knotted corn husks or leaves may have been tied in overhand knots to form loops. In terms of temporal significance, the overhand knot is used throughout the sequence, although the knotted corn leaves and cotton appear late in the sequence. This latter occurrence is probably a reflection of the later use of corn and cotton.

Slip Knots for Loops or Snares

49 specimens excavated.

Slip knots are common in excavated sites. They are made by tying one end of a strand in a simple overhand knot over the other portion. Thirty-three slip knots were made in hard-fiber strands, seven in bark strips, four in softer bast fibers or chewed maguey, and one in S-twist hard-fiber yarn or string. One piece of braided rope

Fig. 153. Knots, balls, and coils. *Row 1:* overhand knot in 2-ply, S-twist corn cord. *Row 2:* loop fashioned with a granny knot; granny knot in a fibrous strand; cord joined to a stalk with two half hitches. *Row 3:* ball of hard agave fiber; ball of agave yarn; hank of cotton yarn; cotton yarn wound around a folded leaf; maguey fiber, some of it spun into yarn, wound around a stick. *Row 4:* maguey fiber coiled around a lock of human hair; a bark coil; coil of braid; fragment of braid.

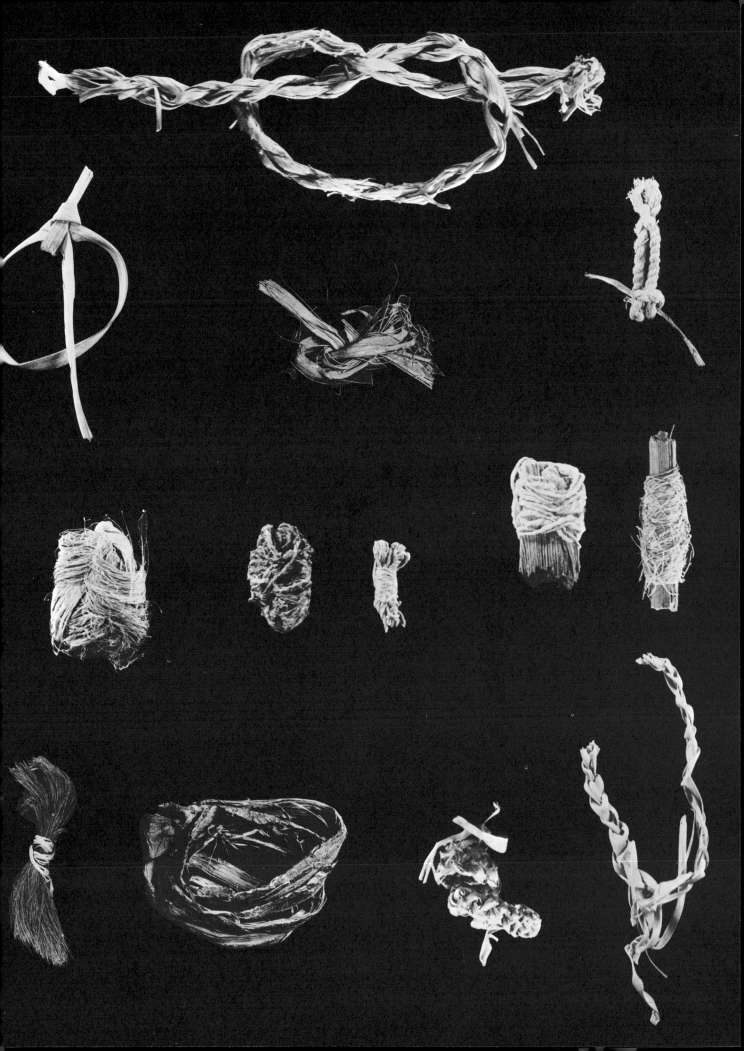

tied in a slip knot may have been part of a slip loop. All of these specimens may have been parts of snares or carrying loops. Slip loops also were tied in three strands of two-ply, Z-twist hard-fiber string.

Two Half Hitches

Figs. 152d, e; 153
19 specimens excavated.

Six agave strands have been tied into loops with two half hitches. A strand of bark tied to a stick and two pieces of Z-twist hard-fiber cord, one of which is fastened to a thin stalk, were also found with two half hitches. These loops could have served as snares or carrying loops. Six small fragments of maguey strands joined with two half hitches to other strands could have been parts of similar tools. Four pieces of two-ply, Z-twist cord tied to another cord by two half hitches may be fragments of nets. All the specimens are from the early ceramic periods.

Square Knots with (Carrying) Loops

Figs. 152, 153, 154
63 specimens excavated.

Thirty-seven strands of maguey have been tied with square knots to form either a single loop (29 specimens) or two loops (8 specimens). Twelve pieces of two-ply, S-twist string of soft yarn were tied with square knots to make single loops (6 specimens) or two loops (6 specimens). Four loops were made by tying both ends of two-ply, Z-twist bast-fiber string together with square knots, and two strands of bark and four pieces of corn-leaf string were also made into loops by tying the ends in square knots. One strand of maguey string braid was tied in a square knot. A strand of agave had been made into a slip knot by using a square knot. An S-twist, bast-fiber yarn and a two-ply, Z-twist maguey cord had their ends tied into single loops with square knots.

Square Knots without Loops

Figs. 152, 153, 154
102 specimens excavated.

Square knots with no discernible loop are popular from the Santa Maria through the Venta Salada phase,

although one earlier specimen appeared in a component of the Coxcatlan phase. It must be noted, however, that many of the fragments of square knots without loops are extremely small and their original use can no longer be discerned. These knots appear in a number of mediums, singly and in series. There were eighty-five square knots found in maguey strands, six knots in grass strands, six in corn cords, three in pieces of bark, and two in soft fibers.

Granny Knots

Figs. 152i, 153
20 specimens excavated.

Five maguey strands were each tied in granny knots, seven more were tied with granny knots to form single loops at one end, and two others were tied into loops at both ends. Two examples of two-ply, Z-twist bast-fiber cord were tied into loops with granny knots. Nineteen of the twenty specimens are from ceramic levels. Most of them must have served as carrying loops.

Bowline Knot

Fig. 152k
1 specimen excavated.

A loop was formed in an S-twist maguey string from a Palo Blanco level by a bowline knot.

Coils of Fiber

Figs. 152l, 153
16 specimens excavated.

We found thirteen coils of maguey strands and one coiled strip of bark. Also, a two-ply cord of Z-twist maguey fiber had been formed into a coil, and a lock of human hair was encircled by a small maguey coil. One of the pieces of braid mentioned in the preceding section was coiled.

Balls of Fiber or String

Fig. 153
9 specimens excavated.

There were five balls of wrapped hard agave fibers, some of which has been spun. One bundle of maguey fiber, a portion of which was spun into S-twist yarn, was

Fig. 154. Square knots tied in various materials, including fibers, bark, and corn-leaf cord.

Table 31. Knots, Coils, and Other Strands from Excavated Components according to Phase

	EL RIEGO			COXCAT-LAN				ABEJAS			AJALPAN	SANTA MARIA		PALO BLANCO												VENTA SALADA							TOTAL VARIETIES	TOTAL TYPES
	Tc 50, XVI	Tc 50, XV	Tc 50, XIV	Tc 50, XIII	Tc 50, XII	Tc 254, E	Tc 50, XI	Tc 254, D	Tc 50, IX	Tc 50, VIII	Tc 254, C	Tc 272, F	Tc 50, VII	Tc 50, VI	Tc 272, E	Tc 272, D	Tc 272, C	Tc 272, B	Tc 272, A	Tc 50, V	Tc 254, C	Tc 254, B	Tc 50, IV	Tc 35e, E	Tc 35e, D	Tc 35e, C	Tc 255, A	Tc 50, III	Tc 35e, B	Tc 50, II	Tc 50, I	Tc 35e, A		
Loops of wound hard fibers																														3			3	3
Leather strands																										2					3		5	5
Balls of fiber or yarn:																																		
cotton yarn, around leaves																														1	1		2	
hank of S-twist cotton yarn																															1		1	
spun and unspun maguey fiber, around stick																								1									1	
hard fibers, spun or unspun														2										2			1						5	9
Coils:																																		
strands of hard fiber								2						3					1			1	3							2	1		13	
2-ply, Z-twist hard-fiber cord																				1													1	
bark										1																							1	
maguey strand, around lock of hair										1																							1	16
Necklace: 2-ply, Z-twist hard-fiber cord	1																																1	1
Bowline knot tying single loop in maguey string														1																			1	1
Granny knots:																																		
in hard fibers, without loops				1										4																			5	
tying single loops in 2-ply, Z-twist bast-fiber cord																	1		1														2	
tying single loops in S-twist hard-fiber yarns																		1															1	
tying single loops in Z-twist hard-fiber yarns																													2	1			3	
tying double loops in hard-fiber strands												1										1											2	
tying single loops in hard-fiber strands														1						1		1	1			1	2						7	20
Square knots, without loops:																																		
in grass stalks																											1		1	4			6	
in bast fibers																		2															2	
in corn leaves														1												2			2	1			6	
in bark strands														1																2			3	
in hard-fiber strands			1										5	24	5				6			16				2	8	10	6	2			85	102
Square knots, with loops:																																		
in braid																			1														1	
in bark strands																			1								1						2	
in 2-ply, Z-twist corn-leaf string																			1										1	2			4	
in 2-ply, S-twist bast-fiber string					1									7					4														12	
in 2-ply, Z-twist bast-fiber string																				1	1	1	1										4	
in S-twist bast-fiber yarn								1																									1	
as slip knot in hard-fiber strand												1																					1	
in 2-ply, Z-twist maguey cord																																1	1	
in hard-fiber strands				1	1			1		1	1		3	2	1				4			2	1		3	1	1	5	1	6	2		37	63
Two half hitches:																																		
in bark strand tied to stick																										1							1	
in hard-fiber strands tied to strands														3								1					2						6	
in hard-fiber strands, forming loops											1				1			1	1	2													6	
in 2-ply, Z-twist hard-fiber cord, forming loops																							1	1									2	
in 2-ply, Z-twist hard-fiber cord tied to cord or strands	4																																4	19
Slip knots for loops or snares:																																		
in braided rope																																1	1	
in root or bark strands									1				5	1																			7	
in hard-fiber (agave) strands	1					1			2				1	1	1			1		1		20	2			1	1						33	
in S-twist hard-fiber yarn								1																									1	
in 2-ply, Z-twist hard-fiber string	1																					1							1				3	
in bast fibers or strands																1	1		1														3	
in 2-ply, S-twist bast-fiber cord	1																																1	49
Overhand knots:																																		
in corn leaves																										1	2						3	
in bark strip																											1						1	
in bark cloth											1																						1	
in Z-twist cotton yarn																								1								1	2	
in 2-ply, S-twist cotton string																			2														2	
in Z-twist hard-fiber yarn								1																									1	
in 2-ply, Z-twist hard-fiber string		1																					1										2	
in 2-ply, Z-twist bast-fiber cord		1																					1					1					3	
in 2-ply, S-twist bast-fiber string	1																																1	
in bast fibers					2									2					1	1	1				1		1						10	
in hard (agave) fibers	1								1	3				2					1	1	1	18	2		1	1	2		2		1		33	59
TOTAL	1	2	9	1	1	2	4	3	5	8	2	1	19	51	8	1	4	1	1	15	7	53	35	3	7	12	1	26	11	30	14	9	347	347

wrapped around a stick which served as a spool. A corn leaf had two-ply, Z-twist cotton string wrapped around it. Unevenly S-twisted cotton yarn was wrapped around a folded maguey-leaf spool, and fine, tightly S-twisted cotton yarn was wound into a small hank.

Leather Strands

5 specimens excavated.

Five strips of leather, about 1.0 cm. wide and 0.5 to 1.0 cm. thick, were found in Venta Salada levels of El Riego Cave.

Fibers Wound for a Loop

3 specimens excavated.

Loops were formed in three agave strands by coiling one end of a strand around the other portion.

Necklace of Threaded Seeds

Fig. 150f

1 specimen excavated.

A very fine two-ply, Z-twist string of hard agave fiber was threaded through a number of small pierced seeds, less than 0.3 cm. in diameter. The necklace is from Zone XIV of Coxcatlan Cave, an El Riego component. The seeds were so brittle and powdery that most of them fell away from the string after the necklace was excavated.

Sandals

Only twelve sandals, or fragments of sandals, were uncovered in the Tehuacan excavations. All but one of these, a small doubtful fragment from the Santa Maria level of Coxcatlan Cave, were unearthed in Palo Blanco and Venta Salada components. The relative scarcity of sandals from late horizons at Tehuacan, as well as their complete absence from early phases, is surprising, particularly since this kind of footwear occurs in some profusion and at early periods in the Southwest of the United States (Martin *et al.* 1952, pp. 259–99), the Great Basin area (Cressman, Williams, and Krieger 1940, Cressman *et al.* 1942, Libby 1955, Jennings 1957), Coahuila in north-central Mexico (Taylor 1956, p. 231), and also in northwestern Mexico (Zingg 1940). Further, the principles involved in the manufacture of our southern Puebla sandals, in which a frame strung with both warp and weft cords was used initially, seem to have been unknown or at least not employed in the Desert Culture area (Cressman *et al.* 1942, pp. 57–61; Jennings and Norbeck 1955). These Mexican sandals thus raise more historical problems than they solve.

One of the first questions we must ask is whether we have an adequate sample of footgear from Tehuacan,

and if not, why not. Can it be that in spite of the large amounts of preserved food stuffs, baskets, cordage, and textiles from the Tehuacan caves, we were just not lucky enough to find more than a dozen sandals? Or could it be that sandals were worn mainly by the "upper class" and that our cave remains were deposited by people of lower status? It seems relevant to note that on murals and in the codices of the Classic and Post-classic periods the majority of the people are shown barefooted, while the gods and important personages sometimes are depicted wearing sandals. These observations perhaps indicate that sandals were rare in Meso-america and were worn mainly by people of high status, but obviously this hypothesis needs to be investigated further.

Other problems arise from the fact that sandals do not appear early in the Tehuacan sequence. Is this a question of sampling, or did sandal-wearing simply begin late in Mesoamerican history? The complete lack of footwear on Middle American clay figurines of early or middle Formative times, the depictions in Olmec art of barefooted individuals only (Drucker 1959), and the absence of any type of early footwear among the abundant perishable remains from the dry caves of Tamaulipas (MacNeish 1958) seem to indicate that sandal-making probably developed late in Mesoamer-ica. If this is true, is this absence of early sandals in southern Mexico—as opposed to their early presence in the Southwest and the Great Basin areas of North America—a fundamental difference between early Mesoamerican cultural traditions and the Desert Culture tradition? Thus we have another problem worthy of further investigation.

Before going on to classify and describe the few sandals from the Tehuacan caves, I would like to emphasize that this is of necessity a preliminary report, based upon an inadequate sample of incomplete sandals, which poses more problems than it solves. It should also be remembered that this study was undertaken by an investigator who had never previously analyzed sandals.

The sample of twelve sandals consisted of three types. (1) Possibly the earliest type were sandals with multiwarp and multiweft concentric-twined soles with rounded toes. These sandals had only one toe tie. Two specimens of this type came from a Palo Blanco level, and a third but questionable fragment was found in a Santa Maria level. (2) Square-toed sandals with multiwarp and multiweft concentric-twined soles are represented by six specimens, three each from Palo Blanco and Venta Salada levels. These sandals had two toe ties. (3) Sandals with multiwarp and multiweft horizontally twined soles and rounded toes are represented by three specimens, all from the Venta Salada horizon. These sandals apparently had two ties, although no ties were preserved. The three types are illustrated in Fig. 155. No sandals similar to these types have been uncovered in other areas of Mexico, or anywhere else. The second type resembles the sandals depicted in both Aztec and Mixtec codices. Drawings in the Borgia (Mixtec) Codex seem to resemble the third type. All the Tehuacan sandals differ fundamentally from sandals of the Southwest and other regions in that they were twined over a web of multiple wefts as well as multiple warps and this web must have been supported by either a solid or an open-sided frame.

Round-toed, Multiwarp-multiweft,
Concentric Twined Sandals

Fig. 155 *a, b*
3 specimens excavated.
Dimensions in cm.: maximum length (1 specimen), 25; maximum width (2 specimens), 8.0, 9.0; thickness (3 specimens), about 1.0.

One almost complete sandal and one central sole section were found in Zone VI, Tc 50. A tiny curved edge fragment of what seems to be a portion of the concentric ball-of-the-foot section of a sandal (or part of a basket?) was found in Zone VII, Tc 50. The sole elements of all three specimens are of coarse agave fibers, most of which are Z-twisted to form yarn. Some of these yarns, as well as some of the coarse tie elements, are S-twisted into 2-ply cord.

Soles. The soles were twined across a lattice of warp and weft elements apparently held by an oval solid (stick) frame. Both elements consist of relatively fine, 2-ply, S-twist, agave cord; probably a single cord was continuously looped about the frame or within it to form both warp and weft. There were from 8 to 12 warps in the heel of the sole and from 10 to 16 warps in the somewhat wider toe. Apparently owing to the curved frame, the central warp loops in the toe of the sole were longer than the outer loops. The warp cords are between 0.5 and 1.0 cm. apart and are from 20 to 25 cm. long.

The weft elements are about the same distance apart as the warp cords, and they measure between 8 and 10 cm. across. Their number varies from 23 to 30. They seem to have been looped continuously around the sides of a frame or around the outermost warps, or around both.

The sole was then woven with coarser cord, which was twined around the junction of the weft and warp elements. The twining was begun in a counterclockwise direction in the center of the forward section of the arch area, until a spiral of twined knots was formed that was about 6 to 10 warps wide. Next a small section beneath the spiral, consisting of about six rows, was twined back and forth across the central warp elements. The twining then turned upward along one of the edges of the spiral until it was above it. Again the weaver twined back and forth for several rows, until the ball of foot and toe areas were filled in. The twining now turned downward along the opposite side of the woven area and then continued in a back and forth direction to fill in the heel. When the last weft was reached, a small rectangular or oblong mat had been woven, with loops extending out along the four sides. Three or four rows were then twined around the edges, through weft loops and warp loops, making a border.

Ties. Sandals of this type had one toe tie, an ankle loop, and two heel supports for the ankle loop. Only the most complete specimen has the toe tie intact (Fig. 155 *a*), although the other large specimen shows part of a centered hole in the upper portion of the sole. Two pieces of 2-ply cord are tied in a single overhand knot on the lower side of the sole, and both are brought up through the single medial hole in the toe to the upper side of the sole. The tie probably came up between the wearer's second and third toes, and then was knotted around the ankle loop. The ankle loop of the complete specimen is composed of a doubled, coarse, 2-ply, S-twist agave cord about 20 cm. long, the ends of which are tied in a complicated manner at the front. The ankle strap runs through two heel supports, one on either side of the sole. Each of these consists of a series of loops made of tightly Z-twisted agave cord, the ends of which are woven into the sole. The other fairly large

Fig. 155. Round-toed, concentric twined sandals (*a, b*). Square-toed, concentric twined sandals (*c, d*). Round-toed, horizontally twined sandals (*e, f*).

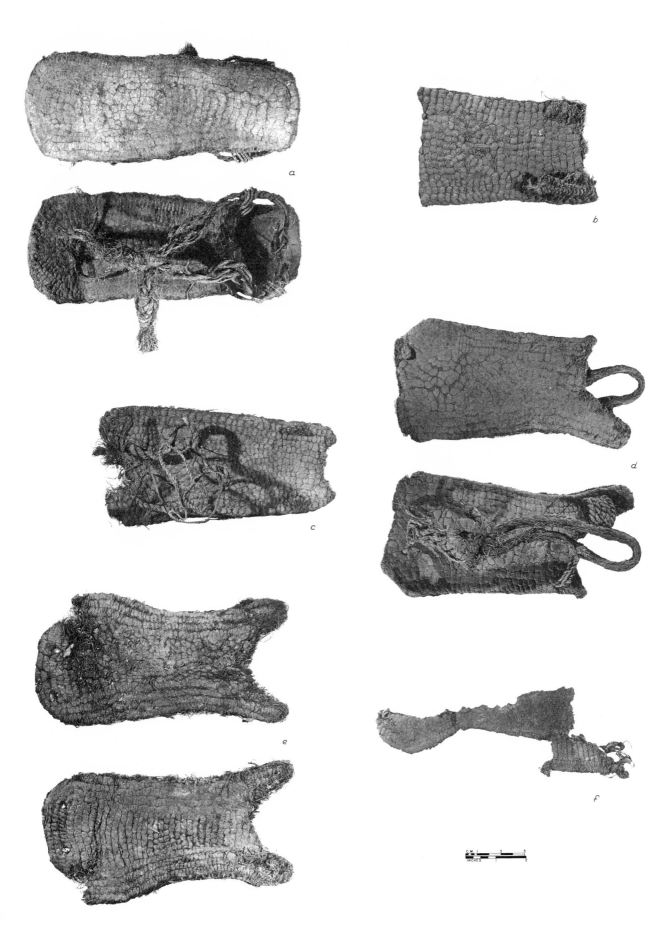

a

b

c

d

e

f

specimen (Fig. 155 *b*) has only a portion of one heel support remaining. It was a wider and more substantial support consisting of a woven, or twined, strip attached to the sole; it was probably twined to the ankle loop as well.

Square-toed, Multiwarp-multiweft, Concentric Twined Sandals

Fig. 155 *c, d*
6 specimens excavated.
Dimensions in cm.: maximum length (4 specimens), 16, 20, 20, 23; maximum width (5 specimens), 9, 10, 10, 11, 12; thickness (all specimens), 1.0–1.5.

Three fairly complete specimens came from Tc 50, Zones VI, III, and I; and three fragments were uncovered in Zones B and D of Tc 272 and Zone I of Tc 50. The weft and warp elements of these sandals are relatively thin S-twist agave yarns. The twining elements of the soles are coarse 2-ply, Z-twist cords. The ties are also of agave yarn but vary greatly as to size; some are Z-twisted and others S-twisted.

Soles. As in the manufacture of the previous type, a lattice of fine warp and weft cords was formed first. The lattice, however, was probably not made on a solid rectangular or oval frame, but on a structure resembling a simple belt-loom arrangement. The warp elements were made from a single cord apparently looped around two sticks and were spaced about a centimeter apart. They number from 10 to 18. The wefts were of the same type of cord, or the same cord, and were about the same distance apart as the warps. They appear to have been looped over the last warps on either side, and not over lateral sticks of a solid frame. There were from 25 to 45 weft elements. As in the construction of the previous type of sole, the twining across warp and weft elements initially formed a spiral through all but the outermost two or three warps on either side. The weaving, however, began in the area of the ball of the foot, rather than the arch, so that once this central forward section was woven, the back and forth twining proceeded only toward the heel. Once the central rectangular mat was woven, the sole was finished by a border of three or four rows of twining around the four sides. These sandals are squared off at toe and heel.

Ties. Each sandal originally had two toe ties that joined the ankle loop, which was held in place by supports on each side of the heel. On two of our specimens (see Fig. 155*c, d*) the toe ties are of thick, coarse, 2-ply, Z-twist agave cords. Each is knotted on one end with a simple overhand knot, to keep it from pulling through the sole. The unknotted ends were each threaded through one of two holes about 3.5 or 4.0 cm. apart in

the toe of the sole. They must have come up between two pairs of the wearer's toes. Both ties were secured around the ankle loop a few centimeters back from the front end, thereby dividing it into a small decorative loop or tab over the instep, and into a much larger loop to encircle the ankle. In the specimen shown in Fig. 155 *d* the ankle band is a thick loop of braided agave fiber. It is divided by the toe ties into a small front loop measuring 2.5 cm. across, and into a long back loop with a circumference of about 25 cm. The two heel supports for the ankle loop of this specimen are made of five vertical rows of S-twist cord, woven into the edges of the sole at one end and into the braided ankle loop at the other end. The heel supports of the other specimens are missing.

Round-toed, Multiwarp-multiweft, Horizontally Twined Sandals

Fig. 155 *e, f*
3 specimens excavated.
Dimensions in cm.: length (2 specimens), over 22 and 25; maximum width (1 specimen), 9.5; thickness (3 specimens), 0.8–1.2.

One specimen from Zone III of Tc 50 is an almost complete sole. Another specimen, from Zone II, Tc 50, is only a small toe portion, and the latest fragment, found in Zone A of Tc 35e, represents a lateral edge with one heel support attached. The twined sole elements of these sandals are 2-ply cord, the yarns of which are coarse, S-twist agave fibers. The smaller tie elements and the even finer weft and warp strings are of the same type of cord.

Soles. There are 10 to 16 fine warp elements and 30 to 46 weft elements; these formed a lattice as in the manufacture of the other two types. Although the toe of this type is rounded, it is difficult to tell whether the sole was woven on an oval solid frame or on an open-sided construction with a curved holding stick at the toe end. I suspect it was the latter. The twining began in the upper left-hand corner of the toe, at the junction of the fourth warp from the left and the fourth weft from the toe end. The twining then continued along the fourth weft to the right, until it reached the third warp from the right side. Then the twining continued from right to left along the fifth weft, and so on back and forth along the wefts until a small rectangular mat was constructed. Finally the twining proceeded round and round the edges of this mat, three or four times, to produce a border like those on the other types of sandals.

Ties. No toe ties were preserved, but two specimens each have two holes in the toe area, at the inner edge of the twined border, and the third specimen shows the edge of a hole. These holes seem to indicate that two cords came through the sole, ran up between two pairs of the wearer's toes, and then joined the ankle band. On the bottom of the sole of the latest specimen, a small piece of coarse yarn is tied in an overhand knot. This is probably the lower end of one of the toe ties.

A small piece of ankle strap is woven to the heel support of this fragment; it is a very thick, coarse cord of two heavy, S-twist agave yarns. The heel support, which is no longer quite complete, is a small rectangular piece of one-over-one woven cloth of fine agave fiber, with the longer sides of the rectangle attached to ankle loop and sole. The warps are looped around the ankle band at one end, and at the other end around the outer edge of the side of the heel. There must have been a similar support on the opposite side. The earlier specimens show a few strings emerging through the sole that may have been parts of similar heel supports.

REFERENCES

COSGROVE, C. B.
  1947 *Caves of the Upper Gila and Hueco Areas in New Mexico and Texas.* PMAE-P, Vol. 24, No. 2.

CRESSMAN, L. S., *et al.*
  1942 *Archaeological Researches in the Northern Great Basin.* CIW. Publication No. 538.

CRESSMAN, L. S., HOWELL WILLIAMS, AND A. D. KRIEGER
  1940 *Early Man in Oregon: Archaeological Studies in the Northern Great Basin.* University of Oregon Monographs, Studies in Anthropology, No. 3. Eugene.

DRUCKER, PHILIP
  1959 *Excavations at La Venta, Tabasco, 1955.* BAE-B, No. 170.

JENNINGS, JESSE D.
  1957 *Danger Cave.* SAA-M, No. 14.

JENNINGS, JESSE D., AND EDWARD NORBECK
  1955 "Great Basin Prehistory: A Review," *Am. Ant.,* 21:1–11.

KIDDER, ALFRED V., AND S. J. GUERNSEY
  1919 *Archaeological Exploration in Northeastern Arizona.* BAE-B, No. 65.

LIBBY, WILLARD F.
  1955 *Radiocarbon Dating.* 2nd ed. University of Chicago Press.

LOUD, L. L., AND M. R. HARRINGTON
  1929 *Lovelock Cave.* UCPAAE, Vol. 25, No. 1.

MACNEISH, RICHARD S.
  1958 *Preliminary Archaeological Investigations in the Sierra de Tamaulipas, Mexico.* APS-T, Vol. 48, Part 6.

MARTIN, PAUL S., *et al.*
  1952 *Mogollon Cultural Continuity and Change.* Fieldiana: Anthropology, Vol. 40. Chicago: Natural History Museum.

TAYLOR, WALTER W.
  1956 "Some Implications of Carbon-14 Dates from a Cave in Coahuila, Mexico." *TAS-B,* 27:215–34.

TOLSTOY, PAUL
  1963 "Cultural Parallels between Southeast Asia and Mesoamerica in the Manufacture of Bark Cloth." *Transactions of the New York Academy of Science,* Series II, 25:646–62.

ZINGG, ROBERT M.
  1940 *Report on Archaeology of Southern Chihuahua.* Contributions to the University of Denver. Denver.

PART IV: TEXTILES

by Irmgard W. Johnson

CHAPTER 13

Textiles

CLIMATIC conditions in the Tehuacan Valley have been unusually favorable for the preservation of archaeological materials; in particular, this dry area has yielded a series of remarkably well-preserved textiles and other artifacts subject to decay. This situation is of special importance for our knowledge of the Mesoamerican textile industry: first, it gives much needed evidence of technological processes employed by the ancient inhabitants; second, it provides valuable comparative data with the weavings from other regions.

To date, few areas in Mesoamerica have given such ideal archaeological proof of the antiquity of textiles as has this region of Tehuacan. Although Candelaria Cave in Coahuila yielded a far greater number of textiles, there was no possibility of carrying out stratigraphical excavations, nor does the antiquity of the finds go back as far as it does in the Tehuacan Valley.

Elsewhere, much of the textile material is of unknown provenience, or it is from sites for which stratification records are poor or lacking. The only safe way of dating textiles is to find them associated with imperishable artifacts, in the same level of excavation. Owing to the use of systematic methods and to a series of radiocarbon dates, the excavations in Tehuacan yielded neat sequences of chronological finds. Consequently, they leave no doubt that there was a well-established knowledge of true loom-weaving at least as early as the Santa Maria period (about 900–200 B.C.). A textile imprint on a pottery sherd from the Ajalpan period (about 1500–900 B.C.) pushes the evidence even further back. Basketry and netting appear even earlier, in components of the El Riego period (about 6500–4800 B.C.).

Of fundamental importance are fragments of a boll of cotton (*Gossypium hirsutum* L.), which, according to Smith and MacNeish (1964: 675–76) prove that this species existed before 5000 B.C. in the Tehuacan Valley.

The bulk of the material with which we are dealing comes from components of the Palo Blanco period (about 200 B.C. to A.D. 700) and the Venta Salada period (A.D. 700–1500). Although no recognizable weaving tools were found which might give archaeological evidence of the type of loom set-up, there seems little reason to doubt that the standard backstrap loom, known throughout most of Mesoamerica, was used. Mention should be made in this respect of a unique find recovered a few years ago from one of the El Riego caves: a small wooden weaving sword which exhibits a carved design along its top edge, and which has a horizontal slot filled with seven round seeds. Though it has the form of a weaving sword, the artifact presumably served as a rattle which must have had some ceremonial significance. It was deposited as an offering in the cave and was found in association with pottery of the Mixteca–Monte Alban V type (I. W. Johnson 1960: 75–85, Figs. 1, 2).

The basis of this study consists of technical descriptions of various noncotton and cotton fabrications. The information has been divided into two main parts: nonloom fabrications, which describes different kinds of netting and weft-twining techniques, and loom-woven materials, which deals with various types of weaving procedures and techniques. Not included are baskets, mats, sandals, and the bulk of the cordage material, which have been discussed in the preceding chapters. Wherever possible, a few notes on comparative data are included.

The study deals only in part with a discussion of fibers, because a complete analysis for fiber identification was not obtainable. As Mrs. Peck Kent (1957: 465) has pointed out: "Fiber analysis is a sadly neglected aspect of the textile studies so far undertaken for the Southwest." With few exceptions, the same may be applied to textile finds in Mexico.

Another neglected aspect is the lack of chemical

191

analysis of dyes for the colored textile materials. The few dependable studies available for Mexico are the ones presented by Michael Kasha (1948: 151–57) on the textiles of pre-Columbian Chihuahua, and the recent studies by Peter Gerhard (1964a: 26–31; 1964b: 177–90) on the purple shellfish dye.

Most of the loom weavings are in the form of small pieces of cloth. The most spectacular find was the mummy wrapped in two blankets, both preserved almost intact. These noncotton blankets give valuable evidence of the type, size, and patterning of fabrics produced in the early Palo Blanco phase. They were found associated with a burial in Coxcatlan Cave.

The custom of wrapping the dead in blankets seems to be widespread and ancient. Numerous examples were recovered from Candelaria Cave and from the Casas Grandes region (I. W. Johnson, n.d.; O'Neale 1948: 99–100). For this reason, frequent comparisons are made between the Tehuacan specimens and those from Coahuila and Chihuahua. In all these sites, the specimens are remarkably well preserved, and detailed descriptions are available.

Mummy-bundle burials are known from the Pueblo region of the Southwest (Kent 1957: 462), and it was also the custom in ancient Peru (Bird and Bellinger 1954: 8, 10, 13–17, et seqq.). The trait of wrapping the dead in cloth survives today among some Indians of Mexico; for instance, the Zapotec Indians of the Yautepec District in Oaxaca weave fine mortuary sheets for burial of their dead (I. W. Johnson, field notes, 1951).

Fibers

The yarns of textiles recovered from caves in the Tehuacan Valley were constructed of cotton and non-cotton fibers. The latter seem to have been obtained from a variety of sources. Initial examination showed that certain cloths contained yarns seemingly belonging to different species of noncotton plants; some had the aspect of being stiff and coarse and harsh, with a lustrous sheen; others were soft and pliable and fuzzy-surfaced, with less sheen. Some of the yarns even resembled cream-colored, cotton-like fibers, so that they were not always easily differentiated unless subjected to a thorough fiber examination.

Unfortunately, it was not possible to obtain a complete botanical analysis of the noncotton fibers. Only a few samples, taken from a selected group of specimens, were sent for identification to Dr. C. Earle Smith, of the United States Department of Agriculture. Dr. Smith (letter to R. S. MacNeish, February 5, 1964) reported the following:

192

I stripped a few fibers from the leaf of a *Hechtia* specimen and compared them with the non-cotton fibers and they compare very well. I thus suspect the non-cotton fiber is from *Tillandsia* or *Hechtia* in the Bromeliaceae but this is not proven, of course. Since I don't know what treatment may have been used to separate the fibers, how old the foliage might have been when gathered, whether inflorescence stalks might have been used, etc., the many variables can't be accounted for. It might even be possible that the fibers are the local *isote* or one of the magueys (it would have to be very young leaves, I think), but again I cannot say. Problems of this sort could be resolved by experimentation on the scene, but they can't be resolved up here since all sorts of material would not be available from herbarium specimens. . .

As shall be discussed below, there is a certain variability in the spinning technique of noncotton fibers. These differences cannot merely be accounted for by their occurrence in the various levels, because the variability seems to run through all periods. On the other hand, it is possible that different motor habits were employed for various vegetal fibers. However, a definite pattern of spinning habits cannot be worked out until additional knowledge has been assembled.

As an example of established motor habits, we may mention the textiles of Candelaria Cave, Coahuila, which showed a clear distinction between the spun yarns used in nonloom fabrications and those employed for woven cloths. The Laguneros used *Yucca carnerosana* and *Yucca treculeana* fibers almost exclusively in the manufacture of loom weavings; with few exceptions, these fibers were spun into 2-ply, S-twist yarns (Z-twist singles). On the other hand, *Agave lechuguilla* was used for all kinds of cordage materials and netted artifacts; the 2-ply elements were predominantly spun with a final Z-twist (S-twist singles). Thus, different fibers were spun in different directions and the resulting elements were used for specific purposes (I. W. Johnson, n. d.)

According to Drs. Smith and MacNeish (1964: 675–76), there is now proof that the antiquity of cotton (*Gossypium hirsutum* L.) goes back to 5000 B.C. Since this discovery is of utmost importance, parts of their study are quoted as follows:

Gossypium remains in the form of cloth, string, assorted bits of fiber, and boll fragments are common among plant remains from upper levels of four of the caves. . . .

In earlier levels of the deposits, the fragments of cotton become less frequent, but they are found in association with obviously cultivated plant remains as early as the Abejas period, which MacNeish dates between 2300 B.C. and 3400 B.C. Preservation of plant remains is excellent: identifications of the material are unequivocal. . .

The most remarkable cotton find is the two segments of a cotton boll excavated in Coxcatlan Cave in Zone XVI, an El Riego floor level dated between 7200 B.C. and 5000 B.C. Three carbon-14 dates for Zone XVI are all around 5800 B.C. . . .

The fundamental significance of the Coxcatlan cotton boll fragments is that *Gossypium hirsutum* was present in North America at an archaeologically early period and that it was well differentiated from the other tetraploid American species of Gossypium. . .

Yarns

Nonloom Fabrications

The finds seem to indicate that noncotton yarns were generally used in the manufacture of nonloom textiles. These include items such as netting, twining strands, cordage for comb(?), tump line(?), and a seed necklace.

Although the examples are too few to point out definite spinning habits, they seem to have in common 2-ply, Z-twisted cordage. Only two atypical forms were found. With the possible exception of the very fine cordage, the elements used for twining, plus the "warp" and "weft" of various artifacts, were probably twisted by hand, without the aid of a spindle.

1. *Netting.* There are seven fragments of netting. With the exception of one, the cordage is 2-ply, Z-twist; singles are S-spun. The exception happens also to be the earliest net fragment and comes from the El Riego phase of Coxcatlan Cave (Zone XV). Its cordage exhibits very fine 2-ply, S-twist elements; the singles are Z-spun. The fiber, which is light colored, seems to be from a different plant source than the fibers appearing in the next levels. Of interest, here, is the fact that the cordage is spun in the opposite direction.

Zone XIV of the same site and same period produced four netted fragments; their cordage is 2-ply, Z-twist, and tightly spun. An example from Burial 2 is exceptionally fine, hard, and evenly twisted; it is comparable to some of the extremely fine and resilient cordage found at Candelaria, Coahuila (I. W. Johnson, n.d.). The cordage used in the piece of full-turn knotless netting, from Zone XI, is also 2-ply and tightly Z-twisted.

2. *Twining Strands.* The earliest specimen of weft-twining comes from Burial 3, of the El Riego phase of Coxcatlan Cave. Twining strands are single ply, finely S-twisted; the "warp" of this mat(?) is made of finely shredded, unspun vegetal material. A later example (Palo Blanco, Zone IV) of twining is represented by a tassel-like artifact (Fig. 158); again, the "warp" consists of loosely gathered, noncotton fibers which are held together by fine Z-twisted twining strands. Thus, its direction of twist is like that found in the earliest piece

of netting. A Venta Salada artifact, which seems to represent a comb, is made of slender sticks held together by rows of twining. The cordage is 2-ply, Z-twist.

3. *Cordage.* The cordage used in the seed necklace from an early El Riego level of Coxcatlan Cave shows that the seeds were threaded on fine, 2-ply, Z-twist strands (Fig. 150f). Finally, there are what seem to be fragments of a tump line, made of istle-fiber "warps"; these are 2-ply, Z-twisted elements, about 2 mm. in diameter. The "wefts" are simply bunched fibers of istle. Another tump line exhibits 2-ply, Z-twist "warps" which are loosely twisted and thicker in diameter; the "wefts" consist merely of three istle filaments, not spun together. The tump lines belong to the Venta Salada complex. (See Fig. 160).

Loom Weavings

No spindle whorls were found in early levels. Nevertheless, the cotton cloth from the Santa Maria period contains yarns which indicate that they were already spun with a spindle.

1. *Warp and Weft.* Loom-woven cloth was manufactured with cotton or noncotton yarns. Probably all yarn used in loom weaving was spun with the aid of a spindle. With few exceptions, single-ply yarns were employed for the warp and the weft. The majority of cotton yarns show that they were Z-spun, while non-cotton yarns tend to be S-spun. However, there are specimens in which the opposite occurs; i.e., cotton weaves exhibiting S-twisted yarns, and noncotton cloth woven with Z-twisted yarns. To give some examples: a gauze fragment from Coxcatlan Cave (Zone II) is woven of single-ply, S-twisted cotton yarns, dyed dark brown; the yarns are hard to crepe spun. The opposite was observed in the mummy blankets, which were woven with single-ply, Z-twist noncotton elements.

As mentioned before, it is not possible to work out a pattern of motor habits without having the complete information on fiber identification. There are too many instances where a positive statement about the source of the fiber remains in doubt. On the whole, the cotton yarns seem to be more consistent in the direction of twist than the noncotton elements. The constancy of this feature is illustrated by the fact that of sixty-three cotton yarns examined, fifty-two evidenced Z-twist spinning, seven were S-twist, and four were 2-ply, S-twist. Of twenty-nine noncotton specimens analyzed, seventeen exhibited S-twist, ten were Z-twist, and two were 2-ply, S-twist. (I am assuming, of course, that all these yarns were correctly classified as to source of fiber.)

The few examples which show 2-ply, S-twist yarns,

193

were employed as follows: in two cases they served as reinforcement of the selvage warp in a cotton plain weave, and they served as regular weaving elements in a plain-weave cotton cloth. These specimens come from the Palo Blanco levels of El Riego Cave. Also from the same site, but from the Venta Salada phase, came a noncotton cloth woven with 2-ply, S-twist yarns. This particular piece may represent an example of the deliberate combination of different fibers; i.e., the warp(?) is thick in diameter and reddish-brown in color, while the weft(?) is finely spun of tan-colored fibers.

In short, 2-ply weaving yarns seem to be the exception rather than the rule.

Of particular interest are two specimens which combine S-twist warps and Z-twist wefts in their weavings. This method appeared in two fragments from Zone I of Coxcatlan Cave (Venta Salada period). Both are semi-basket weaves; one is made of cotton, the other of noncotton fibers. The degree of twist varies from medium hard to very hard to crepe. The difference in the direction of twist in warp and weft gives the texture a crepelike and resilient effect.

Another variant turned up in a fragmentary cotton cloth from the same site, but from Zone II; here, Z-twisted wefts are combined with S-twisted wefts. The warp is finely Z-spun all the way through; the weave combines plain and semi-basket variations.

The amount of twist given a yarn affects, to a certain degree, the quality of a loom-woven cloth. In Tehuacan textiles there is considerable variability, which often depends on the kind of fiber employed and the use to which it was put. The earliest piece of weaving, recovered from a Santa Maria level, has single-ply, Z-twist yarns of cotton; the degree of twist is hard to crepe.

In the Palo Blanco horizon, most of the cotton yarns are spun medium hard to very hard; some show tight crepe twist. Ordinarily, the method is to give the warp a somewhat tighter twist than the weft; this results in a finer diameter and added strength for the warp. The mummy-bundle wrappings exhibit differently colored warps which are medium to hard spun. Diameters are fairly fine, though the inner blanket shows a range from very fine to thick. One fragile cotton specimen from El Riego Cave has very fine and hard-twist yarns, dyed reddish brown; the weft cording elements are more loosely spun and thicker in diameter. The combination of plain weave and weft cording is voile-like in texture. From the same site comes a cotton fragment with S-twisted, crepe-spun yarns.

In the Venta Salada complex there are a number of yarns which show great range in the degree of twist. A plain-weave fabric from Coxcatlan Cave (Zone III) is woven of what seems to be shredded yucca fibers. Though the yarns are fairly coarse and thickly spun, the weave is not uneven; it may have served as a sturdy carrying cloth. As a contrast, an all-over gauze weave, from the same cave (Zone II), exhibits very fine and hard-spun yarns, which are dyed dark brown. The tightly twisted yarns give a creped appearance to the finely woven cloth. Another brocaded-gauze piece combines single-ply cotton yarns, which range from very hard to crepe twisted and are fine in diameter; the contrasting brocading weft of double yarns is loosely spun. Another advanced weave, represented by a twill cloth, employs yarns which have a medium hard to very hard twist and, in some parts, are even tightly creped.

2. *Twining Elements.* These consist of heavier yarns which are formed by twisting together two or more singles; the final twist is, as a rule, in the opposite direction from the initial spinning of the singles. The twining elements used in the mummy blanket are 2-ply, S-twist noncotton elements, which were loosely twisted together. The strands employed in the twined weft-fringe are also 2-ply, S-twisted; but they are hard-spun, strong cotton yarns.

3. *Seams and Mends.* As described above, single-ply yarns are the typical yarns employed in weaving. But yarns used for seaming and mending are generally multiple-ply strands, to give them more strength. Thus, Tehuacan seaming yarns of cotton include 2-ply, S-twist and 3-ply, S-twist yarns; in each case, the singles are Z-spun. Examples of noncotton sewing yarns vary from single-ply, Z-twist to 4-ply, S-twist elements. Worth mentioning is a 3-ply, S-twist yarn used for mending the inner mummy blanket; it represents a two-tone yarn in which each of the three plies is composed of a white and a blue strand; these are twisted together to form three Z-twist elements which, in turn, are made up of two Z-twist singles.

Another multiple-ply cotton cordage, found in the Venta Salada phase, is composed of a 2-ply, Z-twist element about 2 mm. in diameter. Each ply is formed of approximately fourteen singles, which are S-twisted together; the singles are finely Z-twisted. This specimen also represents a two-tone yarn; each ply contains about five or six blue singles; the rest are white.

Colors and Dyes

The bulk of the collection is made up of plain-weave cloth, generally woven of natural color yarns and left undecorated. Patterning through color first appears in the Palo Blanco complex, the common method being to dye the thread before it is woven.

Coxcatlan Cave yielded three specimens decorated

with warp-striped patterns. The best preserved and most outstanding examples are the two blankets found wrapped around the mummy from Zone VI. These two noncotton specimens have preserved their color to an astonishing degree, the outer wrapping undoubtedly being the newer cloth at the time the body was buried.

It is often difficult to distinguish accurately the dye colors of an archaeological textile. Sometimes it is even impossible to tell whether the color is due to accidental staining or to intentional dyeing. Frequently, the original shade has changed through fading; thus, one must guess whether a light brown and a medium-dark brown originally came from the same or from different dye lots. Or, they might have come from the same dye lot, but one sample could have been dyed first, when the dye was more concentrated, while the lighter shade might have been obtained later, when the dye was already diluted. This, in fact, seems to have occurred with some of the brown- and blue-dyed yarns of the outer blanket. The medium dark blue and blue-green yarns may be from a single dye lot, and the medium dark brown yarns may have come from the same lot as the light brown yarns. Taking these possibilities into account, there follows a list of the eight—or six?—colors distinguished on the outer wrapping, arranged according to the frequency of use. The number of stripes of a color are in parentheses and are multiplied by two because the wrapping consists of two webs. The shades are: medium dark blue (9 × 2), blue green (5 × 2), blue black (5 × 2), medium dark brown (8 × 2), light brown (2 × 2), tan (6 × 2), natural or creamy (6 × 2), rusty (orange) red (7 × 2). The rusty-red color gives evidence of having deteriorated the fibers, since many of these yarns have fallen out.

The inner wrapping exhibits a warp-striped pattern with the following combination of five—or four?—colors: blue green, blue, light brown, tan, natural (creamy). This blanket has more blue in its pattern than the outer blanket, which emphasizes brown and rusty-red shades. Because of the better state of preservation of the latter, it was easier to work out its color sequence. For the inner wrapping, which was already faded and worn when used as a burial robe, it was practically impossible to obtain an accurate order of frequency.

The third specimen showing color is a cotton fragment from Zone IV of Coxcatlan Cave. One set of yarns is dyed gray; the opposite set has a barely visible warp-striped pattern in gray and brownish yarns. The latter may well represent natural-brown cotton.

El Riego Cave yielded four colored specimens. From Zone D (Palo Blanco) came a cotton weave with a warp-striped pattern in blue and white. Zone C yielded two cotton weaves which have both the warp and the weft dyed reddish brown; one specimen is exceedingly fragile, the other is so brittle that it is practically reduced to powder. Once more it is the reddish-brown (or rusty-red) color which, whatever its source, wears out the yarns first. The fourth specimen has brown-colored warps and wefts, but here again the fiber may be natural-brown cotton.

In contrast to the Palo Blanco specimens, none of the Venta Salada examples are characterized by warp-striped patterns. The majority have both sets of yarns dyed the same color. This phase produced several pieces of gray-dyed yarns. At Coxcatlan Cave, five such specimens appeared in Zone II: four were cotton cloths with warp and weft dyed in varying shades of light and medium gray; one was a 3-ply cotton cord, light gray in color. The second color shown by examples from Zone II is dark brown, exemplified by a fragmentary gauze weave of cotton and also by a piece of 3-ply cotton cord, which may have been dyed intentionally or stained accidentally. Zone III contained three colored specimens. One plain-weave piece has cotton yarns that are dyed a smoky gray-black. Another bunch of cotton yarns is gray colored. A third weave exhibits mainly blue-gray cotton yarns, which are mixed with a few brownish yarns (natural-brown cotton?); it is not clear whether this represents a striped pattern or not.

The Postclassic levels of El Riego Cave yielded a few woven specimens exhibiting reddish-brown dyed yarns; they are extremely fragile and practically reduced to a powdery substance. One more gray-colored cotton weave was found in Zone A. Of special interest for the identification of dye sources is a sample of red hematite, found wrapped in a piece of cloth and also recovered from Zone A (Fig. 156).

Two nonloom specimens having color are exemplified by: a two-toned cotton cord from Tc 268 and a noncotton mending yarn from Coxcatlan Cave (Palo Blanco). Both are made up of blue and white elements (see above, Yarns).

Complete information on dyes and dyeing processes used by the ancient inhabitants of Mesoamerica would be of the greatest interest to students of archaeological textiles. Unfortunately, very little has been done to determine the sources of prehistoric textile dyes. For Mexico, there are very few reliable reports which contain scientific data on coloring matter. Peter Gerhard thoroughly discusses the history and distribution of the famous shellfish dye in America (Gerhard, 1964b:177–90). Dr. Kasha presents a detailed chemical analysis of the coloring matter in pre-Columbian textiles of Chi-

Fig. 156. Lump of red hematite found wrapped in plain-weave cloth.

huahua. He was the first to subject colored textile material to a spectrophotometric analysis. The results of his study are of considerable value, particularly in respect to this study. According to Dr. Kasha (1948:156), the Chihuahua textile worker produced

... orange colors by a purely *inorganic* pigment resulting from precipitation of ferric hydroxide within the fiber; a greenish-black by means of a purely *organic* dyestuff, plant indigo, using a relatively complicated "vat-dye" process ... and blue-black and brown colors by means of an *organic dye mordanted by metallic hydroxides,* namely alizarin mordanted by ferric hydroxide and (chiefly) aluminum hydroxide, respectively. The colors in each case were somewhat modified by the natural yellow-brown of the Apocynum.

In this connection, it is of considerable interest to mention that the colors found in the yucca-fiber warp-striped mantles from Candelaria Cave, show striking similarities with those of Chihuahua; i.e., the predominant colors are various shades of dark and light browns, reds, and pale bluish grays (I. W. Johnson, n.d.).

Although a thorough analysis of the Tehuacan textile dyes remains to be done, we may surmise that the dark blues, blue-greens, blacks and browns, rusty reds, and so forth, might well prove to be from sources such as those found in the Chihuahua materials.

Nonloom Fabrications

Netting

The Tehuacan finds contain several specimens which come under the classification of single-element tech-

niques, that is, only one element is used to construct a fabric. The finds include the following types: knotless netting and knotted netting. The examples are so small and fragmentary, however, that nothing can be deduced as to their original shape and utility. They may have been carrying nets, pouches, string aprons, or have served some unknown purpose.

1. *Knotless Netting.* Two variants of this technique were recovered: simple looping (or plain coiling) and full-turn looping (or loop-and-twist technique). In simple looping, the technique is to work successive rows of coils into the loops of the preceding row (Fig. 157). The mesh may be closely set together, or it may be open and widely spaced. Only one example of plain-coiled small-mesh netting was recovered; it came from Zone XIV of Coxcatlan Cave, an El Riego component.

Full-turn looping is derived from simple looping in that an extra twist is given to the basic loop (Fig. 157). The full-turn variant is exemplified by two fragments; one from Burial 4, of the El Riego period, and another from the Coxcatlan phase. The cordage is 2-ply, Z-twist, tightly and evenly spun of noncotton fibers. The mesh is approximately 0.5 cm. high. The earlier fragment was found on top of a basket, which was inside another basket, all of which was placed on top of the skeleton's skull.

2. *Knotted Netting.* This technique is represented by six fragments, which exhibit two different types of knots in their construction.

Two examples were tied with overhand knots (Fig. 157). These pieces come from El Riego levels of Coxcatlan Cave. The earliest one (Zone XV) is made of 2-ply, S-twist cordage; the singles are finely Z-twisted, noncotton fiber. The mesh of this small piece is approximately 2.5 cm. square. The second example, found in Zone XIV, has a fine mesh measuring about 1.0 cm. square. Its noncotton cordage is 2-ply, Z-twisted; singles are S-twisted.

Four specimens illustrate the use of the lark's head knot. (Fig. 157.) Three appeared in an El Riego component (Zone XIV) of Coxcatlan Cave. One fragment, caught in lumps of earth, shows a fairly large mesh. Another small piece has a mesh of 2.5 cm. square; its noncotton cordage is 2-ply, tightly Z-twisted. With Burial 2 was found a third specimen constructed in this manner. The cordage is 2-ply, Z-twisted; singles are S-spun. Though extremely brittle, it is very fine in diameter, and hard and evenly spun. The mesh of the net fragment measures approximately 1.1 cm. square. It was found over the pelvic region of a child burial, underneath a basket. This example is comparable to some very fine cordage material found at Candelaria Cave.

196

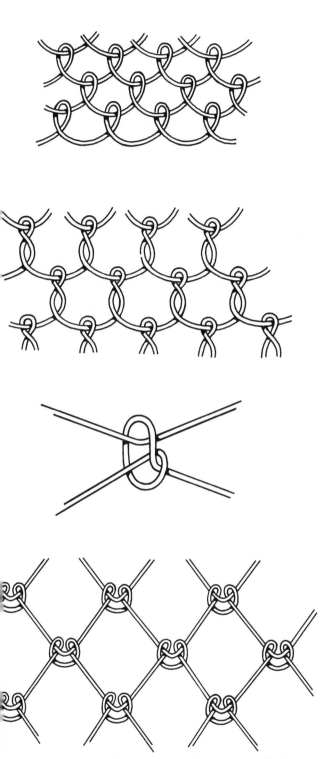

Fig. 157. Netting techniques. *Top to bottom:* Simple looping or plain coiling; full-turn looping or loop-and-twist technique; overhand knot; lark's head knot.

Another fragmentary net tied with lark's head knots comes from a Palo Blanco component. The cordage is 2-ply, Z-twisted. It is too fragmentary to measure its mesh, but the diameter of the knotting element is thicker than that of the previous specimens.

Coiled netting technique is widespread in time and space, both in South and North America (Davidson 1935:123–24, 131–32). As in the Tehuacan region, two types are known from various Coahuila sites: plain coiling and full-turn looping. The first type predominates. Coiled netting was used in the construction of patterned bands, "purses" with wooden frames, plain pouches, open-mesh bags, and so on (I. W. Johnson, n.d.). In Tamaulipas, the technique was used to make bags and a semicircular "kilt"; the latter was found in a preceramic level in Romero Cave. From the same site came large burial baskets exhibiting coiled netting stretched within oval-shaped wooden frames (Whitaker, Cutler and MacNeish 1957: 352–58; I. W. Johnson, unpubl. notes).

Full-turn looping is found in Coahuila specimens in the form of patterned bands and pouches (I. W. Johnson, n.d.). The technique is also known from the La Perra culture, in the Sierra de Tamaulipas (MacNeish 1950:92–93; I. W. Johnson, unpubl. notes).

Knotted netting technique is represented at Candelaria Cave by the square knot, for large-mesh nets, and by the sheet bend, for small-mesh nets (I. W. Johnson, n.d.). No examples of knotted netting were found in the Tamaulipas caves.

The presence of the overhand knot and the lark's head knot in the Tehuacan region seems, therefore, to be of particular interest.

Weft-twining Technique

Analysis revealed that bits of textile material, obtained from the El Riego phase at Coxcatlan Cave, had been constructed of weft-twining technique. In Burial 2 bits of twined matting were found along the sides and underneath the legs of a skeleton. More pieces were discovered with Burial 3, partly at the left and the right sides of the skeleton, while others came from in between the ribs and down toward the hips. Whether the fabric was placed on top of the skeleton was no longer discernible, but the matting could have been wrapped all around it. In Burial 4, fragments of a twined textile were found over the chest of the skeleton.

The warp of the twined matting is made of finely shredded vegetal material. These elements are held together by a series of weft-twined rows; i.e., paired wefts are twined across the set of warps. The twining is finely and tightly worked, the rows being less than 0.5

Fig. 158. Tassel-like artifact of noncotton strands.

cm. from each other. Twining strands are fine single-ply, S-twisted elements. The remains are so fragile, however, that it was impossible to take adequate thread counts.

In Zone IX of Coxcatlan Cave, an Abejas component, two more small pieces of twined matting were found. Again the rows of twining are about 0.5 cm. apart.

The Palo Blanco complex contains a tassel-like arti-fact, made of noncotton strands (Fig. 158). The "warp" consists of loosely gathered, unspun fibers. The twining strands are fine Z-twisted elements of the same material. There are only four rows of weft-twining. The artifact looks quite clean, white, and new, but it is difficult to suggest its former usage.

The Venta Salada assemblage contained another arti-fact constructed by twining technique. It seems to be a small comb, made of five slender sticks and held to-gether by rows of weft-twining. The weft element is 2-ply, Z-twist, noncotton cordage. The whole thing is 6.5 cm. long.

Twining, as a textile-manufacturing technique, ap-peared in Romero Cave, Sierra Madre de Tamaulipas, in the form of a noncotton weft-twined robe. The robe dates from the pre-pottery Guerra culture. Later exam-ples of weft-twined fabrics occurred in the San Lorenzo and San Antonio cultures (Whitaker, Cutler and Mac-Neish 1957:354–57; Johnson, unpubl. notes). The tech-nique is also known from the El Zape caves in Durango; the twined specimens date from the historic period (Delgado, n.d.). There is no evidence of twined cloth from Candelaria, but it is reported from Frightful Cave, Coahuila (Taylor 1948: Tables 2, 3). Finally, a very fragile and possibly charred twined specimen was found near Xico (District of Chalco) which seems to be made of istle fibers and probably dates from the Late Teotihuacan period (specimens in A. A. Heflin Collec-tion).

Loom Weavings

Dimensions

The great majority of Tehuacan textile specimens are smallish fragments. They are not considered in this section because nothing conclusive about their original dimensions can be inferred. Most have no remaining selvages at all. Others show part of a preserved edge, either a side or an end selvage.

The total number of loom-woven fabrics for which full dimensions could be established is three; all come from the Palo Blanco phase. El Riego Cave yielded two fragments of a narrow band; since most of its side sel-vages are preserved, the complete breadth can be es-tablished as being 6 cm. Lengths are fragmentary. The pieces represent warp-faced weaves of noncotton fibers.

Coxcatlan Cave furnished the only examples of com-plete blanket-size cloths. They are the two mummy-bundle wrappings from Zone VI. (Figs. 159, 160). The outer wrapping is a two-breadth cloth which measures 1.33 m. in length, and 25 cm. plus 25 (26) cm. in width. One web is more completely preserved than the other. One end selvage looks like a raw edge, but may very well represent the original end selvage; although frayed, it is evenly straight. The opposite end is a fringed sel-vage (see below, Selvages). The estimated length of the blanket can be established by taking into consideration that the selvage end has worn off through hard wear. The proof of a finished end selvage is to detect warp loops along the edge; but loops may break with age and brittleness.

The inner wrapping is larger; the complete length is 1.58 m. and its two-web width is 45 cm. plus 45 cm. About 4 cm. along one side selvage is folded over and hemmed. Since this cloth is more fragmentary and brit-tle and is folded in several places, only approximate measurements can be given. One end represents a finished selvage; the opposite edge has a "knotted" fringe (see Fig. 173).

The two blankets are warp-faced, warp-striped weaves elaborated with noncotton yarns. The two-breadth cloths, which are rectangular in shape, are the only examples which give us an idea of sizes and shapes woven at this time.

Fig. 159. Outer mummy wrapping. (Photo courtesy Mission Archéologique et Ethnologique Française au Mexique.)

Fig. 160. Inner mummy wrapping. (Photo courtesy Mission Archéologique et Ethnologique Française au Mexique.)

For comparative purposes, it might be pertinent to mention the dimensions of mantles from Candelaria Cave (Johnson, n.d.). They too were woven of noncotton yarns, represent warp-faced warp-striped weaves, and were made by seaming together two webs. Complete lengths fall within the range of 1.10 to 1.82 m. Although there is a great variation in the single webs, at least thirty of them measure from 40 to 48 cm. in width. Complete breadths fall within the range of 67 and 115 cm. for two full breadths.

Among the pre-Columbian Chihuahua textiles, only three were found with complete dimensions. But, unlike the Candelaria and Tehuacan four-selvage cloths, their widths appear to be greater than their lengths (O'Neale 1948:105, 148, Tables 1, 2).

In Tehuacan, complete width measurements for non-loom fabrications are preserved for only three specimens. They come from different sites of the Venta Salada phase. These textiles are not classed with the blanket group because of their narrowness, and because they are nonloom structures exhibiting different techniques. Thus, from El Riego Cave comes a frag-

mentary "three-warp" specimen, made of istle fiber, and perhaps representing part of a tump line; its complete width is about 0.75 cm., its length is fragmentary. Tc 268 yielded two other incomplete specimens, which may also have formed parts of tump lines. One is a "two-warp" istle fabrication, measuring 0.8 cm. in width, and is the narrowest web found among Tehuacan textiles. The other, a somewhat wider over-one-under-one weave of istle, measures 1.8 cm. These three specimens are shown in Fig. 161.

1. *Two-Breadth Cloths.* It is difficult to know whether it was standard procedure among people of the Tehuacan Valley to seam together two webs to form blankets. There are only two examples—the mummy wrappings —which give direct evidence that this procedure was known, at least in the Palo Blanco period. The outer blanket consists of two webs, sewn together lengthwise, each measuring 25 to 26 cm. The inner wrapping is wider, each web being about 45 cm. (see above, Dimensions).

No earlier evidence exists, and the later periods merely give us tenuous indirect evidence. Analysis re-

200

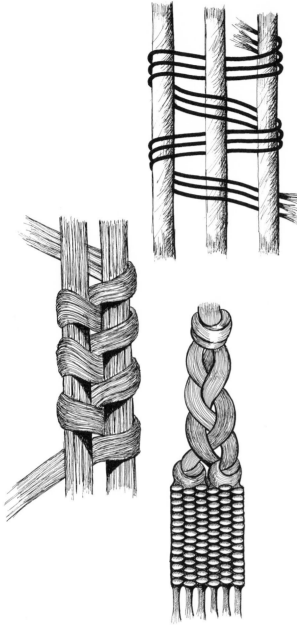

Fig. 161. Nonloom fabrications of istle fibers. *Top to bottom:* "two-warp" band; "three-warp" band; over-one-under-one fabrication with "warps" braided and tied into a knot at the top.

is knotted to a bunch of gray-colored yarns. The fact that the fragment is stitched to a second piece along an end selvage does not necessarily indicate that the textile served as a two-breadth blanket. But it may represent another type of garment, which required the joining of two or more webs.

The other example has traces of a hard-spun yarn still in place on the cloth, but not along a selvaged edge; it could be interpreted as forming part of a seam or mend.

Seaming together two webs appears to have been the conventional procedure of the Laguneros of Coahuila to obtain mantles. There were at least forty-three instances to support this assumption (I. W. Johnson, n.d.). On the other hand, O'Neale (1948:105) reports that, with two exceptions, the Chihuahua cloths are all single-breadth weavings.

Thread Counts and Textures

The fineness or coarseness of a weave is generally indicated by the number of warp and weft yarns per unit of measurement (2.5 cm.); furthermore, one must also consider the texture of a fabric when speaking of quality.

Tehuacan textiles are woven of noncotton or of cotton fibers. The majority are formed of plain-weave variants. There are a few samples of gauze and twill structures. All these different forms of interlacing give variability to the texture and pattern of a fabric and affect, to a certain degree, the thread count.

Thread counts were not taken of the very small pieces, often in a poor state of preservation, because such counts would not give accurate judgment respecting Tehuacan weaving. Besides, many yarns have shifted from their original position, thereby loosening the weave, which would produce an inaccurate count.

In spite of the relatively few counts obtained, a characteristic of Tehuacan textiles seems to be the preponderance of warps over wefts; that is, the majority of fabrics are warp-faced weaves. There are no true weft-faced specimens, and only a few examples have a square count.

Analysis showed that the warp counts fall within the range of 15 to 57 warps per 2.5 cm. The lowest warp count is 15. Only one piece has the exceptionally high count of 78 warps (by 24 wefts) per unit of measurement. Weft yarns range between 12 and 37 yarns per 2.5 cm.

Square counts are concentrated between 19 and 37 yarns for the warp, and 18 and 37 yarns for the weft. Similarly, the warp-faced weaves are concentrated between 29 and 57 warps per unit of measurement.

The earliest cotton weave, from the Santa Maria

vealed two instances which show traces of stitching along an edge, thus indicating that the cloth may have been sewn to another breadth. The examples come from Coxcatlan Cave and belong to the Venta Salada period. Both are fragmentary plain weaves of cotton. One exhibits a preserved end selvage which is whipped to another, smaller piece of selvage, both woven in the same manner. For some reason, one end of this selvage

phase, has an almost perfect square count of 32 by 30 yarns per 2.5 cm.

The specimen with the exceptionally high warp count (78 warps by 24 wefts) comes from the Palo Blanco period; it is a plain weave, finely and tightly made of cotton. About four square counts were recorded for this period; the rest are predominantly warp-faced weaves. The warp-striped mummy cloths belong in this period. Textures vary considerably. Some are made of rather coarse materials, but they may be evenly and strongly woven. Others are canvas-like and may be grouped with the so-called utility cloths. Still others exhibit finely woven and fairly open textures. Special mention must be given to one piece which is a very fragile, extremely even and fine weave; it is comparable with voile-like fabrics. Its yarns are characterized by their reddish-brown color, which tends to deteriorate the fibers. The thread count is 32 warps by 30 wefts per 2.5 cm.

Different weaves turn up in the Venta Salada phase; that is, to the plain-weave variants are added some gauze and twill types. As before, the trend is to produce fabrics showing a higher number of warp over weft yarns. There are three square-count pieces, and two specimens in which the weft yarns are slightly in excess over the warps. To give a few examples: 18 single warps by 21 double wefts per 2.5 cm.; and 15 single warps by 19 double wefts per unit. Textures vary considerably: there are fairly open weaves, of noncotton fibers, which resemble present-day *ayate* constructions; some weaves are sturdy and canvas-like; others are plain coarse cloths, with unevenly spun yarns; there are several examples of close, even, and fine weaving; at least two specimens resemble grosgrain ribbon, and thus are true warp-faced fabrics; and there are a couple of fine, almost voile-like cloths, with their tightly spun yarns producing crepe-like textures; one noncotton specimen, with a square count of 37 by 37 per 2.5 cm., is a fairly fine, almost linen-like weave.

Three fragments represent gauze weaves. One is finely woven, its tightly twisted yarns producing a crepe-like texture. Another fragile piece of plain all-over gauze contrasts noticeably with its thick plain-weave borders.

Finally, the twill weave shows that it must have been a sturdy cloth at one time; the count is 29 double warps by 23 double wefts.

Candelaria and Chihuahua noncotton mantles are definitely classified as warp-faced weaves (I. W. Johnson, n.d.; O'Neale 1948:130). This type was also recovered by MacNeish from Romero Cave in the Sierra Madre de Tamaulipas (MacNeish 1950:79–96; I. W. Johnson, unpubl. notes). The Laguneros of Coahuila

did not attempt to excel in fine weaves; their interest was oriented toward the ornamentation of fabrics which certainly show a great variety of handsome warp-striped patterns.

Weaving Procedures

1. *Selvages.* The Tehuacan fabrics were probably woven on the backstrap loom in much the same manner as found elsewhere in Indian communities of Mesoamerica. The standard method, even to-day, is to weave rectangular webs singly on the loom. Each web represents a separate warping operation which establishes its length and width. The warp skein is held by loom-strings and is bound to the loom bars by winding cords. After completion of the weave these cords are united and the result is a four-selvage fabric. Evidence of such weaving procedures is deduced from the presence of the following features, even though preserved on mere portions of a weave.

a. Side selvages. The majority of cloths examined for selvage treatment have no preserved edges at all. In a few cases, only small sections of a finished selvage are available. From these we learn that no special arrangement was made to strengthen the side edges. Most are of the plain-edge variety. This is true for the Palo Blanco and Venta Salada specimens, for which we have the evidence. In general, the outermost selvage yarn is composed of a single warp and there is no congestion, or only a slight one, near the edges. There is no difference in the weave, either.

No examples of a twined selvage, which produces a strong and cordlike edge, were found.

In the Palo Blanco period there are two plain-weave specimens, made of cotton, which differ from the others. They exhibit a kind of reinforcement provided by the introduction of double warps at the side edges; in one, the edge warp consists of a 2-ply, S-twist element, which is followed by a double warp. These features give them an unusual selvage treatment. Two frayed selvages were mended by rolling under the edges and fastening them with whipping stitches, to keep them from raveling further. (See above, Seams and Mends).

The Venta Salada period continues to show similar procedures, although some interesting variants turn up. One semi-basket weave shows that the last warp is double; in another, the last two warps are double. The gauze fragment gives evidence of the only sturdy and unusual reinforcement seen on a side selvage; a group of ten thick warps, each a 2-ply, S-twist yarn (singles, Z), form a band almost 2 cm. wide. This heavy side edge contrasts markedly with the fragile weave of the gauze section (see Fig. 168).

202

b. End selvages. With a single exception, the specimens with partially preserved end selvages have the same technical features in common. They appear in both the Palo Blanco and Venta Salada phases. The method consists of strengthening the edges by introducing thicker wefts in the first two, three, or four sheds; some of these thick elements are double wefts, others are thick 2-ply, S-twist or Z-twist cords. One specimen has a unit of four wefts in the first shed; another variant shows a unit of four wefts in the first shed and this is followed by nine rows of double wefts.

Once more, the two mummy blankets are the only examples furnishing complete details. One end selvage of the outer wrapping resembles a raw edge, except for the fact that the whole edge is still fairly straight; the warp loops may have broken or worn off or become frayed. The opposite end selvage represents a loop-fringed end; a weft-twined decorative finish is worked in just above the fringe (Fig. 172). The inner blanket shows that one edge has the cut warp ends worked into a "knotted" finish (Fig. 173). Its opposite end selvage represents a finished selvage, with the warp loops going over a thick loom-string cord, of four singles. The fact that this edge is a true selvage, favors the view that the outer blanket had a similarly finished end selvage, even though it is no longer discernible.

The only specimen that illustrates a different method of selvage construction comes from a Palo Blanco level of El Riego Cave; it seems to be a true weft-twined reinforcement. The twining elements contain approximately sixteen to eighteen cotton strands; individual ones consist of at least two yarns. There are about four rows of tightly worked regular twining; the following three rows contain double wefts. Since this is the only preserved example of a twined edge finish, it is impossible to know whether it was a common or an atypical form of selvage treatment.

There were no specimens which showed stitchery to keep frayed edges from raveling.

Comparing these methods with those employed on mantles from Candelaria Cave, it should be pointed out that the Laguneros furnished their noncotton cloths with countertwined end selvages (I. W. Johnson, n.d.). The archaeological cloths from Chihuahua, on the other hand, have both the end and side selvages finished by rows of plain twining (O'Neale 1948: 121, 129).

2. *Heading and Join.* In four-selvage webs the "heading strip" is the first piece of weaving done on the backstrap loom. Heavier yarns or double wefts are usually introduced in this narrow section. The strip regulates the width of the cloth and secures the spacing of the warps. Some heading strips are deeper than others.

Fig. 162. Plain-weave cotton cloth; the edge opposite the side selvage is folded under and hem-stitched.

Then the weaver reverses her loom and starts a second time at the opposite end. She weaves the whole length of the warp, until she comes within a short distance of the heading strip. The weaving which closes this gap is known as the "join"; it is generally recognized by the looseness and irregularity of its weave and, sometimes, by the introduction of fill-in wefts or thick yarns.

Among Tehuacan textiles there is not one piece from which we may gather information as to how the heading strips were constructed. Nor can anything definite be said regarding the manner in which the join was closed; only one specimen retained what could be construed as the join area. This fragment, an example of basket-

Fig. 163. Enlargement showing plain weave of cotton. The specimen has barely visible warp stripes of gray and brown.

weave cloth from the Palo Blanco phase, is shown in Fig. 165.

One specimen preserves what seems to be a "second start." It is the cotton gauze (Venta Salada period) which has a weft-fringe whipped to an end selvage. The strip is about 1.5 cm. deep. The first shot contains four wefts; the next twelve rows have closely battened double wefts. Each weft is a single-ply, softly Z-twisted yarn. The "second start" is followed by the fine and fragile section of gauze (Fig. 168).

3. *Fill-in Wefts.* Not one instance of a fill-in weft was detected in the specimens analyzed. Much of the technical information has been lost on account of the fragmentary condition of most pieces. Fill-in wefts are incomplete wefts which are entered only part way into the shed; they are frequently employed to straighten a slanting working edge and for closing the join.

The method is still common practice among contemporary weavers. Candelaria and Chihuahua prehistoric cloths exhibit an unusually large number of fill-in wefts (I. W. Johnson, n.d.; O'Neale 1948:125–26).

Weaving Techniques

1. *Variations of Plain Weave.* The simplest method of constructing a fabric on the loom is that of interlacing two sets of yarns, the warp and the weft, in an over-one-under-one manner. This is the basic form of plain weave. Variations are obtained by crossing single warps with double or triple wefts, or paired warps with single wefts, and so on. These variants are known as semi-basket weaves. The technique of crossing paired (or triple) warps with paired (or triple) wefts is known as a basket weave. Textural differences are created by the use or combination of these variants.

Tehuacan loom-woven cloths show that the predominant form is the basic over-one-under-one weave (Figs. 162, 163, 164). The earliest direct evidence of a plain-weave cotton cloth comes from the Santa Maria phase in Coxcatlan Cave. Only one example was recovered. There is, however, indirect evidence that the weave occurred earlier; a piece of pottery with the impression of a fabric was found in the Ajalpan phase.

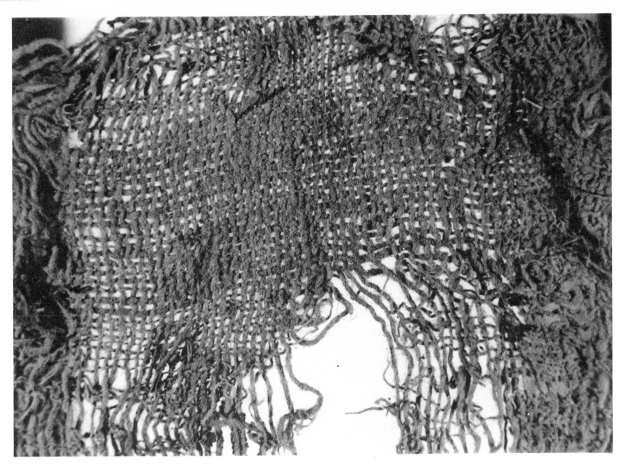

Fig. 164. A portion of a plain-weave utility cloth.

The Classic and Postclassic periods produced the majority of examples of plain-weave technique, all rendered in noncotton or cotton fiber yarns. The Palo Blanco phase had twenty-nine examples, the Venta Salada period twenty.

Even though the predominant method shown is the basic over-one-under-one type, there is considerable variety of textural differences. By employing yarns with fine or thick diameters, by spacing the yarns closely together or widely apart, by using different fiber materials, and so forth, the specimens exhibit a wide range of textures and qualities. For example, there are very fine, voile-like fabrics, there are open weaves, crepe-like cloths, tightly and evenly woven materials, linen-like weaves, canvas-type cloths, sturdy utility-type fabrics, *ayate*-like structures, and so on. The majority is monochrome colored.

Noticeable is the fact that the majority of weavings exhibit a decided preponderance of warp yarns over the weft. These are followed by a category which exemplifies a nearly balanced yarn count. On the other hand,

there are no examples of a true weft-faced fabric. (See above, Thread Counts).

The most frequently used plain-weave variation is the one which has single warps interlaced by paired wefts. This semi-basket weave is represented by eight samples from the Classic period and by eleven from the Postclassic, indicating a slight increase in the later levels. Among these pieces are a few which have a grosgrain-like texture.

Basket weave is represented by the variant of crossing paired warps with paired wefts (Fig. 165). Again, the evidence seems to indicate that this form was oftener employed in the later period; the Classic phase yielded two examples, the Postclassic five. Some of these fragments have a ribbed effect; i.e., the warp-faced weave covers the thick weft element.

A distinct pattern is obtained by the combination of basic plain weave with one of the semi-basket variants. Only five samples of this kind were recovered, almost equally from Classic and Postclassic times. There seems little doubt that this combination was used with the

the warp, or both. A weft-corded row is made by using a supplementary bobbin which carries the extra wefts together. Warp cording, on the other hand, must be pre-arranged during the warping process.

In all, six specimens showing corded patterns were found. Three instances are from the Palo Blanco period and three from the Venta Salada period. All the earlier specimens illustrate the cross-striped type. The first examples are on the mummy blankets from Coxcatlan Cave. Two paired rows of thick corded wefts were placed near the fringed edge of the outer wrapping. The first unit is 1.5 cm. from the end, the second unit is 5.0 cm. distant from the former. A thick ridge is formed by introducing a group of five to six single wefts together. The arrangement is the same for both webs of the blanket.

The inner mummy blanket exhibits a similar procedure: a cross-corded group, composed of thick wefts, is introduced near the fringed end; only one unit of cording is made. At the opposite end, there is a finished selvage with a thick weft cord serving as the loomstring; this is followed, at short intervals, by two more weft cords. At a distance of 3 cm., another two rows of cross-cording are inserted. In this case, the weft-cording served to strengthen the end selvage rather than to decorate the cloth.

From a later level of Coxcatlan Cave (Zone V), there is another fragment with an interesting combination of two plain-weave variants (i.e., basic plain weave and single warp crossed by double weft) alternating with rows of weft-cording.

From the Postclassic period at El Riego Cave (Zone C) comes a very fragile cloth, made of finely spun reddish-brown yarns, and exhibiting the following set-up:

6	rows of semi-basket weave
	(single warp/double weft)
8	rows of plain weave
6 (7?)	rows of semi-basket weave
4	rows of plain weave
5 (6?)	rows of semi-basket weave
4	rows of plain weave

Thus, the plain-weave ground has fine cross stripes of corded yarns, made by putting double wefts through the shed. The pattern consists of a repetition of heavier cords, introduced at shorter and longer intervals. This is an extremely fine and fragile web, and may easily be compared with our finest voiles.

The same site yielded two more fragments showing the same structure: (1) a small and fragile piece with a section of weft-cording on its plain-weave ground; (2) the *only* example combining a corded weft and warp pattern (Fig. 166). The latter deserves special atten-

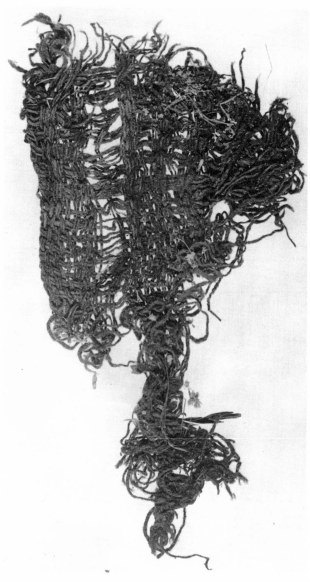

Fig. 165. Basket weave, of cotton, showing a preserved side selvage and a section of what may be the join.

idea of creating different decorative patterns, some of which are weft-corded designs (see below). However, there are other instances where this effect occurred accidentally, either through faulty shedding, or through errors in the warp arrangement, or through mistakes in the heddle set-up.

2. *Weft and Warp Cording.* A type of weave which changes the texture of a material is obtained by grouping together several yarns and putting them through the same shed. This group of yarns, which is treated as a single unit, results in a corded effect which contrasts well with the plain-weave ground. The structural patterning may be worked in the direction of the weft or

206

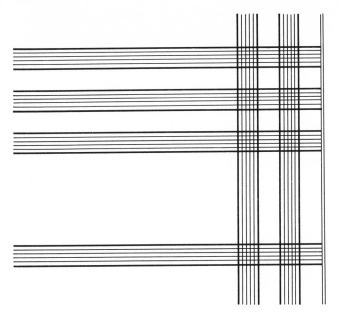

Fig. 166. "Plaid" pattern of a corded warp-weft weave.

tion: the plain ground, of white cotton, has an irregular "plaid" pattern resulting from heavier weft and warp units which are introduced as follows:

(*a*) The weft pattern unit is made up of two thick cords (four wefts in the same shed), placed along the outer edges of the unit and having four finer cords (two wefts in the same shed) between them. Three of these pattern units alternate with narrow stripes in plain weave; the whole group forms a wide cross band near the upper selvage(?).

(*b*) The warp pattern unit is similarly arranged. Corded groups of two different weights are formed: groups consisting of four warps per unit for the outer rows of cording, and groups with two warps per unit for the rows between them. Two of these pattern units alternate with two narrow stripes in plain weave. The whole pattern is placed along a preserved side selvage. Unfortunately, the specimen is too fragmentary and torn to give us the full arrangement of the "plaid." Seemingly, the corded warp pattern is only found near the outer selvages. There is indication, however, that the cross-corded motif may have been repeated, at irregular intervals, several times throughout the length of the fabric.

Another form of cording is seen in fabrics with heavy transverse rows, resembling grosgrain ribbon. A tiny sample from a Postclassic level, Zone III of Coxcatlan Cave, has a thread count in which the warp yarns outnumber the wefts; it has a texture in which the wefts are corded and the close-set warps cover them com-

pletely. The warps are fine in diameter, the wefts are thick and loosely spun.

A cotton piece from Zone II of the same site exhibits a semi-basket weave with a count of 42 warps by 15 wefts per 2.5 cm.; although its weave is coarse, it is decidedly corded.

There is not much evidence concerning the use of weft- or warp-cording in connection with prehistoric cloths. The few known instances in which the technique appears as a decorative feature are: (*a*) a small ceremonial cotton *huipil* (woman's garment), recovered from Cerro de San Lorenzo, Coahuila. This garment has painted floral motifs and cross-stripes in red and black; the latter are bordered by thick weft cords. The specimen dates probably from around the time of the Conquest (Barlow 1946:266–67; Johnson 1958–59:115–22, Pl. 3). (*b*) Again, on some miniature votive *huipiles* of cotton, found in a cave in the Mixteca Alta,* weft-cording was employed as a decorative motif. This suggests that the technique was probably employed regularly on garments worn by the women of that time. Even today, weft-cording is often used as a device to give textural variation to different kinds of loom-woven fabrics.

3. *Warp Striping.* Warp-striped patterns, as opposed to weft-striped design, have to be planned and arranged before the warp skein is fastened to the loom. That is, the color sequence is measured and counted off during the warping procedure. Warping for stripes represents a certain amount of effort and forethought, because the weaver has to visualize the result of the combinations before the weaving has even started. When the pattern is an all-over design, it requires frequent changes of colors. Finally, the pattern is more or less established by the time the skein is bound to the loom bars. Weft-striping, on the other hand, does not need as much ingenuity, because the weaver creates the stripes as she goes along; if the pattern does not appeal to her, she can easily unravel the portion and start over again.

In general, warp-striped fabrics are also warp-faced weaves; the closer the warps are spaced together, the clearer will the striped pattern show up. In an all-over design, it takes skill to plan the combination of colored stripes and to contrast them effectively with the background color. A great variety of patterns may be achieved by the introduction of different colors, by the expansion, repetition, or combination of basic pattern units. The units may consist of a single yarn which, in the finished weave, looks like a series of short lines

* The exact place of the site is unknown; the specimens are in a private collection.

against the background color, or, a pair of warps will show up as a thin line; or, by increasing the number of colored warps, narrow or wider monochrome sections are the result; or, different effects are created by alternating two (or more) warps of one color with two (or more) warps of another color; and so forth.

The earliest striped patterns are from the Palo Blanco period. Four of the analyzed specimens are patterned by this method. The most remarkable and outstanding ones are the two mummy wrappings from Coxcatlan Cave. Both fabrics are warp-faced, noncotton weaves. Since practically the complete blankets have been preserved, it is possible to analyze the color sequence across the whole width; however, this was more successfully achieved for the outer than for the inner blanket. The outer one contains about six to eight recognizable colors. Its two webs have the same all-over color sequence, but in reverse order; i.e., there is a bilateral arrangement of color stripes which are repeated in the same order from the center seam toward the outer side selvages. Some of the basic design units are symmetrical both in arrangement and in color proportion. The weft is all of one color, rusty red or natural color with a reddish tinge.

The colors of the warp stripes still preserve much of their original bright shadings. The complete warp set-up of Web I is given here to show the details of the pattern arrangement. The sequence runs from the outer to the inner selvage; it is repeated in Web II in reverse order. The set-up is as follows: 6 blue black—2 light brown—4 tan—32 blue black—4 light brown—46 rusty red—4 medium dark brown—18 blue black—16 medium dark blue—5 medium dark brown—1 tan—32 medium dark blue—4 medium dark brown—42 natural color (creamy white)—4 medium dark brown—44 tan—4 rusty red—4 creamy white—4 rusty red—4 creamy white—4 rusty red—4 creamy white—4 rusty red—4 creamy white—4 rusty red—42 tan (plus 2 which are double—should be 44 tan)—3 medium dark brown—44 creamy white—4 medium dark brown—27 medium dark blue—3 blue green—4 tan—2 blue green—1 medium dark blue—12 blue green—1 medium dark blue—1 blue green—12 medium dark blue—2 blue green—1 medium dark blue—4 medium dark brown—22 rusty red—4 medium dark brown—18 medium dark blue—16 blue black—6 tan—6 blue black—1 medium dark blue.

The inner blanket shows evidence of having been frequently worn before it was deposited in the grave. Its warp pattern has the following colors: natural, tan, light brown, blue, blue green. Sometimes it is difficult to decide which is the original color, because many of the yarns have faded considerably. This fabric contains more blue in its set-up than does the outer blanket; the latter emphasizes rusty reds.

Coxcatlan Cave yielded another small piece (Zone IV) showing a simple striped pattern. This cotton specimen, voile-like in texture, barely shows alternating stripes in gray and brown. The weft(?) is all gray colored; consequently, the gray warp(?) stripes appear solid-colored, while the brown ones are a mixture of the two colors (Fig. 163). From El Riego Cave (Zone D) comes a cotton fragment, having a weave that is tightly warp-faced. One can still distinguish a rather faded blue stripe, 3 cm. wide, followed by a natural-color section. Unfortunately, it is no longer possible to tell whether this pattern is repeated.

The Postclassic yielded only one specimen with a striped pattern. The cotton cloth was found in Coxcatlan Cave, Zone III; its weave is fairly open and crepe-like. The main part is woven with blue-gray yarns, but there are two sections containing brownish yarns. It is not clear whether they were introduced to produce a striped pattern, or whether the striping was accidental.

At Candelaria Cave, warp-striped blankets outnumber cloths which were patterned by other methods, thus indicating that this type of decoration was representative of Lagunero weavings. Although few design units were employed, a great variety of patterns were achieved. In contrast to the elaborately patterned stripes encountered in Candelaria specimens, Coxcatlan patterns contain mainly solid-color stripes. The most striking feature of Candelaria mantles is the choice and arrangement of colors which make up the stripes. The available range is not extensive but it is sufficient to create a variety of pattern effects. Aside from the natural color yarns, the most frequently occurring colors are various shades of browns, reddish-browns, and rusty reds. A faded bluish-gray is used occasionally. The combination of dark browns, rusty reds, and faded bluish-grays creates extremely rich and beautiful patterns (I. W. Johnson, n.d.). Though less elaborate, similar effects were achieved on the mummy blankets of Coxcatlan.

The apocynum blankets of Chihuahua described by O'Neale (1948:134–38) are also decorated by warp-striped patterns. However, the Candelaria patterns represent a development far in advance of anything suggested by the Chihuahua striped cloths.

There are a few examples from other sites: one, a cotton cloth with plain pin stripes, was found at Chametla, Sinaloa. Some bast-fiber cloths from El Zape Cave, Durango, also showed a warp-striped pattern. These pieces date from the Postclassic to the historic period (Delgado, n.d.).

4. *Twill.* Twill weave is characterized by the diagonal lines or wales which extend across the fabric, from one side to the other. The wales are made by floating the wefts over a determined number of warps. Different types of twills are obtained, depending upon the direction of the float sequences.

The Tehuacan specimen from Coxcatlan Cave dates from the Venta Salada period (Zone II). The irregularly shaped fragment of cotton measures approximately 21 by 9 cm.; it has no preserved selvages. The weave represents a two-and-two twill. Both warp and weft are composed of double yarns, i.e., two singles are treated as a unit. The weave is one in which the weft floats over two warps, under two warps, over two warps, and so on. The characteristic of this even twill is that it forms a reversible fabric (Fig. 167).

Today, twills are woven on the backstrap loom in a number of Indian communities of Middle America. In addition to the basic loom parts, the set-up is equipped with the necessary devices to produce the twill variant. For a two-and-two twill, contemporary weavers set up their loom with three heddles, one shed-roll, and two complementary pattern sticks.* These devices control the warps in the order given below; manipulation is from the bottom upward.

Unit of repeat:

```
12 - - 9 8 - - 5 4 - - 1      Shed roll
12 11 - - 8 7 - - 4 3 - -     III. Heddle
12 11 - - 8 7 - - 4 3 - -     II. Pattern stick
 - 11 10 - - 7 6 - - 3 2 -    II. Heddle
 - 11 10 - - 7 6 - - 3 2 -    I. Pattern stick
 - - 10 9 - - 6 5 - - 2 1     I. Heddle
```

In the Coxcatlan specimen, the wales cross the cloth from lower right to upper left, at an angle of approximately 53 to 57 degrees. This irregularity is due to the fact that since the cloth is fragmentary, the yarns have shifted somewhat from their original position. The average warp count per 2.5 cm. is 29 (double yarns); the weft number 23 (double yarns). It is not possible, now, to know what use this sturdy cloth might have had; its weave is fairly even, and the yarns exhibit a twist which ranges from hard to very hard to crepe. Otherwise, the all-white textile is completely unadorned.

Thus, the methods used today by some of the Mixteca Alta weavers are probably representative of those employed in Postclassic times in the Tehuacan Valley.

* As exemplified by the set-up of a twill loom from Teotongo, Tamazulapan, Oaxaca (Mixteca Alta region); it is used by Chocho Indians for weaving wool blankets. Twill looms are also used by the Nahuatl Indians of San Bernardino, a town above Teotitlan del Camino, Oaxaca.

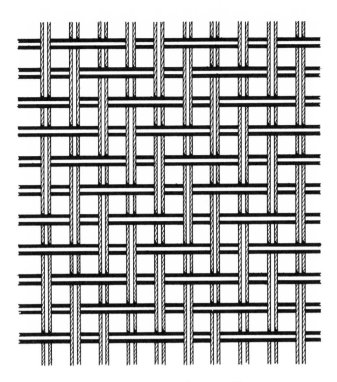

Fig. 167. Two-and-two twill.

Twill-weaving was carried out with the aid of heddles; although finger-weaving could have been employed, it is an exceedingly laborious process.

One other twill specimen was recovered from the Tehuacan region (Tc 267). It is a one-and-two twill. However, since the yarns are spun of wool fibers, there is little doubt as to its post-Conquest origin.

Several variants of archaeological twills have been recovered in Mesoamerica. Two-and-two twill cotton cloths were found in La Perra Cave, Sierra de Tamaulipas. They are said to date from the Laguna culture of 500–300 B.C. MacNeish found another cotton twill of the same variant in Romero Cave, Sierra Madre de Tamaulipas; it dates from the Palmillas culture of A.D. 150–850 (MacNeish 1950:79–96; 1961:94–96). In a Postclassic site at Chametla, Sinaloa, there appeared an interesting piece of reversed twill of cotton, which was preserved through contact with copper (Delgado, n.d.). At Yagul, in the Valley of Oaxaca, a warp-faced one-and-three twill of cotton was found; though the specimen is probably of pre-Conquest times, its exact date could not be ascertained (Johnson, 1957:77–81, Figs. 34–36). From the earliest burial at Tlamimilolpa, at Teotihuacan, some of the cotton fragments were revealed as compound-twill weaves (Strömberg 1942: 157–60, Fig. 298). And from the Maya region, we have knowledge of another compound-twill of cotton, re-

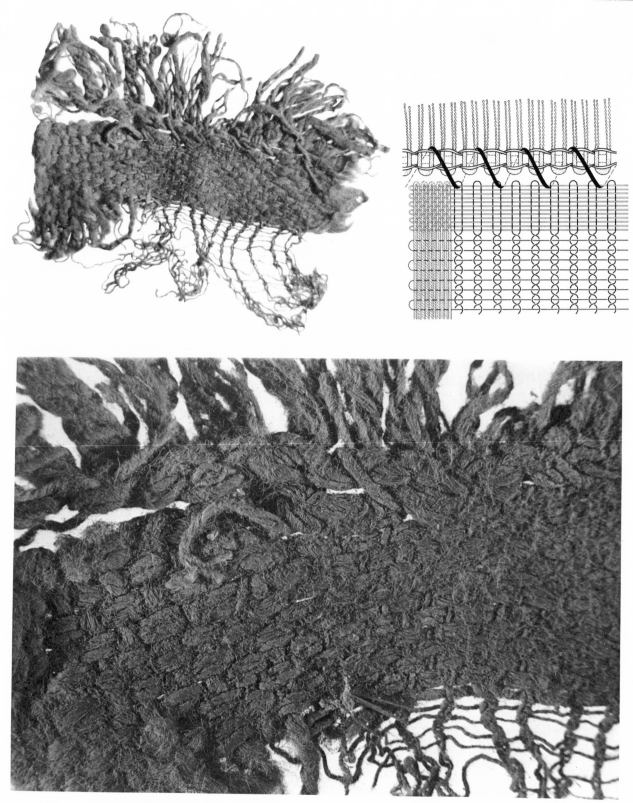

Fig. 168. Corner fragment of gauze weave, *upper left,* with twined weft fringe attached to end selvage. Shown with schematic drawing and enlarged section.

Fig. 169. Brocaded gauze, with plain-weave cross bands.

covered from the Sacred Cenote at Chichen Itza (Haury 1933, unpubl. MS, Fig. 5).

All these textile remains indicate that the ancient weavers of Mesoamerica must have had considerable knowledge of twill techniques, which represent rather an advanced form of structural patterning.

5. *Gauze.* True gauze is an open, lacelike weave which is achieved by crossing and recrossing two adjoining warps, and holding them in place by a passage of the weft. There are different types of gauzes, depending on the way in which the warps are grouped. Some are classified as plain, others as fancy or figured gauze. Contemporary weavers in Middle America elaborate certain gauze types on the backstrap loom, with the aid of a shed roll and a heddle. The latter is strung in such a manner as to control the crossings of the warps systematically; the resulting gauze is usually of the plain type. This method of setting up the loom to weave plain gauze may well have been known in Postclassic times in the Tehuacan region. In order to produce fancy or figured gauze, indigenous weavers generally use the finger-weaving method, i.e., consecutive rows of gauze are laboriously manipulated by finger work. Figured gauzes require a good deal of skill.

a. Plain gauze. Only three fragments of gauze-woven cloths are contained in the present collection, but they are among the finest and most interesting weavings of the whole group. All come from Coxcatlan Cave, and are assigned to the Venta Salada period. They are woven of single-ply cotton yarns, and fall within the classification of plain all-over gauze. In this case, single warps are regularly crossed and recrossed over adjacent single warps, and held in place by single wefts. The regular sequence of these two manipulations form vertical rows of crossed warps.

The first specimen is a fragment from Zone II, measuring 19 cm. in length and 6 cm. in width; it is made of cotton yarns which are dyed dark brown. In contrast to the other gauzes, this piece employs S-twist singles. A preserved end selvage is followed by a strip of semi-

211

basket weave, which contains nine rows of double wefts. The section of plain all-over gauze has no pattern to vary its texture, but the high twist of the yarns gives this finely woven fabric a crepe-like effect.

Another small fragment, from a somewhat later level (Zone I), measures 7.5 cm. in length and 6.5 cm. in width. It exhibits a preserved end selvage, which has a separately woven weft fringe whipped on to its edge (see below, Weft Fringe). This end seems to be the "second start"; its twelve rows of double wefts are closely battened together, thereby forming a thick and sturdy crossband. Also preserved is a portion of the side selvage, which, together with the end selvage, forms an intact corner. The warps along the side edge are made up of thick 2-ply, S-twisted yarns; ten such warps form a sturdy border. Within this reinforced corner is a small section of plain all-over gauze; its lacy and fragile texture contrasts markedly with the compact weave of the flanking borders (Fig. 168). The warp and weft of the gauze section are tightly Z-twisted, very fine in diameter, and used singly.

b. Brocaded gauze. Perhaps the most interesting example comes from Coxcatlan Cave, Zone II. It measures approximately 14 cm. in length and 23 cm. in width. This relatively small piece of cotton fabric exhibits a combination of *three* contrasting textures: (i) cross bands in semi-basket weave, (ii) decorative bands of plain gauze, and (iii) brocaded spot motifs on a ground of plain all-over gauze (Figs. 169, 170, 171).

The technique is analyzed as follows: (i) The two cross bands of semi-basket weave are approximately 1.4 cm. wide. Single warps are interlaced with double wefts for the most part, except along the outer edges where the weave is cordlike (i.e., single warps crossed by a unit of four wefts). Owing to the double wefts and the tight weave, the cross bands are solidly textured. The first band forms part of the preserved end selvage. (ii) Between these two cross bands there is a narrow strip, about 1.0 cm. wide, of plain all-over gauze (nine weft rows). The warp and weft are composed of single, finely and tightly spun yarns, which create an open, lacy texture. The second area of gauze is a wide section containing a row of brocaded spot motifs (see below). The all-over gauze ground measures 4.0 cm. in width (thirty weft rows). Following this patterned area, there is a third cross band of semi-basket weave (1.1 cm. wide), which alternates with a third strip of narrow gauze (nine weft rows); the latter is bordered by a fourth band of plain weave. Although there is evidence of a further gauze section, it is not possible to tell whether it should represent a plain narrow strip, or a wide area with brocaded motifs. (iii) The plain all-over gauze

weave is very effective as a ground for brocading, because the open and sheer weave contrasts strikingly with the heavier, solidly inwoven decoration. The spot motifs, which are rendered with thick strands of double brocading wefts, cause the design to stand out clearly on the transparent ground. The brocading technique is elaborated as shown in Fig. 171. The horizontal row of brocaded motifs contains three geometric units, each varying slightly in size and shape. The variations are due to weaving irregularities, none of which are particularly noticeable. The average size of the motif is about 4.5 cm. in width and 3.0 cm. in height. It seems to represent a stylized flower form.

Since these open-work textiles are mere fragments, nothing definite about their original use can be said. It is only from the texture and decorative features that we may venture an opinion. For example, the gauze piece with attached weft fringe may have been part of a ceremonial cloth, or *servilleta*. Such a textile, of undetermined date, was discovered in a cave near Tenancingo, State of Mexico (now in Museo Nacional de Antropología, Mexico). Its plain-weave ground is adorned by negative painting; it measures approximately 45.5 cm. by 45.5 cm. A separately woven weft fringe, constructed in very much the same manner as the example from Coxcatlan Cave, is sewn all around the fabric. The fringe, furthermore, is identical in structure to a specimen from the Sacred Cenote at Chichen Itza (Haury 1933: Fig. 19). Another textile, found in one of the caves in the Mixteca Alta region, also exhibits a twined weft fringe (Johnson, unpubl. notes). And the technique survives today among Indians in the Valley of Toluca, among the Amusgos of Guerrero, and others.

The brocaded gauze specimen may have formed part of a *huipil*, a woman's tunic-like garment still worn in many parts of southern Mexico and Guatemala. The same form of inwoven decoration is practiced by Chinantec, Cuicatec, Mazatec, and Trique Indians of Oaxaca, and by certain Nahua of the Sierra de Puebla. In addition, it is found in Guatemalan textiles (O'Neale 1945: 74–75).

Archaeologically, gauze was an important technique in Peru (O'Neale and Clark 1948:147–53) and in the Southwest of the United States (Kent 1957:506–10). It may also have been an important weave in Mesoamerica. Judging from the evidence at hand, it was probably widespread and fully developed. Examples of plain gauze have been found in the Sacred Cenote at Chichen Itza (Haury 1933: Fig. 7). At Chametla, Sinaloa, pieces of plain gauze and brocaded (or embroidered?) gauze were preserved through contact with copper (Delgado, n.d.).

Fig. 170. Silhouetted brocade designs; reverse side of Fig. 169.

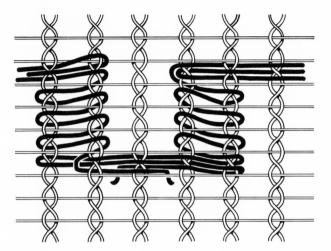

Fig. 171. Detail showing brocading technique.

6. *Weft Twining*. An unusual decorative feature was observed on the warp-striped outer mummy blanket from Coxcatlan Cave. It consists of a weft-twined pattern done near the fringed edge of the fabric. Two types of twining are represented: plain and countertwining. They were executed while the fabric was being woven on the loom; creamy white and black yarns were utilized as twining elements.

a. Plain twining. The method is to take a pair of twining elements and twist them about groups of warps; i.e., with each half turn about one another, they enclose a unit of six warps. The white twining elements are formed of four strands, softly twisted together; each is a 2-ply, S-twist yarn. The rows of twining are worked on the bare warps between two passages of the weft. Two narrow twined rows are made (see Fig. 172, *A* and *C*). One is just beyond the reinforced edge of the web. To start this row (*A*), the two halves of the twining elements were looped about the outer group of six warps, at the right side-selvage, and then successively twined around the following warp units. At the opposite, left side-selvage the two raw ends are knotted together. Thus, the direction of manipulation of the twined row is from right to left; and the diagonals slant from the upper right to the lower left. The second row (*C*) of weft-twining is done in the same manner, except that: (i) it is placed at a short distance away from the first one, (ii) the direction of manipulation is worked from the left side-selvage toward the right side-selvage. Its finishing knot is at the opposite edge, and the slant of the twining strands is from the upper left to the lower right of the pattern unit.

b. Countertwining. In the space between the two

rows of plain weft-twining, there is a center motif (see Fig. 172, *B*) which is worked in countertwining technique. The method is the same except that: (i) two rows of twining are placed next to each other; (ii) each row is worked in the opposite direction; (iii) the twining elements twist about groups of twelve warps; (iv) the countertwined rows are worked with a two-color combination: namely, one pair of black yarns works with a pair of creamy-white yarns. The latter contain from eight to ten strands, each formed of 2-ply white yarns; in contrast, the black twining element is composed of nine strands, each of which is a single-ply yarn. In Web I a secondary pattern is effected by the countertwined row; i.e., small chevrons are formed by alternating the dark and light colors. In Web II, the weaver must have made a mistake, because the chevron pattern is lost. Compared with the rows of plain twining, the countertwined motif is larger, thicker, and more noticeable on account of its two-color scheme.

Weft-twining technique is a familiar feature of both archaeological and present-day fabrics. Prehistoric textiles from Chihuahua exhibit end and side selvages which are reinforced by rows of plain twining (O'Neale 1948a:115). Present-day Tarahumara Indians work twined edges along the four sides of their wool blankets (Johnson, field notes, 1953). Archaeological mantles and narrow bands from Candelaria Cave are furnished with twined end selvages only, which are produced by countertwining technique (I. W. Johnson, n.d.). A fragment of a twined "robe" from Romero Cave, Sierra Madre de Tamaulipas, exhibits an unusually sturdy selvage reinforcement, worked with nine twining elements. The specimen dates from the preceramic Guerra culture (MacNeish 1957:352–58; I. W. Johnson, unpubl. notes). Some plain-weave cloths from Chametla, Sinaloa, are reported as having twined selvages. The same method appeared on plain-weave fabrics recovered from various caves in Durango (Delgado, n.d.). Of particular interest, with regard to the Tehuacan samples, is a miniature three-selvage web of cotton, found in one of the Mixteca Alta caves and now in a private collection, which shows a loop-fringe edge reinforced by a row of twining.

Painted(?) Design

A cotton cloth with red spots painted(?) on one surface was found in Purron Cave. Since the spots are barely visible, one can not distinguish clearly whether they formed part of a painted motif, or whether the surface was accidentally colored. The cloth, though evenly and sturdily woven, is not of particularly fine texture. It dates from the Classic period.

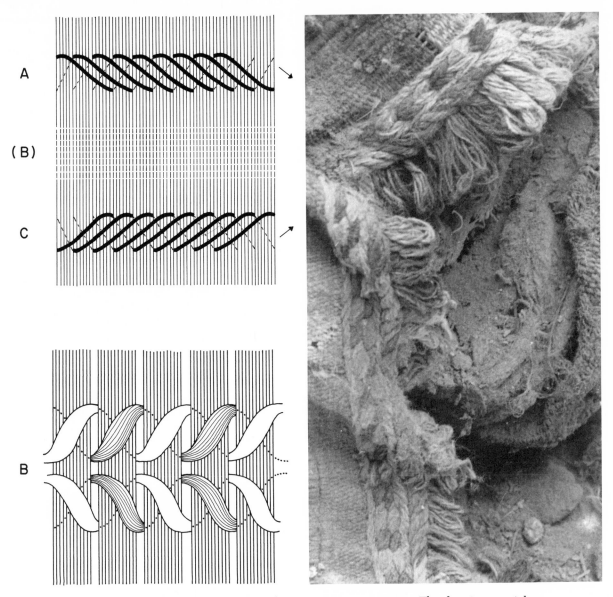

Fig. 172. Decorative end treatment of outer mummy wrapping. The drawings at right represent plain weft-twining technique (rows A and C); two rows of countertwining technique (B), used between rows A and C; and the loop-fringed end selvage. (Photo courtesy Mission Archéologique et Ethnologique Française au Mexique.)

Weft Fringe

Only one example of a weft fringe was recovered; it came from a Venta Salada level (Zone I) of Coxcatlan Cave and was attached to a fragmentary piece of gauze weave. The fringe, which was separately woven, is whipped to a preserved end selvage with a 3-ply, S-twist cotton strands (singles, Z). The wefts are held together by two rows of warp-twining; each twist of the twining strands encloses a pair of weft yarns. Since the two sets of warp pairs are twined in opposite directions, the

variant results in countertwining technique (Fig. 168). The fringe is approximately 2.0 cm. wide. Wefts are paired S-twist elements (singles, Z); twining strands are 2-ply, S-twist, hard and strong yarns. Whether or not the weft fringe was originally sewn all around the four sides of the fabric, is no longer detectable.

The find is of considerable interest, because similar constructions were found at Chichen Itza (Haury, 1933: Fig. 19), and on the painted cotton cloth from Tenancingo, state of Mexico (Museo Nacional de Antropología; Johnson, unpubl. notes), and on three minia-

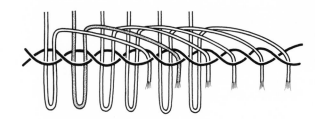

ture votive garments found in a cave in the Mixteca Alta and now in a private collection. Furthermore, the technique survives among the Amusgo Indians of Guerrero, the Otomi and Mazahua Indians of the State of Mexico, and others.

Loop-fringed Ends

The mummy blankets from Coxcatlan Cave exhibit a very particular form of reinforcement along the end selvages. On the outer blanket, this type is worked with uncut warp loops. Since the blanket has a warp-striped pattern, the fringe shows sections of differently colored warps. The decorative finish is a sort of "loop-fringe," worked as shown in Fig. 173. A row of weft-twining holds the groups of warps which form the fringe. Twining elements consist of a pair of black strands, each having three single yarns. Individual units of the fringe are made up of about six single warps, approximately 6.5 cm. in length. First, each unit is caught between a twist of the twining strands; second, the unit is brought back up and through the same twined hole, thereby forming a loop at the lower end; third, the unit is passed on and through the third twined hole, further along the row. In this manner, the fringe exhibits long looped yarns, which remain along the front side of the blanket, and cut warp ends, which are placed along the back side. In one web, the last bunch of warp strands is knotted together at the right side-selvage; in the other web, the last bunch of strands terminates in the last loop of the twined row.

The inner blanket has a different reinforcement at the end selvage. Here, the "knotting" elements are composed of three single-ply, Z-twisted strands. These are tightly "knotted" or wrapped around groups of warps (approximately 12 per group), as shown in Fig. 173. The short fringe has cut warp ends, and there is nothing to indicate how long they may once have been.

Both types of reinforcement are not only effective in keeping the ends from raveling, they also give the fabrics a decorative edge finish.

So far as is known, there is no archaeological evidence of a "loop-fringed" edge, nor of a "knotted" finish. Contemporary weavings from the Mixteca Alta sometimes have warp fringes with a similar, though not identical finish. Popoloca Indians weave wool *ponchos* which are finished with a "loop-knotted" fringe, not unlike the type described for the Coxcatlan blanket (information gathered by Carmen Cook de Leonard in Los Reyes Mezontla, Puebla). Also, some Zapotec weavers of the Miahuatlan District, Oaxaca, produce *rebozos* (shawls) and *servilletas* with decoratively finished warp ends; in some cases, the effect is almost the same as

216

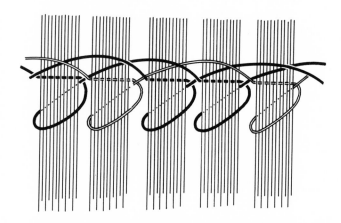

Fig. 173. Diagram of "knotted" reinforcement along end selvage of inner mummy wrapping, shown in Fig. 161.

that of the loop-fringed end of the Coxcatlan outer mummy wrapping (Johnson, field notes, 1952).

Mends and Seams

The loom-weavings show that many were already used cloths by the time they were employed as wrappings for the dead or were left behind in the caves. The evidence for this are the mends and repairs along the outer edges and within the webs.

The earliest evidence of mending comes from the Palo Blanco period. From El Riego Cave there are two cloths, one of cotton and the other of noncotton, which show remains of mended selvages; one is partly rolled under and hemmed, the other is rolled and reinforced by whipping stitches.

Purron Cave produced two sturdy utility-type cloths showing mending. One of them has a tiny piece of cloth sewn to a larger fragment. Only two whipping stitches remain as evidence; they were worked with 3-ply, S-twisted yarns (singles: Z). The other fragment has a raw edge which is turned under and hemmed with carelessly executed stitchery; the fine sewing yarn is 2-ply, hard S-twisted.

The Palo Blanco phase of Coxcatlan Cave yielded three specimens showing reinforcement and repair work. One plain-weave cotton cloth has a frayed and worn edge selvage folded under and hem-stitched with 2-ply, S-twisted yarn. This folding of frayed edges gives more strength to the selvage, but it also creates bulky and thick borders.

The inner wrapping of the mummy bundle must have been quite worn by the time it was employed as a burial blanket. Several mends are worked with running stitches. Both wrappings, composed of two webs, were seamed together along the center side selvages. Fine yarns were employed; they are single-ply, Z-twisted, natural-color noncotton. The stitches are fairly wide apart, about 2.5 cm. from each other.

From the Venta Salada phase of Coxcatlan Cave come four samples of plain weave that show evidence of mending and stitching. One piece has a preserved end selvage whipped to a fragmentary second selvage; since both are woven in the same manner, it may be that the fragments are remains of a two-web textile. Another cloth is folded diagonally and a fragment of a separate side selvage is whipped to the edge of the fold; the sewing yarn is 2-ply, S-twisted. One basket weave of cotton has been stitched to another cloth; the 2-ply, S-twist, hard-spun seaming yarn is still in place. Finally, the small section of cotton gauze weave having part of a preserved side and end selvage (Fig. 168), illustrates the method by which a weft fringe is whipped to the end selvage. The yarn is 3-ply, S-twisted cotton (singles, Z) and quite fine in diameter.

The practice of mending blankets was common among the Laguneros of Coahuila. Frayed edges are reinforced with rather carelessly executed whipping or blanket stitches (I. W. Johnson, n.d.). The worn edges of Chihuahua cloths were also mended by whipping stitches (O'Neale 1948:131–32).

Conclusions

The perishable remains from the Tehuacan Valley have given us a unique opportunity to study a textile industry which goes far back in time. The long chronological sequence of textile finds commences in the El Riego period and continues to produce artifacts of a perishable nature up to the historic times. Needless to say, this ideal situation is rarely found in Mesoamerica where climatic circumstances have generally been so unfavorable for the preservation of such evidence.

The oldest remains are in the form of loose cordage, netting, basketry, and twined matting, which appear first in the El Riego period and continue on through the Abejas period. Netting with and without knots was practiced. Knotless netting appeared in two forms: plain and full-turn looping. Knotted netting was pro-

duced by the overhand knot and the lark's head knot. Nothing much can be deduced as to the nettings' original function, because all examples are mere fragmentary remains. We can only surmise that they must have served as carrying nets or pouches or for some other purpose suitable to a people living a nomadic life. The fragments of twined matting found in early burials suggest the ancient custom of burying the dead in some kind of wrapping.

Of greatest importance for the study of textile development in the New World is the archaeological proof that *Gossypium hirsutum* L. existed in this region about 5000 B.C.

Loom weaving probably existed in the early Formative Ajalpan period, but the only evidence thereof is the indirect one of a textile imprint on pottery. The first direct evidence of cloth dates from the late Formative Santa Maria phase. There is no doubt that the earliest piece of cotton weave already shows a well-established knowledge of true loom weaving.

The bulk of the textile material was recovered from the Classic and Postclassic Palo Blanco and Venta Salada phases. Both cotton and noncotton fibers were used in the manufacture of cloth. Although some form of finger weaving was probably employed, all major procedures of backstrap-loom weaving were undoubtedly well known. The cloths represent several techniques and the weaving standards are, as a whole, fairly high.

The predominant form of interlacing is plain weave and its variants: semi-basket and basket weaves. A characteristic of Tehuacan textiles is the preponderance of the warp yarns over the weft yarns. There are no true weft-faced weaves. Only a few examples exhibit square counts. But a variety of effects are achieved: some cloths are made of rather coarse materials and resemble strong carrying cloths; others are sturdy and canvas-like; some exhibit fine, even, and open weaving; others are fragile and voile-like; there are linen-like textures and some that resemble grosgrain ribbon, etc. Thus, although the weave is basically plain, a diversity of textures is derived from the kind of material used and the skill and proficiency employed in spinning and weaving. In short, it seems evident that the function of the cloth was considered at the time of its manufacture.

The most remarkable fabrics of the Classic period are the two mummy-bundle wrappings from the early levels of the Palo Blanco phase. They are the only complete fabrics recovered and, therefore, supply most of the information on weaving procedures; they are also the only cloths that are elaborately decorated with vertically striped patterns. These wrappings contain the fullest range of colors in any of the specimens found: various hues of black, brown, tan, rusty-red, blue, and blue-green. This gives proof that the people of Tehuacan were proficient in their dyeing methods, even though the rest of the finds consist predominantly of natural-color, or single-color, or plain-striped patterns. No textiles with outstanding colored patterns were recovered from the Postclassic components.

In most cases, the weavings were primarily manufactured to withstand heavy wear and should be classed with the so-called utility cloths. In contrast to them, there are a few outstanding fragments representing gauze and twill weaves. One gauze is very finely woven of tight-twist yarns which produce a crepe-like texture. Then there is the brocaded gauze which, undoubtedly, represents a highly sophisticated weave. Two-and-two twill weaving indicates a high stage of technical development. The Venta Salada complex has also yielded twined weft-fringes and fine corded patterns. Judging from available evidence, the emphasis seems to be on structural patterning instead of colored designs.

By this time the people of the Tehuacan Valley had settled in villages or towns, which were oriented around ceremonial centers. It is quite possible that the various crafts—such as spinning, dyeing, weaving—were in the hands of specialists.

List of Textile Specimens by Type
I. Nonloom Fabrications

Knotless Netting, Simple Looping

Specimen 65–11n, Tc 50, Zone XIV. El Riego period. Fragment of knotless netting: simple looping or plain coiling. Fig. 157. Cordage: 2-ply, Z-twist, fine noncotton fiber. Mesh: 1.0 cm. square.

Knotless Netting, Full-turn Looping

Specimen 1. Tc 50, Zone XIV, Burial 4. El Riego period. Fragment of knotless netting: full-turn looping or loop-and-twist technique. Fig. 157. Cordage: 2-ply, Z-twist, hard and evenly spun, noncotton. Mesh: approximately 0.5 cm. in height. Remarks: found on top of an interlocking coil basket, which was inside another basket, which lay on top of skeleton's head.

Specimen 2. Tc 50, Zone XI, No. 134–12n. Coxcatlan period. Very small fragment of knotless netting: full-turn looping or loop-and-twist technique. Cordage: 2-ply, Z-twist, tightly spun, noncotton.

Knotted Netting, Overhand Knot

Specimen 1. Tc 50, Zone XV, No. 75–11nn. El Riego period. Fig. 157. Fragment. Cordage: 2-ply, S-twist (singles, Z), very fine, light colored. Example of a different fiber and different twist. Mesh: about 2.5 cm. square.

Specimen 2. Tc 50, Zone XIV, No. 65–11n. El Riego period. Fragment. Cordage 2-ply, Z-twist (singles, S), bast (?) fiber. Mesh: about 1.0 cm. square.

Knotted Netting, Lark's Head Knot

Specimen 1. Tc 50, Zone XIV, Burial 2. El Riego period. Fig. 157. Fragment. Cordage: very fine 2-ply, Z-twist (singles, S), hard and evenly spun, noncotton fiber; fine diameter, very brittle. Mesh: about 1.1 cm. square. Remarks: found under a basket and over pelvic region of child burial; one portion was underneath heavier cord (rope? belt?). Also, twined matting at sides of legs and underneath skeleton.

Specimen 2. Tc 50, Zone XIV, No. 65–11n. El Riego period. Fragment. Cordage: 2-ply, Z-twist, tightly spun, bast (?) fiber. Mesh: about 2.5 cm. square.

Specimen 3. Tc 50, Zone XIV, No. 65–11n. El Riego period. Fragment. Cordage: 2-ply, Z-twist, bast fiber. Fairly large mesh; net caught in lumps of earth.

Specimen 4. Tc 50, Zone V, 25–4n. Palo Blanco period. A small piece of net; seemingly end of net?. Cordage: 2-ply, Z-twist, thick diameter.

Although most of the specimens appeared in the latest El Riego level of Coxcatlan Cave, the one specimen from the Palo Blanco level suggests that this type may have had a long life span in the Tehuacan Valley.

Twined Matting

Specimen 1. Tc 50, Zone XIV, No. 145–12n. El Riego period. Very small fragment of textile material; bits of yarn and perhaps a twined section can be distinguished; difficult to say what specimen represents.

Specimen 2. Tc 50, Zone XIV, Burial 3. El Riego period. Fragment of twined matting: finely shredded vegetal material serving as "warp"; closely spaced, unspun elements. Held together by series of weft-twined rows; twining is finely and tightly worked; rows spaced less than 0.5 cm. from each other. Twining strands are finely S-twisted singles. Remarks: found partly at L and R sides of skeleton (infant); fragments also found between ribs and down to hips; mat may have been wrapped all around it.

Specimen 3. Tc 50, Zone XIV, around legs of Burial 2. Same as Specimen 2.

Specimen 4. Tc 50, Zone XIV, Feature 62. Same as Specimen 2.

Specimen 5. Tc 50, Zone XIV, Burial 4, 5, 6. Same as Specimen 2.

Specimen 6. Tc 50, Zone XIV, Burial 2, 3. Same as Specimen 2.

Specimen 7. Tc 50, Zone XIV, Burial 4. Fragment of twined matting, found over chest of skeleton. Cordage: 2-ply, Z-twist, noncotton, 6 mm. in diameter.

Specimen 8. Tc 50, Zone IX, Feature 42. Coxcatlan period. Fragment of twined matting. Same as Specimen 2.

Specimen 9. Tc 50, Zone IX, No. 69–9n. Coxcatlan period. Fragment of twined matting. Same as Specimen 2.

Specimen 10. Tc 50, Zone VIII, No. 141–9n. Abejas period. Fragment of twined matting; rows about 0.5 cm. apart.

Various Artifacts

Specimen 1. Tc 268/1–2m. Venta Salada period. Fig. 161. Three small fragments of a tump line(?); probably belong with Specimen 2 below; structure very similar. Fragments are approximately 0.8 cm. wide; lengths are 1.9 cm., 1.9 cm., and 2.9 cm. Represent a "two-warp" fabrication: unit of eight istle fibers woven around two "warps"; these cores are composed of a bunch of istle-like fibers, slightly Z-twisted.

Specimen 2. Tc 268/1–2m. Venta Salada period. Fig. 161. Three fragments of what seems to have been a tump line or a sling or part of a sandal. Very brittle and fragile. When the three fragments are placed end to end, the specimen measures over-all approximately 17 cm. in length (from upper knob to lower fragment edge). Maximum width, 1.8 cm. "Warps" consist of 2-ply, Z-twist, istle-fiber (?) elements, about 0.2 cm. in diameter; there are six "warps." The "wefts" are made of bunched istle fibers (?) and are closely spaced (about 11 wefts per inch). The two elements are interlaced in an over-one-under-one fashion. At the upper end, the loose warps are divided into three parts and braided for about 4.0 cm., ending in a big thick knot.

Specimen 3. Tc 268/1–2m. Venta Salada period. Small piece of cotton cordage: 2-ply, Z-twist, 2 mm. diameter. Each ply is made up of about 14 singles S-twisted together (singles, finely Z-twisted). Cordage is two-toned: each ply has about 5 or 6 blue singles; the rest are white.

Specimen 4. Tc 50, Zone IV, No. 74–3n. Palo Blanco. Tassel-like artifact. Fig. 158. White noncotton fibers are loosely gathered together S-fashion (not spun). Twining strands are fine, Z-twist elements of the same material. This flat object looks very clean, white, and new. Use?

Specimen 5. Tc 50, Zone III, No. 82–4n. Venta Salada period. Very small tassel-like fragment of cotton. From a top knot radiate five thick S-twist "warps," each of which consists of about four Z-twist singles. These are interlaced by finer, double "wefts" in an under-one-over-one fashion; raw ends continue outward. There are ten fairly closely spaced rows. Originally, there may have been more "spokes," because there are two more short ends protruding from the upper knot, which was seemingly formed by folding and tying the "warps."

Specimen 6. Tc 35e, Zone B, No. 38–3n. Venta Salada period. Fig. 161. Istle-fiber specimen: 3.0 cm. long by 0.75 cm. wide. Yarns: "warps" are 2-ply, loosely Z-twisted, thick in diameter; "weft" consists of three unspun fibers. Technique: the three closely spaced "warps" are interlaced by the "weft" in an over-one-under-one weave. Remarks: use?

part of a tump line? Found knotted around one end of a narrow band—see Specimen 8, Semi-Basket Weaves.

II. Loom-Woven Cloths

Plain Weave, Over-One-Under-One

Specimen 1. Tc 50, Zone VII, No. 76–8n. Santa Maria period. Fragmentary plain-weave cloth. Yarns: warp and weft are single-ply, Z-twist, hard to crepe spun, white cotton. Count: 32 by 30 per 2.5 cm.

Specimen 2. Tc 272, Zone B, No. 75–2n. Palo Blanco period. Fragmentary plain-weave, warp-face cloth. Yarns: warp and weft are single-ply, S-twist, medium-hard-spun cotton. Count: 52 warps by 26 wefts per 2.5 cm. Selvage: one plain side selvage preserved. Remarks: one surface of cloth shows red spots, very weak and barely visible, perhaps worn off. May be part of painted motif or may be accidental coloring. Cloth not particularly fine, though evenly and sturdily woven; rather like canvas in texture.

Specimen 3. Tc 272, Zone B, No. 6–2n. Palo Blanco period. Very small fragment of sturdy, utility-type plain-weave cloth; some cordage is attached to it. Yarns: warp and weft are single-ply, S-twist, medium-hard-spun cotton(?). Cordage or sewing element: 3-ply, S-twist (singles, Z); same fiber as weave. Remarks: specimen represents an instance of mending; a tiny piece is sewn to a larger fragment with the cordage described; only two whipping stitches remain.

Specimen 4. Tc 272, Zone C, No. N7E5. Palo Blanco period. Fragment of plain-weave cloth; though yarns are fairly evenly distributed, weave is rather coarse, like sacking material. It is *ayate*-like, except that the fiber is much softer than istle. Size: about 29 by 49 cm. Yarns: single-ply, S-twist, medium to crepe spun, natural color noncotton; not smoothly spun. Count: 19 warps (?) by 18 wefts (?) per 2.5 cm. Remarks: Though specimen is fairly large, cloth is quite worn and edges are raw; some yarns have shifted; there are several holes.

Specimen 5. Tc 50, Zone V, No. 80–3n. Palo Blanco period. Very small fragment of plain-weave cloth; yarns more closely spaced in one direction, probably warp faced. Yarns: single-ply, S-twist, hard-spun noncotton.

Specimen 6. Tc 254/1–1n. Palo Blanco period. Small fragmentary plain-weave cloth. Yarns: single-ply, S-twist noncotton (yucca-type fiber). Remarks: stuck to cloth is fragment of very finely spun cordage different from fabric fiber; it is single-ply, S-twist, shiny, hard fiber.

Specimen 7. Tc 254, Zone B[1], No. 27–1n. Palo Blanco period. Radiocarbon date, A.D. 330. Fragmentary plain-weave cloth, warp (?) face. Yarns: single-ply, Z-twist, medium hard to hard to crepe spun, seemingly cotton. Remarks: very small piece of cordage attached, of different fiber from cloth; 4 ply, Z-twist (singles, S).

Specimen 8. Tc 254, Zone B[1], No. 12–1n. Palo Blanco period. Radiocarbon date, A.D. 330. Fragmentary plain-weave cloth; weave very evenly distributed, texture of sheeting material. Yarns: single-ply, Z-twist, evenly spun cotton.

Specimen 9. Tc 50, Zone IV, No. 129–2n. Palo Blanco period. Fragment of plain-weave cloth. Yarns: warp and weft are single-ply, Z-twist, medium hard to very hard spun, white cotton. Count: 24 warp by 26 weft per 2.5 cm., approximately square. Selvage: part of what seems to be an end selvage; first four shots are thick, 2-ply, S-twist yarns. Remarks: cloth is folded parallel to selvage; underside is frayed and worn and stitched together with hemming stitches in 2-ply, S-twist yarn. At one point, a short piece of yarn is knotted to edge of end selvage.

Specimen 10. Tc 50, Zone IV, No. 129–2nn. Palo Blanco period. Small fragment of plain-weave cloth; noncotton yarn; preserved side selvage.

Specimen 11. Tc 50, Zone IV, No. 129–2nn. Fragmentary cloth in plain-weave technique, though there are instances of double wefts interlacing with single warps—if direction of weft is correctly interpreted. Yarns: single-ply, S-twist, medium to very hard spun noncotton.

Specimen 12. Tc 50, Zone IV, No. 7–2n. Palo Blanco period. Fig. 163. Piece of plain weave, even but open, voile-like. Size: 30 cm. (max.) by 20 cm. (max.). Yarns: single-ply, Z-twist, fairly fine spinning. Yarns in one direction seem to be finer; they are hard-twist cotton, dyed gray. Yarns in opposite direction are thicker; they seem to be brown cotton (?). Pattern: barely visible striped pattern; if it is a warp-striped pattern, then all wefts are gray and the warps are gray and brown. Thus the gray stripes are solid gray; the brown stripes are brown and gray combined.

Specimen 13. Tc 35e, Zone E, No. 4–8n. Palo Blanco period. Fragment of plain-weave cloth, tightly woven of non-cotton yarns. Specimen was mixed with various cord fragments, which range from fine, 2-ply, S-twist cords (evenly spun istle?), to loosely spun 2-ply, Z-twist cord of thick diameter and different fiber, to 2-ply, Z-twist cord of medium-thick diameter and different noncotton fiber.

Specimen 14. Tc 35e, Zone D, No. 4–5n. Palo Blanco period. Batch of seven or eight related cloth fragments; plain weave, warp face, finely and tightly woven. Yarns: 2-ply, S-twist noncotton. Count: 78 warps by 24 wefts per 2.5 cm. Selvages: side selvages partly rolled under and hemmed (mended). End selvage shows special finish: a hard-fiber cordage is whipped around a section of it; evidently represents a weft-twined reinforcement, involving about 16 or 18 strands; individual twining elements consist of at least two yarns; there seem to be about four rows of regular twining; the next three rows contain double wefts. Pattern: warp-striped, very much faded, consists of a blue stripe 3.0 cm. wide followed by a natural-color area; it is impossible to tell whether this combination is repeated. Remarks: fragments may have been parts of a mantle? or a band? A hard-fiber cordage (istle?) was attached: 2-ply, S-twist (singles, Z).

Specimens 15 and 16. Tc 35e, Zone D, No. 38–4n. Palo Blanco period. (15) Fragment of plain-weave cloth, finely woven. Yarns: single-ply, Z-twist, fine cotton (?). (16) Fragment of plain-weave cloth, fairly open weave. Yarns: cotton; wefts are single-ply, Z-twist, fine diameter; warps are single-ply, Z-twist, somewhat thicker diameter. Selvage: plain side selvage preserved.

Specimen 17. Tc 35e, Zone D, No. 33–4n. Palo Blanco period. Very small and frayed cloth fragment, plain weave. Yarns: single-ply, S-twist, crepe-spun cotton. Remarks: found with batch of cotton-like fibers with seeds.

Specimen 18. Tc 35e, Zone C, No. 5–5n. Venta Salada period. Fragment of plain-weave cloth, warp face—if close-set yarns are warps. Yarns: single-ply, Z-twist, medium hard to crepe spun, cotton.

Specimen 19. Tc 35e, Zone C, No. 11–3m. Venta Salada period. Small piece of plain-weave cloth. Yarns: single-ply, Z-twist cotton. Selvages: corner intact with end and side selvages. Edge warp of side selvage is 2-ply, S-twist, and next warp is double; unusual form of side reinforcement. End selvage: first 3 shots contain double warps; one of them seems to have become S-twisted.

Specimen 20. Tc 35e, Zone C, No. 11–4n. Venta Salada period. Tiny fragment of plain-weave cloth; yarns are single-ply, S-twist noncotton.

Specimen 21. Tc 35e, Zone C, No. 11–3nn. Venta Salada period. Tiny piece of plain-weave, warp-face cloth. Yarns: single-ply, Z-twist cotton. Remarks: found with small batch of unspun and spun cotton yarn (single-ply, Z-twist).

Specimen 22. Tc 35e, Zone C, No. 28–4m. Venta Salada period. Small piece of plain-weave cloth; some yarns create a semi-basket variant, probably accidental (i.e., double warps crossed by single weft, or single warp crossed by double weft). Yarns: single-ply, S-twist, noncotton.

Specimen 23. Tc 35e, Zone C, No. 33–3n. Venta Salada period. Two long fragments of a narrow (6 cm.) band; plain weave, warp face. Yarns: single-ply, S-twist noncotton (?). Selvage: most of side selvages preserved; ends raw.

Specimen 24. Tc 35e, Zone C, No. 10–5n. Venta Salada period. Small fragment of plain-weave cloth, closely woven in one direction, warp face (?). Yarns: single-ply, S-twist noncotton (?).

Specimen 25, 26, and 27. Tc 35e, Zone C, No. 37–3n. Venta Salada period. (25) Fragmentary cloth, fairly even plain weave. Yarns: single-ply, S-twist, seemingly noncotton. Count: 29 by 36 yarns per 2.5 cm. (26) Fragment of plain-weave, warp-face (?) cloth. Yarns: single-ply, S-twist noncotton. (27) Fragment of cloth, plain weave, noncotton. Selvage: remains of a mended selvage (?), rolled up and fastened by whipping stitches.

Specimen 28. Tc 35e, Zone B, No. 40–2n. Venta Salada period. Fragments of extremely fragile and powdery plain-weave cloth; impossible to determine whether it is patterned in any way. Yarns: single-ply, S-twist, noncotton, reddish-brown color. Remarks: resembles very fine semi-basket-weave specimen from Tc 35e, Zone C (No. 9–2n), described below under Semi-Basket Weaves.

Specimen 29. Tc 35e, Zone B, No. 29–3n. Venta Salada period. Small piece of plain-weave cloth. Yarns: single-ply, Z-twist, cotton.

Specimen 30. Tc 35e, Zone B, No. 24–5n. Venta Salada period. Small fragment of plain-weave cloth. Yarns: single-ply, Z-twist, hard to crepe spun, cotton. Remarks: found with batch of unspun fibers.

Specimen 31. Tc 35e, Zone B, No. 1–2n. Venta Salada period. Largish fragment of plain-weave cloth, open textured. Yarns: 2-ply, S-twist, noncotton (?); warp (?) is thicker in diameter and reddish-brown; weft (?) is finer and tan colored. Selvage: part of end selvage, contains double wefts. Remarks: similar to an *ayate* weave; example of a combination of different fiber yarns?

Specimen 32. Tc 50, Zone III, No. 86–5n. Venta Salada period. Very small fragment of plain-weave cloth. Yarns: single-ply, S-twist, fairly coarse and thick spinning, but not unevenly done; shredded yucca fiber?. Remarks: perhaps part of coarse carrying cloth?

Specimen 33. Tc 50, Zone III, No. 87–5n. Venta Salada period. Small cloth fragment, plain weave—must have been a fine, almost voile-like cloth; tightly spun yarns give it a texture like crepe. Yarns: single-ply, Z-twist, hard to crepe spun, fine diameter, white cotton. Remarks: one corner is gathered into a knot, tied with a loosely S-spun istle-fiber cord.

Specimen 34. Tc 50, Zone III, No. 36–3n. Venta Salada period. Batch of single-ply, Z-twist cotton yarns, mixed with fragments of bark cloth (beaten kind?) and a piece of cloth done in plain-weave technique, fairly open and crepe-like. Main part of weave seems to be woven with blue-gray yarns; in two instances brownish yarns are introduced to give a striped pattern—or is patterning accidental? Yarns: (1) single-ply, Z-twist, fine diameter, hard to crepe spun, dyed blue-gray; (2) single-ply, Z-twist, thicker in diameter, brownish color (brown cotton?).

Specimen 35. Tc 50, Zone III, No. 86–5n. Venta Salada period. Fragmentary plain-weave cloth, not too finely woven. Yarns: single-ply, Z-twist, medium to hard, not too finely spun cotton; warp and weft the same; dyed smoky gray-black. Count: 12 by 21 yarns per 2.5 cm.

Specimen 36. Tc 50, Zone III, No. 86–5n. Venta Salada period. Fragmentary plain-weave cloth (found with Specimen 35), not very finely woven. Yarns: single-ply, Z-twist, medium to hard, diameter varies from fine to thick, white cotton; both warp and weft seem to belong to same lot. Selvages: first two sheds of an end selvage contain thick, 2-ply, Z-twist cord (singles, S) of white cotton. This selvage is whipped to a fragmentary second selvage woven in the same manner (though its weave is almost all gone), one end of which is knotted to a bunch of gray-colored yarns. Function? May indicate remains of a two-web textile.

Specimen 37. Tc 50, Zone III, No. 86–3n. Venta Salada period. Cloth fragment, plain weave, very even and fairly fine. Yarns: single-ply, Z-twist, soft-spun, noncotton fiber.

Square count: 37 by 37 yarns per 2.5 cm. Remarks: almost linen-like in texture.

Specimen 38. Tc 35e, Zone A, No. 6–3n. Venta Salada period. Tiny fragment of closely woven cotton cloth, plain weave. Plain side selvage.

Specimen 39. Tc 35e, Zone A, No. 11–1n. Venta Salada period. Piece of red hematite found wrapped in a fragment of plain-weave cloth.

Specimen 40. Tc 35e, Zone A, No. 12–5n. Small fragment of cloth, plain weave, with a few over-one-under-two shots. Yarns: single-ply, Z-twist, noncotton.

Specimen 41. Tc 35e, Zone A, No. 17–1n. Venta Salada period. Fragment of plain-weave, warp-face (?) cloth. Yarns: single-ply, Z-twist, cotton.

Specimen 42. Tc 35e, Zone A, No. 21–5n. Venta Salada period. Fragments of plain-weave, warp-face (?) cloth. Yarns: single-ply, S-twist, noncotton.

Specimen 43. Tc 35e, Zone A, No. 36–1n. Venta Salada period. Fragmentary plain-weave, warp-face (?) cloth. Yarns: single-ply, Z-twist, gray-colored cotton (?).

Specimen 44. Tc 50, Zone II, No. 83–3n. Venta Salada period. Fragment of plain-weave, warp-face cloth. Yarns: single-ply, Z-twist, fairly fine and evenly spun, medium gray cotton. Count: 41 warp by 25 weft per 2.5 cm. Selvage: plain side selvage. Remarks: cloth has been folded diagonally and a narrow fragment of another side selvage is whipped to the upper edge of the fold. A mend? Sewing yarn is 2-ply, S-twist.

Specimen 45. Tc 50, Zone II, No. 181–2n. Venta Salada period. Fragmentary plain-weave cloth, stuck together in form of a ball. Yarns: single-ply, S-twist, noncotton.

Specimen 46. Tc 50, Zone II, No. 82–3n. Venta Salada period. Small fragment of plain-weave cloth, fairly open weave. Yarns: single-ply, Z-twist, noncotton; fairly thick diameter.

Specimen 47. Tc 50, Zone II, No. 10–1n. Venta Salada period. Largish fragment of plain-weave cloth. Yarns: single-ply, Z-twist, noncotton.

This was the most common type of weave in the Tehuacan Valley. The plain-weave type lasted at least from Santa Maria times to the Spanish Conquest. A piece of pottery with the impression of a fabric on it may indicate that the type started even earlier, in the Ajalpan period.

Semi-Basket Weave, One over Two

Specimen 1. Tc 272, Zone E, No. 69–5n. Palo Blanco period. Fragmentary utility-type cloth, approximately 20 cm. wide by 7 cm. long; semi-basket weave, single warps crossed by double wefts. Yarns: cotton; warp is single-ply, Z-twist, hard to crepe spun, fine diameter, used single; weft is same type, but has looser twist and is used double. Selvage: no finished selvage remains; one horizontal edge shows that raw edge was turned under and hemmed with fairly crude and careless stitching; sewing yarn: 2-ply, S-twist, hard and fine. Remarks: Yarns have shifted from original position and some have fallen out; an exact yarn count could not be taken.

Specimen 2. Tc 272, Zones A-B, No. 30–1n. Palo Blanco period. Fragmentary cloth, approximately 9.0 cm. wide by 13.5 cm. long; fairly fine and even semi-basket weave; single warps interlaced by double wefts. Yarns: white cotton; warp is single-ply, Z-twist, fine diameter, hard to crepe spun, used single; weft is the same, but used double. Count: about 42 single warps by 30 double wefts per 2.5 cm.

Specimen 3. Tc 272, Zone B, No. N7E5. Palo Blanco period. Fragmentary strip of strong, sturdily and evenly woven utility cloth, approximately 2 cm. wide by 34 cm. long; semi-basket weave, single warps interlaced by double wefts. Yarns: white cotton; warp is single-ply, Z-twist, hard spun, fairly fine in diameter, used single; weft is single-ply, Z-twist, medium spinning, thicker in diameter, used double. Count: 22 single warps by 22 double wefts per 2.5 cm. Selvage: part of one side selvage; last warp along outer edge is double.

Specimen 4. Tc 50, Zone V, No. 36–5n. Palo Blanco period. Textile fragment; closely spaced semi-basket weave, single warps crossed by double wefts. Yarns: white cotton, single-ply, Z-twist. Count: 50 single warps by 22 double weft. Remarks: One corner of fragment is gathered into a finger knot.

Specimen 5. Tc 50, Zone V, No. 37–4n. Venta Salada period. Textile fragment; semi-basket weave, single warps crossed by double wefts. Yarns: single-ply, Z-twist, white cotton. Remarks: may have represented closely woven cloth, now too frayed and worn to take a count.

Specimen 6. Tc 35e, Zone C, No. 33–2n. Venta Salada period. Fragment of semi-basket-weave cloth, single warps interlaced by double wefts. Yarns: cotton?

Specimen 7. Tc 35e, Zone C. No. 37–2n. Venta Salada period. Tiny fragment of cloth; semi-basket weave, single warps crossed by double wefts, yarns loosely spaced. Yarns: single-ply, Z-twist, cotton. Remarks: found with small amount of single-ply, Z-twist, loosely spun cotton yarn.

Specimen 8. Tc 35e, Zone C, No. 9–2n. Venta Salada period. Tiny piece of cloth; semi-basket weave, single warps crossed by double wefts. Yarns: single-ply, Z-twist; brown cotton?.

Specimen 9. Tc 35e, Zone B, No. 38–3n. Venta Salada period. Longish narrow band, 4 cm. wide by 20 cm. long; semi-basket weave, single warps crossed by double wefts, finely woven. Yarns: single-ply, Z-twist, cotton; warp finer than weft. Remarks: one end wrapped and knotted around a fragmentary istle specimen.

Specimen 10. Tc 35e, Zone A, No. 25–1n. Venta Salada period. Fragmentary cloth; semi-basket weave, single warps crossed by double wefts. Yarns: single-ply, Z-twist, cotton.

Specimen 11. Tc 50, Zone III, No. 86–3n. Venta Salada period. Bandlike sturdy and evenly woven textile, approximately 4 cm. wide by 33 cm. long; semi-basket weave, single warps crossed by double wefts. Yarns: single-ply, Z-twist,

fine and hard spinning. Count: 53 single warps by 23 double wefts per 2.5 cm.

Specimen 12. Tc 50, Zone II, No. 74–2n. Venta Salada period. Small piece of closely woven cloth, 4 cm. wide by 5 cm. long; semi-basket weave, single warps interlaced with double wefts. Yarns: single-ply, Z-twist, finely spun medium hard to hard, dyed gray, cotton. Count: 48 single warps by 32 double wefts per 2.5 cm. Selvage: plain side selvage.

Specimen 13. Tc 50, Zone II, No. 75–2n. Venta Salada period. Small fragment of cloth, semi-basket weave, single warps interlaced with double wefts, warp face. Yarns: single-ply, Z-twist, cotton; weft more loosely spun. Count: 42 single warps by 15 double wefts per 2.5 cm. Remarks: fabric has grosgrain-like texture, but coarser.

Specimen 14. Tc 50, Zone II, No. 83–3n. Venta Salada period. Two fragments of same piece of cloth, semi-basket weave, single warps crossed by double wefts. Yarns: single-ply, Z-twist, cotton. Remarks: yarns have shifted from original position, making count useless.

Specimen 15. Tc 50, Zone II, No. 181–2n. Venta Salada period. Fragmentary cloth, semi-basket weave, single warps cross double wefts. Yarns: single-ply, Z-twist, medium-gray colored, cotton. Remarks: part of a plain-weave cloth is stuck to this specimen; both are medium gray in color.

Specimen 16. Tc 50, Zone I, No. 28–1m. Venta Salada period. Small textile fragment, semi-basket weave, single warps cross double wefts, closely spaced yarns. Yarns: warp is single ply and S-twist; weft is single ply and Z-twist; both are evidently spun of *same* fiber! Count: 18 single warps by 21 double wefts per 2.5 cm.

Specimen 17. Tc 50, Zone I, No. 81–1n. Venta Salada period. Largish piece of cloth, 36 cm. (max.) wide by 36 cm. (max.) long; semi-basket weave, single warps cross double wefts. Yarns: cotton? Warp is single ply and S-twist, medium hard to very hard spun; weft is single ply and Z-twist, hard to crepe spun. Different directions of twist seem to give texture a crepe-like and "springy" effect. Count: 14–16 single warps by 18–19 double wefts per 2.5 cm. Selvage: last two warps at side selvage are doubled.

Specimen 18. Tc 268/1–2n. Venta Salada period. Small fragment of cloth, about 5 by 6 cm.; semi-basket weave, single warps cross double wefts, finely and evenly woven. Yarns: single-ply, Z-twist, hard spun, even and fairly fine in diameter, cotton. Count: 45–48 single warps by 28 double wefts per 2.5 cm. Selvage: plain side selvage.

Basket Weave, Two over Two

Specimen 1. Tc 50, Zone IV, No. 129–2n. Palo Blanco period. Fragment of basket-weave cloth, double warps crossed by double wefts. Yarns: single-ply, Z-twist, medium to hard to crepe spun, white cotton; both elements used double. Selvage: one plain side selvage. Remarks: fragment may represent part of "join" area; there are a series of heavy, irregularly introduced weft shots, each of which contain groups of 8—4—4—4—4—4 yarns. May also represent a weft-corded pattern, but this is doubtful.

Specimen 2. Tc 35e, Zone C, No. 27–2n. Venta Salada period. Tiny fragment of cloth, basket weave, double warps cross double wefts. Yarns: single-ply, Z-twist, cotton (?).

Specimen 3. Tc 50, Zone III, No. 13–3n. Venta Salada period. Small fragment of basket-weave cotton cloth, double warps interlace with double wefts. Found with several pieces of 2-ply, Z-twist cordage.

Specimen 4. Tc 50, Zone III, No. 81–3n. Venta Salada period. Tiny fragment of basket-weave cloth, double warps cross double wefts. Yarns: single-ply, Z-twist cotton; warp is very fine in diameter; weft is quite thick and more loosely spun. Difference in yarn size produces a warp-face weave resembling grosgrain ribbon; that is, the thick wefts completely covered by close-set warps give a ribbed effect.

Specimen 5. Tc 50, Zone II, No. 75–2n. Venta Salada period. Fragmentary basket-weave cloth, 10 by 8 cm., with canvas-like texture. Double warps cross double wefts; along upper (?) edge the weave changes to double warps crossed by four wefts for seven rows. End of weave? Weft cording? Yarns: single-ply, Z-twist, cotton. Count: approximately square, 22 double warps by 21 double wefts per 2.5 cm.

Specimen 6. Tc 50, Zone II, No. 127–2n. Venta Salada period. Fragment of basket-weave cloth, double warps interlace double wefts. Yarns: single-ply, Z-twist, cotton (?). Remarks: poor condition, yarns pulled out of position.

Specimen 7. Tc 50, Zone I, No. 82–1n. Venta Salada period. Fragmentary basket-weave cloth, double warps cross double wefts. Yarns: single-ply, Z-twist, cotton; weft (?) somewhat more loosely spun than warp (?). Remarks: may have been stitched to another (?) cloth; a 2-ply, S-twist, hard-spun yarn is still in place on cloth. Found with small amount of single-ply, S-twist, cotton (?) yarn.

Weft and Warp Cording

Specimen 1. Tc 50, Zone V, No. 101–3n. Palo Blanco period. Small fragment of cloth, much damaged. Yarns: single-ply, S-twist, noncotton. Technique: combination of plain-weave variations (plain and semi-basket) with a corded-weft decoration. The corded weft is composed of about six yarns grouped in a single shed. Pattern: as far as can be determined, the set-up is a corded weft—followed by a shot of plain weave—followed by a corded weft—followed by a shot of plain weave—followed by a corded weft—followed by a shot of semi-basket weave. . .

Specimen 2. Tc 35e, Zone C, No. 9–2n. Venta Salada period. Small piece of very fragile cloth. Yarns: cotton, dyed reddish-brown. Warp is single-ply, Z-twist, very fine and hard spun, used single. Weft is the same, also used single. Weft cording is same type and color, but much more loosely spun and thicker; it is used double. Count: 32 single warps by 30 wefts (single and double) per 2.5 cm. Technique: combination of plain weave and weft cording in the form of cross stripes. Pattern: 6 rows of weft cording—8 rows of plain weave—6 (7?) rows of weft cording—4 rows of plain weave—5 (6?) rows of weft cording—4 rows of plain weave.

Remarks: an extremely fine, even, and fragile weave, comparable with finest voile-like webs.

Specimen 3. Tc 35e, Zone C, No. 401–2n. Venta Salada period. Fragment too brittle and powdery for analysis. Seems to be same type as preceding specimen; i.e., technique may be combination of plain weave and weft cording.

Specimen 4. Tc 35e, Zone A, No. 12–5n. Venta Salada period. Small piece of fragile cloth. Yarns: single-ply, Z-twist, cotton (?). Technique: plain weave with weft-corded cross stripes (?).

Specimen 5. Tc 35e, Zone A, No. 16–1nn. Venta Salada period. Fragmentary cloth. Yarns: cotton. Warp is single-ply, Z-twist, fine diameter; corded warp has same structure but is more loosely spun. Weft and weft cord are the same. Selvage: last warp of side selvage is double. Technique: plain weave with corded warp and weft stripes. Pattern unit, weft-wise: cross bands are bordered by thick weft cords, containing four wefts per shot; between them are four rows of weft cords, containing double wefts per shot. Pattern unit, warp-wise: vertical bands of warp cording set up in same manner. (See Fig. 166.) Remarks: cloth too torn and fragmentary for full arrangement of pattern to be seen; seems to represent an irregular "plaid" pattern along side and end (?) selvages.

Specimen 6. Tc 50, Zone II, No. 82–3n. Venta Salada period. Small fragment of cloth, in poor condition. Yarns: cotton. Warp is single-ply, Z-twist, fine diameter; weft is partly single-ply, Z-twist, and partly single-ply, S-twist, gray-colored. Technique: combination of plain weave and semi-basket weave (weft cording?). Remarks: interesting use of Z-twist and S-twist wefts.

Warp Striping

Specimen 1. Tc 50, Zone VI, Burial 1, No. 129–6n. Palo Blanco period. Outer wrapping of mummy bundle, a two-breadth, noncotton fabric. Figs. 159, 172, 173. Size: length, 1.33 m.; complete width of Web I varies from 23.5 to 25.0 cm.; complete width of Web II varies from 25.0 to 26.0 cm. Web I is more completely preserved than Web II. Web I yarns: noncotton. Warp is single-ply, Z-twist, medium soft to hard spun, fine diameter; for different colors, see warp set-up below. Weft is single-ply, Z-twist, medium to hard spun, fine diameter; see below for color. Web II yarns: same as Web I. Count, Web I: 52, 58, 58 warps by 22, 19, 18 wefts per 2.5 cm. Web II: 56, 54, 60 warps by 20, 19, 20 wefts per unit.

Selvages: plain side selvages; in some places the warp is more closely spaced, but not consistently so. One end selvage represents a fringed end (see below); has uncut warp ends. The opposite end seems to be a raw edge, but since the whole edge is fairly straight, it could have been a finished edge originally; the end loops of the warp may have broken or worn off.

Technique: warp-face plain weave; warp-striped pattern. Near fringed edge there are two double rows of thick weft cords. Warp set-up for Web I, from outer side selvage to inner (seam) selvage: 6 blue-black—2 light brown—4 tan—32 blue-black—4 light brown—46 rusty red—4 medium dark brown—18 blue-black—16 medium dark blue—5 medium dark brown—1 tan—32 medium dark blue—4 medium dark brown—42 natural color (creamy white)—4 medium dark brown—44 tan—4 rusty red—4 creamy white—4 rusty red—4 creamy white—4 rusty red—4 creamy white—4 rusty red—4 creamy white—4 rusty red—42 tan (plus two which are double; should have been 44 tan)—3 medium dark brown—44 creamy white—4 medium dark brown—27 medium dark blue—3 blue-green—4 tan—2 blue-green—1 medium dark blue—12 blue-green—1 medium dark blue—1 blue-green—12 medium dark blue—2 blue-green—1 medium dark blue—4 medium dark brown—22 rusty red—4 medium dark brown—18 medium dark blue—16 blue-black—6 tan—6 blue-black—1 medium dark blue. Web II has the same color sequence, but in reverse order.

Weft cording, Web I: placed near fringe edge; first unit is 1.5 cm. from edge, second unit is 5.0 cm. from first unit. Thick ridge is formed by introducing groups of five to six weft strands together in one shed. Since corded wefts show loops along side selvages, their ends must have been finished off within the second shed; a thickening along the corded row seems to give evidence of this procedure. Weft cording, Web II: same arrangement; first unit is 1.0 cm. from fringe edge, second unit is 4.0 cm. from first one.

Fringe edge: weft-twined decoration utilizes very light tan (or creamy white) and black yarns. (1) Plain twining: has a pattern unit of four yarns which are twined over groups of six warps; each strand is 2-ply, S-twist, softly twisted together; forms upper edge. (2) Countertwining: forms the center motif. Pattern forms small chevrons, which show up clearly on Web I; weaver must have made a mistake in Web II, because the countertwined pattern is lost. (3) Plain twining: same as above, but direction of manipulation is reversed; forms narrow white edge at bottom of decorative motif. Finish of twined rows along side selvage: when twining is from upper left to lower right, the strand at left selvage is looped; it is knotted at right selvage. Web I: last bunch of strands seems to end in last loop of twined row, at right selvage. Web II: last bunch of strands is knotted together at right selvage. The reinforcement along the edge is worked with uncut warp loops. Fringe shows sections of different colors set up in the warp stripes. Seam: sewing yarn is single-ply, Z-twist, natural color, fine diameter; stitches are fairly wide apart (about 2.5 cm.).

Remarks: "medium dark brown" and "light brown" are probably from same dye lot. Though the shading changes in various sections, "rusty red" represents the color which gives most evidence of having disintegrated the fiber; consequently, these yarns have fallen out in a number of places. The combination of medium dark blue and blue-green warp striping is very irregular; the lighter shade may have been dyed later, in the same dye lot. The weft yarns are rusty red

in most sections; in others they are natural colored with a reddish tinge.

Specimen 2. Tc 50, Zone VI, No. 129–6nn. Early Palo Blanco period. Inner wrapping of mummy bundle, two-breadth noncotton fabric. Figs. 160, 173. Cloth is fragile and folded in numerous places. Size: Length, 1.58 m. Width, 41 cm. (plus 4 cm. fold) plus 45 cm. Measurements are approximate. Yarns: noncotton. Warp is single-ply, Z-twist, medium to hard spun, very fine to thick in diameter; for colors, see below. Weft is single-ply, Z-twist, medium to hard spun, fairly fine diameter, blackish gray. Count, Web I: 45, 42, 47 warps by 15, 13, 12 wefts per 2.5 cm. Count, Web II: 52, 52, 51 warps by 15, 14, 15 wefts per unit.

Selvages: plain side selvages, perhaps slightly coarser for reinforcement. One end selvage is a finished selvage; warp loops go over a thick loomstring cord, composed of 4 singles. The opposite edge has cut ends, finished with a "knotted" reinforcement (see below).

Technique: warp-faced plain weave. Warp-striped pattern. Weft cording. "Knotted" fringe. Warp stripes: pattern contains natural, tan, light brown, blue, blue-green colors. Difficult to determine which were the original shades; garment is quite faded and was old and worn when used as burial robe. It has more blue in its pattern than the outer wrapping; the latter exhibits more rusty red, which the inner robe seems to lack.

Weft cording: one group near the fringe end is composed of thick weft element (about five yarns together); the method is the same as in the outer wrapping, except that there is only one group of cording. Opposite end: a finished selvage with a thick weft cord serving as loomstring, plus two more weft cords at short intervals; after 3 cm. there is another group of weft cords (2 rows); cloth at this end is very brittle, thus difficult to discern details.

Fringe: "knotting" elements are composed of three singly-ply, Z-twist strands. Tightly knotted units. All warp ends have been broken off and original length cannot be determined.

Mending: robe was undoubtedly well worn by the time it was used as a wrapping for the mummy; it has several mends. Most of the inner side selvage of Web I is folded under and hemmed with running stitches. Folded section has two rows of stitching: one along present outer edge, the other along inner (originally, selvage) edge. There are several tears which were haphazardly mended. The stitches are crudely done and widely spaced. Yarns used: (1) two-tone yarn that is 3-ply, S-twist, each ply composed of a white and a blue yarn Z-twisted together (singles, also Z). (2) Single-ply, Z-twist, brown-colored yarn. (3) 4-ply, S-twist, brownish black yarn.

Twill

Specimen 1. Tc 50, Zone II, No. 74–2n. Venta Salada period. Fragmentary cloth, approximately 21 cm. (max.) by 9 cm. (max.) Fig. 167. Yarns: white cotton. Warp (?) is single-ply, Z-twist, medium hard to very hard spun, sometimes creped, used double. Weft (?) shows same structure but is less tightly spun, also used double. Count: 28, 29, 30 double warps by 24, 23, 22 double wefts per 2.5 cm. Selvages: all edges raw. Technique: two-and-two twill. Angle of the wale, approximately 53 to 57 degrees. In some places warp or weft is single—owing to a mistake in the shedding manipulation or breakage of yarns and worn condition of fragment. Remarks: specimen must have been part of a sturdily woven cloth; weave is fairly even and yarns exhibit very hard twist, even creped in part. An all-white textile, apparently without decoration.

Specimen 2. Tc 267/1–2n. Post-Conquest? Small fragment of cloth. Yarns: single-ply, Z-twist, medium hard spun, reddish brown, apparently wool! Technique: one-and-two twill; yarns are closely spaced and the piece is evenly woven. Remarks: surely not pre-Spanish?

Gauze

Specimen 1. Tc 50, Zone II, No. 60–2n. Venta Salada period. Fragmentary cloth, about 14 cm. long and 23 cm. wide. Figs. 169, 170, 171. Yarns: white cotton. Warp is single-ply, Z-twist, very hard to crepe spun, fine diameter. Weft, in gauze sections, is same as basic warp; weft in plain-weave stripes is single-ply, Z-twist, medium soft spun, used double. Brocading weft is composed of double strands of loosely spun, single-ply yarns. Count, plain-weave section: 12 single warps by 12 double wefts per 1.25 cm. Selvages: one end selvage, plain, except for unit of 4 wefts introduced for strength at edge; other edges are raw.

Techniques: (1) plain weave, (2) gauze weave, (3) brocading on gauze ground; used in alternating horizontal stripes. (1) Plain-weave stripes are done in two variants of semi-basket weave: single warp crossed by double wefts and single warp crossed by four wefts. (a) End-selvage stripe contains sequence of one shot of 4-weft unit, followed by twelve shots of double-weft unit, ending with one shot of 4-weft unit. This cross stripe measures 1.3 cm. (b) After a narrow gauze section, a second plain-weave cross stripe follows; it consists of one shot of a 4-weft unit, followed by eleven shots of double-weft unit, ending with one shot of 4-weft unit. This stripe measures 1.4 cm. (c) Following a wide brocaded gauze section, comes a third plain-weave cross stripe; it has one shot of 4-weft unit, followed by nine shots of double-weft unit, ending with one shot of 4-weft unit. This stripe measures 1.1 cm. (d) Following another narrow gauze section comes a fragmentary plain-weave stripe similar to the other three; its exact width cannot be determined because the weave has become loose and frayed. This stripe was followed by another gauze section—whether a wide brocaded one or a narrow one cannot be discerned. All plain-weave bands are solidly woven, owing to doubled wefts and tight battening. (2) Gauze weave: narrow and wide cross stripes are rendered in plain, all-over gauze weave; warp and weft yarns are single, fine, tightly spun,

and create a fine, lacelike texture. (a) First gauze stripe is narrow (about 1.0 cm.), consists of nine weft shots, and is unadorned. (b) Second gauze stripe is wide (about 4.0 cm.) and consists of thirty weft shots; it contains brocaded spot motifs. (c) Third stripe is narrow, has nine weft shots, and is unadorned. (3) Brocading on gauze ground: thick, double strands of brocading weft are used to build up design motifs, each of which forms a separate unit. The design stands out clearly, thickly, and sharply on the lacelike gauze ground. Design: motif consists of a geometric unit, repeated three times horizontally. Weaving irregularities cause slight variations in size: units vary from 4.25 to 4.75 cm. in width and from 2.75 to 3.00 cm. in height. In the alternating plain-weave cross stripes, each shot preceding and following the gauze sections consists of a 4-weft unit, probably both to reinforce edges and to contrast plain-weave sections more clearly with the finer gauze weave.

Remarks: This all-white cotton textile must have been a handsome fabric. The combination of gauze and brocading evinces skillfullness and advanced knowledge of weaving manipulation. Spinning also shows high skill and sureness. Sophisticated handling of patterning is shown by the contrast of the lacy gauze weave with the rather heavy and thick design units, and the alternation of these gauze stripes with tightly woven plain-weave bands. Though the specimen is fragmentary and frayed, it is still remarkably well preserved.

Specimen 2. Tc 50, Zone II, No. 82–3n. Venta Salada period. Fragmentary cloth, 19 cm. long by 6 cm. wide (max.). Yarns: cotton; single-ply, S-twist, hard to crepe spun, dyed dark brown. Selvage: preserved end selvage consists of a first shot of a 4-weft unit, followed by 9 shots of a double-weft unit. Technique: plain all-over gauze, finely woven, no patterning. Remarks: hard twist of yarns gives weave a crepe-like texture.

Specimen 3. Tc 50, Zone I, No. 81–1n. Fragmentary cloth, 7.5 cm. long (including fringe) and 6.5 cm. wide. Fig. 168. Yarns: white cotton. Warps are single-ply, tightly Z-twisted, very fine in diameter. Wefts are single-ply, more softly Z-twisted elements. Warps at side selvage are thick 2-ply, S-twisted yarns (singles, Z). Selvages: corner intact; end selvage is about 1.5 cm. deep. The first shot is a 4-weft unit; the next eleven rows contain double-weft units, closely battened together. Side selvage is approximately 2.0 cm. wide; the ten thick 2-ply warps in this section create a sturdy reinforcement. Technique: semi-basket weave along selvages; plain all-over gauze section; twined weft-fringe. There is marked contrast between the thick and heavy weave along the side and end selvages and that of the fine, fragile, gauze part. (See Fig. 168.) Fringe: a separately worked weft fringe is whipped to the end selvage; whipping yarn is 3-ply, S-twist (singles, Z), fine diameter. The weft fringe is constructed with a pair of warp-twined rows, which result in countertwining technique. The wefts are single-ply, Z-twist; in the finished fringe pairs of yarns twist about each other

S-fashion; twining strands are 2-ply, S-twist, hard and strong elements. The fringe is about 2.0 cm. deep. It is no longer possible to determine whether the fringe was also whipped

along the side selvage; there is no evidence of stitching. However, the fringe is broken (raw) at the preserved corner of the fabric, indicating that it may have been longer.

REFERENCES

BARLOW, R. H.
1946 "Cerro de San Lorenzo, Coahuila: Dos Sitios Arqueológicos." *RMEA*, 8:266–67. Mexico.

BIRD, JUNIUS B., AND L. BELLINGER
1954 *Paracas Fabrics and Nazca Needlework: 3rd Century B.C.—3rd Century A.D.* Washington: National Publishing Company.

DAVIDSON, D. S.
1935 "Knotless Netting in America and Oceania." *AA*, 37:117–34.

DELGADO, HILDA S.
n. d. "Archaeological Textiles from Durango, Zacatecas and Sinaloa." Unpublished MS.

GERHARD, PETER
1964a "Emperor's Dye of the Mixtecs." *Natural History Magazine*, 73:26–31. American Museum of Natural History, New York.
1964b "Shellfish Dye in America." *XXXV Congreso Internacional de Americanistas, Actas y Memorias, 1962*, 3:177–90. Mexico.

HAURY, EMIL W.
1933 "Maya Textile Weaves." Unpublished MS.

JOHNSON, IRMGARD W.
n. d. "Candelaria Cave Textiles." Unpublished MS.
1957 "An Analysis of Some Textile Fragments from Yagul." *Mesoamerican Notes*, No. 5, pp. 77–81. Department of Anthropology, Mexico City College, Mexico.
1958–59 "Un Antiguo Huipil de Ofrenda Decorado con Pintura." *RMEA*, 15:115–22, pl. 3. Mexico.
1960 "Un *Tzotzopaztli* Antiguo de la Region de Tehuacán." *Anales del INAH, 1957–1958*, 11:75–85.

KASHA, M.
1948 "Chemical Notes on the Coloring Matter of Chihuahua Textiles of Pre-Columbian Mexico." In O'Neale 1948 (see below).

KENT, K. P.
1957 *The Cultivation and Weaving of Cotton in the Prehistoric Southwestern United States.* APS-T, Vol. 47, Part 3.

MACNEISH, RICHARD S.
1950 "A Synopsis of the Archaeological Sequence in the Sierra de Tamaulipas." *RMEA*, 11:79–96.
1961 "Recent Finds Concerned with the Incipient Agriculture Stage in Prehistoric Mesoamerica." *Homenaje a Pablo Martínez del Río*, pp. 91–101. INAH, Mexico.

O'NEALE, LILA M.
1945 *Textiles of Highland Guatemala.* CIW, Publication No. 567.
1948 *Textiles of Pre-Columbian Chihuahua.* CIW, Publication No. 574. Contributions to American Anthropology and History, No. 45.

O'NEALE, LILA M., AND B. J. CLARK
1948 *Textile Periods in Ancient Peru.* III. The Gauze Weaves. UCPAAE.

SMITH, C. EARLE, AND R. S. MACNEISH
1964 "Antiquity of American Polyploid Cotton." *Science*, 143:675.

STRÖMBERG, E.
1942 "Technical Analysis of Textiles Recovered in Burial I." In S. Linné, *Mexican Highland Cultures*, pp. 157–60. Ethnographical Museum of Sweden, New Series, Publication 7. Stockholm.

TAYLOR, WALTER W.
1948 *A Study of Archeology.* American Anthropological Association Memoirs, No. 69.

WHITAKER, THOMAS W., H. C. CUTLER, AND R. S. MACNEISH
1957 "Cucurbit Materials from Three Caves near Ocampo, Tamaulipas." *Am. Ant.*, 22:352–58.

Conclusion

THE TYPES of nonceramic artifacts found in the Tehuacan Valley have been described and illustrated in the preceding pages. Some of the types, as we have pointed out, are better time markers than others, and for various reasons. Inadequate or unrepresentative samples keep some of the types from being completely acceptable. The textile, wood, bone, basket, and petate types, for example—as well as the cordage, knots, cores, and some of the ground-stone tools—all appear to be relatively good time markers, but their usefulness is limited because they are represented by inadequate samples. Only when adequate surveys reveal more representative sites, and their investigation yields more materials for study, can it be determined how satisfactory these particular types actually are.

Another problem in typology is that certain categories of artifacts are not as susceptible to change as others. When the features of various classes of artifacts alter little over time, it becomes difficult to establish types that are characteristic of specific periods. The unifacial side-scrapers, some of the choppers, and the bifacial knives are cases in point. Once these particular tools were invented, they continued to be made and used with little alteration over thousands of years. Thus, the first inhabitants of the Tehuacan Valley used the majority of these artifact types, and their descendants continued to use them, changing their manufacturing techniques but little. Among the unifacial side-scraper types, therefore, only the burins, gravers, and spokeshave-like tools, which were more popular in early levels, showed any temporal significance. In fact, all the utilized or retouched flakes described in Chapter 3 could be considered as a single type rather than the eight trial types we established in the hope that they will have some value in future investigations.

The ellipsoidal, discoidal, and blocky-core choppers and the thin ovoid bifaces, or knives, were also found throughout the sequence, except in the earliest levels where samples were small. Other of the bifacial types,

however, had definite significance in time. Flake and slab choppers were more popular in the lower levels; battered pebbles, pebble choppers, large and small disks, and the cruder square-based knives are associated with middle levels; and finely made knives and half-moon side-blades were found in the later levels. The bifaces, which are represented by adequate samples, therefore provide some reasonably good time markers and some very poor time markers.

There are four groups of nonceramic artifact types which were derived from large samples and which are excellent time markers. These are the projectile points, with 1,212 specimens from excavation and 1,101 from the surface; the blades, with 1,832 specimens from excavation and 1,288 from the surface; the grinding implements, with 1,454 specimens from excavation and 707 from the surface; and the end-scrapers, with 1,799 specimens from excavation and 1,143 from the surface. Of these good marker categories, the end-scrapers are least satisfactory as time markers. Even so, they follow temporal trends. Crude, keeled end-scrapers, for instance, appear first in the sequence and are followed shortly by the crude, ovoid, plano-convex end-scrapers and the long, flat-flake end-scrapers. These are followed in turn by multifaceted scraper-planes, domed and flat-topped scraper-planes, and gouges. Slightly later thin-flake and crude discoidal end-scrapers appear. As the keeled end-scrapers and multifaceted scraper-planes diminish, end-of-blade scrapers begin to replace them. And as the crude, ovoid, plano-convex end-scrapers go out of style, the finely chipped, small, ovoid end-scrapers make their appearance. The latter type is followed by finely made flat-topped end-scrapers, and in the final part of the sequence, by finely chipped thumbnail end-scrapers.

The prismatic blades struck from fluted polyhedral cores are good time markers, in spite of their tendency, once they appear, to linger through the rest of the sequence—albeit in diminishing amounts. The fact that

227

the blades are found in proportionately diminishing numbers over later time periods offsets the problem of their continued manufacture, which in the case of the side-scraper, chopper, and bifacial-knife types was a limiting factor. In the earliest levels crude prismatic blades with unprepared striking platforms are found, and they are followed by crude blades with prepared platforms and then by crude blades with pointed striking platforms. Then come fine blades, usually of obsidian, with unprepared striking platforms. Fine blades with pointed platforms then appear and become dominant, to be followed closely by a minority type of fine blades with prepared striking platforms. About the time that this minority type diminished in popularity, fine snapped blades with two worked edges and fine blades with ground striking platforms enter the sequence. The last-mentioned type reached its greatest popularity in the latest levels.

The thirty-two projectile-point types appeared in an even more definite chronological sequence. Projectile points are better time markers than many of the other types, not only because they are represented by a large sample, but also because each type tends to have exclusive attributes. Furthermore, each type tends to have a specific beginning point, a period of being numerically dominant over other types, and a period of decreasing importance; usually there is also a terminal date after which the type no longer appears. To review very briefly: Lerma and Abasolo points appear in the earliest levels, followed respectively by Plainview, El Riego, and Flacco points, and then by Nogales, Tortugas, Trinidad, and Hidalgo points, and finally by La Mina and Agate Basin points. About the time that Lerma, Tortugas, El Riego, and Plainview points are disappearing, San Nicolas, Tilapa, and Abejas points appear. These are followed by Coxcatlan, Almagre, Garyito, Shumla, and perhaps Pelona points; some crude examples of Catan points are also found in the same period. After Flacco, Agate Basin, La Mina, Hidalgo, Almagre, Abejas, and Tilapa points die out, the Zacatenco type appears, to be followed shortly by Salado points and the disappearance of Trinidad points. Coxcatlan and Pelona points probably disappear at the time Matamoros points enter the sequence, followed by the Tehuacan type. Abasolo points seem to disappear shortly thereafter, along with Garyito, Shumla, Zacatenco, and Salado points, while Teotihuacan, Morhiss, Ensor, and Tula points come in. Perhaps about the time that Palmillas, Catan, Nogales, and San Nicolas points are no longer made in significant proportions, Texcoco, Harrell, and Starr points are first manufactured.

Occasionally, the fact of being confined in time to a specific period makes an artifact type important regardless of the size of the sample—as in the case of burins, which are exclusive to early periods. Sometimes too the fact that an artifact type does not exist at specific time periods makes the type important as a time marker— as in the case of the ground-stone tools for grinding and pounding, which are absent from early levels. The first types among the ground-stone artifacts to appear, but in very limited numbers, were tecomate mortars and cylindrical pestles, and one small fragment of a pebble which could have been either a muller or a mano. Then, in the order named, boulder metate–milling stones, metates, ovoid mullers, hemispherical mortars, mortars with flaring rims, and conical and rectangular pestles make their appearance. Somewhat later ovoid manos and trough metates appear. Oblong manos, tecomate bowls, cuboid pestles, hemispherical bowls, and spherical manos then enter the sequence in the order mentioned. Stone bowls with flaring rims, ovoid plano-convex metates, and long manos that are lenticular in cross section appear at a still later date. Lipped, saucer-shaped metates appear in still more recent levels and are followed by four new types: oblong lipped metates, long manos that are triangular in cross section, and bell-shaped and truncated-cone pestles. In later levels, flat-iron smoothers or pestles, basin-shaped metates, and cylindrical manos appear in that order, while most of the earlier mortar, pestle, and stone-bowl forms are disappearing. As the earlier mano and metate types are dying out, rectangular tripod metates and cuboid manos come into existence, followed shortly by stave-shaped manos. Dog-bone manos and effigy bowls enter the sequence next, and the last type to appear is the thumb-tack pestle.

All in all, we have about eighty to a hundred nonceramic types from the Tehuacan Valley which are excellent time markers. As Volume I points out, some of the domesticated plants also serve as marker types, and Volume III will show that the ceramic types are even better time markers. In preceramic times, however, all we really have to work with are the nonceramic artifacts, and these serve not only as time markers for the longest period of the valley's pre-Hispanic history, but also as a basis for correlating the different preceramic zones. The correlation of the various site components of the Tehuacan Valley is based primarily upon comparisons of the various sites with the well-documented, stratigraphically determined preceramic sequence of types from Coxcatlan Cave (Tc 50).

Chronological Alignment of Preceramic Components

When we compared the diagnostic artifacts—that is,

228

the good time markers—from all zones of all other sites with those from the earliest Coxcatlan occupations (Zones XXVII–XXIII), only one, Zone 6 of the West Niche of El Riego Cave (Tc 35w), was comparable. It was similar to Zones XXVII–XXIII of Tc 50 in having only crude blades with unprepared striking platforms; Abasolo and Lerma points; crude keeled, crude ovoid plano-convex, and crude long, flat-flake end-scrapers; and only flake and blocky-core choppers. However, Zone 6 of Tc 35w appears to be later than Zones XXVII–XXIV of Tc 50, for it lacked any associated extinct animal bones, and it contained a Plainview point. Plainview points were not found in Tc 50 until Zone XIX. Furthermore, Zone 6 of Tc 35w had a tecomate mortar, a type which first appeared in Zone XXI of Tc 50. Thus, it would appear that Zone 6 of Tc 35w, in terms of artifact trends, fits in the period between Zones XXIV and XXI of Tc 50. The lack of scraper-planes, blades with prepared striking platforms, multifaceted scraper-planes, gouges, ellipsoidal choppers, battered pebbles, and El Riego points in Zone 6 of Tc 35w would seem to indicate that it is earlier than Zone XXII of Tc 50, where all these artifacts are found, while the Plainview point and the tecomate mortar show that Zone 6 of Tc 35w is later than Zone XXIII of Tc 50. Thus, Zone 6 of Tc 35w, on the basis of the artifact trends of Tc 50, seems to fall in the period between Zones XXIII and XXII of Tc 50.

The next earliest component in terms of comparisons with Tc 50 seems to be Zone C of Tecorral Cave (Tc 255). The presence of extinct antelope bones certainly indicates that it is early. However, this component has more crude blades with prepared than with unprepared striking platforms, a pattern that does not occur in Tc 50 until Zone XVIII. Zone C of Tc 255 also has ovoid bifaces, which do not appear in Tc 50 until Zone XIX, and thin-flake end-scrapers, which do not appear in Tc 50 until Zone XX. Thus, Zone C of Tc 255 probably is not earlier than Zone XXI of Tc 50. The relatively larger proportion of crude flake end-scrapers and the absence of keeled and crude ovoid end-scrapers, plus the extinct animal bones, suggest that it is of about the same period as Zone XIX of Tc 50 or just slightly earlier. The relatively small number of tools from Zone C of Tc 255 makes it difficult to position it exactly in terms of the trends from Tc 50.

This is equally true of Zone H of Abejas Cave (Tc 307). The lack of extinct animal bones and the presence of ovoid bifaces and an ovoid muller would seem to show that its occupation occurred after those of Zone XIX of Tc 50 and Zone C of Tc 255. However, the keeled end-scrapers and the blades with unprepared

striking platforms show that it probably was earlier than Zone XVIII of Tc 50.

The small number of artifacts from the three lower levels of Purron Cave (Tc 272, Zones S, T, U) make it almost impossible to place these zones in their exact chronological position. Therefore, perhaps the earliest occupation of Tc 272 that can be compared with Tc 50 is Zone R, and even this zone's sample of artifacts is small. The Trinidad point, the multifaceted scraper-plane, and the many ovoid metates and ovoid mullers from this level suggest that it comes after either Zone XVIII or Zone XVII of Tc 50, while the complete lack of domesticated plants in Zone R probably places it before Zone XVI of Tc 50. Thus, Zone R of Tc 272 may fall between Zones XVII and XVI of Tc 50. Because Zones S, T, and U of Tc 272 have the same high proportion of boulder metate–milling stones, as well as other similarities to Zone R, these zones seem to be close together in time, and I would guess they all fall within the same span.

The placing of Zone 5 of Tc 35w just before Zone DE of Coxcatlan Terrace (Ts 51) and of both levels between Zones XVI and XV of Tc 50 is based upon a much firmer foundation. Zone 5 of Tc 35w contained Agate Basin points, an ovoid mano, and a stone bowl fragment, and therefore must be later than Zone XVI of Tc 50. However, the La Mina, El Riego, and Lerma points, together with the very small number of crude pointed blades and thin-flake end-scrapers found in Zone 5, place it before Zone XV of Tc 50. Zone DE of Ts 51 also must be later than Zone XVI of Tc 50 and Zone 5 of Tc 35w, since it has La Mina, Agate Basin, and San Nicolas points, a square-based biface, and an ovoid mano.

Zones F and G of Tc 307 appear to come next when compared with the trends of types from Tc 50, but unfortunately the sample of tools is small and the "fit" in the sequence is not nearly so convincing. The presence of a Tilapa point in Zone F and of a trough metate and an Abejas point in Zone G, certainly seems to show that both zones are little if any earlier than Zone XV of Tc 50. The relatively high proportion of boulder metate–milling stones in Zone G and the spokeshave-like tool found there, considered together with the absence of crude blades with pointed striking platforms, certainly are evidence that it is not much earlier than Zone XIV of Tc 50 and only possibly slightly earlier than Zone XV. All in all, then, the two zones are roughly contemporaneous with Zones XVII or XVI of Tc 50, and I would guess that they were somewhat earlier.

Zones D^1–D^2 and E of Tc 307 are equally hard to place in chronological position because of small samples. However, since level D^1 contained a multifaceted scraper-plane, it seems likely that all three were occupied before Zone XIII of Tc 50. The higher proportion of crude blades with pointed striking platforms in Zone E suggests that it is later than Zone XVII of Tc 50. The larger proportion of scraper-planes in all three levels tends to place them relatively early in this time range, between Zones XVII and XIII of Tc 50.

The artifacts from the large roasting pit of Ts 381w also fit into a similar position. Again the multifaceted scraper-planes place it before Zone XIII of Tc 50, while the square-based bifacial knives, the ovoid mano, the Abejas point, and the fact that the only blade found was a crude one with a pointed striking platform indicate that Ts 381w probably was occupied considerably after Zone XIV and perhaps after Zones E and D^1–D^2 of Tc 307. Zone Q of Tc 272, although the evidence is poor, may have a similar position in time, for it too contained a multifaceted scraper-plane. Thus, it may be earlier than Zone XIII of Tc 50. An ovoid mano in Zone Q may indicate that it followed Zone XIV of Tc 50, as well as Zones D^1–D^2 and E of Tc 307.

Zone D of Tc 307 can next be placed in its chronological order, since the Coxcatlan point it contained indicates that it is probably not earlier than Zone XIII of Tc 50. The presence of an Abejas and a Tilapa point confirms such minimum dating, as does the lack of multifaceted scraper-planes. Whether it comes before Zone XII of Tc 50, which has many new types, is open to question, but I would guess that it might fit into such a chronological position.

Zone 4 of Tc 35w does, however, fit very easily into the sequence after Zone XII of Tc 50, for it contained Garyito, Catan, Shumla, and Almagre points, a fine-blade fragment, and a square-based bifacial knife—all of which do not appear any earlier than Zone XII in the Tc 50 sequence. The El Riego and Plainview points, the limited number of discoidal scrapers and square-based knives, and the lack of stone bowls and Pelona points in Zone 4 of Tc 35w, would seem to place it before Zone XI of Tc 50.

Probably close in time to these components are Zones F and E of San Marcos Cave (Tc 254), but it is difficult to prove this on the basis of the limited number of artifacts uncovered in these levels. The small fragment of a tecomate or hemispherical bowl, the discoidal scraper, the two-ply coarse cord, and the atlatl foreshaft found in these zones would place them among the occupations between Zones XII and XI of Tc 50. However, when we look at the types of corn in Zone E, which include many wild and a few early cultivated types, one begins to feel that Zones F and E of Tc 254 fall into place just between Zones XI and XII of Tc 50. On the basis of the tecomate

or hemispherical bowl, I would be inclined to place them after Zone 4 of Tc 35w.

Seemingly, the next components would be Test 1 of Ts 365, Zone C of Tc 307, and Zones Q^1, P, and O of Tc 272, but all have only small samples of good marker types. Zone P of Tc 272 seems to be later than Zone XI of Tc 50, since it contained a spherical mano; and Zone O with a Trinidad point and a keeled end-scraper seems to be earlier than Zone X of Tc 50. Zone C, Tc 307, with a fine-blade fragment and a fine blade with an unprepared striking platform, probably is not earlier than Zone XI of Tc 50, and the presence of a hemispherical mortar fragment makes it logical to place Zone C before Zone X of Tc 50. The small test in Ts 365 containing Shumla and Catan points certainly should be dated later than Zone 4 of Tc 35w; on the basis of its fine-blade fragment, it probably comes after Zone XI of Tc 50 and the other zones just mentioned. Its Abejas point fragment seems to suggest that it existed even earlier than Zone X of Tc 50.

The similarity of the corn in Zone D of Tc 254 to the corn in Zone X of Tc 50 indicates they are close in time. The fine blade with an unprepared striking platform in Zone D of Tc 254 indicates that it might date slightly after Zone X, and the thin bifacial disk it contained may mean that it is earlier than Zone IX of Tc 50. Zone B of Tc 307 and Zones N and N^1 of Tc 272 seem to be of the same general period, for all three contained fine blades and cuboid pestles. Furthermore, a large bifacial disk from Zone B, Tc 307, indicates that this level probably existed before Zone IX of Tc 50. Zone C of Ts 51 may also be of this period, since it contained a fine blade and a bifacial disk as well as a stone bowl fragment.

In a later chronological position than Zone IX of Tc 50 would be the pit house and surrounding refuse from Ts 381e. The artifacts from this site—a hemispherical stone bowl, a flaring-rim bowl, a fine blade with an unprepared striking platform, a long mano with a lenticular cross section, a paint palette, oblong manos, and Shumla and Garyito points—also indicate a late preceramic period, probably following the period of Zone IX of Tc 50. An Abejas point and a tecomate bowl may indicate that it existed even before Zone VIII of Tc 50.

The final three preceramic components of the Tehuacan excavations, Zones M, M^1, and L of Tc 272, are very difficult to classify. The pebble choppers and other bifacial choppers in these zones suggest that they fall somewhere between Zones XIII and VIII of Tc 50. However, only the rubbed pebble and paint palette of Zone L are temporally diagnostic. These artifacts may indicate that these three zones of Tc 272 followed Zone VIII of Tc 50.

230

Thus, in terms of trends established by nonceramic artifacts, we are able to align the preceramic components or zones in chronological order, from earliest to latest. Zone XXVII, Tc 50, seems to be our earliest occupation. Zones XXVI, XXV, XXIV, and XXIII of Tc 50, Zone 6 of Tc 35w, and Zones XXII and XXI of Tc 50 followed in that order. Although the placement is based on a small sample, there is reason to believe that Zone C of Tc 255 existed next. Zones XX and XIX of Tc 50, Zone H of Tc 307, and Zones XVIII and XVII of Tc 50 assuredly followed it. Zones U, T, S, and R of Tc 272 seem to have been occupied in that order. I estimate that these components were followed by Zone XVI of Tc 50, which probably was followed in turn by Zone 5 of Tc 35w and Zone DE of Ts 51.

The exact placement of the next four zones is difficult, but I suspect that Zones G, F, E, and D^1–D^2 of Tc 307 probably preceded Zone XVI of Tc 50, and that the roasting pit of Ts 381w may have followed Zones XV and XIV. There is good reason for believing that Zone XIII of Tc 50 follows, and it is possible that Zone Q of Tc 272 and Zone D of Tc 307 came next, before Zone XII of Tc 50. The artifact trends together with trends based on agricultural plants indicate that Zone 4 of Tc 35w, Zone E of Tc 254, and Zone XI of Tc 50 followed in that order. Possibly Ts 365, Test 1; Zones Q^1, P, and O of Tc 272; and Zone C of Tc 307 were next in order. Then comes Zone X of Tc 50, followed by Zone D of Tc 254, Zone B (and B^1) of Tc 307, Zone N and possibly Zone N^1 of Tc 272, and Zone C of Ts 51. Following these are Zone IX of Tc 50, the pit house at Ts 381e, and Zone VIII of Tc 50. Although we have little artifactual proof of it, Zones M, M^1, and L of Tc 272 seem to be our last preceramic components. Some confirmatory evidence for this chronological sequence is provided by the trends in domesticated plants and the trends in animal bones, both of which are discussed in Volume I. Later volumes will show that studies using completely different lines of investigation, such as pollen and radiocarbon determinations, also align many of these components in the same order.

Table 32, with the ordinate the aligned preceramic components and the abscissa the aligned more sensitive and better represented artifact types, not only serves as proof of cultural continuity and of the chronological alignment of the components, but also demonstrates that there were major periods when new artifact types or new complexes of types were introduced or invented. These major periods of artifactual increments are, of course, the basis for dividing our preceramic sequence. Further, once these new complexes of traits appear in the sequence, they continue to appear throughout a series of chronologically aligned components. These reoccurring complexes of traits from a number of components which segment our sequence thus provide the basis for our cultural periods—or phases, as we shall call them in the following discussion.

The Establishment of Cultural Phases on the Basis of Nonceramic Artifact Types and Complexes

The earliest cultural phase seems to have occurred in Zones XXVII through XXIII of Tc 50 and Zone 6 of Tc 35w. Of these, Zones XXIV and XXIII of Tc 50 and Zone 6 of Tc 35w have the most adequate samples of traits, as well as a similar complex of traits. The traits include crude blades with unprepared striking platforms, crude keeled end-scrapers, crude ovoid end-scrapers, flake choppers, Lerma points, blocky-core choppers, scraper-planes, crude flat-flake end-scrapers, and spokeshave-like tools. Two of these three components also possess flake gravers, Abasolo points, burins, and slab choppers. These are the diagnostic traits of the Ajuereado phase, which was first recognized as a distinctive cultural complex while we were digging Ajuereado Cave, although during the earlier part of the excavation it was usually referred to as the Lerma-point complex. A number of more general traits were also evident in these pure Ajuereado components, including thick and thin flakes with one or two retouched or utilized edges, cobble hammers, and crude-blade fragments. These are such very general traits, however, that they can hardly be considered diagnostic of a single phase. A Plainview point, a muller fragment, a mortar fragment, and a pestle fragment were each present in different components and probably are not diagnostic Ajuereado traits. Zones XXVII, XXVI, and XXV of Tc 50 have much smaller congeries of artifacts, and although possessing some of the general traits, they have among the diagnostic traits only keeled end-scrapers and crude blades—as well as extinct faunal remains similar to those of Zone XXIV. Zones XXVII, XXVI, and XXV are, therefore, tentatively classified as Ajuereado. In addition, Ts 372, Ts 381, Ts 391, and Ts 380, all nonexcavated sites found in survey, possessed some of these Ajuereado diagnostic traits and are possible components of this period.

Ten new traits appear in Zone XXII of Tc 50: crude blades with prepared striking platforms, El Riego points, mortar fragments, boulder metate–milling stones, multifaceted scraper-planes, domed and flat-topped scraper-planes, gouges, ellipsoidal choppers, and spherical battered pebbles. Gradually other traits are added to this new complex from Zone XXI of Tc 50, Zone C of Tc 255, Zones XX, XIX, XVIII, and XVII of Tc 50, and Zone H of Tc 307. These traits include Flacco points, ovoid mullers, discoidal choppers, thin-flake end-scrapers, ovoid bifaces, crude blades with pointed striking platforms, Nogales points, flaring-rim and hemispherical mortars, crude discoidal scrapers, abrader-hammers, Tortugas points, Trinidad points, Hidalgo points, conical and long rectangular pestles, and possibly Agate Basin and La Mina points. Most of these traits are diagnostic of a new phase, which we called El Riego after El Riego Cave, and which originally was called the mortar and scraper-plane horizon. Carrying on into this phase from the Ajuereado period were crude keeled and ovoid end-scrapers, cylindrical pestles, spokeshave-like tools, flake choppers, and tecomate mortars; these traits are also considered to be a part of the El Riego complex. The continuing use of retouched or utilized flakes and hammerstones are not diagnostic of the El Riego phase, nor are such new traits as Nogales points, boulder metate–milling stones, mullers, gouges, crude discoidal scrapers, thin-flake end-scrapers, Abasolo points, ovoid bifaces, discoidal choppers, and battered spherical pebbles, because they all persist throughout the sequence and are not distinctive of any particular chronological segment or segments. Some of the knots, nets, cordage, and basket types may also be diagnostic of the El Riego phase, but it is difficult to tell from our inadequate samples of these objects. However, the El Riego diagnostic traits do appear in varying numbers from Zone XXII of Tc 50 through fifteen subsequent components. Zones XVIII, XVII, and XVI of Tc 50, Zone 5 of Tc 35w, Zone DE of Ts 51, Zone G of Tc 307, Zones XIV and XV of Tc 50, Zone D¹–D² of Tc 307, and the roasting pit of Ts 381w— all possess a majority of these El Riego diagnostic traits and may be considered to be pure components. Zones XXII through XIX of Tc 50 have lesser numbers of these traits, as does Zone C of Tc 255, but they are still valid components. Zone H of Tc 307, Zone R of Tc 272, and Zones E and F of Tc 307 are considered to be probable El Riego components. Zones U, T, and S of Tc 272 display even fewer diagnostic traits and are possible components, as are the following surface sites: Ts 387, Ts 390, Ts 388, Ts 377, Ts 379, Ts 384, Ts 252, and Ts 374.

As the discussion of agricultural plants in Volume I points out, Zones XIII-XI of Tc 50 contain substantial evidence of plant domestication; remains of corn, gourds, amaranth, moschata squash, common beans, black sapotes, and white sapotes appear rather suddenly. As might be expected, these agricultural innovations are accompanied by a number of new non-ceramic artifact types, such as Coxcatlan points, oblong

manos, anvil stones, tecomate stone bowls, pebble choppers, and Almagre, Garyito, and Shumla points. Appearing frequently with these new traits are a number of traits which had appeared only spasmodically late in the El Riego phase, and these include San Nicolas, Agate Basin, Abejas, and Tilapa points; crude blades with pointed striking platforms; trough metates and ovoid manos; discoidal scrapers and gouges; and discoidal choppers. Also, seemingly diagnostic of this new phase, which we named Coxcatlan, are a number of types that carry on from the El Riego phase, such as ovoid manos, hemispherical mortars, flake choppers, Flacco and Trinidad points, spokeshave-like tools, flake gravers, and crude blades with or without prepared striking platforms. Other possible diagnostics would be various wooden atlatl parts, full-turned coiled nets, and interlocking-stitched and split-stitched coiled baskets, but all of these types are not well represented. Many of the more general artifacts from the two earlier phases also appear in Coxcatlan components, but, of course, are not diagnostic.

Most of the traits of this new complex are found in Zones XIII, XII, and XI of Tc 50 and Zone 4 of Tc 35w. These zones are considered to be pure components of the Coxcatlan phase. The test at Ts 365, and perhaps Zone E of Ts 254, may be considered probable components because of their agricultural plant assemblages. However, owing to limited samples, Zones Q, Q¹, P, and O of Tc 272 and Zone D of Ts 307 must be classified as possible components, along with the archaeological reconnaissance sites Ts 338, Ts 385, Ts 373, Ts 371, Ts 348, and Ts 376.

The final preceramic phase, Abejas, was not recognized as quickly as the earlier ones during the excavation, and this was partly because of the continuing presence of many artifacts characteristic of the Coxcatlan phase—although these artifacts appeared in very different proportions. However, as Volume I shows, there was a fundamental shift in the proportions and uses of domesticated plants in Zone D of Tc 254, as well as in Zones X–VIII of Tc 50, and the settlement pattern was also very different, as Volume V will demonstrate.

Completely new nonceramic artifacts in Zones X and IX of Tc 50 include fine blades with unprepared striking platforms, fine snapped blades, long manos that are lenticular in cross section, cuboid pestles, polishing pebbles, ovoid metates, and stone bowls with flaring rims. Also accompanying this complex of new types are a series of traits which originated earlier, but which now appear in significant proportions in a larger number of components. These are end-of-blade scrapers, large bifacial disks, Catan points, hemispherical stone bowls, Pelona points, spherical manos, and perhaps Almagre and Garyito points and trough metates. Other traits that continued from the earlier phase or phases and are also diagnostic of the Abejas period are spoke-shave-like tools; Coxcatlan, San Nicolas, Shumla, Abejas, Tilapa, and Trinidad points; oblong and ovoid manos; tecomate stone bowls; crude blades; anvil stones; flake and discoidal choppers; and square-based bifaces. Possible new Abejas traits are small bifacial disks, spherical stone beads, paint palettes, rubbed pebbles, a few wooden tools, and cotton Z-twist yarn. This complex of traits, although it contains many Coxcatlan characteristics, has lost many others that started in the El Riego period and continued into the Coxcatlan period. The Abejas trait assemblage is well represented in the following pure components: Zones X, IX, and VIII of Tc 50, Zone C of Ts 51, and the pit-house village of Ts 381e. Probable components are Zone D of Tc 254, Zone B of Tc 307, and Zone N of Tc 272. Possible excavated components with very limited examples of Abejas traits include Zones N, M, M¹, and L of Tc 272. The surface collections from sites Ts 386, Ts 375, Ts 388, Ts 253, Tc 273, Tc 274, and Tc 156 should also be considered possible components.

Thus, in preceramic times in the Tehuacan region we have four phases—Ajuereado, El Riego, Coxcatlan, and Abejas—with definite evidence of cultural continuity involving changing concepts. The final five phases of the Tehuacan sequence are all represented by pottery, and their definition is largely based upon ceramic attributes.

The poorly defined Purron phase with two probable components has a few crude and fine blades, oblong manos, and trough metates, plus only two new nonceramic traits—saucer-shaped metates with lipped rims and fine blades with prepared striking platforms. It would be difficult to recognize this period as a separate entity without its distinctive, poorly made pottery.

The later ceramic periods do, however, have many distinctive nonceramic artifact types, although the ceramic artifacts, of course, are far more numerous and provide a number of excellent diagnostic types. Nonetheless, there are many more types of nonceramic than types of ceramic artifacts for each of these periods, and these alone are almost distinctive enough to divide the rest of the sequence into four periods. Thus these later phases are based upon total known trait complexes, not just upon changing ceramic attributes.

The Ajalpan phase is characterized by such new and distinctive nonceramic traits as fine blades with pointed striking platforms, Zacatenco and Salado points, oblong lipped metates, long manos that are triangular in cross section, bell-shaped and truncated-cone pestles, fine ovoid and fine flat-topped end-scrapers, abrader smoothers, square-polled celts and adzes, metapodial awls with the distal end as a handle, rib-bone spatulas or weaving tools, tubular ear plugs, twilled petates, and perhaps cotton cloth. Besides these diagnostic traits, the Ajalpan phase is represented by traits that carry on from earlier horizons, such as large and small bifacial disks, square-based bifaces, discoidal choppers, anvil stones, paint palettes, rubbed and polished pebbles, fine snapped blades and fine blades with unprepared striking platforms, crude blades of all types, discoidal end-scrapers, lipped saucer-shaped and ovoid plano-convex metates, long manos that are lenticular in cross section, ovoid and oblong and spherical manos, cuboid pestles, spokeshave-like tools, and San Nicolas, Pelona, Garyito, Shumla, and Catan points. In fact, the ceramic Ajalpan period has a more impressive and more convincing re-occurring complex of nonceramic artifacts than do some of the preceramic phases.

The components of the following phase, Santa Maria, have fewer new or re-occurring nonceramic types. These include Palmillas, Matamoros, and Tehuacan points, fine snapped blades and snapped blades with two edges retouched, basin-shaped metates, flat-iron pestles or smoothers, flattened stone ear plugs, one-over-one cotton cloth, and perhaps pressure-flaked bifacial knives, cylindrical manos, pointed-poll celts, lip plugs, four-ply cotton rope, coarse braid, three-ply cord, and corn-leaf cord. Although there are a large number of new and distinctive ceramic types which distinguish the Santa Maria from the Ajalpan phase, and although some of these types shift considerably in popularity within the Santa Maria phase, the majority of the diagnostic and re-occurring nonceramic types seem to be carry-overs from the Ajalpan period. These types include Salado, Zacatenco, Catan, Shumla, Garyito, Pelona, and San Nicolas points; bell-shaped and truncated-cone pestles; long manos that are either triangular or lenticular in cross section; ovoid and oblong manos; lipped oblong, lipped saucer-shaped, and ovoid plano-convex metates; fine flat or plano-convex end-scrapers; crude discoidal end-scrapers; fine blades with pointed or prepared or unprepared striking platforms; crude blades; paint palettes; abrader saws; polished or rubbed pebbles; twilled petates; and pressure-flaked bifacial knives.

The Palo Blanco phase, although it shares some types with the Santa Maria phase, is represented by many new nonceramic artifact types. These diagnostic traits include fine blades with ground striking platforms;

Ensor, Morhiss, Teotihuacan, and Tula points; half-moon bifacial knives; rectangular tripod metates; cuboid and stave-shaped manos; the racket type of bark-beater with a rectangular, grooved stone head; bark cloth; wooden drills and hearths for fire-making; arrows; combs made of sticks lashed together; twilled baskets; colored warp-striped blankets; one-over-two and two-over-two woven cotton cloth; round-toed sandals; and disk beads. Diagnostic traits continuing from the Santa Maria phase are less numerous but include San Nicolas, Catan, Matamoros, Palmillas, and Tehuacan points; fine blades of all types; pressure-flaked bifacial knives; cylindrical manos; truncated-cone pestles; pointed-poll celts; twilled petates; and one-over-one cotton cloth. In many respects, the nonceramic artifacts of the Palo Blanco period are more distinctive than the ceramic types.

The final Venta Salada phase has an almost completely different set of ceramic types, but many of its diagnostic nonceramic artifact types are carry-overs from the Palo Blanco phase. These are Matamoros, Tehuacan, Teotihuacan, and Tula points; truncated-cone pestles; cylindrical, cuboid, and stave-shaped manos; tripod metates; drills and hearths for fire-making; polishing pebbles; fine blades of all types; bark cloth and racket-type barkbeaters; twilled baskets; arrows; round-toed sandals; and cotton cloth of one-over-one, two-over-one, and two-over-two weaves. Diagnostic traits that first appear in Venta Salada levels include Harrell, Starr, Texcoco, and San Lorenzo points; dog-bone manos; stone effigy bowls; thumbtack pestles; thumbnail end-scrapers; trapezoidal hoes; copper bells; wooden paddles; cane fire tongs; decorated combs; gauze and twilled cloth; wicker baskets; human-hair yarn; and, perhaps, the club-shaped stone barkbeater.

We have altogether eight distinctive breaks in our archaeological sequence when a series of new nonceramic types first appear and then reappear in a number of sequential components. These breaks are in large part the basis for establishing the Ajuereado, El Riego, Coxcatlan, Abejas, Ajalpan, Santa Maria, Palo Blanco, and Venta Salada phases or periods. Although the Purron phase is meagerly represented by artifact types and its components contained few diagnostic nonceramic types, the stratigraphy and two distinctive pottery types indicate that it is a poorly defined complex that exists in our sequence between the Abejas and Ajalpan phases. Besides making it possible to divide our sequence into periods, the nonceramic artifacts indicate that there was cultural continuity in the Tehuacan Valley. This indication is supported by our studies in physical anthropology, which reveal that the valley

was populated by a relatively uniform racial group during most, if not all, of the sequence. It should also be noted that the periods of innovation when new artifact types appear correspond to periods when there were changes in the subsistence patterns caused by the introduction of new agricultural plants or practices. A later volume will show that the agricultural and nonceramic artifactual shifts which permit us to establish eight tentative phases and one complex correlate very closely with the shifts in ceramic types and settlement patterns.

External Relationships Based on Preceramic Phases

The final part of this study of nonceramic artifacts will examine the relationships of the four preceramic phases or periods of the Tehuacan sequence to other preceramic assemblages of Mesoamerica. The external relationships of the ceramic phases will be left to Volume III, which will show how the ceramic types and trade sherds are far more sensitive indicators of external relationships than are the nonceramic artifacts. In making comparisons during ceramic periods between the Tehuacan sequence and those of surrounding regions, one is, in fact, forced to use only ceramic features, because descriptions of the nonceramic artifacts from the other ceramic periods are usually lacking.

Unfortunately, Mesoamerican preceramic materials are also very limited, but this situation is about to change, for Mesoamerican archaeologists are showing a growing interest in the preceramic field and good students are being trained to specialize in it. Before long, I hope they will out-date the section to follow and provide a quantity of material to serve as a basis for more definite conclusions. However, being impatient and not valuing my academic neck very highly, I shall present what we know as of 1963. I will discuss the preceramic remains from the southern part of Mesoamerica first and then gradually shift my discussion in a northerly direction.

At Copan in Honduras, J. M. Longyear (1948) reported finding a series of obsidian chips without ceramics in an erosional cut under the Acropolis, and large collections of preceramic artifacts from the mountains of Honduras have recently been reported (Bullen and Plowden 1963). In the Zacapa Valley in Guatemala, I picked out a few chips and a possible chopper from a bank of the Motagua River. At a site nearby, Michael D. Coe and Kent V. Flannery have reported large surface collections of obsidian quarry materials and tools (1964). In southernmost Mexico near Teopisca, Chiapas, José Luis Lorenzo (1961) undertook excavations and

Table 32. Sequence of Prec[...]

(Based on 79 sensitive artifact types[...])

	TOTAL ARTIFACTS	Flake gravers	Crude keeled end-scrapers	Spokeshave-like tools	Crude blade fragments	Crude blades, unprepared platforms	Nicholas burins	Crude ovoid end-scrapers	Slab choppers	Flake choppers	Lerma points	Crude flat-flake end-scrapers	Scraper-plane fragments	Blocky-core choppers	Abasolo points	Plainview points	Muller fragments	Cylindrical pestles	Tecomate mortars	Crude blades, prepared platforms	El Riego points	Mortar fragments	Boulder metate-milling stones	Multifaceted scraper-planes	Domed scraper-planes	Flat-topped scraper-planes	Gouges	Ellipsoidal choppers	Spherical battered pebbles	Flacco points	Ovoid mullers	Discoidal choppers	Thin-flake end-scrapers	Ovoid bifaces	Crude blades, pointed platforms	Nogales points	Biface fragments	Flaring-rim mortars
ABEJAS																																						
Tc 272, L	8													2			1						3															
Tc 272, M¹	0																																					
Tc 272, M	0																																					
Tc 50, VIII	131	2		3	1	6			1	2		4	1	1	2		6			3		1	5	1	1	1	4	1			4	6	4	1	12		8	
Ts 381e	38			1																2				1	1	4						1		4	2			
Tc 50, IX	286		3	5	16	13		2	1	6		6	3	4	6		7			4		1	1				3	3	3		5	12	5	3	29	1	16	
Ts 51, C	27								1	1		2	3							1		1	2				4										1	
Tc 272, N¹	2																																					
Tc 272, N	20									5				4			1									1			1				1				2	
Tc 307, B	53	4		2	1		4					6					10						4						3	1	4	2	1					
Tc 254, D	21			1								2	1	1			1			1					1	2	2							2				
Tc 50, X	280	1		6	16	5			3	11		4	4	2	3		6			4			6		1	2	3	1	1	1	8	6	4	1	27	3	13	
COXCATLAN																																						
Tc 307, C	13			1			1										2						4	1								1	1					
Tc 272, O	2						1																															
Tc 272, P	5														1		1							1										1				
Tc 272, Q¹	0																																					
Ts 365, test	7								1																													
Tc 50, XI	308	6		6	13	15		1	4	10		13	7	1	4		13			6			14	2	3		10	4			5	15	3	4	20	4	14	
Tc 254, E	8			1																1				1	1							1	1					
Tc 35w, 4	142	3		4	3	4			1	2		10	7	3	1	1	7			3	1	2		1	4		6	3			1	9	5	2	6	1	7	
Tc 50, XII	123	4		1	9	8				3		2	5	1	1		8			4		4	4		2	1	4			1	2	7	2	2	7		6	
Tc 307, D	12			1								1		1			2													1					1		1	
Tc 272, Q	7																1							3	1			1										
Tc 50, XIII	111	5	1	4	7	6			1	5		2	1	3	1		5					2					1	4	3		2	6		1	1	1	5	
EL RIEGO																																						
Ts 381w, pit	27		2						1		1			2	3							1	1	3	2	3						1		2	1			
Tc 307, D¹D²	28					1			1		1	2	3	1			1				1		4	2		3	2				2	1	1				1	
Tc 307, E	26		1	2		5					2				1		1		2							5							1	2	4		1	
Tc 50, XIV	296	5	3	15	17	12		5	4	10		11	20	15	1		5	2		10		4	6	7	12	11	12	7		2	8	9	10	4	6	1	8	
Tc 50, XV	311	8	5	18	3	11		2	3	9		16	22	10	2		23	1	1	25		6	5	9	22	14	8	7	1	3	4	8	9	1	7		9	
Tc 307, F	17				1	1	1					1					4				1			2	1	1	1	1			1							
Tc 307, G	42		1	2	2							3					2					5	8	1	2	2	1	2	1		1						4	1
Ts 51, DE	210	8	2	13	5	9		6		6	1	9	17	9	5		3	1		10		5	2	12	12	11	5	9				1	3	4	1		17	2
Tc 35w, 5	107	2	2	6	4	1			1		3	1	13	10	6	2	2	3		6		5	5		1	1	5	1					5	1			4	
Tc 50, XVI	301	3	7	4	6	15		4	6	17	5	28	20	16	1	1	9	1		26	3	2	8	15	20	11	9	7	3	3	4	10	1	4	4	1	6	
Tc 272, R	80											1					29					1	34	1	1						12							
Tc 272, S	14										1			1			2						9								1							
Tc 272, T	2																2						2															
Tc 272, U	2																2						2															
Tc 50, XVII	101	1	1	5		1			2	1	5	8	10	8	1					3		5	1	5	13	8	1	7	1	3	1		1	2				1
Tc 50, XVIII	229	3	7	7	5	12	1	7	6	9	4	18	23	17	3	1	5	2	1	8	1	4	5	3	12	19	11	6	1		3	3	7	2	3		2	
Tc 307, H	12		1	1		1							1				1					1									1			2			1	1
Tc 50, XIX	64		2	1		6			6	3	2	5	6	8		1	4			3	1		1		1	4	1				1	2	2					1
Tc 50, XX	40		2	2	2	4		4	1	1	1	2	3		1					1			1	2			2		3		1	1	2		1	1	2	
Tc 255, C	38				2	2					1	7	2	8						4				1	3	1	2	1	1					2	1			
Tc 50, XXI	25	1	1	1		1			1	1	2	2	2			1	1		1	2	1				1	1				2	1	2					5	
Tc 50, XXII	23	1	1						1		1	2	3	1			1	2		1	2	2	1	1	1	2	1	1	1									
AJUEREADO																																						
Tc 35w, 6	18		2	1	1	2	1	1		1	1	2	1	2	1	1		1					1															
Tc 50, XXIII	55	1	9	1	1	6		4	3	3	4	12	5	2	1		1	1					1															
Tc 50, XXIV	26	3	8	2		2		2	1	1	1	3	1	2																								
Tc 50, XXV	7		1	1	2	1	1			1			1																									
Tc 50, XXVI	2		1	1																																		
Tc 50, XXVII	2		1	1																																		

surface collections on what seem to be preceramic, or certainly, nonceramic sites.

It might also be mentioned that Barnum Brown found a petrified bone of a sloth in the Peten district of Guatemala in which were incisions that might have been made by man (Shook 1951). A large concave-base point was collected near San Rafael west of Guatemala City (Coe 1960), and a similar point from Costa Rica has been reported (Swauger and Mayer-Oakes 1952). A collection of crude bifaces was gathered by Jorge Engerrand (1912) at LaConception in Campeche, near the Guatemala border. None of these materials come from archaeological context, however, and there is no definite evidence that they are preceramic, let alone some of them of *cazadores paleoindios* (Aveleyra 1962).

So far, the only adequate sample of preceramic artifacts from southern Mesoamerica to have been found in archaeological context comes from the Santa Marta Cave near Ocozocoautla, Chiapas (MacNeish and Peterson 1962). Here carefully controlled excavations revealed ten superimposed occupations, and four of the floors have been dated by radiocarbon determinations. The top five floors contained ceramics. The earliest ceramic occupation contained the earliest ceramic types (called the Cotorra complex) so far found in southern Mesoamerica, as well as the earliest radiocarbon date (1330 B.C. ± 200 [M-978]) for pottery in that area. The five earlier occupations however, were definitely preceramic; Occupation 2 was dated 6780 B.C. ± 400 (M-980), and Occupation 4 was dated 5370 B.C. ± 300 (M-979). It seems probable that all five of these earlier occupations belong to the same cultural complex, but this conclusion is extremely tentative, since a total of only fifteen artifacts came from the three earliest floors. Occupations 4 and 5, however, were represented by an adequate sample of ninety-one artifacts, and these are comparable with the nonceramic artifacts of the Tehuacan Valley.

The projectile points of the Santa Marta Cave include two Nogales points, three San Nicolas points (reported [*ibid.*] as Almagre points, since that classification was not then subdivided into the Almagre and San Nicolas types), a small Tortugas point which was reported as a Matamoros point (*ibid.*), and a fragment of what could have been a Trinidad point (reported as perhaps a Gary point, *ibid.*). Although the first three types could appear in any of the preceramic phases of the Tehuacan sequence, the five types in combination could only appear in the El Riego phase, and late in the phase at that. Obviously, the Santa Marta complex lacks many of the projectile-point types of the El Riego period—such as Flacco, La Mina, Hidalgo, and Tilapa—but all the

point types found in the Santa Marta Cave were also found in the El Riego components of the Tehuacan Valley. The Santa Marta scraper types—such as domed and flat-topped scraper-planes, crude ovoid end-scrapers, gouges, thick and thin side-scrapers, and spokeshave-like tools—also were common to the El Riego components, although the Santa Marta end-of-blade-scraper type does not appear in the Tehuacan sequence until Coxcatlan times.

All the crude-blade types of the Santa Marta Cave are found in El Riego components and none of the later Tehuacan blade types appear in either. The blocky-core or nodule choppers, slab choppers, flake choppers or slab bifaces, and the ovoid bifaces of the Santa Marta Cave are found in El Riego levels also, as are the pebble mullers and manos, pebble hammers, split-bone awls, and boulder metate–milling stones. In fact, the Santa Marta complex yielded only two artifact types, sinew stones and anvil or nut stones, which are not present in the El Riego components. The El Riego phase, however, based on a much larger sample, is represented by over twenty artifact types not found in the Santa Marta Cave. The burial practices in the two regions are very different as well. Nevertheless, the many traits in common indicate that the Santa Marta complex and the El Riego complex are closely related. Further research in Chiapas may eventually indicate just how close this relationship is.

On the coast of Chiapas, in the region of Islona de Chantuto, shell mounds that appear to have preceramic deposits have been reported by José Luis Lorenzo (1955) and Philip Drucker (1948). Alfonso Medellin Zenil and Lorenzo have told me about similar shell mounds on the Gulf coast near Alvarado in Vera Cruz, and in 1962 Ellen S. and Charles F. Brush found preceramic remains under early pottery in shell mounds on the Guerrero coast. In 1963 James A. Ford and Medellin Zenil took me to see their surface blowout sites on the Vera Cruz coast near Cempoala; these yielded crude scraper-planes, choppers, flake tools, and Matamoros, Garyito, and Pedernales projectile points. Whether these tools are preceramic or not remains to be demonstrated, but I have the impression that they may be related to artifacts of the Coxcatlan and Abejas phases of the Tehuacan region. My general feeling is, however, that these coastal preceramic remains are rather different from those in the interior, with regard to both artifact complexes and settlement patterns. Certainly, here is a field deserving further investigation, and the findings could perhaps revolutionize our ideas about preceramic and early village life in Mesoamerica.

We move back inland now, in our survey of preceramic materials, to the state of Oaxaca, which lies between Chiapas and the Tehuacan Valley. From brief studies of nonceramic materials in the museum at Mitla, as well as from various unofficial stops at sites along the Pan-American Highway, I received the impression that southern Oaxaca abounds in preceramic sites. Unfortunately, only the Yuzanu site near Yanhuitlan has been excavated, and it has produced few diagnostic artifacts (Lorenzo 1958). However, my perusal of the collections in the Mitla Museum, of recent surface collections near Mitla, and of the preceramic sites along the highway revealed that most of the Tehuacan projectile-point types, except for Lerma and El Riego, exist in the region, as do many of the scraper and chopper types. But without excavations of large samples of preceramic artifacts, nothing definite can be said about preceramic relationships between Oaxaca and Tehuacan. However, I am willing to hazard the guess that the El Riego, Coxcatlan, and Abejas complexes extended southward into Oaxaca, at least as far as Mitla.

Recent investigations in northern Puebla, although still incomplete and unreported, reveal that some of the Tehuacan phases, or phases extremely like them, do extend into that region. Seemingly, the earliest remains so far found in northern Puebla are those uncovered by Cynthia Irwin-Williams on the north side of the Valsequillo reservoir. Her excavations at San Baltasar and Tetela have yielded about twenty artifacts in association with extinct mastadon, mammoth, horse, antelope, dire wolf, and some smaller mammal or bird remains. The artifacts include a number of side-scrapers, biface fragments, flake choppers, burins, gravers, pestles, and a few fragments of what seem to be Lerma points. This complex of tools is very like the Ajuereado complex. The principal differences seem to be that some of the Valsequillo artifacts show evidence of more burin blows and that the faunal assemblage is richer. Be that as it may, the Ajuereado remains and the earliest Valsequillo remains are closely related. Although the geological studies of the Valsequillo finds are not definitive, it may be that the relationship is one in which the Ajuereado phase developed out of a complex similar to the Valsequillo phase of northern Puebla.

The later preceramic assemblages of northern Puebla were still being studied as I wrote this section, so what I write is not final. However, during the summer of 1963 and winter of 1964, Castillo Tejero, under the direction of José Luis Lorenzo, head of the Departamento de Prehistoria of the Instituto Nacional de Antropología e Historia, excavated the Texcal rock shelter on the southern shore of Valsequillo reservoir across from where Irwin-Williams had dug. Zone 5 of this cave, one of the lowest levels having cultural remains, contained a number of artifacts, including scraper-planes, gouges, ellipsoidal and blocky-core choppers, crude blades, and Flacco and Abasolo points. All these artifacts are diagnostic of the El Riego phase of the Tehuacan sequence, and Zone 5 of Texcal Cave, if it is not actually an El Riego component, seems to be very closely related to that phase.

In the levels or zones above these remains, Flacco, Catan, Garyito, and Coxcatlan points were found, along with bifacial disks, oblong manos, and other general tools. It seems that here a Coxcatlan component or one closely related to that phase has been uncovered.

Although some remains that possibly are preceramic have been reported in both Vera Cruz and Morelos, the next group of early materials closest geographically to the Tehuacan region are from the Valley of Mexico. Here many more investigations have been undertaken, and a number of reports have been written—including articles for the popular press—but as yet the archaeological picture is far from clear. A number of finds have been attributed with varying degrees of certainty to the Paleo-Indian or Big Game Hunting stage. Descriptions of the remains and comments on the validity of the attribution can be found in Aveleyra 1962. About a dozen of the finds show possible evidence of man, possibly at an early time period. These include alleged human footprints in rocks found in 1891 near Rincon de Guadalupe; a fossilized human jaw bone possibly associated with extinct fauna found in 1893 near Xico; two stone chips found with mammoth bones near Los Reyes Acozac; possibly man-made cuts on mammoth bones found in a location between Tepexpan and Totolzingo; an obsidian flake found with mammoth bones near Tepexpan; a skeleton uncovered in a rather poorly documented and poorly excavated site near Tepexpan; a mammoth tooth from Tepexpan that possibly was worked by man; a human tooth possibly associated with a mammoth found near the hospital at Tepexpan; a carved camel bone, a pointed piece of fossilized bone, and a stone chip from an irrigation ditch near Tequixquiac; a series of worked flakes and a few crude bifaces (?) from the Barranca de Acatlan near Tequixquiac; a chip from a deep excavation in the Cerro de Las Palmas near Tacubaya; some fossil human bones from El Peñon de los Baños near Mexico City; and fifty-nine fine chips from an excavation near the Barrio de San Bartolo Atepehuacan in the northern suburbs of Mexico City. None of these scattered finds, however, provides acceptable evidence of any early cultural complex, nor can they be the basis for comparisons with the Tehuacan materials.

236

Three other sets of materials from the Valley of Mexico may be as early as the above. One of these is Helmut de Terra's San Juan industry, established on the basis of ten "artifacts" from three different localities near San Francisco Mazapa, near Tequixquiac, and at El Risco (De Terra 1949). These materials consist of a worn, pointed piece of bone that may very well have been formed naturally; two so-called gravers, only one of which could conceivably have been intentionally chipped by man; a pointed obsidian pebble and two obsidian flakes, none of which shows definite evidence of human workmanship; a small, oblong, plano-convex blade with a dulled edge from San Francisco Mazapa that could have been produced by nonhuman agencies; a triangular obsidian flake from Tequixquiac, one edge of which may have been utilized; a so-called hammerstone; and a chipped pebble. Even if all of these are artifacts—and only four of them can be so described after much stretching of the imagination—they are so lacking in diagnostic characteristics that no relationship with Tehuacan can be established.

A second very large sample of chipped-stone artifacts, mainly of basalt, came from the strata under and surrounding the skeleton of Santa Maria Astahuacan. These were found by George O'Neill in 1953. The high florine count of the skeleton (Heizer and Cook 1959), as well as the artifact types that I saw associated with it, such as Lerma points and many crude choppers and scrapers, leave little doubt in my mind that here indeed was an early site with a large sample of artifacts. Unfortunately, following the discovery of the skeleton, the artifacts disappeared, and no report on them is available.

Other early finds from the Valley of Mexico came from two localities near Santa Isabel Iztapan, both of which have mammoth remains. The first excavation produced seven artifacts and the second three (Aveleyra and Maldonado-Koerdell 1953; Aveleyra 1956, 1962). A radiocarbon determination on the first site gave a date of 7050 B.C. ± 250 (L-191). It seems probable that both of these mammoth kills were roughly contemporaneous, and for convenience I shall discuss the artifacts associated with them as if they came from a single site. Of the projectile points, I believe two to be Lerma points—although one was called a knife in the original report—of the type which appears in Ajuereado and early El Riego components in the Tehuacan Valley. Another projectile point, first reported as an Angostura point, resembles an Agate Basin point, a type found in middle El Riego levels. The remaining point originally was called a Scottsbluff point, and this it assuredly is not. It is a difficult projectile point to classify because

the lateral edges near the base are ground, which gives it a stemmed appearance and makes it unlike any of the projectile points excavated in the Tehuacan Valley. If the lower edges had not been ground, I would have had little hesitation in classifying it as a Nogales point, a type existing in the Tehuacan Valley from early El Riego times to the Venta Salada period. In this same assemblage there was a triangular object whose base was pressure-flaked into a steep bevel. Although it is called an end-scraper, in our Tehuacan typology it would be classified as a gouge, for it is like those that first appeared in early El Riego levels. Another object classified as a retouched blade is clearly a finely made fragment of a keeled end-scraper of the type found in Ajuereado or early El Riego components, although part of its cutting edge had been removed by a so-called "intentionally made open break." The Iztapan spoke-shave-like tool is also like those common to the El Riego and Ajuereado phases. The two crude blades and the double-edged thin side-scraper of Iztapan would fit into any of the Tehuacan preceramic phases.

Artifacts of the above types, with the exception of the miscalled Scottsbluff point, appear in either or both of the two earliest phases in the Tehuacan Valley. Certainly these finds are related to either the Ajuereado or the El Riego phase, or to both, and except for the so-called Angostura and Scottsbluff points, these sites could be thought of as possible late Ajuereado components. The number of artifacts from Iztapan is, however, too small to plot definite cultural relationships, and the artifacts are too difficult to visualize in terms of a total cultural complex, since they obviously come from mammoth kills. For these very reasons, conclusions based on the Iztapan data about an early stage of Paleo-Indian Big Game Hunters for Mesoamerica should be regarded only as speculation.

The more recent preceramic materials from the Valley of Mexico are even more difficult to understand and to compare with those of Tehuacan. De Terra, on the basis of about fifty artifacts and chips from a beach in the vicinity of the Tepexpan skeleton, established an industry called Tepexpan, which he estimated followed the San Juan industry (De Terra 1949). On the basis of a much larger sample of artifacts collected from the surface of several other sites, he also predicated a Chalco industry following the Tepexpan industry (ibid.). Both of these industries are represented by artifacts that are similar to the preceramic artifacts from Tehuacan. Included in the Tepexpan collection are points that appear to be of the Tortugas and Nogales types, a possible graver, a possible keeled end-scraper, a crude ovoid end-scraper, a crude flake end-scraper, a cobble hammer, and possibly some small plano-convex end-scrapers. Although most of these are rather general types, they resemble artifacts in our El Riego complex. The artifacts of the Chalco industry also resemble the El Riego assemblage, for there are possible Abasolo and Agate Basin points, discoidal scrapers, crude flat-flake end-scrapers, multifaceted scraper-planes, flat-topped and domed scraper planes, ellipsoidal and discoidal choppers, cobble hammers, flake gravers, and ovoid mullers. The Chalco assemblage also reputedly includes oblong manos of the the type found in the preceramic phases in the Tehuacan Valley. Although artifacts of both the Tepexpan and Chalco industries display similarities to those of the El Riego complex, they lack a host of El Riego diagnostic types; the most that may be said is that there are hints of relationships. Before the Tepexpan and Chalco "traditions" can be seriously considered as distinct cultural complexes, it is necessary to have a better sample of artifacts from excavated archaeological contexts, rather than from surface collections.

Perhaps the most reliable later materials from the Valley of Mexico available for comparisons with the Tehuacan findings are those from Chicoloapan (De Terra 1959). These remains are too meager to establish firm relationships, but the assemblage does include fragments of what were possibly Almagre points, end-of-blade scrapers, spokeshave-like tools, boulder metate–milling stones, biface fragments, large plano-convex end-scrapers, domed scraper-planes, a pebble mano or hammer, blocky-core choppers, and flake side-scrapers. This particular complex of tools also appears as a complex in the early Coxcatlan phase of the Tehuacan sequence. Again, many of the Coxcatlan traits are missing, but there are hints of a connection. Generally speaking, however, comparisons of the Tehuacan preceramic phases with remains from the Valley of Mexico are not very satisfactory, and although there are hints of relationships, more reliable data from the Federal District are awaited before definitive statements may be made.

In Hidalgo and Queretaro the situation is somewhat better owing to the efforts of Cynthia Irwin-Williams in 1959. Earlier Florence Müller had reported preceramic remains and had found a Flacco point—called a Meserve point by Aveleyra (1962)—in a context suggesting considerable antiquity (Müller 1962). Irwin-Williams' excavations in what she calls Tecolote Cave (or what Aveleyra, 1962, calls Cueva Calcinada del Chivo), located near Huapalcalco, displays good stratigraphy and includes preceramic artifacts in three distinct zones. These materials have been classified into two sequential phases or complexes—the earlier Hidalgo and the later

Tecolote (see manuscript dated 1964 in the files of the Dirección de Prehistoria, Instituto de Antropología e Historia, Mexico). Although the complexes have not been totally described, the earlier Hidalgo complex has in common with El Riego of Tehuacan at least such artifact types as Abasolo, Tortugas, Hidalgo, Agate Basin, Flacco, and perhaps El Riego points, as well as scraper-planes, ellipsoidal bifacial choppers, flake burins, crude blades with or without prepared striking platforms, and boulder metate–milling stones. The overlying Tecolote complex seems more closely aligned with the Coxcatlan phase of the Tehuacan sequence. Common to both of them are Trinidad, La Mina, Abejas, Coxcatlan, and Pelona points; crude blades with unprepared or pointed striking platforms; discoidal scrapers; and bundle group burials. Although many Tehuacan types are absent from the Tecolote Cave sequence, and although I am not familiar with other Tecolote types, there is good evidence of a close relationship between the two areas.

In Queretaro in the San Nicolas Cave near San Juan del Rio, Irwin-Williams uncovered preceramic materials also closely related to those of Tehuacan. Among the artifacts from her earlier phase or complex, San Juan, are Lerma points; crude blades with unprepared striking platforms; an abundance of Nicolas, Fort Liard, and artifact burins; flake and slab choppers; and snub-nosed end-scrapers like those of the Tehuacan Ajuereado phase. The later San Nicolas phase is similar to the Abejas phase of Tehuacan and is represented by Pelona, Catan, Coxcatlan, San Nicolas, Garyito, and Palmillas points; all types of crude blades, as well as some fine blades; ovoid and oblong manos, mullers, and perhaps metates; small end-scraper types; indications of the use of the domesticated dog; and evidence of the custom of cremation.

Irwin-Williams considers that the phases from the two areas may be combined in a single sequence roughly as follows: San Juan, Hidalgo, Tecolote, and San Nicolas. In terms of relationships between the Tehuacan Valley and these two more northerly excavations, San Juan and Ajuereado seem linked, as do Hidalgo and El Riego; perhaps early Coxcatlan is connected with Tecolote and San Nicolas with late Coxcatlan and Abejas.

This evidence of a strong relationship between Queretaro, Hidalgo, and Puebla further points out the inadequacies of preceramic investigations in the Valley of Mexico. It also demonstrates the kinds of artifactual materials that one can expect to be uncovered eventually, once "prehistoric" archaeological research is undertaken in that much publicized zone. Further, the artifacts—particularly the projectile-point types from excavations in Hidalgo and Queretaro—may serve to link the larger samples of points from excavations in both Puebla and Tamaulipas, especially since most of the same types have been found at least on the surface or in poorer archaeological contexts from the in-between areas such as the Federal District and San Luis Potosi.

We turn now to southern Tamaulipas, where two regional archaeological sequences are based upon stratigraphy and on sixteen radiocarbon dates (MacNeish 1958; Kaplan and MacNeish 1960). The Infiernillo phase, the earliest phase of these sequences, was uncovered in the Infiernillo Canyon near Ocampo in the Sierra Madre region of southwestern Tamaulipas. Two radiocarbon determinations place it between 7000 and 5000 b.c., roughly contemporaneous with the El Riego phase of Tehuacan. Infiernillo's Hidalgo and Abasolo points also appear in the El Riego phase, although Infiernillo's Almagre type does not appear in the Tehuacan Valley until Coxcatlan times, and the Infiernillo point is absent from the Tehuacan sequence. Infiernillo also has in common with El Riego crude keeled and ovoid plano-convex end-scrapers; flat-topped, domed, and multifaceted scraper-planes; gouges; blocky-core, slab, flake, and ellipsoidal choppers; boulder metate–milling stones; twined blankets; a possible cylindrical pestle; and a number of more generalized types of scrapers, as well as ovoid bifaces, hammerstones, split-bone awls, and the like. The Infiernillo subsistence pattern is also similar to El Riego's in a general way. There are, however, many differences. For example, most of the Infiernillo net and basketry complex is distinctive, but Infiernillo lacks the El Riego polyhedral core and blade, mortar and pestle, and weaving complexes. Nevertheless, the two phases do seem related, and they exhibit many more resemblances than do the later phases of each region.

The subsequent Ocampo phase of southwestern Tamaulipas and the Coxcatlan or Abejas phases of the Tehuacan sequence have less in common, although they are roughly contemporaneous. Subsistence complexes are similar in a general way, and both phases have pebble manos, boulder metate–milling stones, Abasolo points, Nogales points, Tortugas points, full-turned coiled nets, atlatls, cane atlatl mainshafts and slotted pointed foreshafts; spring traps; anvil hammers; similar scraper-plane types; discoidal scrapers and bifaces; similar chopper types; square-based knives; and gouges. However, the differences are more numerous, and most of the blade, projectile-point, mano, muller, and metate types of the Coxcatlan or Abejas phases do

not appear in Ocampo. I might add that the Chalco-complex site reported from San Luis Potosi by De Terra (1949) and Aveleyra (1950) is probably another component of the Ocampo phase.

The final preceramic phases of southwestern Tamaulipas, Flacco and Guerra, are later than any preceramic remains in the Tehuacan region, and they have even fewer traits in common. The few shared tool types usually appear earlier in Tehuacan. They include San Nicolas, Flacco, Catan, Matamoros, and Trinidad points; crude blades with unprepared, prepared, and pointed striking platforms; discoidal choppers, bifaces, and scrapers; mullers and mortars; split-stitched coiled bundle-foundation basketry; a few heavy scraper and chopper types; and a few of the more general artifact types.

The other sequence in southern Tamaulipas was uncovered in the Sierra de Tamaulipas (MacNeish 1958). Here the earliest remains are termed the Diablo complex, but because of the limited sample of artifacts, it is difficult to relate it definitely to any other phase—even the following Lerma phase. The Lerma phase is, however, better represented and seems related to its temporal counterpart, Ajuereado, in the Tehuacan Valley. These two phases have in common Lerma points, gravers, flake and slab choppers (reported as "variety 2 choppers," *ibid.*, p. 84), crude keeled and snub-nosed end-scrapers (a Lerma phase end-scraper reported as a "plano-convex snub-nosed end-scraper," *ibid.*, p. 77, Fig. 26, no. 8, is actually keeled), domed scraper-planes, blocky-core choppers ("variety 1 of the bifacial choppers," *ibid.*, p. 84), and other more general traits, such as thick side-scrapers and pebble hammers. Differences between the two phases are that the Lerma complex alone possesses stemmed end-scrapers, a Tamaulipas triangular point, and ovoid, square-based, and half-moon bifacial knives, and that the Ajuereado phase alone has crude prismatic blades, spokeshave-like tools, a Plainview point, and Abasolo points. Some of the Lerma examples of Lerma points are extremely wide and flat and have such a poorly pointed base that they very closely approach some examples of the Abasolo type.

In the Sierra de Tamaulipas a long temporal gap occurs in the sequence between the Lerma phase and the next phase, Nogales. If, during this gap, a phase comparable to Infiernillo existed, then there could have been affinities between a cultural complex of the Sierra de Tamaulipas and the El Riego phase of the Tehuacan Valley. Suppositions aside, when the final three preceramic phases of the Sierra de Tamaulipas—Nogales, La Perra, and Almagre—are compared with the Coxcat-

239

lan and Abejas phases of the Tehuacan region, the dissimilarities far outweigh the similarities.

In northern Tamaulipas, a tentative sequence exists that is mainly based upon reconnaissance, but it is somewhat confirmed by limited stratigraphy. The complexes have been named Nogales, Repelo, Abasolo, and Catan. They seem closely connected with materials found in the salvage excavations of the Texas portion of the Falcon Dam, as well as with the more recent complexes found in Nuevo Leon (Epstein 1961). These latter excavations, although unfortunately based on the "arbitrary level" technique, have been in part confirmed by a series of radiocarbon dates, which also in part confirm my original dating estimates (MacNeish 1958). The latest culture, represented by the Catan phase and the upper levels of Epstein's cave, are similar in having Harrell, San Lorenzo, Tortugas, Starr, and Fresno points and half-moon side-blades. Although most of the above traits are found with Postclassic remains, the more northerly complexes lack the other vast number of Postclassic traits, such as those associated with metates, ceramics, architecture, and the various complex settlement patterns.

The Abasolo complex of northern Tamaulipas and the middle levels of Epstein's cave, although sharing some of the projectile-point types of the Classic period of southern Tamaulipas, both appear unrelated to preceramic cultural areas further south. The next phase, Repelo, is characterized by Repelo points. Repelo and the lower levels of Epstein's Nuevo Leon cave both show some resemblances to the preceramic Flacco and Almagre phases of southern Tamaulipas, and perhaps as well to the latest materials from the La Perra and Ocampo phases. They have in common San Fernando, Tortugas, Hidalgo, and Trinidad points, as well as gouges, disk choppers, and disk scrapers. These two related northern complexes seem little connected with cultural complexes in central Mexico. This is equally true of the earlier related northeastern Mexican manifestations such as Ocampo, Nogales, La Perra, the San Isidro site of Nuevo Leon, and much of the material from the Falcon Dam site, in spite of its abundance of Tortugas and Abasolo points, gouges, choppers, and scraper-planes.

We now turn westward in our survey of preceramic materials, to the state of Coahuila in northern Mexico. In this state a number of excavations have been undertaken in caves and rock shelters. Two complexes have been named, Cienegas and Coahuila, but the inadequate reports available consist largely of references to the kinds of awls and quids found in some of the cave levels (Taylor 1956). A brief article also demonstrates

how inaccurate preliminary temporal estimates may be in terms of later radiocarbon dates (Taylor 1948). From a brief examination of some of the Coahuila materials, I believe that they connect more closely with the remains found in caves in the Big Bend region of Texas than they do with the more southerly preceramic Mexican complexes previously mentioned. However, Coahuila seems to be archaeologically rich; skilled excavations should be undertaken there in the future.

Still further west in Mexico preceramic remains have been noted in Durango, Sinaloa, Sonora, and Chihuahua. These materials for the most part have not been reported fully, and from what little has been said about them, they seem to relate to the Cochise materials of southern Arizona and New Mexico, rather than to the materials of Tehuacan or Tamaulipas. The materials from lower California also show little relation to cultures of the south or east, with the possible exception of the San Dieguito complex, which shows some resemblances in point types to the Lerma and Ajuereado phases. For the most part, however, the lower California materials are related to those of southern California and southwestern Arizona.

Speculations

This brief survey of Mexican preceramic complexes makes evident the limitations of reliable data that can be compared with the Tehuacan findings. In spite of this, a beginning can be made to align, tentatively, the early sequences of a number of different regions of Mexico. At the present pioneer stage, we have sequences of preceramic remains—some of which have been dated and some of which come from acceptable archaeological context—in Chiapas, southern Oaxaca, northern Puebla, the Valley of Mexico, Hidalgo, Queretaro, Tamaulipas, Nuevo Leon, and Coahuila. In Figs. 174 and 175 I have attempted to align these materials and to assign them possible positions in history.

In terms of general time levels, five of the six cultural complexes existing in the period before 7000 B.C. appear to be related. Ajuereado, Valsequillo, Iztapan, the lower levels of San Nicolas Cave, and Lerma all have Lerma points. Further, Ajuereado and Valsequillo have in common Fort Liard and Nicolas burins, keeled end-scrapers, and possibly crude blades. Common to Ajuereado and Iztapan are blades and possibly burins; Lerma and Ajuereado both share flake and blocky-core choppers, crude plano-convex and keeled end-scrapers, and possibly, crude blades. This represents a considerable number of similarities when the small number of artifacts found in most of these complexes is taken into account.

240

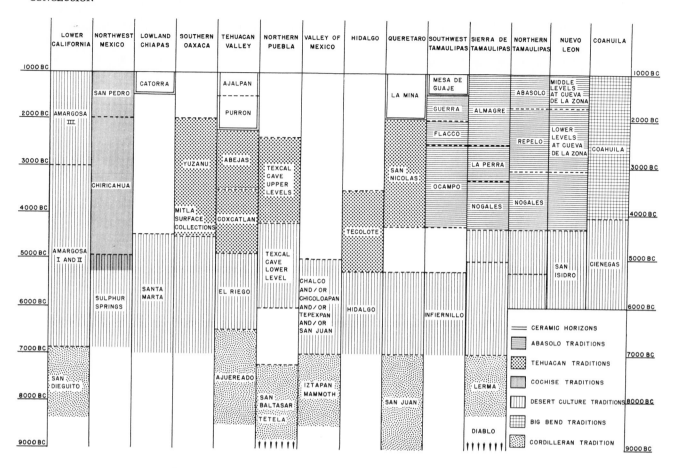

Fig. 174. A tentative correlation of preceramic phases and traditions in Mexico.

In the period from 7000 to 5000 B.C. even more cultural similarities existed over much of Mexico. Furthermore, the larger number of cultural complexes involved are also represented by larger samples. Represented in this time period are Santa Marta in Chiapas, El Riego in Puebla (and probably Oaxaca), the lower levels of Texcal Cave in the Valsequillo basin, the various industries of De Terra in the Valley of Mexico, the lower two levels of Tecolote Cave in Hidalgo, Zone B of San Nicolas Cave in Queretaro, Infiernillo in southwest Tamaulipas, probably San Luis Potosi, possibly Nogales in the rest of Tamaulipas, and possibly Nogales or a similar culture in Nuevo Leon. The Cienegas complex of Walter W. Taylor may also be of this period. Common to most of these complexes or phases are a number of varieties of scraper-planes and choppers, mortars and pestles, gouges, grinding stones and mullers, possibly blades with prepared striking platforms, and a number of projectile-point types with contracting stems, as well as large triangular and leaf-shaped points. The general similarity to the Cochise culture of the Southwest of the United States makes me suspect that some

of the meager remains from western and northwestern Mexico might also be related.

The Mexican materials from the period between 5000 and about 2000 B.C., however, do not seem to be quite so closely related. On the basis of point types, southern Oaxaca, northern Puebla, Hidalgo, and Queretaro appear to be connected, but the materials from northeastern Mexico, although related to each other, do not seem to be directly related to the more southerly materials. Nor do the Coahuila or Pecos River materials of north central Mexico, nor the Cochise artifacts of northwestern Mexico, seem to be associated with southern materials.

The question becomes, then, can definite conclusions about the prehistory of Mexico be drawn on the basis of these data? Definite or final conclusions, of course, cannot yet be contemplated, for our information in most cases is very meager. There is, nevertheless, just enough data to permit speculations. Such speculations are necessary—not to foster false conclusions, as Aveleyra (1962) fears—but to lead to working hypotheses that can be tested, accepted, rejected, or modified into more

241

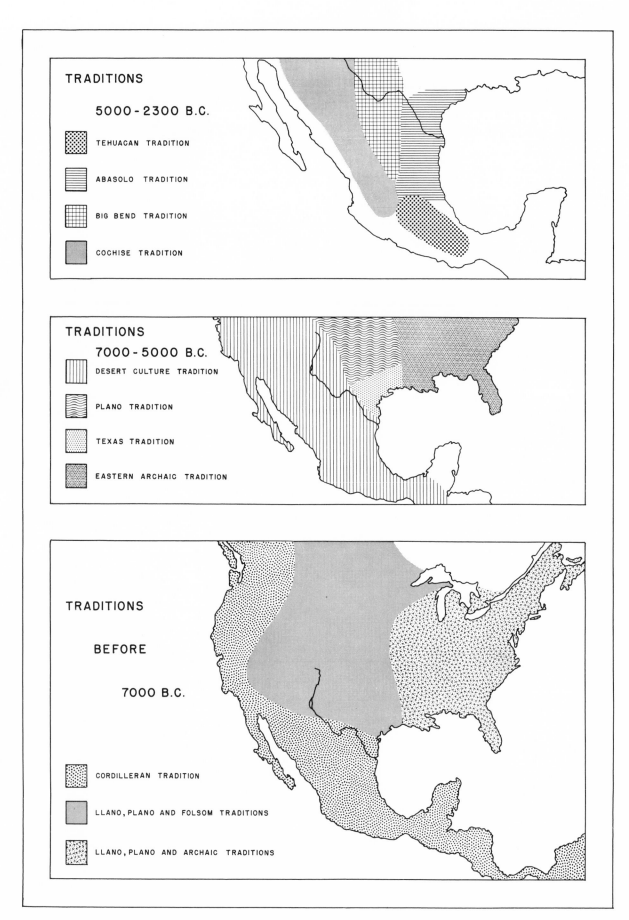

Fig. 175. Geographical range of Mesoamerican preceramic cultural traditions.

valid hypotheses, which eventually will lead to more soundly based conclusions. In speculating about the possible meanings of the preceramic sequences in Mesoamerica and their relationships and inter-relationships, I shall use the "tradition" concept as an integrating device. I am defining cultural tradition to mean a way of life, as manifested in the archaeological artifactual record, which persists through time and in space.

It is my opinion that the earliest remains so far uncovered in Mexico are closely related to one another, with the possible exception of the poorly documented Diablo complex of Tamaulipas, and I also suspect that they probably all belong to the same cultural tradition. I call this early tradition Cordilleran. It has a relatively continuous distribution in western America from Venezuela to Alaska. Representative cultural complexes belonging to this tradition might be El Jobo of Venezuela, Ajuereado of southern Puebla, San Baltasar in northern Puebla, Iztapan in the Valley of Mexico, the earliest remains of San Nicolas Cave in Queretaro, Lerma of Tamaulipas, possibly the earliest remains in Val Verde County of Texas, San Dieguito of southern Arizona and California, the earliest materials at Five Mile Rapids in Oregon and Lind Coulee in Washington, some of the "Old Cordilleran" remains of Idaho, the materials from the lowest levels of the Fraser Canyon site in British Columbia, the Klondike complex in the Northwest territories, the Kluane complex of the southern Yukon and the Flint Creek complex of the Northern Yukon, possibly the Kayuk complex of the Brooks Range of Alaska, and probably too some of the recent finds William Irving uncovered along the Navatuk River in western Alaska.

Traits that are common to many of these cultural complexes and which are diagnostic of the Cordilleran tradition include double-pointed Lerma-like projectile points, crude blades struck from conical polyhedral cores, burins made on flakes or artifacts, spokeshave-like tools, choppers (usually made of flakes), scraper-planes, flake gravers, some type of snub-nosed end-scraper, and a large proportion of flake tools. The subsistence pattern of the Cordilleran tradition was probably equally distinctive in that it may have been adapted to environments of mountainous valleys.

This particular way of life and its characteristic cultural traits would contrast sharply with contemporaneous traditions in North America. Certainly, the traditions of the Great Plains and the eastern Rockies—such as Llano, Folsom, Plano, and others, with their distinctive points and blades and their emphasis on bifacial tools and subsistence based on hunting big game—would have been very different. Further, both the traits

and the way of life of the traditions of the eastern Woodlands, such as the Archaic, eastern Fluted, eastern Plano, and others, must necessarily have been even more unlike that of the Cordilleran tradition.

The Cordilleran tradition, with its burins, double-pointed bifacial projectile points, many flake tools, blades, chopping tools, and crude scrapers, obviously has many relationships with the Siberian Paleolithic that the big-game-hunting Llano and Plano traditions and others of this period do not have. I would further suggest that the Cordilleran tradition existed in Mexico until about 7000 B.C.

I would think, too, that as the Pleistocene waned, man would have made new adaptations to his gradually changing environment. In the Great Basin area of the United States, in the greater Southwest, and in much of Mexico, this led to a new way of life that has been called the Desert Culture tradition. This tradition seems to have existed in Utah, Colorado, Arizona, New Mexico, most of Mexico, and possibly, some of west Texas. Redefining this tradition so that it includes the available Mexican materials, I would describe its traits as follows: milling stones and mullers, mortars and pestles, scraper-planes, choppers of many types, leaf-shaped projectile points, contracting-stemmed and large triangular points, and an emphasis on bifacial tools. Perhaps more important than these artifactual characteristics would be the new kind of subsistence pattern which emerged. At the end of the Pleistocene the subsistence of people of this tradition seems to have shifted; during the lusher seasons they gathered in macrobands to collect plants, but during leaner seasons they split into microbands to hunt, collect plants, and starve. This way of life contrasts with the traditions of other peoples in North America between 7000 and 5000 B.C., for subsistence of the eastern Archaic people was oriented toward forests and rivers, while the people of the Great Plains still were hunters. More northerly groups were oriented toward lakes or coastal waters. The Arctic group may have been making still another adaptation to a tundra environment.

Gradually, however, the developing cultures within this larger Desert Culture tradition began to lose their cultural unity and evolved into new traditions. For example, in central highland Mexico, from Oaxaca to Hidalgo and Queretaro, a tradition based in part upon an embryonic agriculture founded on corn, beans, and squash began to develop. This tradition, which we might call the Tehuacan tradition, has as its diagnostic characteristics true manos and metates; stone bowls; Coxcatlan, Tilapa, and Garyito points; crude and fine blades; gouges; and the use of pit houses. This way of life contrasts with other developments arising from the Desert Culture tradition, such as the Cochise, Repelo, and Pecos River traditions. The Cochise tradition continued its food-gathering activities and the use of choppers, scraper-planes, and contracting-stem projectile points, but it added more elaborate types of milling stones, pit houses, and yet another kind of emergent agriculture. In northeastern Mexico the Repelo tradition—characterized by gouges, mullers, an emphasis on triangular and leaf-shaped points, the use of smaller scrapers, a slightly different agricultural base, and a semi-nomadic way of life—constitutes another development. In north central Mexico and western Texas still another tradition, which I shall call Big Bend, may have developed without agriculture but with Shumla and Ensor points, gouges, distinctive kinds of sandals and baskets, small end-scrapers, and few, if any, milling stones or pestles. James A. Ford's new data from the Vera Cruz coast, as yet unpublished, hints that still another tradition may have evolved on the Gulf coast during this period.

By the emergence of ceramic periods in the Tehuacan Valley, the Tehuacan tradition (and probably some of the others as well) gradually changed into yet another tradition, which is already known as Mesoamerican. This tradition is characterized by the development of a more stable agricultural system involving greater use of many plant hybrids; the making of pottery and figurines; the evolution of village life, elaborate ceremonialism, and social stratification; the rise of full-time specialists and of writing and calendar systems; as well as many other complex and distinctive traits.

This hypothetical reconstruction has, I hope, placed the preceramic phases of the Tehuacan Valley in a more general light. In terms of the limited evidence, it seems to make sense. I do not believe for a minute that it is the final word, although I will defend these tentative hypotheses with considerable vigor against any armchair archaeologist who is not armed with facts and artifacts. I do, however, hope that my hypotheses will stimulate others to test them and to obtain more information about the preceramic period of Mexico. To those who are so stimulated, I wish them good digging and a great deal of luck, but I use the word "luck" in the Ralph Waldo Emerson sense, meaning "tenacity of purpose."

REFERENCES

AVELEYRA ARROYO DE ANDA, LUIS
  1950 *Prehistoria de México*. Mexico: Ediciones Mexicanas.
  1956 "The Second Mammoth and Associated Artifacts at Santa Isabel Iztapan, Mexico." *Am. Ant.*, 22:12–28.
  1962 *Antigüedad del Hombre en México y Centroamerica*. Cuadernos del Instituto de Historia, Serie Antropólogica, No. 14. Mexico.

AVELEYRA ARROYO DE ANDA, LUIS, AND
MANUEL MALDONADO-KOERDELL
  1953 "Association of Artifacts with Mammoth in the Valley of Mexico." *Am. Ant.*, 18:332–40.

BONCH-OSMOLOVSKY, G., AND V. GROMOV
  1936 "The Paleolithic in the Union of Soviet Socialist Republics." *International Geological Congress, XVIth Session, 1933*. Washington.

BORDEN, C. E.
  1960 "DjRi 3, An Early Site in Fraser Canyon, British Columbia." *Contributions to Anthropology, 1957*. National Museum of Canada, Bulletin No. 162. Ottawa.

BULLEN, R. P., AND W. W. PLOWDEN
  1963 "Preceramic Archaic Sites in the Highlands of Honduras." *Am. Ant.*, 28:382–85.

BYERS, DOUGLAS S.
  1959a "The Eastern Archaic: Some Problems and Hypotheses." *Am. Ant.*, 24:233–56.

CAMPBELL, JOHN M.
  1959 "The Kayuk Complex of Arctic Alaska." *Am. Ant.*, 25:94–105.

COE, MICHAEL D.
  1960 "A Fluted Point from Highland Guatemala." *Am. Ant.*, 25:412–13.

CRESSMAN, LUTHER S.
  1960 *Cultural Sequences at The Dalles, Oregon*. APS-T, Vol. 50, Part 10.

CRUXENT, J. M., AND IRVING ROUSE
  1956 "A Lithic Industry of Paleo-Indian Type in Venezuela." *Am. Ant.*, 22:172–79.

DAUGHERTY, RICHARD D.
  1956 "Archaeology of the Lind Coulee Site, Washington." *APS-P*, 100:223–78.

DRUCKER, PHILIP
  1948 *Preliminary Notes on an Archaeological Survey of the Chiapas Coast*. Middle American Research Records, Vol. 1, No. 11. New Orleans: Tulane University.

EPSTEIN, JEREMIAH F.
  1961 "The San Isidro and Puntita Negra Sites: Evidence of Early Man Horizons in Nuevo Leon, Mexico." *Homenaje a Pablo Martínez del Río*, pp. 71–74. INAH.
  1963 *Centipede and Damp Caves: Excavations in Val Verde County, Texas, 1958*. TAS-B, Vol. 33.

244

FAY, GEORGE E.
1956 "Peralta Complex—A Sonoran Variant of the Cochise Culture." *Science*, 124:1029.

GROMOV, V. I.
1945 "Twenty-five Years of the Quaternary of the U.S.S.R." *AJS*, Vol. 243.

HAURY, EMIL, *et al.*
1950 *The Stratigraphy and Archaeology of Ventana Cave, Arizona.* Tucson: University of Arizona Press.

HEIZER, ROBERT F.
1951 "Preliminary Report on the Leonard Rockshelter Site, Pershing County, Nevada." *Am. Ant.*, 17: 89–98.

HEIZER, ROBERT F., AND S. F. COOK
1959 "New Evidence of Antiquity of Tepexpan Man and Other Human Remains from the Valley of Mexico." *SJA*, 15:36–42.

JENNINGS, JESSE D.
1957 *Danger Cave.* SAA-M No. 14. Salt Lake City.

KAPLAN, LAWRENCE, AND R. S. MACNEISH
1960 *Prehistoric Bean Remains from Caves in the Ocampo Region of Tamaulipas, Mexico.* BML, Vol. 19, No. 2.

LONGYEAR, JOHN M.
1948 "A Sub-Pottery Deposit at Copan, Honduras." *Am. Ant.*, 13:248–49.

LORENZO, JOSÉ LUIS
1955 "Los Concheros de la Costa de Chiapas." INAH *Anales*, 7:41–50.
1958 *Un Sitio Precerámico en Yanhuitlán, Oaxaca.* Dirección de Prehistoria, Publication No. 6. INAH.
1960 *La Revolución Neolithica.* Dirección de Prehistoria, Publication No. 11. INAH.
1961 "Un Buril de la Cultura Precerámica de Teopisca, Chiapas." *Homenaje a Pablo Martínez del Río*, pp. 75–90. INAH.

MACNEISH, RICHARD S.
1958 *Preliminary Archaeological Investigations in the Sierra de Tamaulipas, Mexico.* APS-T, Vol. 48, Part 6.
1959 "Man out of Asia: As Seen from the Northwest Yukon." *Anthropological Papers of the University of Alaska*, 7:41–59. Fairbanks.
1961 "Recent Finds Concerned with the Incipient Agriculture Stage in Prehistoric Mesoamerica." *Ho-*

menaje a Pablo Martínez del Río, pp. 91–101. INAH.
1964 "Archaeological Excavation, Comparisons, and Speculations." *Investigations in the Southwest Yukon.* Papers of the Robert S. Peabody Foundation for Archaeology, Vol. 6. Andover.

MACNEISH, RICHARD S., AND F. A. PETERSON
1962 *The Santa Marta Rock Shelter, Ocozocoautla, Chiapas, Mexico.* Papers of the New World Archaeological Foundation, No. 14. Provo, Utah.

MAYER-OAKES, WILLIAM J.
1952 "A Central American Clue to Early Man." *Carnegie Magazine.* Carnegie Museum, Pittsburgh.

ROGERS, MALCOLM J.
1939 *Early Lithic Industries of the Lower Basin of the Colorado River and Adjacent Desert Areas.* San Diego Museum Papers, No. 3. San Diego.

SAYLES, E. B., AND ERNST ANTEVS
1941 *The Cochise Culture.* Medallion Papers, No. 22. Globe, Arizona.

SHOOK, EDWIN M.
1951 "The Present Status of Research on the Pre-Classic Horizons in Guatemala." *Selected Papers of the XXIXth International Congress of Americanists*, 1:93–100.

SWAUGER, J. L., AND W. J. MAYER-OAKES
1952 "A Fluted Point from Costa Rica." *Am. Ant.*, 17:264–65.

TAYLOR, WALTER W.
1948 *A Study of Archaeology.* American Anthropological Association Memoirs, No. 69. Menasha.
1956 "Some Implications of Carbon-14 Dates from a Cave in Coahuila, Mexico." *TAS-B*, 27:215–34.

TERRA, HELMUT DE
1949 "Early Man in Mexico," *Tepexpan Man.* Viking Fund Publications in Anthropology, No. 11. New York.
1959 "A Successor of Tepexpan Man in the Valley of Mexico." *Science*, 129:563–64.

TSCHOPIK, HARRY, JR.
1946 "Some Notes on Rock Shelter Sites near Huancayo, Peru." *Am. Ant.*, 12:73–80.

VAILLANT, GEORGE C.
1930 *Excavations at Zacatenco.* AMNH-AP, Vol. 32, Part 1.

ABBREVIATIONS USED IN THE BIBLIOGRAPHY

AA	*American Anthropologist*, Lancaster and Menasha.
AJS	*American Journal of Science*, New Haven.
Am. Ant.	*American Antiquity*, Menasha and Salt Lake City.
AMNH-AP	American Museum of Natural History, Anthropological Papers, New York.
APS-P	American Philosophical Society, Proceedings, Philadelphia.
APS-T	American Philosophical Society, Transactions, Philadelphia.
BAE-B	Bureau of American Ethnology, Bulletin. Washington, D.C.
BML	Botanical Museum Leaflets, Harvard University, Cambridge, Mass.
CIW	Carnegie Institution of Washington, Washington.
CIW-CAAH	Carnegie Institution of Washington, Contributions to American Archaeology and History, Washington.
CIW-NMAAE	Carnegie Institution of Washington, Notes on Middle American Archaeology and Ethnology, Cambridge.
INAH	Instituto Nacional de Antropológia e Historia, Mexico.
PMAE-M	Peabody Museum of Archaeology and Ethnology, Memoirs, Cambridge, Mass.
PMAE-P	Peabody Museum of Archaeology and Ethnology, Papers, Cambridge, Mass.
RMEA	*Revista Mexicana de Estudios Antropológicos*, Mexico.
SAA-M	Society for American Archaeology, Memoir, Menasha and Salt Lake City.
SJA	*Southwestern Journal of Anthropology*, Albuquerque, New Mexico.
TAPS-B	Texas Archaeological and Paleontological Society, Bulletin, Abilene and Lubbock.
TAS-B	Texas Archaeological Society, Bulletin, Austin.
UCPAAE	University of California Publications in American Archaeology and Ethnology, Berkeley.

BIBLIOGRAPHY

ALEXANDER, HERBERT L.
1963   "The Levi Site: A Paleo-Indian Campsite in Central Texas." *Am. Ant.,* 28:510–28.

AVELEYRA ARROYO DE ANDA, LUIS
1951   "Reconocimiento Arqueológico en la Zona de la Presa Internacional Falcón, Tamaulipas y Texas." *Revista Mexicana de Estudios Antropológicos,* 12:31–59. Mexico.
1956   "The Second Mammoth and Associated Artifacts at Santa Isabel Iztapan, Mexico." *Am. Ant.,* 22: 12–28.
1962   *Antigüedad del Hombre en México y Centroamerica.* Cuadernos del Instituto de Historia, Serie Antropólogica, No. 14. Mexico.

AVELEYRA ARROYO DE ANDA, LUIS, AND
MANUEL MALDONADO-KOERDELL
1953   "Association of Artifacts with Mammoth in the Valley of Mexico." *Am. Ant.,* 18:332–40.

BARLOW, R. H.
1946   "Cerro de San Lorenzo, Coahuila: Dos Sitios Arqueológicos." *Revista Mexicana de Estudios Antropológicos,* 8:266–67. Mexico.

BIRD, JUNIUS B.
1943   *Excavations in Northern Chile.* AMNH-AP, Vol. 38, No. 4.

BIRD, JUNIUS B., AND L. BELLINGER
1954   *Paracas Fabrics and Nazca Needlework: 3rd Century B.C.—3rd Century A.D.* Washington: National Publishing Company.

BONCH-OSMOLOVSKY, G., AND V. GROMOV
1936   "The Paleolithic in the Union of Soviet Socialist Republics." *International Geological Congress, XVIth Session, 1933.* Washington.

BORDEN, C. E.
1960   "DjRi 3, An Early Site in Fraser Canyon, British Columbia." *Contributions to Anthropology, 1957.* National Museum of Canada, Bulletin No. 162. Ottawa.

BULLEN, R. P., AND W. W. PLOWDEN
1963   "Preceramic Archaic Sites in the Highlands of Honduras." *Am. Ant.,* 28:382–85.

BUTLER, B. R.
1961   *The Old Cordilleran Culture in the Pacific Northwest.* Idaho State College Museum, Occasional Papers, No. 5. Pocatello, Idaho.

BYERS, DOUGLAS S.
1954   "Bull Brook—A Fluted Point Site in Ipswich, Massachusetts." *Am. Ant.,* 19:343–51.
1959a   "The Eastern Archaic: Some Problems and Hypotheses." *Am. Ant.,* 24:233–56.
1959b   "Radiocarbon Dates for the Bull Brook Site, Massachusetts." *Am. Ant.,* 24:427–29.

CAMPBELL, JOHN M.
1959   "The Kayuk Complex of Arctic Alaska." *Am. Ant.,* 25:94–105.

CASON, JOE E.
1952   "Report on Archaeological Salvage in Falcon Reservoir, Season of 1952." *TAPS-B,* 23:218–59.

COE, MICHAEL D.
1960   "A Fluted Point from Highland Guatemala." *Am. Ant.,* 25:412–13.
1961   *La Victoria: An Early Site on the Pacific Coast of Guatemala.* PMAE-P, Vol. 53.

COE, MICHAEL D., AND KENT V. FLANNERY
1964   "The Pre-Columbian Obsidian Industry of El Chayal, Guatemala." *Am. Ant.,* 36:43–49.

COSGROVE, C. B.
1947   *Caves of the Upper Gila and Hueco Areas in New Mexico and Texas.* PMAE-P, Vol. 24, No. 2.

CRESSMAN, LUTHER S.
1960   *Cultural Sequences at The Dalles, Oregon.* APS-T, Vol. 50, Part 10.

CRESSMAN, LUTHER S., et al.
1942   *Archaeological Researches in the Northern Great Basin.* CIW. Publication No. 538.

CRESSMAN, LUTHER S., HOWELL WILLIAMS, AND
A. D. KRIEGER
1940   *Early Man in Oregon: Archaeological Studies in the Northern Great Basin.* University of Oregon Monographs, Studies in Anthropology, No. 3. Eugene.

CRUXENT, J. M., AND IRVING ROUSE
1956   "A Lithic Industry of Paleo-Indian Type in Venezuela." *Am. Ant.,* 22:172–79.

DAUGHERTY, RICHARD D.
1956   "Archaeology of the Lind Coulee Site, Washington." *APS-P,* 100:223–78.

DAVIDSON, D. S.
1935   "Knotless Netting in America and Oceania." *AA,* 37:117–34.

DELGADO, HILDA S.
n. d. "Archaeological Textiles from Durango, Zacatecas and Sinaloa." Unpublished MS.

DRUCKER, PHILIP
1948 *Preliminary Notes on an Archaeological Survey of the Chiapas Coast.* Middle American Research Records, Vol. 1, No. 11. New Orleans: Tulane University.
1959 *Excavations at La Venta, Tabasco, 1955.* BAE-B, No. 170.

EKHOLM, GORDON F.
1942 "Excavations at Guasave, Sinaloa, Mexico." *AMNH-AP,* 38:23–139.
1944 "Excavations at Tampico and Panuco in the Huasteca, Mexico." *AMNH-AP,* 38:321–509.

ENGERRAND, JORGE
1912 "La Huella Más Antigua Quizá del Hombre en la Península de Yucatán." *Reseña de la 2ª Sesión del 17º Congreso Internacional de Americanistas,* pp. 89–100. Mexico.

EPSTEIN, JEREMIAH F.
1960 "Burins from Texas." *Am. Ant.,* 26:93–97.
1961 "The San Isidro and Puntita Negra Sites: Evidence of Early Man Horizons in Nuevo Leon, Mexico." *Homenaje a Pablo Martínez del Río,* pp. 71–74. INAH.
1963 *Centipede and Damp Caves: Excavations in Val Verde County, Texas, 1958.* TAS-B, Vol. 33.
1964 "Towards the Systematic Description of Chipped Stone." *XXXV Congreso Internacional de Americanistas, Mexico, 1962,* I:155–69. Mexico.

FAY, GEORGE E.
1956 "Peralta Complex—A Sonoran Variant of the Cochise Culture." *Science,* 124:1029.

FORD, JAMES A.
1954 "The Type Concept Revisited." *AA,* 56:42–54.
1962 *A Quantitative Method for Deriving Cultural Chronology.* Technical Manual 1, Pan American Union, General Secretariat, Organization of American States. Washington.

FORD, JAMES A., AND C. H. WEBB
1956 *Poverty Point: A Late Archaic Site in Louisiana.* AMNH-AP, Vol. 46, Part 1.

GERHARD, PETER
1964a "Emperor's Dye of the Mixtecs." *Natural History Magazine,* 73:26–31. AMNH.
1964b "Shellfish Dye in America." *XXXV Congreso Internacional de Americanistas, Actas y Memorias, 1962,* 3:177–90. Mexico.

GLADWIN, H. S., et al.
1937 *Excavations at Snaketown: Material Culture.* Medallion Papers, No. 25. Globe, Arizona.

GREEN, F. E.
1963 "The Clovis Blades: An Important Addition to the Llano Complex." *Am. Ant.,* 29:145–65.

GROMOV, V. I.
1945 "Twenty-five Years of the Quaternary of the U.S.S.R." *AJS,* Vol. 243.

HARRINGTON, M. R.
1933 *Gypsum Cave, Nevada.* Southwest Museum Papers, No. 8. Los Angeles.

HAURY, EMIL W.
1933 "Maya Textile Weaves." Unpublished MS.

HAURY, EMIL W., et al.
1950 *The Stratigraphy and Archaeology of Ventana Cave, Arizona.* Tucson: University of Arizona Press.

HEIZER, ROBERT F.
1951 "Preliminary Report on the Leonard Rockshelter Site, Pershing County, Nevada." *Am. Ant.,* 17: 89–98.

HEIZER, ROBERT F., AND S. F. COOK
1959 "New Evidence of Antiquity of Tepexpan Man and Other Human Remains from the Valley of Mexico." *SJA,* 15:36–42.

HIBBEN, FRANK C.
1941 *Evidences of Early Occupation in Sandia Cave, New Mexico, and Other Sites in the Sandia-Manzano Region.* Smithsonian Miscellaneous Collections, Vol. 99, No. 23. Washington.

HOLMES, WILLIAM H.
1919 *Handbook of Aboriginal American Antiquities.* BAE-B, No. 60.

JENNINGS, JESSE D.
1957 *Danger Cave.* SAA-M, No. 14. Salt Lake City, Utah.

JENNINGS, JESSE D., AND EDWARD NORBECK
1955 "Great Basin Prehistory: A Review," *Am. Ant.,* 21:1–11.

JOHNSON, IRMGARD W.
n. d. "Candelaria Cave Textiles." Unpublished MS.
1957 "An Analysis of Some Textile Fragments from Yagul." *Mesoamerican Notes,* No. 5, pp. 77–81. Department of Anthropology, Mexico City College, Mexico.
1958–59 "Un Antiguo Huipil de Ofrenda Decorado con Pintura." *RMEA,* 15:115–22, pl. 3. Mexico.
1960 "Un *Tzotzopaztli* Antiguo de la Region de Tehuacán." *Anales del INAH, 1957–1958,* 11:75–85.

JOHNSON, L.
1964 *The Devil's Mouth Site.* University of Texas, Department of Anthropology, Archaeological Series, No. 6. Austin.

KAPLAN, LAWRENCE, AND R. S. MACNEISH
1960 *Prehistoric Bean Remains from Caves in the Ocampo Region of Tamaulipas, Mexico.* BML, Vol. 19, No. 2.

KASHA, M.
1948 "Chemical Notes on the Coloring Matter of Chihuahua Textiles of Pre-Columbia Mexico." In

Lila M. O'Neale, *Textiles of Pre-Columbian Chihuahua*, CIW, Publication No. 574. CAAH, No. 45.

KAUFFMAN DOIG, FEDERICO
1963 *Tres Etapas Pre-Chavin*. Lima.

KENT, K. P.
1957 *The Cultivation and Weaving of Cotton in the Prehistoric Southwestern United States*. APS-T, Vol. 47, Part 3.

KIDDER, ALFRED V.
1947 *The Artifacts of Uaxactun, Guatemala*. CIW, Publication No. 576.

KIDDER, ALFRED V., AND S. J. GUERNSEY
1919 *Archaeological Exploration in Northeastern Arizona*. BAE-B, No. 65.

KRIEGER, ALEX D.
1944 "The Typological Concept." *Am. Ant.*, 9:271–28.
1946 "Artifacts from the Plainview Bison Bed." *Bulletin of the Geological Society of America*, No. 58, pp. 927–54.

LANNING, E. P., AND E. A. HAMMEL
1961 "Early Lithic Industries of Western South America." *Am. Ant.*, 27:139–54.

LARSEN, HELGE
1951 "De Dansk-Amerikanske Alaska-ekspeditioner, 1949–50." *Geografisk Tidsskrift*, 51:63–93. Copenhagen.

LEWIS, THOMAS M. N., AND MADELINE KNEBERG LEWIS
1961 *Eva: An Archaic Site*. A University of Tennessee Study in Anthropology. Knoxville.

LIBBY, WILLARD F.
1955 *Radiocarbon Dating*. 2nd ed. Chicago: University of Chicago Press.

LONGYEAR, JOHN M.
1948 "A Sub-Pottery Deposit at Copan, Honduras." *Am. Ant.*, 13:248–49.

LORENZO, JOSÉ LUIS
1955 "Los Concheros de la Costa de Chiapas." *Anales del INAH*, 7:41–50. Mexico.
1958 *Un Sitio Precerámico en Yanhuitlán, Oaxaca*. Dirección de Prehistoria, Publication No. 6. INAH. Mexico.
1960 *La Revolución Neolithica*. Dirección de Prehistoria, Publication No. 11. INAH. Mexico.
1961 "Un Buril de la Cultura Precerámica de Teopisca, Chiapas." *Homenaje a Pablo Martínez del Río*, pp. 75–90. INAH. Mexico.

LOUD, L. L., AND M. R. HARRINGTON
1929 *Lovelock Cave*. UCPAAE, Vol. 25, No. 1.

MACNEISH, RICHARD S.
1948 "The Pre-Pottery Faulkner Site of Southern Illinois." *Am. Ant.*, 13:232–43.
1950 "A Synopsis of the Archaeological Sequence in the Sierra de Tamaulipas." *RMEA*, 11:79–96. Mexico.

1954 *An Early Archaeological Site near Panuco, Vera Cruz*. APS-T, Vol. 44, Part 5.
1958 *Preliminary Archaeological Investigations in the Sierra de Tamaulipas, Mexico*. APS-T, Vol. 48, Part 6.
1959 "Men out of Asia: As Seen from the Northwest Yukon." *Anthropological Papers of the University of Alaska*, 7:41–59. Fairbanks.
1960 "The Callison Site in the Light of Archaeological Survey of the Southwest Yukon." *Contributions to Anthropology, 1957*. National Museum of Canada, Bulletin No. 162, pp. 1–51. Ottawa.
1961 "Recent Finds Concerned with the Incipient Agriculture Stage in Prehistoric Mesoamerica." *Homenaje a Pablo Martínez del Río*, pp. 91–101. INAH. Mexico.
1963 "The Early Peopling of the New World." *Early Man in the Western American Arctic: A Symposium*. Anthropological Papers of the University of Alaska, Vol. 10, No. 2. Fairbanks.
1964 "Archaeological Excavation, Comparisons, and Speculations." *Investigations in the Southwest Yukon*. Papers of the Robert S. Peabody Foundation for Archaeology, Vol. 6. Andover, Massachusetts.

MACNEISH, RICHARD S., AND F. A. PETERSON
1962 *The Santa Marta Rock Shelter, Ocozocoautla, Chiapas, Mexico*. Papers of the New World Archaeological Foundation, No. 14. Provo, Utah.

MARINGER, JOHN
1950 *Contributions to the Prehistory of Mongolia*. Sino-Swedish Expedition, Publication 34, No. 7. Stockholm.

MARTIN, PAUL S., *et al.*
1952 *Mogollon Cultural Continuity and Change*. Fieldiana: Anthropology, Vol. 40. Chicago: Natural History Museum.

MAYER-OAKES, WILLIAM J.
1952 "A Central American Clue to Early Man." *Carnegie Magazine*. Carnegie Museum, Pittsburgh.

MAYER-OAKES, WILLIAM J., AND R. E. BELL
1960 "An Early Man Site Found in Highland Ecuador." *Science*, 131:1805–06. Washington.

MEDELLIN ZENIL, ALFONSO
1960 *Cerámicas del Totonacapan*. Universidad Veracruzana. Jalapa, Vera Cruz.

MEDVEDEV, G. I.
1964 "The Place of the Culture of Verkholenskaia Gora in the Archaeological Sequence of the Baikal Region." *Am. Ant.*, 29:461–66.

MÜLLER, FLORENCIA
1961 "Tres Objetos de Piedra de Huapalcalco, Estado de Hidalgo." *Homenaje a Pablo Martínez del Río*, pp. 319–22. INAH. Mexico.

OAKLEY, KENNETH P.
1957 *Man the Tool-maker.* Chicago: University of Chicago Press.

OKLADNIKOV, A. P.
1950 *Lenskiye Drevnosti,* Vyp. 3 (Antiquities of the Lena, Part 3). Moscow.

OKLADNIKOV, A. P., AND I. A. NEKRASOV
1959 "New Traces of an Inland Neolithic Culture in the Chukotsk Peninsula." *Am. Ant.,* 25:247–56.

O'NEALE, LILA M.
1945 *Textiles of Highland Guatemala.* CIW, Publication No. 567.

1948 *Textiles of Pre-Columbian Chihuahua.* CIW, Publication No. 574. Contributions to American Anthropology and History, No. 45.

O'NEALE, LILA M., AND B. J. CLARK
1948 *Textile Periods in Ancient Peru.* III. The Gauze Weaves. UCPAAE.

ROBERTS, FRANK H. H.
1935 *A Folsom Complex.* Smithsonian Miscellaneous Collections, Vol. 94, No. 4. Washington, D. C.

ROGERS, MALCOLM J.
1939 *Early Lithic Industries of the Lower Basin of the Colorado River and Adjacent Desert Areas.* San Diego Museum Papers, No. 3. San Diego, California.

ROUSE, IRVING
1939 *Prehistory in Haiti.* Yale University Publications in Anthropology, No. 21. New Haven, Connecticut.

SAYLES, E. B., AND ERNST ANTEVS
1941 *The Cochise Culture.* Medallion Papers, No. 22. Globe, Arizona.

SHOOK, EDWIN M.
1951 "The Present Status of Research on the Pre-Classic Horizons in Guatemala." *Selected Papers of the XXIX International Congress of Americanists,* 1:93–100. Chicago: University of Chicago Press.

SMITH, C. EARLE, AND R. S. MACNEISH
1964 "Antiquity of American Polyploid Cotton." *Science,* 143:675.

STRÖMBERG, E.
1942 "Technical Analysis of Textiles Recovered in Burial I." In S. Linné, *Mexican Highland Cultures,* pp. 157–60. Ethnographical Museum of Sweden, New Series, Publication 7. Stockholm.

SUHM, DEE ANN, A. D. KRIEGER, AND E. B. JELKS
1954 *An Introductory Handbook of Texas Archaeology.* TAS-B, Vol. 25.

SWAUGER, J. L., AND W. J. MAYER-OAKES
1952 "A Fluted Point from Costa Rica." *Am. Ant.,* 17:264–65.

TAYLOR, WALTER W.
1948 *A Study of Archeology.* American Anthropological Association Memoirs, No. 69. Menasha.

1956 "Some Implications of Carbon-14 Dates from a Cave in Coahuila, Mexico." *TAS-B,* 27:215–34.

TERRA, HELMUT DE
1949 "Early Man in Mexico," *Tepexpan Man.* Viking Fund Publications in Anthropology, No. 11. New York.

1959 "A Successor of Tepexpan Man in the Valley of Mexico." *Science,* 129:563–64.

TOLSTOY, PAUL
1963 "Cultural Parallels between Southeast Asia and Mesoamerica in the Manufacture of Bark Cloth." *Transactions of the New York Academy of Science,* Series II, 25:646–62.

—— "Stone, Bone, and Antler Tools of Central Mexico from Preclassic to Aztec Times." To be published in *Handbook of Middle American Indians.* Austin: University of Texas Press.

TSCHOPIK, HARRY, JR.
1946 "Some Notes on Rock Shelter Sites near Huancayo, Peru." *Am. Ant.,* 12:73–80.

VAILLANT, GEORGE C.
1930 *Excavations at Zacatenco.* AMNH-AP, Vol. 32, Part 1.

WEBB, WILLIAM S.
1946 *Indian Knoll, Site Oh 2, Ohio County, Kentucky.* University of Kentucky Reports in Anthropology and Archaeology, Vol. 4, No. 3, Part 1. Lexington.

WEBB, WILLIAM S., AND D. L. DEJARNETTE
1942 *An Archaeological Survey of Pickwick Basin in the Adjacent Portions of the States of Alabama, Mississippi, and Tennessee.* BAE-B, No. 129.

WHITAKER, THOMAS W., H. C. CUTLER, AND R. S. MACNEISH
1957 "Cucurbit Materials from Three Caves near Ocampo, Tamaulipas." *Am. Ant.,* 22:352–58.

WORMINGTON, H. M.
1957 *Ancient Man in North America.* 4th ed. Denver Museum of Natural History, Popular Series, No. 4. Denver, Colorado.

YOSHIZAKI, M.
1959 *Tachikawa Preceramic Industries in South Hokkaido.* Hokkaido Municipal Museum Research Bulletin, No. 6. Tokyo.

ZINGG, ROBERT M.
1940 *Report on Archaeology of Southern Chihuahua,* Contributions to the University of Denver. Denver.

INDEX

NOTE: Pages on which definitions or descriptions occur, or on which major material is concentrated, are indicated by bold type.